A CAUTIOUS PATRIOTISM

A CAUTIOUS PATRIOTISM

THE AMERICAN CHURCHES & THE SECOND WORLD WAR

GERALD L. SITTSER

THE UNIVERSITY OF NORTH CAROLINA PRESS / CHAPEL HILL & LONDON

© 1997 The University of North Carolina Press
All rights reserved
Manufactured in the United States of America

Library of Congress Cataloging-in-Publication Data
Sittser, Gerald Lawson, 1950–
A cautious patriotism: the American churches and the
Second World War / Gerald L. Sittser.
p.   cm.
Includes bibliographical references and index.
ISBN 0-8078-2333-3 (cloth: alk. paper)
1. World War, 1939–1945—Religious aspects. 2. War—Religious
aspects—Christianity. 3. World War, 1939–1945—Influence.
4. United States—Church history—20th century. I. Title.
D744.5.U6S58   1997
940.54'78—dc20   96-35005
CIP

01   00   99   98   97   5   4   3   2   1

*To the members of Whitworth College's religion
and philosophy department, who are such
wonderful colleagues and friends:*

Forrest E. Baird

F. Dale Bruner

Terrence McGonigal

Stephen C. Meyer

Roger L. Mohrlang

Michelle L. Seefried

CONTENTS

ACKNOWLEDGMENTS

My friend, mentor, and former professor, Marty E. Marty, the dean of American religious historians and professor at the University of Chicago, first directed my attention to the subject of American religion and World War II. He suggested that I investigate how much serious research had been done on religion and the war. I discovered, much to my surprise and delight, that very little had been done, and nothing done comprehensively. He later read the entire manuscript and offered substantial suggestions. Two other Chicago faculty, Jerald Brauer, professor emeritus, and the late Arthur Mann, also offered helpful criticisms. I am deeply grateful to all of them for their investment of time, energy, and expertise. John Yoder and Dale Soden, professors at Whitworth College, read selected chapters and commented insightfully about ways that my argument could be nuanced better.

I also wish to thank the dozens of librarians in the dozens of libraries across the Chicago area that I visited so regularly for what seemed at the time to be decades. They directed me to sources, answered my many questions, and expressed genuine interest in what I was doing. Two librarians at Whitworth College, Gail Fielding and Nancy Bunker, were quick to obtain books, articles, and other sources when I needed them. These bibliophiles transformed my research from an exercise in frustration into a journey of discovery.

Lewis Bateman, executive editor at the University of North Carolina Press, upheld the highest standards of forthrightness, promptness, and excellence through the two years we were in conversation about the book. He demanded much and encouraged more. His guidance and persistence made those two years seem like two months. Pamela Upton, assistant managing editor, and Leslie Henry, copyeditor, dazzled me with their attention to detail and commitment to excellence. They caught numerous errors and inconsistencies that escaped me, and they helped the manuscript become more readable and accurate.

My late wife, Lynda, cheered me on in the early stages of this project. She gave me time and showed me patience, all the while repeating words that are now imprinted in my brain, "Do it well and get it done!" Well, I have tried to do it well, and I have gotten it done. I know she would be very proud. My three children, Catherine, David, and John, are still too young to be interested in books of this kind. They helped me immeasurably, however, by keeping me from becoming a fanatic about such a project. In their minds, what is the value of writing a book when I could be shooting baskets with them?

Finally, I wish to acknowledge my indebtedness to the members of the religion and philosophy department at Whitworth College. This unusual collection of competent, kind, and loyal colleagues and friends shows me what the academy was meant to be. I dedicate this book to them with gratitude and respect.

A CAUTIOUS PATRIOTISM

THE CRISIS

It has often been called "the last good war." Most people who lived through the Second World War drew a straight and clear line between the side that was right and the side that was wrong. Evidence was easy to come by. Germany and Japan were the guilty aggressors: totalitarian, expansionist, evil. America and its allies, with the exception of Russia, were the innocent defenders: democratic, peaceful, good. There was little doubt in the minds of most Americans about the justice of their cause.

World War II was the kind of war that the American churches could have supported without reservation. Clearly the United States was above blame, or so it was assumed at the time. It had avoided belligerency and, until 1940, lagged behind in military preparation. It had tried to remain neutral and refrained from practicing brinkmanship. It took a Pearl Harbor to force the nation to fight. Never had America been pushed so relentlessly toward war. Never had America been so slow to respond. The churches, then, had every reason to be singlemindedly patriotic. Considering their record in other wars, such patriotism would have been the expected response.

It was surely the response of the vast majority of Americans. Business leaders, journalists, entertainers, and politicians did not hesitate to proclaim America's innocence, extol its virtues, and denounce the enemy. They only reinforced the pressure put upon Christians in general and church leaders in particular to give unquestioning and uncritical support to America's war effort. Any hint of questions, criticism, and caution would have been interpreted as disloyalty and betrayal, especially in the eyes of America's super-patriots, of which there were many.

The churches, however, were not fanatically patriotic, nor were they unpatriotic. For perhaps the first time in the history of America at war, they lived in the tension of a "cautious patriotism." They were devoted to the nation but not without ambivalence and reservations. Church leaders in particular did not want to let the war undermine their greater loyalty to God, justice, humanitarianism, and peace. However severe the crisis, they tried to resist being overcome by patriotic fervor. As we shall see, they could have followed very different courses of action.

The End of Christian Civilization?

That a crisis was looming before America seemed beyond question. Reinhold Niebuhr, a professor at Union Seminary, prolific author, and ubiquitous presence in American religion, was one of many who saw it coming. In February 1941 a small group of Christian leaders, Niebuhr among them, founded a new journal called *Christianity and Crisis*. Niebuhr argued in the first issue of the journal that the name was appropriate considering the times in which Americans were living. Having already faced a series of crises over the past thirty years, America was facing another crisis that was more serious and severe than any that had gone before. It was a crisis that challenged the future of Western civilization. He explained: "We mean *the* Crisis itself; not the crisis of some segment of the social order, but of the whole social order. We mean that as Protestant Christians we stand confronted with the ultimate crisis of the whole civilization of which we are a part and whose existence has made possible the survival of our type of faith and our type of church. . . . The inconceivable has happened. We are witnessing the first effective revolution against Christian civilization since the days of Constantine."[1] The crisis, Niebuhr went on to argue, was precipitated by the ideology and aggression of Nazi Germany, which was threatening such cherished American traditions as democracy and freedom. It was exacerbated by America's reluctance to enter the war and defend Christian civilization. The crisis exposed America's loss of nerve, shallow thinking, cautious leadership, and lack of political realism.

This crisis had been a long time coming. It began with the close of the First World War. America had entered that war to make the world safe for democracy. It became clear in the postwar settlement emerging from Versailles, however, that the world had not been made safe for democracy but for nationalism, greed, and vengeance. In the war's aftermath America was plunged into a period of political disillusionment and isolationism, social experimentation, and financial prosperity. It also experienced cultural conflict. Having won the war in Europe, Americans declared war on each other. Different groups tried to claim America exclusively for themselves. The battle between fundamentalists and modernists may be the most notable now, but it was certainly not unique then. Conflicts raged between radicals and conservatives, newcomers and old-stock Americans, bohemians and traditionalists, religious confessionalists and positive thinkers. The Scopes trial, the Red Scare, the Ku Klux Klan, the Sacco-Vanzetti trial, speakeasies, Al Capone, and self-help religion captured the attention of the country and created points of tension in American society.

The Stock Market crash mitigated, but did not erase, those conflicts. It also created a crisis of another kind. The Great Depression appeared to show that Americans were facing troubles that could not be overcome by traditional—supposedly Protestant—values. Hard work, common sense, and fair play were apparently not enough to reverse the descent toward economic ruin. The repeal of Prohibition and the popularity of Hollywood, mass marketing, and consumerism only confirmed the impression that America was slowing slipping away from the influence of traditional values. By the middle of the decade the shadow of Nazism, Stalinism, and Fascism began to fall over Europe. Soon most of Europe was engaged in war. Eventually the greater part of it was absorbed or conquered by the Nazi war machine.

Thus the Second World war followed closely behind a series of crises in American society, as Niebuhr intimated in the first editorial of *Christianity and Crisis*. Christian leaders were certain, however, that the war was not simply another in that series of crises, the last and perhaps worst of a string of catastrophes. They used the word "crisis" frequently and self-consciously to show that the Second World War was unlike any event that had occurred in Western history. They believed that the war was inaugurating a new phase in history. It was an event of such violence, trauma, and portent that Western civilization would never be the same, would be forever changed for good or evil, would be forced, by the sheer magnitude of the conflict, to determine its destiny once and for all. It was, as the word implies, a judgment and a turning point.

Religious leaders regarded the war as a unique event, different in kind and worse in degree than other periods of upheaval in history because it symbolized a clash between two opposing ideologies. The whole world had been gradually divided between two ways of life. Only one would emerge the victor. "One way of life," a statement from the Council of Bishops of the newly created Methodist Church read, "exalts the State as supreme, subordinates the individual to its demands, makes men selfless cogs in a relentless machine crushing out all semblance of personal worth and freedom. The other, based upon the principle of the sacredness of personality, proclaims the intrinsic worth of every man, and for every human being the fullest freedom consonant with the same freedom for all others." The democratic way of the West was engaged in a battle to the death against the forces of totalitarianism. "The totalitarian way would unify and organize by conquest, the democratic way by consent. The former is bent not only upon the conquest of territory, but mastery also over the minds of men. . . . It clashes with the fundamental principles of our Christian faith and seeks deliberately to destroy Christianity as its avowed enemy."[2]

Writing for the *Commonweal*, a Catholic weekly, British historian Christopher Dawson propounded the idea that Nazism represented a resurgence of the kind of paganism that had overrun Rome in the fifth century. Yet there was a difference. The "old barbarism" of the invaders of the Roman world was culturally inferior to Roman culture and could therefore be won over to a different, better way of life. The new powers were "armed with all the resources of modern scientific technique which are inspired by a ruthless will to power that recognizes nothing save that of their own strength."[3] Editor L. O. Hartman of *Zion's Herald*, an independent Methodist weekly, believed that "paganism and Christianity are at each other's throats." "Both," he added, "cannot survive. One or the other is destined to perish from the earth, if not forever, at least for thousands of years to come."[4]

Such pronouncements came from many religious quarters. Leaders of the United Lutheran Church in America passed a resolution saying that the crisis symbolized a new and dangerous capitulation to godlessness. "God has been left out of the lives of men," the statement read. "Therefore, mankind is reaping the harvest of its apostasy, in judgment, discipline, and vicarious suffering."[5] To John Mackay, president of Princeton Seminary, the war manifested a trend to substitute "man for God as the ultimate object of loyalty, and to enthrone human relativities in the place of the divine absolutes." He predicted that the war would bring about changes in society so radical that he and his contemporaries were witnessing the "end of an era."[6] Other church leaders argued that the war was precipitating a crisis on a whole range of fronts—in the ecumenical movement, in missions, in the progress of liberal religion, or in the spread of religious liberty.[7] Whatever the nature of the consequences, the crisis of the Second World War was as severe as anything that Western civilization had ever witnessed.

It was natural that church leaders should compare the Second World War to the First, which had come to a bloody conclusion only twenty years earlier. They concluded that it was both worse and different. John Mackay suggested that the real meaning of the war was not simply that the lights were going out in Europe for awhile, as they had during the First World War. "On this occasion it is not a question of lights going out; it is a question of fires belching from beneath, which are predestined, ere they burn low again, to alter the substance and shape of things wheresoever they burn. Not the blackout, but the tongues of flame that leap from Libyan sands and Arctic snows, from tropical jungles and teeming cities, are a symbol of our present situation." Mackay believed that the war was not simply a conflict between rival imperialisms, as had been the case in the First World War. "This war is a conflict between rival understandings of life, which struggle not primarily for things, but for the souls of men."[8] Editor Hartman of *Zion's Herald* called it "more serious" than any crisis that civilized people had faced before.[9] Nathan R. Melhorn, editor of the *Lutheran*, suggested that the Second World War, unlike previous wars, erupted because common people had been deluded by the vain promises of demagogues who had aroused evil passions in their followers and led them to forsake their convictions about God.[10]

Theologians often looked past World War I to search for other crises, more tumultuous still, to which the Second World War could be compared. A statement issued by the administrative board of the National Catholic Welfare Conference began with the bold assertion: "Christianity faces today its most serious crisis since the Church came out of the catacombs."[11] Christopher Dawson argued that the West had not faced such upheaval since Augustine of Hippo lived.[12] William T. Manning, Episcopal Bishop of New York City, declared that the ruthless ambition of Hitler rivaled the rapacity of Genghis Khan.[13] No event in the ravaged and reeling history of Western civilization, in other words, was sufficiently horrible to rival the Second World War, which towered above them all.

The war was seen as a warning to Americans. It exercised such significant influence largely because of what the American people did *not* have to face. Though affecting virtually every aspect of American life, the crisis of World War II was kept safely on foreign soil. Thousands of miles separated most

Americans and the theaters of operation. The distance between America and the arena of conflict afforded Americans the opportunity—the luxury, really—to think about the meaning and implications of the conflict without having to fight for their very lives. For Americans the outcome of the war never boiled down to a question of survival. They had the freedom therefore to ask bigger questions about the war. They could be more reflective, philosophical, and visionary. That the crisis occurred "over there," and not in America, reminded the American people of what *could* happen to their nation if its people were not alerted to and protected from the forces, both military and ideological, that were destroying Europe. The war was close enough to threaten the American way of life—too often taken for granted—but far enough to give Americans the chance to change before it was too late.

This opportunity to reflect on the nature of the crisis motivated the American people to take inventory of America's soul. To conquer the enemy, the nation would have to marshal its resources as never before. Many Christians believed that these resources would have to be both physical and spiritual. Military might was not sufficient in itself to repel the foe and save Western civilization, for the war was not primarily a conflict between rival armies. Spiritual and moral renewal was even more necessary to win the greater battle of ideas. Religious leaders believed, therefore, that the Second World War provided the church with a rare opportunity to reaffirm Christianity's importance in America. If democracy symbolized the American way of life, then Christianity was the bulwark of democracy. If liberty occupied the principal place in the American creed, then Christianity was the source, defender, and protector of that liberty. If moral goodness embodied the American character at its best, then Christianity was the foundation of morality.

Christian leaders recognized that the war was pivotal for religion because religion was essential to winning the real war. They wanted the Christian faith and the church to play major roles in the war effort because they believed that religion and patriotism were partners in a divine purpose. They sensed intuitively that Christianity, the assumed cornerstone of America's heritage, was ripe for revitalization or doomed to failure and ruin. As John Mackay stated, "The destiny of this country is inseparably bound up with loyalty to its national heritage. Apart from faith in God the history of America has no meaning." Sensing that an epochal moment in history had arrived, Mackay announced: "There are times in the history of persons and peoples, particularly times of tomorrow, when the awakening of a sense of heritage becomes a portent determinant of destiny."[14]

Religion and War

Religion and war have been on friendly terms throughout Western history. In the name of God armies have marauded rival cities, invaded rival nations, and fought against rival empires. That has been true for a religion like Islam. It has been no less true for Christianity. While a small stream of pacifism has fed itself into the Christian church since the Apostolic age, the major currents of Christianity have rejected pacifism in favor of a more militarist position. Charlemagne was both a great conqueror and the Holy Roman Emperor, the first of many who were able to combine the two functions without a violation of conscience. Countless popes were not hesitant to marshal military power to defend or expand their authority. Pope Urban II, for example, was the first of several popes who pronounced a divine blessing upon the crusades. The European wars of the sixteenth and seventeenth centuries were also fought in the name of religion.

American history has followed the same pattern. North and South were divided religiously as well as economically and militarily during the Civil War. Before the war erupted at Fort Sumter, Presbyterians, Methodists, and Baptists broke fellowship over the issue of slavery. During the war both northern and southern branches of these great denominations gave succor and support to their respective governments and armies. In the First World War the churches embraced a similar patriotic mission. Many clergy were eager to invoke the name of God for the great crusade of making the world safe for democracy. In their enthusiasm the clergy stirred the American people to paroxysms of patriotism.

Scholars have studied the role religion played in every major war in which Americans have fought, with World War II as the one exception. For some reason scholars have overlooked how the churches participated in the war and how the war affected the churches. Why the apparent neglect? First, the more recent past has not received the scholarly attention from historians of religion that it will with the passage of time and the growth of the relatively new discipline of American religious history. Time and expansion will allow religious historians to explore what has already been investigated from other points of view, perhaps shedding new light on old subjects. A religious perspective may help historians to see familiar haunts with fresh eyes, World War II being no exception.

Second, study of the war itself—foreign policy, mobilization, campaigns and operations, postwar settlement—has so dominated scholarly attention that other areas of scholarly investigation have gone largely unnoticed.

Some of these neglected topics, like working women and conscientious objectors, have recently attracted the interest of historians. An avalanche of books has followed. But not so in the case of religion and the war. In the eyes of many historians, religion was simply and unobtrusively present during the war, functioning blandly, if at all, to inspire, comfort, and strengthen the American people. But it did not appear to play the kind of conspicuous and major role that, say, conscription, the Roosevelt presidency, or the Holocaust did. Thus scholars have passed it over because its importance seems to pale in comparison with other topics. Even social historians concentrating on the American home front have largely ignored the topic of American religion and the war. Scholars have thereby assumed that religion and the war were only loosely or accidently related, neither one having much impact on the other. It has been customary, in other words, to study American religion in the 1940s and overlook the war, or to study the war and overlook religion.

American Christianity, however, did play a role in the war. It was vital, complex, and creative. It contributed significantly to the war effort. The war also affected American Christianity, in some cases by sending it in new directions, in other cases by correcting the course it had already chosen for itself. Like rationing, religion's presence and influence was so diffused and universal that it was often taken for granted. But, again like rationing, its impact during the war was enormous.

The primary and secondary sources on the war are overwhelming. The wealth of sources poses a problem for historians. Given the many stories that historians could tell about the war, how should they organize the material so that they tell one story well without saying too little or too much? Since historians cannot tell the whole story, how can they tell one part of the story and still tell the whole truth?

The purpose of this book is to tell the story of the American churches and the Second World War. As if flying a reconnaissance mission over vast stretches of unchartered territory, it will read the terrain in only one way and sketch only one kind of map. This map will introduce a new question into the study of the Second World War: what was the nature of the church's patriotism during the war?

Patriotic Options

There would appear to be three possible answers. First, the churches could have been fanatically patriotic. Such indeed was the nature of the churches' patriotism during the First World War, at least as church leaders remembered it in the 1920s and 1930s. The American churches could have followed a similar course during the Second World War. They could have been jingoistic and self-righteous, a posture that comes naturally to religious people who invoke the blessing of God upon a national crusade. Sometimes there appears to be a good reason for such national enthusiasm. The union of church and state benefits both parties during wartime. The state wins the support of a powerful institution and the sanction of an ultimate authority. The church, in turn, wins public respect and the state's approval, protection, even patronage.

To defend this point of view, church leaders could have appealed to hard, cold realism. They could have argued that Christianity itself would not survive unless Nazism was defeated and democracy preserved. The necessity of such a realistic perspective has often been and will continue to be a cogent argument during wartime, especially if the enemy is obviously evil. Hitler seems to have met this criterion.

Church leaders could have maintained that it was the church's duty during wartime to play a priestly role. They could have reasoned that a generous demonstration of support and encouragement was more appropriate, considering the stress of the conflict, than an unmitigated dose of criticism. They could have simply decided to postpone a prophetic ministry until after the war was over.

Religious leaders could have used the war as the perfect opportunity to demonstrate their patriotism to a doubting public. Religious pacifism had been popular between the wars, especially among mainline church leaders. Having later abandoned peacetime pacifism, as many of them eventually did, these leaders could have felt embarrassment over their "naive idealism" and reacted to it by becoming fanatically patriotic, thus proving to the public that they had "recovered" from their pacifism and were unconditionally loyal to America, war or no war.

Church leaders could have assumed that the war itself needed a religious legitimation because the public was not altogether sure that the war was worth fighting, at least before Pearl Harbor. They could have tried to show that the stakes were much higher than the popular mind thought. Indeed, religious legitimation has swayed the public in many wars. It has created an aura of divine blessing around war that few have dared to question. If God is the final authority and he sanctions a war—now a "holy" war—then how can anyone appeal to a higher authority to question such a decree?

Church leaders could have assumed that the church was poised to gain definite advantages by joining the side of war mania, thereby ingratiating itself to the nation's leaders. They might have sensed that the church was on the verge of advancing its own interests—say, in missions or social action or world peace—if America won the war. Total victory could have provided unimaginable opportunity and power for the church, under the one condition that the church silence all criticism of the nation during the war. The other alternative—unpopularity and gradual decline—would have been considered too costly. The specter of unmitigated evil in Europe was so ominous and the opportunity for the churches with an allied victory so great that church leaders would seem to have been inclined to be incautiously patriotic. As we shall see, however, with only a few exceptions they did not follow this course.

Second, the churches could have been unpatriotic. Like the prophets of old, church leaders could have castigated a nation that thought itself righteous enough to wage war against an evil enemy when its own faults, if not worse than the enemy's in an absolute sense, were at least as bad as the enemy's in a relative sense, considering the special favor God had bestowed on the nation. They could have chided America for neglecting to solve its social problems during a time when these problems were flaring up in new and ugly ways. They could have adduced that fighting a war abroad was hypocritical when racism, injustice, and corruption still thrived at home. Religious leaders had plenty of evidence at their disposal to make such a case against America. Over 110,000 Japanese Americans were interned in relocation camps during the war, though the majority of them were American citizens. African Americans were segregated in the armed services and discriminated against in war industry. Giant corporations were making huge profits from the war while small businesses were being squeezed out. How could America have dared to condemn another nation's sins and yet overlook its own?

Christian leaders could have contended that true Christians ought to be internationalists, the citizens of a fellowship that encompasses the globe. Their loyalty should be to the whole world, not to one nation; to the worldwide community of believers, not to a society of people who just happen to live within the same borders. Christians in America, after all, probably had more in common with most German Christians than they had with American fascists or communists. The war provided the churches with a perfect opportunity to shed the rags of nationalism and put on the robes of internationalism. Surely the first step was obvious: denounce narrow patriotism and embrace the cause of international peace and goodwill.

Church leaders could have affirmed that the Christian faith is simply and unequivocally opposed to war. Jesus said that his followers should love their enemies and return good for evil. He taught that love and war are irreconcilable. Did Christians, then, really have a choice? Surely nonresistance—the way of love—was morally superior to violence—the way of hate. Assuming, as many did before World War II began, that war was ultimate evil, worse even than totalitarianism, Christians could have avowed that the Christian faith requires absolute repudiation of violence, nationalism, hate, revenge, retaliation, even defense against attack. They could have decided to live for peace regardless of what the government ordered them to do.

Then, to repulse attacks from their patriotic opponents, who would have undoubtedly accused them of being traitors, church leaders could well have decided to follow a politically cautious strategy to reach their pacifist goals. They could have practiced prudence in the political arena—say, in urging an immediate peace without victory. They could have used the rhetoric of patriotism to secure the civil liberties they needed as much as anyone did to continue their absolute opposition to the war, thus preserving for themselves the very rights that war imperils. They could have tempered their chastisement of America by lauding the America of idealism, the America of freedom, peace, and goodwill. Such a cautious political strategy would have made their criticism of the other America—the warring America—less conspicuous and offensive.

Third, the churches could have been—and turned out to be, as I will argue in this book—cautiously patriotic. Writing during the war, some religious leaders observed that the churches had assumed exactly that position. In an article written for *Social Action* and later included in a book on religion and war, Roland Bainton, a pacifist and historian, observed that, unlike previous American wars, especially World War I, the churches shunned jingoism and fanaticism during the Second World War. Though pacifism had collapsed by Pearl Harbor, "its place was not taken by a crusade in which the knight could fight without qualm, assured that the cause was holy, that God was with him and Christ beside him, and that victory would be a triumph of the cross. Such a mood recurred but slightly this time and chiefly in secular quarters. Practically every church pronouncement was replete with the note of contrition. . . . The attitude was sober, matter-of-fact, and entirely unsentimental."[15]

Ray Abrams, another pacifist whose book on the clergy and World War I had pricked the conscience of church leaders in the 1930s, reported that the pervasive mood in America was relatively calm. "A few bellicose warmongers, yes, but they were not outstanding, certainly." He concluded: "In general, the clergy were calm about the struggle, and, in fact, in their sermons seem to have paid relatively less attention to the current problems of the war than one might have supposed. The generalization is based on data gathered from all over the United States. The war was a grim necessity—something to be gotten over as soon as possible. Again, a greater toleration of diverse opinions was demonstrated. The Jehovah's Witnesses fared badly, it is true. Yet, the record of civil liberties appears better this time than for the previous war."[16] Columnist G. Elson Ruff of the *Lutheran Standard*, added: "The churches have accepted the war as a fact without much philosophizing about it one way or the other. In 1917 many churches were busy abetting the war fury. In 1943, although pacifist resistance to war has subsided to a whisper, the churches have shown no disposition to devote their talents to inciting war lust. They are finding outlet for surplus energy in a surge of peace planning."[17]

The churches were loyal to America and the American war effort. Their heritage and the nation's, their destiny and the nation's, were too tightly interwoven to make disloyalty a reasonable option for the vast majority of Christians. Most Christians in America had grown up believing that America occupied a special place in God's plan for history. It would have been difficult—virtually impossible, really—for the churches to be unpatriotic.

But the churches did not gravitate to the other extreme either. They were not blindly and fanatically patriotic. They attached certain conditions to their patriotism. These conditions grew out of a belief in the global fellowship of the church, the possibility of international peace and cooperation, the cultural significance of vital religion, and the relevance of biblical standards of justice. Christians were committed to the allied cause but refused to call it a holy crusade or to caricature the enemy. They believed that America had a divine destiny, but only insofar as the church was spiritually vital and the nation was morally good. They affirmed that the allied cause was righteous, but they recoiled from self-righteousness. If the outcome of the war did not establish a righteous peace and create new opportunities for the church, then the war, though successful in its operation, would have been considered a failure in its outcome. The benefits gained by victory would endure only if religion was strong.

This cautious patriotism enabled the churches to rally their resources to fight the war on the side of the allies and yet maintain biblical fidelity and spiritual integrity. They tried to strike a balance between nationalism and internationalism, political realism and religious idealism, priestly concern and prophetic criticism. They wanted to walk the thin line between labeling totalitarianism as the absolute enemy and viewing war as the ultimate evil, between striving for total victory and seeking peace at any price. Throughout the war they kept affirming belief in a transcendent God, in an independent church, and in an authoritative religion. They tried to minister to the needs of the nation, but not at the expense of their commitment to justice and peace.

Cautious patriotism was possible because the churches made religion a more important issue during the war than the war itself. They called the nation to repentance and religious renewal even as they provided comfort and hope to soldier and civilian. Theodore Hume spoke for many when he wrote: "Even if a church is true to its Gospel, there is no assurance that it will survive, in any recognizable form, the whirlwind which is sweeping so many institutions into the discord. But there is a chance, still more greatly to be prized, that the true 'church within the churches' may be used of God as a lens to focus His judgments for men to see, and as a vessel to lift to the lips of a despairing mankind the cup of hope from which men may take refreshing, and find life inwardly renewed."[18] The war was not ultimately a military conflict to be won by superior military power, nor was it a political conflict to be won by a superior system of government. It was a spiritual conflict that called for a resurgence of religion. The war was the church's opportunity to increase its influence in world affairs. Church leaders were confident that the church would rise to the occasion. They believed, as Walter Marshall Horton, professor of theology at Oberlin College, wrote, that "religion has not permanently lost its cultural creativity, that the recent cultural sterility of Western religion and the recent secularization of Western society do but evidence that a particular outburst of religious creativity, on which we had been living for some centuries, has now spent its force; that our civilization can and must experience religious rebirth, which alone can inaugurate a new ascending phase of the culture cycle and save what is salvable in our existing institutions."[19]

How the churches expressed this cautious patriotism varied from issue to issue and from event to event. The churches were not always in agreement. They were often deeply and bitterly divided, especially over the prospects of American involvement in the war. The substance of that debate, however, reveals that the churches, though divided on matters concerning strategy, were united in their basic convictions about American democracy, freedom, and religion (chapters 2, 3, and 4). Church leaders, moreover, gave different religious interpretations of the war. In most cases, however, they looked to a transcendent God who judges all nations, even America, and who calls all peoples, even Americans, to repentance. Wartime theodicy did not so much make the church an accomplice to militarism as made it attentive to truths that transcended the conflict (chapter 5). Similarly, the churches were not always of one mind in determining what the church's proper role ought to be during wartime. But they were united in believing that victory itself would be worth very little if the peace did not strengthen the church and advance the cause of Christianity in America and the world (chapters 6 and 7). Though nearly all the churches helped to fight the war abroad—through, say, the ministries of chaplains and denominational programs for servicemen and civilians (chapters 8 and 9)—they were also committed to fighting other wars at home. Many churches considered it unconscionable to fight against totalitarianism abroad and deny civil liberties at home. That many Christian leaders spoke out against discrimination against African Americans and condemned the internment of Japanese Americans proves that the churches were not blind to America's faults and weaknesses. These Christians, the exception in a culture that was essentially racist during the war, would not let the prophetic voice of the church be silenced, even during wartime (chapter 10). The churches did not always speak with one voice on the moral implications of the war. Yet they were all in agreement that war exacts a horrible cost and were committed to mitigating those costs. They never lost sight of a biblical vision of mercy and justice (chapters 11 and 12). Finally, the churches did not always have a unified vision of the postwar world, but together they devoted themselves to securing a just peace and extending the church's influence in the world, particularly through world missions. Military victory was only a means to the much more important end of world peace, church unity, and spiritual renewal (chapter 13).

There are exceptions to this general argument, of course. Not all church groups in America were patriotic, not all churches were cautiously patriotic, not all churches expressed cautious patriotism in the same way. Not all denominations, for example, tried to protect the civil liberties of Americans at home. Of those that did, not all defended the same liberties. Some were more concerned about freedom of speech, others about freedom of religion. Some supported the Jehovah's Witnesses, others American communists, and still others Japanese Americans. Some churches provided support for orphaned missions, others for Jewish refugees, and still others for prisoners of war. The churches were not always of one mind during the war. There was no shortage of tension and competition. That there was a basic unity of concern, a similarity of patriotic posture, is the thesis of this book. The cautious patriotism of the churches is the story that must be told.

A number of subplots will surface throughout this study. These will be mentioned but not explored exhaustively. The Japanese American internment, the Holocaust, civilian public service camps, the military chaplaincy —these and many other subjects deserve a fuller treatment. Each is a story all in itself. Their coverage in this study will be limited by the boundaries of the thesis. Though important subjects, they will not be central.

I will limit my investigation to the public posture of church groups: what, for example, church leaders propounded in articles and books, what religious groups stated in their public resolutions, what churches and individual Christians actually did to fight the war abroad and the wars at home. Attention will be paid to the public conversation and action of the churches. Obviously the term "the churches" cuts both a wide and a narrow path. "The churches" may not always apply to all churches in America, nor "Christians" to all Christians in America, nor "church leaders" to all religious leaders in America. These terms will be used carefully and defined as precisely as possible, considering the context in which they appear.

The nature of the topic has governed the use of sources. I limited my research to those sources that tell the story of the churches' public life during the war. Primary sources include religious magazines and journals representing the viewpoints of roughly forty different groups, minutes of denominational meetings, and important books published during the war. Secondary sources include books written on different aspects of the American home front, like women and the war, selective service, war relief work, and Jewish refugee organizations, as well as books that tell the story of the churches and the war, such as the histories of various denominations, biographies of important Christian leaders, and studies of specific religious movements and organizations.

The wartime patriotism of the churches enabled them to live in a creative tension. This posture will be the focus of the book. In my mind it is worthy of serious exploration. In post-Vietnam America many Christians found it hard to believe that it was possible for the churches to be patriotic at all. In the post-Reagan era Christians may find it difficult to be anything but patriotic. This dialectical approach—what I am calling a "cautious patriotism"— may help the church become both priest and prophet, loyal citizen and loving critic of America.

CHAPTER TWO

PROMISES TO KEEP

Debate over moral and political issues never occurs in a vacuum. The terms, perspectives, and lines of argumentation are framed by the past. This general rule applies quintessentially to the American churches in the late 1930s when religious leaders and church groups began to debate the prospects of America's entry into the war. What made the debate so passionate, agonizing, and divisive was the huge gap that opened between the ideals of church leaders—their obsession with peace—and the reality of the world situation—the brutality of totalitarianism. The attempt to reconcile personal conviction and political fact explains why the war debate went on for so long and became so heated. It also explains why most churches entered the war with such caution.

From World War I to 1933

Church leaders became disillusioned after the First World War.[1] With few exceptions, they recoiled from the memory of the war and its outcome. Many Christians had witnessed the carnage firsthand. The senseless butchering of humanity horrified them. Poison gas, barbed war, machine guns, airplanes, tanks—technological "advances" over the last war in which Americans had fought—exposed the ugly nature of modern warfare. Clergy in particular wanted nothing more to do with war. The death toll of several millions only exacerbated the sense of revulsion to war that many Christians felt.

Yet the brutality of war—repulsive but hardly surprising—was not the only cause of offense. The wartime atmosphere in America aggravated the reaction. Many clergy were haunted by the memory of their own wartime behavior. They had been unprepared for the war, confused by the pressure of propaganda, deceived by the grandiose vision of a just postwar settlement, taken in by the apocalyptic warnings of a German victory. They had turned the war into a holy crusade and later came to regret it.

Their zeal had not gone unnoticed. In the early 1930s one author set out to tell the story of Protestant clergy and the war. Ray Abrams's book, *Preachers Present Arms*, indicted clergy for their fecklessness, hysteria, and naïveté. His book reminded the clergy of what could happen if they compromised their convictions. It told them of what in fact did happen when they sold their faith down the river of popularity and were swept away by the currents of war hysteria. Abrams did not hesitate to name names and quote sermons. Many leading Protestant clergy, such as Harry Emerson Fosdick, were pilloried before the public. They felt shame, but they also found courage. Abrams's book filled them with resolve. "NEVER AGAIN!" became the battle cry.

Postwar developments like the treaty of Versailles buttressed the clergy's determination to make sure it would not happen again. Initially most clergy considered the treaty a just settlement. The work of revisionist historians, however, persuaded them to change their minds. Within fifteen years clerical criticism of Versailles became as fashionable and passionate as their denunciations of the Hun during the war. It also served as a convenient explanation, though hardly a justification, for the rise of totalitarianism. Clergy believed that the punitive measures of Versailles had set the stage for the emergence of the likes of Hitler a decade later. The allies, in short, had unknowingly shot themselves in the foot, and maybe the head. Historians also began to shift blame for the outbreak of war. France and Russia were at fault, not just Germany. British imperialism was culpable, too.

Other facts came to light as well. The stories of German atrocities that had infuriated Americans during the war were later shown to be bogus. Americans, as it turned out, had been too gullible, an easy prey to propaganda. A report from the Nye Committee revealed that a ring of munitions manufacturers had lent a hand in creating conditions favorable to the outbreak of war and had prolonged the war once the outcome was certain. Powerful industrialists, propagandists, and politicians had thus duped the clergy. Americans had fought World War I in vain. Worse still, Americans had vainly fought the war in the name of God.

Clergy reaction was decisive and extreme. They were chastened, repentant, and determined. They decided to turn their backs on war and embrace peace. World War I became a symbol of the senselessness of war itself. In the name of peace, they declared war on civilization's greatest enemy, war itself. "Never again" was taken literally.

The churches turned their immediate postwar attention to the League of Nations, which was supposed to provide a tool to eliminate future wars and establish international peace. Virtually every major denomination endorsed the league and urged the Senate to ratify it, and religious organizations like the Federal Council of Churches, Church Peace Union, and the World Alliance for International Friendship through the Churches threw their support behind the league and actively campaigned for its passage. Over 14,000 clergy signed a petition calling for its ratification. A new peace agency, the Committee on the Churches and the Moral Aims of War, was formed to inform the public and drum up popular support. Many denominations passed resolutions favorable to the league and religious journals advocated American membership. Many of the churches continued to urge entry even after the Senate failed to ratify it.

The churches gave even greater support to the Permanent Court for International Justice. Though the Senate was reluctant to ratify it, the Protestant churches were not reluctant to urge its ratification. Again, church bodies endorsed the idea of a World Court, and religious organizations like the Church Peace Union and the World Alliance for International Friendship conducted a campaign to arouse popular interest.

The churches appeared to give their most enthusiastic approval to the Pact of Paris, which was signed by fifty-nine nations, including the United States, on August 27, 1928 and approved by the Senate on January 15, 1929. The signatories agreed to renounce war as an instrument of national policy, though defensive wars were still allowed. Since many churches had denounced war as a means of solving international problems as early as 1921, they were stirred into action by the prospects of formulating an international agreement that would outlaw war altogether. The churches were thus early and vocal supporters of the pact. Denominations passed resolutions endorsing the pact, and the Federal Council of Churches (FCC) conducted a vigorous campaign to secure its adoption. Federal Council leaders presented to the president a petition approving the pact with 185,333 signatures on it. Similar petitions were presented to Congress. When the Senate finally approved it, church leaders exclaimed that it was a major victory for peace. A statement from the FCC read, "Let church bells be rung, songs sung, prayers of thanksgiving be offered and petitions for help from God that our nation may ever follow the spirit and meaning of the Pact."[2] Charles Clayton Morrison, editor of the *Christian Century* and a longtime opponent of war, announced, "Today international war was banished from civilization."[3]

The churches also advocated disarmament of offensive, and sometimes defensive, weapons. Many churches paid close attention to the Washington Conference, at which ten nations discussed military problems in the Pacific and set limitations on the construction of certain types of military ships. Denominational groups, church journals, and Christian leaders applauded the agreement and lobbied the Senate for ratification. The FCC, acting in concert with Roman Catholic and Jewish agencies, planned a Reduction of Armament Sunday, blanketed the churches with promotional literature, and pressured Congress to approve the agreement. The Washington Conference was only one of several international meetings at which the issue of disarmaments was discussed. That the churches showed such strong interest revealed the general sentiment within the churches that, because war was considered morally reprehensible, the nations were obligated to rid themselves of the weapons of war. Many voices within the church urged drastic reduction of armaments and protested any political decision that betrayed a militarist mind-set. There were exceptions, of course, particularly in the South. The major current of the churches, however, moved in that direction.

The churches reinforced these political positions with moral resolve. They appealed to the standards of biblical morality and believed that they were right in renouncing war. Hundreds of antiwar resolutions were passed by Christian groups. For example, in 1926 the General Synod of the Reformed Church in America declared: "The Church of Christ as an institution should not be used as an instrument or an agency in support of war." In 1931 the Presbyterian General Assembly testified: "The Church should never again bless a war." In 1929 the Evangelical Synod of North America gave allegiance to the conviction that "to support war is to deny the Gospel we profess to believe." In 1936 the General Conference of the Methodist Church proclaimed: "War as we now know it is utterly destructive. It is the greatest social sin of modern times; a denial of the ideals of Christ; a violation of human personality; and a threat to civilization. Therefore, we declare that the Methodist Episcopal Church as an institution does not endorse, support, or purpose to participate in war." In 1934 the Congregational General Council stated: "We of this Council are convinced that we must now make this declaration: 'The Church is through with war!' We of this Council call upon the people of our churches to renounce war and all its works and ways, and to refuse to support, sanction or bless it."[4]

These resolutions, of course, spoke the corporate mind of each denomination, not the mind of individual Christians. Church leaders recognized that individuals would have to follow their own consciences on the matter. Acknowledging that militarism was far more popular and persuasive during wartime than pacifism, they urged church groups to register and support the conscientious objectors among their ranks while peace still reigned. The Methodists, Episcopalians, Presbyterians, and Congregationalists did. Furthermore, the Presbyterians (in 1931), the Northern Baptists and Episcopalians (in 1934), and the Methodists and Unitarians (in 1936) voted to ask the government to give the same consideration to their conscientious objectors as it had given to the conscientious objectors from the historic Peace Churches during the First World War.

Not all Protestants were as idealistic. Some churches attached conditions to their pronouncements. The Presbyterian General Assembly, for example, proposed to circulate among its members a pledge that read, "I will not cross the borders of any nation except in friendship, nor will I support my country in such action." The statement was intended to voice objection to offensive wars, not defensive ones. In the same year the Northern Baptists proposed that its members pledge: "Reserving the right of national self-defense by such means as may seem to me wise, effective and Christian, I, from now on, definitely repudiate all aggressive war. I will cross no national boundary line to kill and destroy, nor will I support my government in sending its army and navy to do so." Southern Methodists added the defense of ideals as another condition. Christians, they affirmed, were obligated "to oppose by all proper and legal methods the resort to force for the alleged settlement of international controversies, except only in defense of those national ideals for the preservation of which the Republic was organized."[5]

Christian conviction moved not only against war but also for peace. Unlike many other Americans during the 1920s and 1930s, church leaders repudiated isolationism, which they regarded as a foolish reaction to the First World War, and embraced internationalism. Besides advocating entry into the League of Nations, participation in the World Court, and approval of the Paris Pact, church leaders were also busy organizing or joining peace organizations, like the Church Peace Union, the World Alliance for International Friendship through the Churches, and the National Council for Prevention of War. Further, the Federal Council of Churches Commission on International Peace and Goodwill gained wide influence, and many churches established peace groups and committees on international affairs.

Interest in internationalism emerged from the church's rejection of war. The antiwar sentiment that swept the churches in the 1920s found a positive outlet in the advocacy of international peace. Christians did not want to be surprised again by international upheaval and drawn unwittingly into the whirlpool of fanatical patriotism. They had fortified themselves against such temptations, embraced the worthy cause of international peace, and made their promises. They were prepared to resist any encroachment on their beliefs, any assault on their commitments. With olive branch in hand and dove on shoulder, they marched into the 1930s with an antiwar conviction as strong as they assumed their "holy crusade" during World War I had been wrong. They were ready for anything.

Then came Mussolini, Stalin, Hitler, Franco, and Hirohito. With them the real battle began. No one had anticipated—no one could have imagined—the brutality and fanaticism of these totalitarian rulers. The invasion of Manchuria and Ethiopia, the civil war in Spain, the pogroms in Russia, and the annexation of Austria and Czechoslovakia were evidence enough to convince anyone that Western civilization was facing a new threat. Fascism exalted the state above the individual, Nazism one race above others. Stalinism created a dictatorship to usher in a classless society that never appeared and probably never would. Japanese imperialism established a militarist society. How far these ideologies would eradicate liberty and disturb international peace no one knew. That these dictatorships were violent and expansionist no one doubted. The confusion of opinion came over what to do about them.

It would be difficult to exaggerate the problem that totalitarianism created for the churches. Living before World War II, the Holocaust, the atomic bomb, and the Cold War, American Christians were simply unaware of the violence and disruption that was soon to envelop the world. They knew nothing about a large, standing peacetime army, huge military bases dotting the globe, massive defense budgets, and whole industries devoted solely to peacetime weapons production. In 1935 the United States had an army the size of Turkey's; its military arsenals were virtually empty. Church leaders were living in an America that had not yet been awakened to the full potential of its international role in keeping the peace or in making war. They lived in a nation in which it was possible and even popular to reject militarism of any kind and renounce war, once and for all. Having recoiled from everything the First World War symbolized, they had taken a stand unequivocally on the side of peace. They were as serious and sincere as they believed totalitarianism was evil.

That, indeed, was the dilemma. The gap between Christian idealism and political reality, between moral conviction and totalitarian threat, became intolerably wide. Events in the 1930s created a crisis of conscience because these events showed how difficult—possibly even perilous—it would be to defend beliefs that had been formed in a period of peace and optimism. Church leaders were not simply facing a political problem; they were wrestling with what they perceived to be spiritual calamity. They were not simply dealing with foreign aggressors; they were struggling with what they identified as ominous ideologies. They were facing the dilemma of having to reconcile sincere beliefs with what appeared to be hard facts. How could they keep faith in God—a faith wrapped up in the white linens of peace rather than the red flag of war—and still meet head-on the fury that threatened to assault civilization as they knew it?

There were four possible answers to that question. First, they could conclude that totalitarianism had introduced a new element in the history of Western civilization and required a change of conviction. Second, they could reason that totalitarianism symbolized absolute evil and called for the declaration of a holy war. Third, they could identify the emergence of totalitarianism as the kind of apocalyptic event that made moral distinctions irrelevant. Fourth, they could believe that totalitarianism was the source of a new temptation that required Christians to remain strong, true, and unbending. Believing as they did that there was nothing worse than war, most church leaders decided for the fourth alternative. How most of them came to believe that there was indeed "something worse than war" tells the story of the churches between 1933 and Pearl Harbor.

From 1933 to Munich

The process of changing convictions took time. Before Munich the churches interpreted totalitarianism as a new temptation and tried to remain true to peacetime promises. If anything, they redoubled their determination to win a lasting peace in the world. These efforts reflected the earlier internationalism of the churches. Church leaders had not yet retreated into fortress America, as they did after Munich, when the wall between isolationists and antiwar internationalists was broken down to create a larger army of neutralists.

In late 1935 the National Peace Conference was formed to promote world peace. Headed by Protestant ecumenical leader Walter Van Kirk, it functioned as a coordinating agency for some thirty peace groups, including the Fellowship of Reconciliation, the Congregationalists Council for Social Action, the Federal Council of Churches Department of International Justice and Goodwill, the Methodist World Peace Commission, and the World Alliance for International Friendship through the Churches. This new agency brought peace advocates and government officials together, enabling the former to suggest concrete peace proposals to the latter. Members of the agency introduced drafts of peace planks to both political parties in 1936. They urged continuation of reciprocal trade, a stabilized International Labor Organization, opposition to military protection of overseas investments, government control of munitions industry, and cooperation with the League of Nations.

One year later, in 1936, an Emergency Peace Campaign was organized. Many of the outstanding Protestant clergy of the nation were involved, including Harry Emerson Fosdick, Theodore Hume, A. B. Coe, Kirby Page, and Albert W. Palmer. Members of the committee conducted preaching crusades against involvement in foreign wars. They advocated an internationalist platform that included such planks as foreign relief, international trade, and participation in the League of Nations and World Court. Members also thundered against military preparedness, although they conceded that armaments for defense were necessary, and they called for mandatory neutrality legislation, an embargo on munitions, and a "cash-and-carry" plan for all other goods.

Then, in 1938, antiwar internationalists began to call for an economic conference to discuss what they believed to be a significant cause of the conflict brewing in Europe—the allocation of economic resources. A Belgian statesman had submitted a report on a program for general economic reform, and it was this report that rallied the forces of Protestant peace advocates. Even Munich did not dampen their enthusiasm. In November 1938 Federal Council leaders approached the World Council about the possibility of an economic conference but were turned down. A meeting was held anyway, in 1939, to discuss international economic issues. Among the participants were such mainline Protestant leaders as John Foster Dulles, J. H. Franklin, Georgia Harkness, Ivan Lee Holt, John R. Mott, Henry S. Leiper, Roswell P. Barnes, and Albert W. Palmer, who was one of the initiators. As late as 1940 Charles Clayton Morrison of the *Christian Century* was still suggesting that the president send a delegation of twenty American statesmen to the neutral capitols of Europe to assemble a peace conference. He hoped that the conference would continue until the war was over and thus create a significant force for peace.

Church leaders made personal pledges, too. Again, they wanted to fortify themselves against the onslaught of temptation to bless war. Meeting in Riverside Church on May 2, 1935, 251 ministers and rabbis repeated the following pledge before God and faithful witnesses: "In loyalty to God I believe that the way of true religion cannot be reconciled with the way of war. In loyalty to my country I support its adoption of the Kellogg-Briand Pact [Paris Pact] which renounces war. In the spirit of true patriotism and with deep personal conviction, I therefore renounce war and never will I support another."[6] Three years later, when war in Europe seemed imminent, 149 members of this group of distinguished religious leaders repeated the pledge. Members of this same group also formed the Covenant of Peace Group. Its creed stressed absolute pacifism. Over 1,000 clergy had signed the pledge by 1940; 1,900 by 1941. This kind of pledge was typical of the time.

An example of a more moderate pacifist declaration came from the Young Men's Club of the Broadway Tabernacle of New York, where participants repeated:

> I have quietly considered what I would do if my nation should again be drawn into war.
>
> I am not taking a pledge, because I do not know what I would do when the heat of the war mood is upon the country. But in a mood of calm consideration I do today declare that I cannot reconcile the way of Christ with the practice of war.
>
> I do therefore set down my name to be kept in the record of my Church, so that it will be for me a reminder if war should come; and will be a solemn declaration to those who hold to this [pacifist] conviction in time of war that I believe them to be right; and I do desire with my whole mind and heart that I shall be among those who keep to this belief.[7]

In 1935 even Reinhold Niebuhr could say: "I do not intend to participate in any war now in prospect." Though rejecting absolute pacifism, Niebuhr reasoned that he could see "no good coming out of any of the wars confronting us." The relative positions of Germany and Russia, he added, "would not affect my decision."[8]

Polls taken in the 1930s reveal that Christians and clergy were not ready to rally behind another war; they were, in fact, positively opposed to another war. In 1931 Kirby Page sent out a questionnaire to American clergy, 19,372 responding. Sixty-two percent said that the churches should declare publicly that they would not support a future war, over 45 percent declared that they would refuse to serve as military chaplains in wartime, and over 80 percent favored armament reductions, even if unilateral. Page conducted another poll in 1934. Of 20,870 clergy responding, 67 percent believed that the churches should declare opposition to future wars, 62 percent said that they would not sanction a future war or participate as an armed combatant, and the vast majority favored armament reductions.

Similar results came from other polls. In 1936 Bishop James C. Baker of the Methodist Episcopal Church sent out a questionnaire to clergy and received 12,854 replies. Fifty-six percent said that they would not sanction another war; only a minority, 36 percent, approved of the use of force against aggressor nations. In 1936 the Northern Baptist Convention also conducted a poll of its members. Though 42 percent said that they would bear arms if the United States were invaded, a sizable 26 percent declared that they would unconditionally refuse to serve. A similar poll of members of the Disciples of Christ in 1937 reveals that over 60 percent said they would fight if the United States were invaded, while a little over 20 percent claimed that they would not fight in any war. Less than 20 percent said that they would bear arms in every war in which the United States was engaged. Finally, in the largest poll conducted, with nearly 200,000 responding, leaders of the Congregationalists Council for Social Action learned that only 6 percent of the respondents would fight in any war the United States government declared, 33 percent would support a war in which the United States was invaded, 56 percent would not sanction any future war or participate as an armed combatant, and only 36 percent favored use of force against nations deemed as aggressors by the League of Nations.

The Page poll of 1934 shows that membership in particular denominations did influence the repondents' answers. For example, 96 percent of clergy from the Church of the Brethren, responding to the first question, believed that churches should go on record as refusing to sanction war, while only 38 percent of Lutherans did. Clergy from Reformed, Congregational, and Baptist churches took a middle position, all at about 60 percent. There was a similar distribution in the case of the second question, which asked if respondents were prepared to state that it was their conviction not to sanction any future war or participate as an armed combatant. Denominational affiliation therefore did have some predictive value.

Still, it is startling to consider the relatively high percentage of those who seemed to disavow war as a justifiable means of solving international disputes. Had the respondents stayed true to their word, America would have had to deal with well over a million conscientious objectors during the war. These polls reveal the sentiment that permeated the churches in the 1930s, when totalitarianism began to cast its menacing shadow over Europe.

Though this political posture became increasingly difficult to hold, peace advocates continued to be both militantly neutralist and internationalist. As late as 1941 church leaders formed the Ministers No War Committee. Palmer, Holt, Ernest Fremont Tittle, Page, A. J. Muste, and Harkness were among its members. Also organized was the Churchmen's Campaign for Peace through Mediation. Morrison, A. E. Day, E. Stanley Jones, Fosdick, and many others were involved. Some 600 signed a call for a "negotiated peace," which became the watchword of the pacifists.

Church leaders pleaded for neutrality. While the United States drifted toward war and the Axis powers began to gobble up Europe, Africa, and Asia, they opposed nearly every piece of legislation and every governmental policy—amended neutrality, conscription, lend-lease, the destroyer deal, increased defense spending, arms production—that even hinted at involvement in the war. Such was the determination of the "neutralists" to resist the temptation of compromise, to stay true to their promises, to keep America out of the war. Their "Never Again" had become a confession of faith. They would not betray it, and they did their best to defend it, though mounting evidence made their position increasingly difficult to hold.

From Munich to Pearl Harbor

The strain between moral idealism and political fact approached the breaking point after war broke out in Europe. Gradually all but a few denominations, all but a few hundred church leaders, and all but a few thousand Christians (excluding members of the Peace Churches) shifted from advocacy of neutrality to support of interventionism, if, that is, they did not already hold to the historic "just war" point of view. Most of the churches eventually rallied behind the allied cause and supported America's entry into the war. But they came to this decision slowly, carefully, soberly, and tentatively. Meanwhile, between Munich and Pearl Harbor, the churches entered a period of confusion, turmoil, and struggle. Convictions, born out of the horrors and failures of the last war and nurtured to maturity through twenty years of peace activity, confronted an unanticipated problem. It was agonizing for Christians to reconsider their position and reconcile their high ideals with new political realities.

Until 1938 church opinion, pledges, and polls had dealt with war in the abstract, the possibility of war, *should* it arise. Would conviction hold if the question became concrete, if the question of *war in Europe*, war against the Nazis, was raised? The answer appears to be "yes." Again, evidence indicates that church leaders in particular, like the population in general, came to war slowly and cautiously. They were uncertain about, sometimes hostile to, the possibility of American involvement, a position they maintained, with some notable exceptions, all the way to Pearl Harbor. Though religious leaders favored some kind of defense program, sympathized with England, and believed totalitarianism to be evil, they nevertheless strived to keep America neutral because they abhorred the thought of war. Eventually most of them changed their minds. Even then church leaders pledged only a chastened, sorrowful, and measured support. The war was a grim necessity, not a holy crusade.

This hesitation after war broke out in Europe attracted the attention of secular journalists, who criticized the churches for their ambivalence. An editorial appearing in the January 1940 issue of *Fortune* decried the moral relativism and religious compromise of the churches in America. America had been founded upon religious values, the editorial read. But over the last one hundred years the influence of religion had declined, largely because of the weakness of the churches and clergy. "The Church, as teacher and interpreter of those values," the article continued, "is the guardian of our faith in them. And as laymen we do not feel that the faith is being guarded."

To support this criticism, the editorial mentioned what it considered to be the church's worst failure in the twentieth century, its attitude toward war. Before the First World War the clergy resisted American entry because they believed war was evil. Yet after America entered the war the clergy mounted their pulpits and turned furiously upon the enemy, using invective that even surpassed the bitter denunciations made by soldiers. Then later, in peace, the clergy repudiated war as passionately as they had applauded it only two years earlier. They were ashamed of their wartime behavior and retracted all their former statements. A number of clergy even turned to pacifism. When war broke out again in 1939, the clergy were thus back where they had been in 1914, opposed, "almost to a man," to American involvement.

The editorial accused the clergy of two failures: "First, the values used by the Church in reaching its decisions could not have been absolute spiritual values because by no spiritual logic is it possible to get from one of these positions to the other. The threat to Christianity from the Kaiser in 1917 was far less than the threat from Hitler is today. . . . Yet the men who urged United States soldiers in 1917 to face death against an ordinary emperor, whose chief sin was worldly ambition, now conclude that it would be wrong to fight a virtual Antichrist whose doctrines strike at the base of the civilization which the Church has done so much to build." The editorial reported the results of a survey of over 80 pastors. Responding to *Fortune* questions, these clergy sent in long, often troubled answers. They admitted that, contrary to popular opinion, clergy were fallible. Their drastic change of opinion about war was evidence enough of that. They also talked about the tormenting disillusionment that had swept over the clergy in the 1920s and 1930s, to which the editorial quipped, "It is for the flesh to be disillusioned, not for the soul."

If the first failure of the clergy was a crisis of absolute values, as the editorial argued, the second was a crisis of leadership. How, the editorial wondered, could the clergy be trusted this time around, considering their former vicissitudes? "[I]f the pastors were not reasoning from absolute spiritual grounds last time, how can we be sure that they are doing so this time? Their position today is almost exactly what it was in 1914, and their arguments are almost the same. How much will it take to get them over on the other side of the fence? The answer would seem to be clear: the pastors will go over to the other side when, as and if the people go over to the other side." The result, concluded the editorial, was cause for *real* despair. The decline of clergy influence would lead to unbridled materialism. Further, it would give way to *genuine* disillusionment because ordinary Americans, when consulting the church for absolute truth, would "hear only what we ourselves have said."

The only solution to this serious problem was a return to absolute values and a renewal of spiritual leadership—initiated, of course, by the clergy. "The way out is the sound of a voice, not our voice, but a voice coming from something not ourselves, in the existence of which we cannot disbelieve. It is the earthly task of the pastors to hear this voice, to cause us to hear it, and to tell us what it says. . . . Without it we are no more capable of saving the world than we were capable of creating it in the first place."[9]

The editorial was not completely accurate. The situation of 1940 was not "exactly" as it had been in 1914 because the clergy of that earlier period had not had the equivalent of the First World War to look back on, the memory of which haunted them. Nor had they joined ranks to march away from war, chanting "Never Again." Nor had they *prepared* themselves to resist the great temptation of wartime hysteria. Nor had they been holding a fistful of promises, pledges, resolutions, proposals, and plans in their hands to keep them on the straight and narrow. Then again, they had never before had to confront the dilemma of having purposed to live according to ideals while the fact of totalitarianism forced them to face reality. The editorial in *Fortune* called for absolute values but sadly expected only relative values from the clergy, whose constant shifts of opinion supposedly proved how spineless they really were.

In August 1942 an article appeared in *Time* that expressed similar displeasure because the churches had not declared themselves either for or against the war. Once again the editorial claimed that clergy had shown an inability to make sound moral judgments. The article stated that the church's authority in America was diminishing because its leaders could not—or would not—make up their minds about the war. Their neutrality reflected a lack of moral courage. "Few things better illustrate the reason United States churches do not enjoy a more impressive leadership in American life than their shilly-shallying about the war. In the eight months since Pearl Harbor, only one major denomination (the United Lutheran Church) has placed itself unequivocally behind the U.S. war effort. Yet no major church has had the courage to take the opposite stand, and state unequivocally that the church's job is religion, not war." The *Time* article reported on a group of Protestant leaders, acting "as individuals," who came out "unequivocally" on the side of the allies, declaring that the church could not be neutral in a conflict between totalitarian aggression and democracy. The editorial commended the statement, which had been signed by 87 Protestant leaders, but not without raising one question. "Conspicuously absent from this program is any mention of the church's—and the country's—biggest lack in fighting World War II: a great dynamic faith. Only Germany and Russia, the two nations most hostile to Christianity, have shown such a faith."[10]

It is not hard to identify the operative words in the two articles: "absolute" and "unequivocal." Contrary to what these articles concluded, it could be that this "shilly-shallying" of the churches actually reflected an absolute and unequivocal stand rooted in the relativities and ambiguities of a fallen world. It could be that the churches were trying to make a definite statement by *refusing* to endorse in absolute and unequivocal terms either holy war or absolute pacifism. It could be that these articles completely misunderstood the churches. As we shall see in the next chapter, that is what seems to be the case.

CHAPTER THREE

THE FINE LINE

A survey of editorials, articles, and resolutions coming from major religious groups indicates that the vast majority of churches were trying to walk a fine line between yielding to what became the inevitability of war and pursuing what continued to be their commitment to peace. Few religious groups arrived easily at the position of supporting the war effort, and none seemed to support it with enthusiasm.

What follows in this chapter is a series of case studies that explore how several different religious bodies responded to the war in Europe and to America's involvement in that war, which culminated in Roosevelt's plea to Congress to declare war on Japan. In almost every case what is most apparent and startling about these studies is the obvious ambivalence and struggle that characterized the response of religious groups. They resisted coming to the conclusion that America should enter the war. It was not at all apparent to them that American involvement was the best and only option. Thus, what appears clear to many Americans today—and what appeared clear to many Americans even then—remained cloudy to a surprising number of religious groups before, and even after, Pearl Harbor.

Denominational Responses

It is difficult to determine, of course, just how accurately the religious bodies that gathered at annual meetings to discuss the war or the religious periodicals that printed the opinions of church members about the war represented the sentiments of the majority of local clergy and lay people. Were they speaking *for* the churches or simply speaking *to* the churches? Were they reflecting the opinions of ordinary church members or trying to mold their opinion? To what extent did these pronouncements, articles, and editorials voice the convictions of ordinary Christians across America?

That these bodies spoke *to* the churches is beyond dispute. The Disciples of Christ, for example, never spoke as a body for the churches, even at its national meetings. Delegates spoke to the churches; they did not presume to speak for them. They aimed instead to educate and to stimulate discussion. But there is at least some reason to believe that these denominational gatherings and religious periodicals also spoke *for* the churches.

There are several reasons for this assumption. First, the gap between denominational executives and ecumenical leaders, on the one hand, and local clergy and church members, on the other, was not as wide then as it became later on during the civil rights movement and the war in Vietnam. Those two events became lightning rod issues that divided many denominational leaders and local churches. Second, denominational gatherings tended to speak for the churches simply because the people who assembled together were sent as representatives of regional bodies and local congregations. They were more inclined, therefore, to remain loyal to the people who sent them because, when they returned home, they had to answer to those same people.

If anyone was inclined to speak to the churches, it was denominational executives and ecumenical leaders, who were farther removed from weekly communication with ordinary—and usually more conservative—church members. When they discussed issues (like America's entry into the war), they talked more often than not among themselves. Their resistance to America's entry into the war was recorded in such ecumenical publications as the *Christian Century* and the *Federal Council Bulletin*.

But what follows in this chapter is not a string of quotes and pronouncements from the *Christian Century* and the *Federal Council Bulletin*. It contains the pronouncements—and dissenting opinions—that were issued from official *denominational meetings* whose delegates represented the convictions of the faithful back home, and it explores the debates and editorials recorded on the pages of *denominational periodicals*. Their sentiments were not identical to average church members; but they were certainly closer to them than the opinions of executives and ecumenical leaders.

These denominational meetings often became occasions for heated debate about America's entry into the war. In some cases dissenting groups actually filed minority reports. Denominational periodicals in turn printed many articles, editorials, and letters that reflected a similar range of disagreement. Again, that debate surfaced in virtually every denomination across America indicates something of the serious struggle that occurred among Christians in America who wanted to apply Christian principles to their response to the war in Europe.

The Disciples

In 1939 the International Convention of the Disciples passed a resolution that condemned the war and urged American neutrality. Unlike earlier declarations, this one was no longer addressing war in the abstract. "War on a large scale has again become a reality," it read.

> All of us are faced with the necessity of confronting frankly the present implications of our past resolutions in which we have condemned war as a pagan and futile method for the solution of international disputes, and served notice to all concerned that we can never again bless or sanction another.
>
> In this present crisis, we Disciples of Christ seek to maintain unswerving loyalty to our Lord, the Prince of Peace, and to be guided in our thinking and acting by our past commitment.

The declaration then proceeded to give practical consideration to the war in Europe. For example, it stated that no international conflict ever arose from a single, isolated incident but from a series of actions that exposed the guilt of all nations, including the United States. It alerted Americans to exercise careful judgment and to avoid hatred and revenge, especially in the light of how craftily government officials used political propaganda to manipulate the public. Finally, it acknowledged that Christians in all nations had to share the blame for allowing, even perpetuating, political and economic injustices that made war possible. The declaration concluded:

> It is our considered judgment that the United States can make its greatest contribution to world justice and brotherhood by remaining out of the present conflict of arms. Thus she may be in a better position to share her influence and resources in the building of a cooperative world order which can provide the basis for an impartial and genuine peace.

We are agreed that every executive and legislative precaution ought to be taken to keep the United States out of war. We are in favor of placing such limitation upon the credits, trade, and travel of citizens of the United States as may be necessary to prevent the recurrence of incidents which might lead to their government's becoming involved in armed conflict.[1]

The mood of the resolution is clear enough. Not strictly pacifist—few denominations were—but somber, cautious, and repentant. The Disciples wanted a negotiated peace and believed that American neutrality would put it in a position to preside over the making of such a peace. They would not heap all the blame on one party, caricature and hate the enemy, and reduce the problem to one issue—say, imperialism. They tried to present a balanced point of view.

The Disciples approved another resolution at its May 1941 convention. It was more flexible than the 1940 statement, acknowledging, for example, that more than one point of view was possible, though war itself was still labeled unchristian. "While Disciples of Christ are agreed as to the unchristian nature of war," the statement read, "this convention recognizes that there are differences of opinion as to the course which individual Christians should take in the present war situation. . . . These differences of opinion extend to the question of the course that should be pursued by the United States with reference to the present conflict."[2] The statement spelled out the positions of two parties: one advocated aid to the democratic nations, short of war, and the other urged strict neutrality. One side stressed the need to defeat totalitarianism, and the other side emphasized the necessity of securing a just peace. The resolution affirmed that both perspectives were legitimate.

Still, the Disciples did not hesitate to call upon the president to keep America out of the war. "The International Convention of Disciples of Christ respectfully and earnestly petition the President of the United States to use the great powers of his office to keep this nation out of the war now raging in Europe, Asia, and Africa."[3]

The role of the church, however, was more important than the policy of the president. In "A Message to the Churches," which Disciples approved at the same convention, attention was shifted away from the problem of war to the role of the church as an agent for peace. Though the church had not been as faithful as it should have been, the declaration nevertheless protested against unfair criticism of the church. "We refuse to acknowledge that the church is primarily to blame for the situation that prevails in the world. The church has made its protest against war as being un-Christian." The solution to the world's problems depended upon the Christian faith, the future peace upon the work of the church. Any kind of national war effort had to be made subservient to the church's peace effort. "Believing that the hope of civilization rests in no small degree upon the church, we dedicate ourselves to the task of making it worthy to lead." The church thus could never be a party to war. "We believe that war is antagonistic to the spirit of Christ, for his conception of the Fatherhood of God and brotherhood of man would make war impossible. War prevails over a large part of the world at the present time because those ideals have not been accepted. We recognize the futility of war and deplore conditions which lead to war, and regret the inability of the church to prevent it."[4]

This basic posture did not change significantly after Pearl Harbor. A special committee was appointed in May 1942 to study the Delaware proposal on a Just and Durable Peace. The committee presented a statement at the August 1942 convention of the Disciples. Supported by a majority of those attending the convention, the statement was sent to local congregations for study. It said nothing about the war effort, even though Pearl Harbor had already become lodged in the nation's memory. Instead, it discussed peace, love, forgiveness, and repentance. It also mentioned problems at home, like the internment of Japanese Americans, and it stressed America's need for religion. "In times of great crisis man becomes more aware of his need of God, religion, and the church. In a crisis such as the one in which the world is now living, it is our firm belief that the church must declare what is the way and will of God for man, and must help man, individually and corporately, to achieve that spirit of unselfishness and graciousness which will help him to see the other man's and nation's problems and lead him to do what is right, at whatever the cost."[5]

Was this the kind of "shilly-shallying" of which *Time* was accusing the churches? Perhaps so. But such ambivalence did not betray an absolute lack of conviction. The Disciples were concerned about the war. Like most other Christians belonging to other denominations, they invested in bonds, worked in war industry, sent their sons to war, and commissioned chaplains for service in the armed forces. They supported the war effort, but they would not give it thunderous applause. Though loyal to America, they were more loyal still to the church and its unique calling. Such a religious perspective kept the Disciples from making the war a holy crusade.

An editorial in the *Christian-Evangelist*, written by the new editor, Raphael Harwood Miller, communicated a tone that rang true to what most church leaders were saying and how they were saying it. Miller did not hide his hope for victory. "We cannot equivocate as on which side in this world conflict our passionate hope for victory lies. We dare not face the alternative." But he urged that the church not stoop, as it had twenty-five years earlier, to propagate the kind of fanatical patriotism that had compromised the church's witness. The Disciples were called to live in a tension between fulfilling their duties as American citizens and upholding the standards of the Christian faith.

Disciples, therefore, had to "withhold nagging our government with carping criticisms and from adding to public confusion by clamor over matters of minor consequence." Yet they were to resist the temptation of succumbing to war hysteria, "though it is difficult in such a time to draw a fine distinction between the citizen and the Christian." Christians were called to serve their country, but the church could never bless war. "We need not with self-righteous zeal cry out against irrelevant trespass of our preferences, our privileges and our comforts. The church of Jesus Christ cannot bless war, but the church in wartime should have something more significant to contribute than a negative attitude. The church has positive and constructive duties to perform to the nation and to the world. Let us discover and fulfill those duties. America is at war. The call is for unity, loyalty, discipline, sacrifice, and faith that God whose judgments are in the earth will lead us through the fires of judgment."[6]

Such, then, was the struggle among the Disciples between awareness of present needs and faithfulness to past promises, between loyalty to country and obedience to God, between religious idealism and political realism. This dilemma of conscience made them ambivalent up to and even after Pearl Harbor.

The Methodists

Methodists were caught up in the same struggle. The huge size of the denomination (some 8,000,000 after the merger in 1940) and the substantial diversity among its members set the stage for passionate debate over America's role in the war. Among its clergy were articulate pacifists, like Ernest Fremont Tittle and Georgia Harkness, who exercised an influence disproportionate to their numbers. Methodist organizations, like the National Council of Methodist Youth (organized in 1935), the Methodist Federation of Social Service, and the Commission on World Peace, joined the chorus advocating peace and pacifism.

The Methodist Church was one of many denominations that in the 1930s had gone on record repudiating war. This testimony continued when Methodists united in 1940. The official stand of the General Conference read: "We believe that the United States should remain in a position to preserve democracy within its own borders, to provide relief for war-stricken populations, and to assist in the physical and economic rehabilitation of a war-shattered world. We hold, therefore, that the United States should remain out of the present conflicts in Europe and in the Far East."[7] As if to reinforce the resolve of the churches, the Commission on World Peace issued a similar statement in 1940. It began by referring to the severity of the crisis. "The tragic days of war are ever the most difficult period for the church. National loyalties and fears, destruction, sorrow, frustration—these tear the very souls of men apart and tend to divide families and nations. Yet God is with us and God is adequate to every human situation. Our hope is in Him." It went on to oppose entry into the war. Then it advocated specific policies that would contribute to winning peace, such as the formation of an international organization, opposition to peace-time conscription, adherence to strict neutrality, preservation of democracy at home, relief for stricken populations abroad, and negotiation of an immediate peace.[8]

Pearl Harbor created a crisis within the ranks of Methodism. Pacifists and nonpacifists challenged each other at denominational gatherings and on the pages of religious journals. Lynn Harold Hough, for example, called pacifists "modern-day heretics."[9] A former pupil of his, L. R. Templin, responded in kind. "There may be, also, the heresy of judgment. When judgment becomes an absolute, whatever else may happen, the man who holds that position becomes ungodlike. Nowhere in the teachings of Jesus can I now recall that we are commanded to judge. The whole burden of His instruction, and the whole dramatic interpretation of His teaching in His life, is a command to love."[10] Sometimes this exchange of views became so heated that mediators had to encourage mutual tolerance and understanding, respect for pacifist and non pacifist alike. "We shall need cool heads and strong resolution to withstand the forces of bitterness, hatred, and cruelty. Whatever happens, whatever our views, let us maintain the Christian spirit, and respect each other's honest opinions."[11]

Methodist sympathies sided with the allies, but conviction kept them from endorsing war. Church leaders kept warning the faithful about the ease with which they could compromise beliefs and jump on the war bandwagon. Clergy behavior during the last war served as a harsh reminder of what could happen if Christians were not ready to battle the war hysteria.

Warned Roy L. Smith, editor of the *Christian Advocate*: "World War I caught the American clergy napping. They were uninformed on European politics and were unaware of the fact that they were being propagandized."[12] Hence, though the *Christian Advocate* shared "the revulsion of all honorable men who view the record of the Nazi regime," it nevertheless affirmed that "the hope of peace lies, not in damning Hitler and the Nazis, but in setting our own house in order before God."[13] Smith was abhorred by the thought of war. "Nothing in the world is less logical than war. It proposes to make peace with bayonets, bombs, and destruction. It imposes treaties by force in which are embedded the seeds of new wars. It turns ancient friends into frenzied enemies. It expends uncounted treasure in a mad effort to open doors of opportunity to new economic privilege, only to find that the advantages gained at such frightful cost have become actual liabilities." The prospects of war were horrifying, as Smith pointed out so wrenchingly. Still, the ruthlessness of the enemy had to be faced. "We cannot bear the thought of war. But peace is not the only Christian virtue. Indeed, it is not even first in the list of virtues. Certainly love and justice, at least, take precedence over peace, if we read the Bible aright. . . . How can the world have peace, how can love and brotherhood flourish, while a neurotic drunk with power and armed to the teeth is running loose in the world?"[14]

This ambivalence was prevalent in religious journals and denominational pronouncements throughout the war. Church leaders could not quite reconcile themselves to absolute pacifism or zealous interventionism. Aware of the promises they had made in the 1930s, they did not want to stray too far from that earlier stand, but neither did they want to be embarrassed by an idealism that was too rigid to adapt to new circumstances. They wanted to be both firm and flexible, faithful and realistic. They wanted, in short, to be both loyal patriots and peace-loving Christians, the two of which did not, in their minds, always agree. One sentiment had to be higher than devotion to country, and that was devotion to God. Ultimate allegiance to God would prevent Christians from becoming rabid nationalists. As Smith affirmed: "The only solution for the present state of world suicide is for the people of all nations to recognize that there is something higher even than love of country. Patriotism is one of the holiest sentiments known to the human heart. There is only one other sentiment higher—and it is higher—that is loyalty to Jesus Christ. No other sin of our generation has caused so much suffering and strife as nationalism. God cannot be bounded by geographical lines."[15]

Pearl Harbor did not entirely resolve the conflict or mitigate the inner turmoil these Methodists faced. In a statement from the Council of Bishops of the Methodist Church, issued just after Pearl Harbor, the war was spoken of in grim terms. The clear-cut clash of ideas did not justify an uncritical endorsement of war, nor did it absolve America from its responsibility to live up to its faltering ideals. "We condemn the processes of war even while accepting the awful alternative, not of our own making, forced upon us by the selfishness and perversity of men. From a measure of guilt none of us is free. We must, however, maintain conditions which make the continuance of Christian civilization even a possibility."[16]

Methodists continued to wrangle, even as late as 1944. During their convention of that year the majority report recommended by the Committee on the State of the Church was rejected on the convention floor by a narrow margin and replaced by the minority report. This reversal may have reflected the growing ideological tension between more liberal denominational leaders and more conservative lay members that began to surface in most mainline denominations at this time. The majority report declared itself against totalitarianism but withheld the church's blessing of war. The minority report affirmed the justice of the war and pronounced a blessing on the allied cause. "In Christ's name," it read, "we ask for the blessing of God upon the men in the armed forces, and we pray for victory. We repudiate the theory that a state, even though imperfect in itself, must not fight against intolerable wrongs."[17]

Roman Catholics

Religious groups like the Roman Catholics could have used the war as an occasion to prove their patriotism to a largely Protestant—and suspicious—public. They could have sought to enhance their status by ingratiating themselves to the patriotic public. Catholics, however, displayed the same kind of cautious patriotism that characterized most other religious groups in America.

The National Catholic Welfare Conference (NCWC) was one of many Catholic groups that urged neutrality. It did not countenance pacifism, but neither did it urge belligerency. In August 1940 the administrative board affirmed:

It seems that tragic circumstances of the present hour are demanding that we invoke the law of self-protection for our national security. Regretfully, Christians are obliged to realize that adequate national defense demands the training of large numbers of our citizens in the arts of warfare. It is imperative that the extent of the emergency and the consequent need for action should be generally realized. On the other hand, in the interests of sound procedure, it should not be overstated. Because of the character of the times, any program promoted by any group, be it militarist, isolationist or interventionist, should be subjected to critical appraisal and cool, sound judgment.

Though endorsing a strong military to defend America, the bishops nevertheless stressed restraint.[18] They encouraged Catholics to be patriotic, but in a manner worthy of Christian principles. A report of the Committee on National Attitudes of the Catholic Association for International Peace stated: "Before Catholics can perform the role which the Church demands of them—and the world expects—they must be sure that their own patriotism is really Christian, and that they themselves do not espouse a nationalism which is un-Christian or anti-Christian. . . . No one can expect the United States to be preserved from pagan nationalism—or Communism—unless its Catholic citizens do their part."[19]

The bishops who headed up the NCWC did not support belligerency, even if the government itself advocated it. They came out, for example, against peacetime conscription (the Burke-Wadsworth Bill). Their argument was twofold. First, the bill did not exhaust the possibility of a volunteer army before mandating a draft. Second, the bill did not provide adequate protection for religious institutions because it did not grant religious exemptions to preministerial students, thus imperiling the ministry of the church during a time when its clergy would be under acute demand and stress.[20]

The bishops believed that Catholics could serve as catalysts for peace in the world. The pope in particular had a special mission to seek peace, the moral authority to secure peace, and the political power to join with someone like Roosevelt to win the peace in Europe. The bishops applauded the pope's efforts and often made reference to his five-point peace plan.[21]

Catholic journals were not as constrained to speak for the Catholic hierarchy in America as the NCWC and therefore represented a much broader spectrum of opinion. The *Catholic Worker* stood in consistent opposition to American involvement in the war. Founded by pacifist Dorothy Day, it never changed its position during the war, although it did change its basic method of argument. Its writers appealed early on to a "just war" pacifism but eventually, under the influence of Paul Furley, urged "evangelical" pacifism based on the simple example of Jesus. The Catholic Worker movement sup-ported conscientious objectors, helped to found the Association of Catholic Objectors (originally called PAX), and agitated against such wartime abuses of power as obliteration bombing. The *Catholic Worker* was by far the most liberal of Catholic publications during the war.[22]

The *Commonweal* carried articles that advocated both intervention and strict neutrality.[23] The debate became so lively in the *Commonweal* that the editors decided to sign editorials so that they could speak their mind with-out having to represent the official position of the magazine.[24] That "official position" remained pragmatically neutralist up to Pearl Harbor. Editors did not favor blind neutrality, nor did they endorse American entry into the war. "It would be unjust to Britain to cut off the considerable American aid that is already under way, and very few, least of all the Editors of *The Commonweal*, are in favor of withdrawing it. We strongly believe that the best course lies in positive action between appeasement and armed intervention."[25] The edi-tors defined their role as that of a "loyal opposition" to the government. "Those of us responsible for these columns of *The Commonweal*," the editors stated,

> are well aware of the opposition repeatedly expressed here to steps taken by the government in face of the war. In foreign affairs, where issues now align the people with "the government" and with "the opposition," we are frequently in the camp of the opposition. . . . In the most general, and therefore vaguest terms, the Administration policy appears·centered upon the war and conflict to a degree which sacri-fices steps to peace and reconstruction; destruction of the German enemy appears to be the touchstone of policy, rather than reconstruc-tion of political, economic and social affairs in a manner that can build a foundation for peace.

Their opposition, as editor Edward Skillin Jr. said, was "loyal" and "not total." There were conditions that both the administration and its oppo-nents had to meet in order to make the opposition useful to the country. The administration, for example, had to spell out its policy, so that meaningful discussion could take place. Both sides, furthermore, had to be loyal, fair minded, tolerant, and honest.[26]

Like the NCWC, the *Commonweal* opposed peacetime conscription be-cause it would inevitably push the nation closer to war.[27] Its editors adduced that the only kind of intervention acceptable was sending food and clothing to Europe's devastated population. "Americans have one sure means in their power of keeping alive the world's hopes, aspirations and efforts for a humane and lasting peace. Relief for the victims of the scourge of war is an unassailable instrument."[28]

Like most religious leaders, the editors of the *Commonweal* accepted the inevitability of war after Pearl Harbor and reconciled themselves to a long, brutal fight. "When we review what was and what we did, it is indulgent and weakening to sentimentalize about what might have been; it is proper only to have remorse and penitence for our sins, resolve of amendment, and thus to prepare for a hard present and a better future." Yet their declaration of support demonstrated a definite lack of hysteria and wild optimism. "It is human to break the threat to our freedom which has been launched against us. But the freedom we seek cannot eliminate the evil we face. We cannot fight until wrong has left the world. The prospect of our material war can properly be limited by the knowledge that our forces cannot impose freedom on others, and naked power cannot compel anybody freely to decide what is good. Our spiritual warfare will last as long as mankind does, and it must be waged within ourselves."[29]

The Jesuit weekly *America* was more militantly neutralist than the *Commonweal* or the NCWC. Almost weekly the journal contained articles urging neutrality, and these often used strong rhetoric to make their case. Typical of these impassioned appeals for neutrality was the following editorial, written by editor Francis X. Talbot just after the German army had invaded Poland: "There is no external force that can drag us into war against our will. There is no propaganda subtle enough or sentimental enough or brutal enough to move us if we refuse to be moved."[30]

Every step that Roosevelt took toward war was opposed by *America*, including conscription and lend-lease, both of which were seen as signs of impending dictatorship in the United States.[31] Brooke Hilary Stewart argued that any notion of rescuing Europe betrayed a dangerous delusion of greatness in America. "Ever since we attained to power we have constantly patronized the rest of God's world. That this attitude lacks both taste and tact is evident, but it is also dangerous. Other countries, from time to time, have had delusions of superiority, and two of them are presently facing each other in battle today."[32] Neutrality assured that America would be kept safe. It also held the greatest promise of accomplishing the very goal toward which interventionists were striving—the preservation of Western civilization. As John Delaney, frequent contributor to *America*, declared: "The choice that faces us is not between neutrality and the destruction of European civilization. It is a choice between intervention and world civilization. Our intervention cannot save European civilization. Our neutrality may save world civilization by saving American civilization."[33]

Yet even such a consistently neutralist journal like *America* showed cracks in its argument. The first such crack appeared when it grieved over the suffering of Poland, a Roman Catholic stronghold. Hilaire Belloc predicted that civilization would literally stand or fall with Poland. Several months later, after Poland's fate had been sealed, editor Talbot commiserated with the Catholic masses who were suffering under Nazi persecution there. "In Poland, as in every region which has fallen under Nazi domination, the chief object of attack has been the Catholic Church, with her ministers and her people."[34]

Three months later, in June 1940, Talbot was struggling on the pages of *America* again, this time over the portentous power of Hitler. Talbot stated that Hitler simply had to be defeated, because the principles upon which his dictatorship was established were wholly at odds with Christianity. Grievances over past wrongs did not justify the kind of brutality that characterized Hitler's leadership. "Whatever wrongs the German people may have suffered, and it cannot be denied that in the years following the Versailles Treaty they had just grievances, it is equally clear that if civilization and Christianity are to be preserved in Europe, the Hitler Government must be destroyed." Yet Talbot issued a disclaimer. There was no place in Christian morality, he declared, for vengeance against the German people. "The deluded and misled German people must be taught that Hitlerism is incompatible with civilization, but they will never learn that lesson from a conquering foe which, on laying down its arms, adopts as its peace-policy another form of Hitlerism."[35]

More cracks appeared a year later when editorials began to lobby for a sturdy defense. Talbot demanded a defense strong enough to make America impregnable and thus keep it out of the war. He wrote:

> We can build up a defense so powerful that no Government would dare attack us. We have all the natural resources, and we can have all that is necessary to turn these resources into instruments of military defense. In addition, we have the men, and we have the spirit that will urge us to defend our homes. But much of what we have will be lost, if we are led into a foreign war against our will. Reluctant armies do not win victories. . . . A Government that tricks its people into war loses

that without which governments cannot long endure—the support which a people gladly give every Government which they believe to be an instrument for the promotion of the common good.[36]

Four months later Japan attacked Pearl Harbor. Almost overnight *America* became a strong supporter of America's war effort. One editorial stated that it was the duty of good Catholics to respect the decision of the government to enter the war, regardless of how much they disagreed with it, just as it had been the duty of Catholics to voice their opinions before the government had made the decision. In an exhortation aimed at unpatriotic Catholics, Talbot declared: "Without presuming to speak for the theologians and moralists, we venture to assert that there is something awry with the conscience of the American Catholic who refuses to support the Government in the present war."[37] Two weeks later he quoted the bishops' pastoral letter: "If we all do our part in the work assigned to us, we have every reason to believe that victory will ultimately be ours. Our God is a God of justice and of love, and He will not be wanting to those who acknowledge His sovereignty, and humbly implore His all-powerful protection."[38]

Yet even this change of mind did not lead the editors of *America* to use extreme rhetoric to engender Catholic patriotism. Although sincere, their support of the war effort seemed measured and obligatory. They were as concerned about problems at home—like pressures on labor or the influence of communists—as they were about the war abroad. Their patriotism was held in check by other concerns that kept them from fanaticism.

The Christian Reformed

The Christian Reformed Church tells a very different story from the mainline churches. Unlike mainline Protestantism, the Christian Reformed Church did not flirt with pacifism after the First World War. If anything, it was as intolerant of pacifism as many other churches were open to it. In a "Testimony" adopted by the Synod of 1939, the church considered both militarism and pacifism to be heretical options. Militarism glorified the very things that Christians should abhor. "All glorification of war for its own sake must be branded as unchristian and a direct violation of the apostolic injunction cited above." Pacifism, in turn, prevented Christians from fulfilling the duty of defending the nation against foreign aggressors. The responsibility to pursue peace "should at no time be used to cancel [the Christian's] equally solemn duty to defend his country against the attack of the aggressor, to protect the weak in the international family from the wanton assault of the strong, and in general to promote justice and fair dealings between the nations of the world."

Conscientious objection was rejected for the same reasons, with one exception. A Christian can rightfully become a conscientious objector if, "recognizing his duty to obey his government and to defend his country in response to its call to arms, he has intelligent and adequate grounds to be convinced that the given war to which he is summoned is an unjust war."[39]

Ironically, the nation would be more likely to avoid war, whether unjust or just, if it maintained a strong national defense, which was considered by some from the Reformed tradition to be one of the primary duties of government. Writing for the *Banner*, R. B. Kuiper, a pastor in the Christian Reformed Church, advocated a strong defense policy. It was the duty as well as the right of every nation to marshal all of its resources to defend itself against "the unscrupulous attacks of robber nations and killer-governments. It is as criminally negligent for a nation to postpone such preparations as it is for a city not to protect itself in every possible way, by means of the most modern methods available, against organized crime or against the ever present danger of destructive fires, earthquakes, floods or storms."[40]

After Pearl Harbor the *Banner* called the nation to repentance because it had not been prepared for war and therefore was unable to threaten aggressor nations with retaliation, should they violate any nation's neutrality, which they obviously had done. Germany and Japan might not have dared to invade weaker nations if the united nations had not abandoned the responsibility of defending them.

> Our military unpreparedness is one of the sins our nation should confess before God. It may cost us our very existence as a nation. It will mean the loss of thousands of lives whose sacrifice would not have been necessary if we had not gone to sleep closing our eyes to real dangers. That sin cannot be properly confessed unless we confess the errors which lie at its root. God demands a repudiation of the theology of which that unpreparedness was the bitter fruit. Our inability to fight it effectively is the penalty of our sin. Perhaps this war would never have been undertaken by any of the present aggressors if the united nations had not refused to face the facts concerning Japan's sinister designs in the Orient and Germany's rearmament.[41]

In August 1940 H. J. Kuiper, editor of the *Banner*, endorsed the conscription law, departing from the vast majority of the mainline Protestant denominations in America. He admitted that his endorsement might not please parents who quite naturally wished to see their sons spared the horror of fighting in a war. Kuiper argued, however, that it was for the sake of those very sons that he favored conscription. "It has been our conviction ever since the World War that voluntary enlistment is not an effective way to keep our country in a proper state of preparedness. A hastily, improperly trained army is sure to suffer frightful losses in modern warfare."[42]

Yet, like most other Protestant clergy in America, Kuiper initially urged neutrality, though he realized that Americans were bound to sympathize with England, and rightly so. In fact, he acknowledged that "it may even be argued with much show of reason that such personal neutrality is not only impossible but immoral. . . . But whatever our personal sympathies may be," Kuiper went on to argue, "we are resolved that the United States shall maintain a *strict official neutrality at every cost.*"[43]

The *Banner* changed its mind in fall 1940. Events in Europe had convinced editor Kuiper that the United States had to become a belligerent and, at the very least, provide military assistance to England, which now stood alone in the battle against Hitler. "Some time ago we defended the official position of neutrality which our government at first maintained toward the nations now at war. But considering the ever-increasing menace of a world ruled by dictators bent on conquest and Hitler's policy of trampling on every principle of right and justice, we believe our administration is justified in giving all possible aid to England short of war."[44]

Yet three months later, in January 1941, Kuiper accused the government of going too far in aiding England. The administration risked pushing the nation into war. Thus Kuiper was ambivalent. He wanted America to remain neutral; yet he recognized the enormity of evil that was consuming Europe. "We personally, like so many Americans, are driven by two apparently conflicting desires with respect to the European conflict. On the one hand, we do not want Germany to win. Such an outcome would be a calamity not only for democracy but also for the Church. On the other hand, we do not want to see the United States become involved more deeply in this struggle. Both desires, we believe, are not only legitimate but compatible."

Kuiper accused America's leaders of brinkmanship. America, he argued, should not give Germany reason to declare war on America, as Germany had not given America sufficient reason to declare war on it. America had to maintain political neutrality, although Kuiper was quick to add that did not imply moral neutrality. "We hate Hitlerism. We abhor its glorification of force and its ruthless trampling on the sacred rights of small, innocent nations. But let us be fair in our judgment. Let us ask whether Germany has committed a warlike act against the United States. Every one knows that the answer is NO."[45]

The *Banner* supported the allied cause after Pearl Harbor. Its support, however, was hardly enthusiastic. Writing in his weekly column "The World Today," E. J. Tanis devoted most of his first post–Pearl Harbor column to a review of America's faults, as if the nation almost deserved to be at war. His jeremiad on sin, judgment, and repentance is startling, considering the unprecedented attack the nation had only recently experienced. "And every Christian," he stated, "in any part of this war-torn world, must feel that this whole war is a scourge, a chastisement, a judgment upon the sins of the nations." Tanis pleaded that the nations humble themselves, beg for God's forgiveness, and seek the kind of wisdom that would enable them to live in harmony, justice, and peace. "We have all sinned, America, England, France, Germany, China, Japan, and now we are reaping the fruit of our iniquity. Even if there were no sovereign and almighty God who punished the sins of the nations, our way of living as nations, our attitudes and policies and practices, are such that they breed distrust and suspicion and friction, and at last there is a huge explosion and a world-wide catastrophe."[46]

Other Perspectives

This ambivalence and caution appears to have characterized nearly every religious group in America. The arguments were similar: an affirmation of peace and, in some cases, pacifism, a plea for neutrality, a repudiation of totalitarianism, and finally, after Pearl Harbor, measured and subdued support of the war effort.

For example, members of the National Lutheran Council described the prospects of war in harsh language. In a statement issued after war broke out in Europe, they declared: "American neutrality must be the result of high and costly motives; not for physical safety, not to maintain an impossible isolation from world problems, not for economic gains, but rather because we have witnessed the utter futility and degradation of war, because war is power politics to the *n*th degree, because war breeds dissatisfaction and hatreds which bring new and ever more terrible conflicts."[47] After Pearl Harbor the United Lutheran Church of America endorsed a statement that called for supreme dedication, "with every resource of heart and mind and conscience, to the defeat and destruction of this evil," much to the delight of the editors of *Time*, who had cited the Lutherans as one of the few religious groups to rally behind the allied cause. Still, the statement had qualifications, which the story in *Time* failed to mention. It condemned hatred, urged the protection of civil liberties, called for relief of suffering, and summoned Americans to repentance and faith.[48]

In summer 1940 the Congregationalists were so divided over the war in Europe that two contradictory statements were included in the minutes, one defending a pacifist point of view, the other urging national defense.[49] The Northern Baptists condemned the aggression of totalitarian powers but entertained the possibility of a defensive war only.[50] In 1940 the Northern Presbyterians stated that "peoples lacking in military strength are being made the prey of nations which put their trust in armaments," thus showing obvious sympathy for defeated and defenseless nations. Still, they refused to urge American intervention. They edged closer in 1941: "We believe that it is the duty of a Church which worships a God of justice, to recognize a moral distinction between enslaving dictatorships which invade the lands of others, and those peoples which are valiantly defending their liberties and spiritual heritages." Even then they hoped that the United States would remain aloof from military participation, "not in any spirit of selfish isolation, nor of moral irresponsibility, but with a clear view of joining with other nations in constructive efforts toward a lasting peace."[51]

The peace churches were, for obvious reasons, opposed to the war. Typical of their view of war was a resolution passed in 1939 by the Mennonite Brethren:

> We, the members of the Mennonite Brethren Church, love our country and to our best knowledge and ability endeavor to work toward its highest good. Love of one's country does not necessitate hatred of any other country or people. It is our conviction and belief that the honest application of the principles of righteousness, peace, and charity in an effort to establish national and international goodwill, will serve our country best and at the same time promote the best for all mankind. We trust in security through love, and protection through good deeds and righteousness; and for such we are willing to bring the necessary sacrifices.[52]

But they also tried to assure Americans that they were also patriotic. In 1940, for example, the Mennonite Brethren in Christ declared: "[W]e believe that [the Bible] teaches non-resistance in a qualified sense, that it is not the Christian's privilege to take up the sword or to fight with carnal weapons; yet it is his duty to be strictly loyal to the Government under which he lives in all things that do not conflict with, or are not forbidden by the Word."[53] The Mennonites joined the Church of the Brethren and the Friends to operate civilian public service camps at their own expense, hoping that by "going the second mile" and performing service of "national importance" they would be able to live according to the standards of their tradition and still demonstrate their patriotism.

The Southern Baptists present a very different case study. From 1939 to 1941 Southern Baptists moved quickly to support interventionism. Initially they endorsed a defensive war, should it be necessary. "As for ourselves," one of their resolutions stated, "we hate war with an intensity that cannot be expressed in words, but we do not believe that the Christian spirit forbids purely defensive war." The statement condemned military aggression and justified the use of armed resistance. "When wild beasts run at large and tear the flesh of women and children they are to be met and subdued by force." Still, as late as 1940 Southern Baptists insisted that America keep out of the war, even though the rhetoric they used betrayed their sympathy with and allegiance to England.[54] It was not until 1941 that all such caution disappeared. "We know not what course others will pursue, but as for us, we hold it were better to be dead than to live in a world dominated by the ideals of modern dictators. . . . We believe that there are some things worth dying for; and if they are worth dying for they are worth living for, and if they are worth living for they are worth defending unto the death."[55]

For the most part, therefore, religious groups in America came to war slowly and soberly. They were committed to the national cause and wanted to support the government, as long as it set a course of direction with charity, in good faith, and according to just principles, all of which appeared to mandate neutrality. When neutrality was no longer possible, most religious groups supported the war effort in a spirit of humility and restraint.

That they supported the war effort is no surprise. How they did so is another matter altogether. There was a notable lack of enthusiasm for war, a definite absence of invective aimed at the enemy. The churches saw the war as a grim business, necessary perhaps, even unavoidable, but not holy or happy or noble. They could not quite forget World War I and Versailles. They could not quite dismiss the promises they had made in the 1920s and 1930s as so much foolish idealism. They could not quite reconcile themselves to the idea that war was God's way of advancing the Kingdom of God. They were, in short, only conditionally and cautiously committed to the allied cause.

CHAPTER FOUR

THE GREAT DEBATE

The churches were ambivalent about America's entry into the war, and their pronouncements reflected it. Though gradually shifting their position on the war as American involvement became more probable and, by 1941, inevitable, a note of caution and sobriety dominated the entire discussion. Very few groups or individuals rushed into war, relished the thought of war, or called it a holy crusade, even after Pearl Harbor.

Terms of Debate

The actual debate concerning American entry into the war reflected that same agony and ambivalence. Church leaders were deeply divided over the issue. As war became imminent, two basic parties emerged: *neutralists*, who, whether absolute pacifists, practical pacifists, or isolationists, wanted to avoid war at all costs; and *interventionists*, who, like the neutralists, wanted to avoid war but believed that the best way to stay out of war was by aiding the allies. These two groups carried on a hearty—and sometimes bitter—debate from 1939 to Pearl Harbor.

These two religious parties actually participated in a much wider debate in America, the division within the churches mirroring the same division in American society. The two groups comprised members who, in any other circumstances, might well have avoided collaboration at all costs but in this one instance became political allies. Such was the case on both sides, especially among the neutralists (also known as noninterventionists or isolationists). As Charles Lindbergh, one of the more famous isolationists, observed, "We would break up in an instant on almost any other issue."

He appeared to be right. Neutralists sometimes made strange comrades. Consider, for example, the diversity of people who contributed to an early collection of neutralist apologies, entitled *Common Sense Neutrality*: former U.S. president Herbert Hoover, pacifist Rufus Jones, labor organizer and Congress of Industrial Organizations (CIO) president John L. Lewis, aviator Charles L. Lindbergh, socialist leader Norman Thomas, and State Department representative Sumner Welles. Their political and ideological persuasions had divided them in the past; but commitment to strict neutrality united them in 1939.

The same could be said for the America First movement, which included members representing a similar ideological spread, from conservative to socialist. Started in April 1940 by a small group of Yale law students, the America First movement was chaired by Robert E. Wood, retired U.S. Army general and chair of the Sears, Roebuck and Company board of directors, and included such notables as Charles Lindbergh; Edward Rickenbacker, World War I flying ace and president of Eastern Airlines; Robert Ralph Young, multimillionaire railroad magnate and chairman of the board of Allegheny Corporation; and Mrs. Ellen French Vanderbilt Fitzsimons, Republican national committeewoman. It also included the likes of Kingman Brewster Jr., editor of the *Yale Daily News*; Oswald Garrison Villard, the "dean of American liberals" and former editor of the *Nation*; Amos Pinchot, liberal publicist; and Samuel Hopkins Adams, a playwright. It is hard to imagine how any issue could have united such a diverse group; yet militant neutrality did.

The same holds true for William Allen White's Committee to Defend America by Aiding the Allies, formed in 1940 to counteract the isolationist impulse in America. The committee grew quickly, until it had over 600 chapters around the country. Its goal was to mold public opinion, largely by influencing media. An insider group, called the "Century Group," agitated for active intervention. Its members included influential East Coast business executives, politicians, writers, and publishers such as Admiral William H. Standley, Joseph Alsop, Elmer Davis, Robert Sherwood, Lewis Douglas, Frank Polk, and Dean Acheson.

These opposing groups drew lines that made former allies into enemies and former enemies into allies, depending upon how they came down on this one issue, an issue that became, over time, a matter of "either-or." Other concerns, however important, receded into the background.

This one basic issue dominated political debate for two years. "Just another European war" quickly turned into something much bigger. The fall of France in June 1940 showed Americans that the stakes were very high, that Western civilization itself was imperiled. As the war escalated, both neutralists and interventionists began to realize how imperative it was to clarify their positions in order to win the support of the American public. Legislative battles over conscription and lend-lease only aggravated the conflict, hardening the two groups in their respective positions and further polarizing them. Each began to react to the extremes of the other, fearing what would happen if the other side won. Each refused to budge. These two sides represented the polar opposites within which the American people placed themselves. Like any political debate, the extremes defined the terms, while the middle carried the day.[1]

This debate between the two parties surfaced in religious circles, too. Like their secular counterparts, the participants engaged each other in *political* rather than distinctively religious debate. There were two reasons for this. The first is that they joined a debate that involved people from across America who did not necessarily discuss it in religious terms. The second is that early on in the controversy interventionists like Reinhold Niebuhr, never far from the minds of his opponents, accused neutralists of being politically naive, their religious convictions being quite beside the point. Interventionists described their opponents as "perfectionists" and "utopian" and "politically irresponsible" to show how impractical, even dangerous, their position was in the real world of politics. This tactic forced Christian neutralists to defend their position on political grounds. They had to show that their ideas were credible in the real world of politics and not simply in the ideal world of religion.

Whether or not it was possible for church leaders to make such a political argument without reference to their religious assumptions is another question altogether. Niebuhr seemed to think it was both possible and necessary, and he challenged neutralists to make their argument without appealing to Christian assumptions. He wanted them to show that their point of view was good politics, not just good religion. That politics and religion could be separated in the great debate over American entry into the war has itself become a matter of great debate among scholars interested in exploring the interplay between religion and politics. Regardless of Niebuhr's intent, it appears that both parties in the debate—and that includes Niebuhr—ended up basing their political arguments on religious assumptions, their good intentions notwithstanding.[2]

The debate intensified as the Nazis gobbled up Europe and as the government took steps that seemed to lead America closer to war. This turn of events gave an advantage to the interventionists, who could—and did—point to events in Europe as justification for a policy of intervention. The neutralists were gradually forced to change their argument. Their internationalism gave way under the pressure of Europe's crisis and collapse. Their political argument eventually yielded to moral argument, which in turn succumbed to isolationism. While there were exceptions to this pattern, the general progression of thought tended to move in that direction. It became increasingly difficult for neutralists to be credible internationalists in a totalitarian world, to be convincing moralists in a violent world. Over time they began to retreat into fortress America. They justified this retreat by suggesting that the most prudent course of action for America was to defend democracy *at home*, for America's greatest threat was not the invasion of a foreign power but the steady encroachment of presidential power. America could fulfill its responsibility in the world by keeping democracy strong at home, to preserve the American way of life, a way that war threatened and peace would strengthen. That is usually where the argument ended up.

Neutralists as Practical Pacifists

The Political Argument

That is not, however, where the argument usually began. In 1939 neutralists were convinced that America was perfectly situated to win peace in Europe. A policy of strict neutrality, editor Francis X. Talbot of the Jesuit weekly *America* averred, "pledges us to give our best efforts toward effecting peace; but if, in spite of our overtures, they will have none of us except we side with them, then shall we refuse to embroil ourselves in their self-destructive madness."[3] Writing for the *Christian Century*, Harold Fey endorsed the National Peace Conference because he believed that it would serve as a useful vehicle to secure peace in the world. Neutrality, he reasoned, did not necessarily imply isolationism. Instead, neutrality would provide the United States with the opportunity to negotiate a "peace without victory."[4] Charles Clayton Morrison even dared to speculate that Hitler himself wanted peace and would therefore respond favorably to overtures from America.[5] Morrison urged the United States to take the initiative and, avoiding the conflict between the Axis and Allied powers, call a conference among neutrals for the purpose of negotiating a just peace.[6] Morrison never gave up on this plan. When, in 1941, a growing number of Christian leaders were demanding a total rout of the Nazis, he continued to press for a negotiated peace. Victory in itself, he argued, would accomplish little. As long as the United States stayed neutral, it occupied a strategic position for mediation. Neutrality promised opportunity; belligerency would make peace without victory impossible.[7]

The possibility of securing a negotiated peace, however, was not the only advantage that neutrality would give the United States. Neutrality would also keep the United States free from foreign entanglement so that it could aid the victims of war. The chief responsibility of the United States in the war was to provide relief, not wage war. America could never justify belligerency in the face of suffering. Wrote Francis Talbot in *America*: "Certainly we cannot be indifferent to the terrible sufferings of the people in the areas of actual conflict, or to the hardships of those in other parts of the countries now at war. What we should wish to do is to help them by every means in our power, chiefly by our prayers, by personal contributions to be used not for war purposes, but for relief, and by convincing ourselves that by keeping out of this war, we can aid them most effectively in the dreadful years that will begin after the armies and the navies have been destroyed or withdrawn."[8] Neutralists assumed that entry into the war would keep America from fulfilling its humanitarian responsibilities. Thus both before and after Pearl Harbor neutralists urged the United States government to send food and medical supplies to the allies, even to those who had been conquered. A blockade was considered morally reprehensible if it prolonged starvation. Former President Herbert Hoover, head of an agency to assess the need for foreign aid and to propose a plan of action, was hailed a virtual hero by some neutralists because, as Morrison said of him: "In his own person Mr. Hoover has become a symbol of hope to the forty million children of whom he speaks. More important than that, however, he has become the awakener of their consciences to hosts of Christians. Some of these do not yet admit the force of his appeal. They find what they assure themselves are good political reasons for maintaining that what the Hoover plan asks is impractical, for reiterating excuses why it cannot be tried, why it must not be tried, why helpless women and children must be left to starve."[9]

Neutralists also claimed that neutrality would keep America from making the same costly mistakes that it had made twenty-five years earlier. World War II was viewed as simply another episode in the long and bloody history of European conflict pitting one imperialistic nation against another.

Defense of England, many neutralists intimated, was really defense of India and Singapore. The war in Europe was an imperialistic war, with imperialistic powers fighting over imperialistic booty.[10] Morrison was still wondering, even in 1942, whether the United States was accomplishing anything besides fighting for the British Empire.[11] Francis Talbot added that it was fruitless to try to make a moral distinction between Allied and Axis powers and therefore "become moral censors of rival imperialisms."[12] The problem that Russia posed for Americans buttressed the neutralists' argument. They asserted that the United States could hardly support Russian totalitarianism. Stalin's nonaggression pact with Hitler in 1939 only reinforced the deep suspicion that Americans had of Russia. It seemed apparent that most Americans would never sympathize with Russia. Why then did American policy change so quickly after Hitler invaded Russia in 1941? Had Russia suddenly become a worthy ally? Francis Talbot did not think so. Russia's change of status in American foreign policy, unaccompanied, as it was, by a change in Russia's political philosophy, exposed the dilemma of trying to make sharp moral distinctions between allies and enemies.[13] Europe was thus best left to itself. It could settle its own internal disputes while the United States attended to the more important business of perfecting democracy at home.

The Moral Argument

The arguments of neutralists became increasingly moralistic after France fell, as if the possibility of cogent political debate evaporated with the capitulation of France and the Lowlands, making the neutralist position seem less politically persuasive. This change of tone was observable, for example, in the way that neutralists tried to cultivate sympathy for Hitler. Pacifist John Haynes Holmes, a longtime Unitarian pastor in New York City, acknowledged that Hitler's ideology was different, even evil. Still, Hitler was as much a victim as he was a villain. Holmes refused to pronounce judgment on him because he believed that America was just as guilty as Hitler, if not more guilty, since America's economic and political system created the conditions for Hitler's emergence. "I should be the more disturbed by this easy challenge if I saw Hitler with the eyes of so many of my contemporaries—as a unique embodiment of wickedness, a monster intruded upon the earth like Satan come from hell. But I do not see him in this guise. I think it unscientific to isolate a man from the time and place which have together spawned him. To me Hitler is all that is horrible, but as such he is the product of our world, the veritable incarnation of our nationalistic, capitalistic and militaristic era. Whatever is worst in our civilization seems to have come to a vile head in him." Holmes had no confidence in violence as a remedy. It was not violence but goodness that would defeat evil in the world. "How shall we confront tyranny and confound terror? Not by force and violence, arms and blood, but by compassion, mercy, brotherhood, love. Not by fighting and killing but by serving and dying. The prophet has spoken the word, echoed by every religion of mankind: 'not by power, nor by might, but by my spirit, saith the Lord'!"[14]

Francis Talbot gravitated toward the opposite extreme. He acknowledged that Hitler was an evil man, as Hitlerism was an evil ideology. But Hitlerism was an idea that could implant itself in any society, even in America. The only line of defense against such a force was not military but moral and religious. America needed to return to God. Though this argument could have been—and sometimes was—used by interventionists, the fact that it found its way into the arsenal of the neutralists reflected their determination to resist an evil foreign power without advocating the policy of intervention. Summoning America back to religion was tantamount to saying that military belligerency was vain. It would accomplish nothing of what really needed to be accomplished if totalitarianism was ever going to be defeated. If anything, it might lead to the very outcome from which belligerency was intended to protect America. Talbot concluded: "This is a time for sackcloth and ashes. Our first line of defense is God, and without Him, all else is useless."[15]

Like the others, Harry Emerson Fosdick's argument was essentially religious and moralistic rather than political. Its authority was grounded in what he deemed to be religiously right rather than politically prudent or expedient values. Disavowing allegiance to "doctrinaire pacifism," he admitted that the pacifist position, like the belligerent position, was riddled with inconsistencies. There was no easy answer. He had supported America's entry into the last war and later regretted it. Subsequent reflection had led him to reconsider his position and its implications for the Christian faith. In his mind, Christ was seated on the judgment seat, where he condemned all parties that violated what he stood for. "The function of the church is to keep him there, above the strife, representing a manner of living, the utter antithesis of war, to which mankind must return if we are to have any hope. But the Christian ministry does not keep him there by throwing itself, generation after generation, into the support and sanction of the nation's wars." It was not the function of the church to help win the war, to become an "adjunct" to the war department. "The function of the church is to keep Christ where he belongs, upon his judgment seat, condemner of our joint guilt, chastener of our impenitent pride, guide to our only hope."[16]

Neutralists spoke more harshly when they critiqued erstwhile pacifists who had turned to interventionism. Their argument reflected an attempt on their part to expose the moral weaknesses of their opponents. George M. Gibson averred that these turncoat pacifists were wrong because they had allowed new circumstances to justify retreat from former convictions. He noted with alarm the number of pacifists who had changed their minds once Hitler came to power. "We now witness a wholesale *volte face* anticipated for twenty years by peace writers, many of whom are joining in what they themselves have described as the coming rout of the intelligentsia. . . . With a moral and intellectual leadership thus easily disposed toward convenient change, can there be much surprise if politicians fail to stand by their promises like trees planted by the waters?" Gibson named the names of these deserters, among them Karl Barth, Reinhold Niebuhr and John C. Bennett. He accused them of subordinating moral absolutes to historical relativities. "Circumstances! There's the point. A circumstantial morality is the ground where grow the poisonous weeds of Machiavellianism. Fully granted that this common agony of nations brings confusion to minds and moral purposes together, yet one cannot witness this flight of moral leadership from its former strong commitment without recalling the cry of young Herder to a former hero: 'The father that begat me hath no bread for me!' "[17]

The Isolationist Argument

Neutralists bordered on isolationism when they called the nation to address matters closer to home. This line of reasoning actually began to surface quite early in the debate and gained momentum as the Nazi machine rolled over Europe. It was argued that the United States had no moral right to intervene in a foreign war because it had problems enough of its own. The neutralist editor of *America*, Francis Talbot, was especially fond of this argument. Before war broke out in Europe he announced, "Our business is to take care of our domestic affairs." He noted that there were still eleven million unemployed people in America who walked the streets. Many of these were on relief rolls. Yet the government had done nothing in the previous six years to alleviate the problem. "How long is this to last?" he asked. "These terrifying facts must not be veiled by the rumors of war fabricated by bureaucrats at Washington. War is not the road back to prosperity. War is the slaughter of young men, the destruction of industry, now and for another generation."[18] He made a similar plea a year later, in 1940. "But what about our domestic cares and problems? We are worrying about England, France, Belgium, Holland, Finland, Norway, and the Dutch East

Indies. But nobody seems to be worrying about the duties of the American Government to the American people."[19] To prove that he was an internationalist, however, Talbot added that it was by addressing problems in America that the government could perform its greatest service for Europe. "Every American policy, then, should be formed primarily to protect the welfare of the American people. No sympathy, however deep, should alienate the Government from that creed. . . . We cannot help Europe by going to war. We can help the whole world by keeping out of war, and that is the truest pledge of our real friendship for Europe and its oppressed peoples."[20]

Neutralists were alarmed by what they assumed would be the certain loss of freedom to which fighting a war in Europe would lead. War, they declared, would destroy everything in America that had made it great. They had two basic concerns in mind. First, they believed that war would give—in fact, was already giving—too much power to the president. When addressing this issue, a sense of paranoia seemed to pervade their reasoning. They predicted that war would make Roosevelt a virtual dictator in America. Every step toward belligerency—conscription, lend-lease, amended neutrality—gave Roosevelt more power, of which he already had too much. A policy of neutrality was needed to keep America from capitulating to totalitarianism at home, which posed a threat equal to totalitarianism abroad. Commenting on the Industrial Mobilization Plan, for example, Harold Fey of the *Christian Century* declared that dictatorship was being "definitely planned" for the United States in the event of war or of some undefined national emergency short of war. He also charged that political and military leaders had already exceeded their proper functions by "blueprinting" a new social and political system for America and that this blueprint was not favorable to democracy but to totalitarianism. He presaged that these leaders— or better, dictators—were going to imitate fascist countries by using force against external threat and internal dissent.[21]

Charles Clayton Morrison, editor of the *Christian Century*, opposed a third term for the same reason, believing that President Roosevelt had already accumulated too much power after two terms. Though promising to keep "American boys" out of the war, Roosevelt had become too delirious from the war fever to provide trustworthy leadership in American foreign policy. War had gone to his head. His time as president was up.

Developments of the past eight years have thrown into Mr. Roosevelt's lap the "makings" of a one-party system, and he has yielded to the temptation to fuse them and make himself the head of a one-party government. Add up these "makings" of an American fascism: 1) The vast political machine. 2) The solid south. 3) The economic blocs grateful for his special legislation—and his alms—the unemployed, the farmer, organized labor. 4) Peacetime conscription. 5) A national emergency, partly inevitable, partly shaped to political ends, and 6) the doctrine of the indispensable leader, and you have a road to fascism paved even more smoothly than the road by which Mussolini and Hitler came to power.[22]

Francis Talbot agreed that twelve years was too much. "How many years," he asked rhetorically, "will he need to save us?" Talbot believed that America would be saved by no one man, for that would lead to dictatorship. Nor would it be saved by a single governing clique, for that would create an oligarchy. America would be saved only through the due process of democracy, which would put limits on the president. "Twelve years carries us, we fear, straight toward a dictatorship."[23]

Neutralists recoiled from Roosevelt's militarism, and they were alarmed by the gradual erosion of congressional authority.[24] They wondered if Congress, which supposedly had the constitutional right to declare war, had the backbone to resist the president.[25] Francis Talbot urged Congress to assert its authority before it was too late, before the constitutional foundation of America's democratic form of government collapsed. "The sole authority to declare war rests with Congress and any transference of that power, whether virtual or actual, to the Chief Executive is a dangerous precedent that tends to weaken our democratic tradition and forfeit prerogatives belonging to the people which are fundamental in our American system of government."[26]

But there was a second reason why neutralists thought entry into the war would set American democracy back, perhaps irreversibly. They believed that it would lead to a slowdown in social legislation and to a loss, if not the total elimination, of civil liberties in American society. Morrison predicted that an increase in armaments production would undermine the gains made in progressive social programs.[27] He assumed, furthermore, that wartime restrictions would undermine civil liberties like free speech.[28] *Christian Century* contributor William Hubben anticipated that the militarization of American society, of which peacetime conscription was the major catalyst, would also imperil freedom in America. His concerns appear now, in retrospect, to be surprisingly prescient. He warned: "Fashion, music, our magazines, our movies, the Sunday sermon, the plays of our children, Christmas gifts for the youngsters, art and literature—not a single province of thought and endeavor will be left untouched by the new militarism. The very dreams of our boys, once colorful with wild west scenes, will assume the terrifying aspect of modern mechanized warfare."[29]

The salvation of democracy abroad, then, was not worth the sacrifice of democracy at home. "Our participation in war would not establish 'democracies' abroad," argued *America*'s Talbot. "But it would certainly destroy what we have left of democracy at home."[30] Sometimes their prediction of war's impact on democracy in America sounded almost apocalyptic. Declared Paul Blakely: "In the moment that this country goes to war, the guarantees of the American Constitution will be swept aside by a dictatorship. We fight best for this Government by not fighting in Europe. If we go to war, we are bound to lose, for before the first contingent of American boys could be disembarked at some foreign port, government under the Constitution, the American Government of our fathers, would have ceased to be."[31]

Neutralists also predicted that American involvement in the war would surely bankrupt the power of labor and fill the war chests of capitalists. Industrialists were greedy enough as it was. War would only tempt them to increase their profits at the expense of wage-earning Americans. Neutrality was the only policy that would restrain untrammeled capitalism.[32] Neutralists were not even persuaded that the economic boom that was assumed would accompany entry into the war would pull the country out of the depression. Such a recovery would be short-lived. It would continue as long as the war lasted and no longer. Americans therefore had to dismiss the idea that "in preparing for the crusade, we can reopen our factories, decrease unemployment, and amass a goodly sum of money."[33]

Neutralists as Absolute Pacifists

Such were the basic arguments of the neutralists. Most of them—what I would call "practical pacifists"—were opposed to *this* war but not necessarily *all* wars. They marshaled political, moral, and religious arguments to prove that neutrality was the best option for America. It was the best way to achieve a negotiated peace in Europe, the best way to protect America from becoming a dictatorship, and the best way to preserve civil liberties on the home front. The other option—interventionism—would only escalate the war and destroy the very thing at home that Americans were trying to defend abroad.

But absolute pacifists also entered the arena of debate and advocated a point of view that they regarded as equally applicable to politics. They were serious about making their religious and moral ideal the foundation for a realistic and workable policy in a world gone mad. Wrote Nels Ferre for the *Christian Century* in 1941: "There is nothing in the world more practical than Christian principles. When the world is out of joint they are more needed than ever. The cross of Christ must not be pushed to 'the edge of history.' It stands as the very center of God's work in human affairs. Too long have we been practical in the false sense of trusting secular culture and humanistic progress. . . . The vicious circle of wars and more wars keeps revolving in the history of secular civilization. Only resolute faith in the transforming power of the cross of Christ, both preached and practiced, can break that circle."[34]

Of the absolute pacifists who believed that pacifism held real political promise for American foreign policy, none spoke more frequently, forthrightly, and passionately than A. J. Muste, labor organizer in the 1920s and 1930s and, beginning in 1940, executive secretary of the Fellowship of Reconciliation. In a pamphlet he wrote in 1941, Muste launched his attack against interventionists and volleyed his own reasons—what he believed were political reasons—to show why pacifism was the best policy for America. Unlike pacifists from the Peace Churches, he was not content to make his program a mere "witness" to peace and righteousness. He intended to argue for its realism and practicality, believing that his position was politically superior to that of his opponents.

Muste began his argument by asserting that it was a dangerous delusion to think that the united nations would, upon winning the war, do any better this time around than last time. Because the facts seemed to indicate that the Allied powers were following the same course of action again, it was foolish to think that they would win a better peace. A sudden change of attitude and plan was out of the question because the allies were too stubborn and ignorant. "But we tell ourselves that, having arrived with fatal precision at that point, a miracle will happen. The momentum acquired in the terrific plunge downhill into which the nations are pouring all their energies, will evaporate as by magic. We shall suddenly get off this road and strike out boldly in another direction. What reason have we to believe this? Surely we have a right to ask for concrete evidence."[35]

Muste questioned the assumption made by the United Nations that it was possible to go to war without hating. He warned that if it was not impossible, then it was certainly dangerous. In fact, Muste proposed that it would be better from a moral point of view if war and hate remained partners, as they had in most previous wars. "Perhaps," he wondered, "the ordinary mortal who is not free from rages and hate when performing the acts of a soldier is, after all, a better integrated personality and nearer to a state of grace, whether from the standpoint of the psychologist or of the gospel."[36]

Muste wondered whether or not it was possible to determine the exact consequences of moral decisions in complex circumstances. He asserted that pacifists and nonpacifists alike suffered from the limitations of being human and fallible. It was highly improbable, he said, that anyone could see much farther than a short distance into the future to calculate with any kind of reliability the moral consequences of a course of action. Political campaigns, military wars, and peace treaties had seldom led to what the actors involved at the time anticipated. He turned this line of reasoning, often used against pacifists, against his opponents. "If, therefore, non-pacifist friends assert that I may not be fully aware of the consequences of my refusal to support the United States government in war, I readily agree that this is so. But neither can they calculate the consequences of their actions; certain it is that in helping to release the terrible forces of modern warfare, they release forces over which they have no control and the consequences of which, to judge by the experience of the last war, they may live to regret bitterly."[37]

Muste referred to his own past to support his argument. During the First World War he had been a pacifist. Hopelessly uninformed, as he came to realize later on, he nevertheless responded to the forces around him by following his intuition, imbued, as it was, with a sense of the "Inner Light." His intuition proved to be right. After the war, however, he abandoned his pacifism in favor of Leninism. He became more "informed" but less discerning. He later learned valuable lessons from the experience of being a radical. The failure of Leninism taught him that one can see things in sharp focus only by deferring to the basic law of the universe, a law which Leninism violated. That law was the simple truth that evil can be overcome only by its opposite, by a dynamic, sacrificial goodness. Leninism's shortcomings also showed him that if one opts for a policy of "realism," then one must follow it to its logical conclusion. In the case of the "realistic" use of violence, one should never hesitate to use it to reach a desirable goal, however bloody the results. He concluded that such logic only confirmed by negative example the foundational principle of pacifism—that the end cannot be divorced from the means, that the final outcome is already determined by the means used to get there. These two ideas—that only goodness can overcome evil and that the means used always anticipate the ends achieved—persuaded Muste to believe that pacifism really was a good option, a realistic and practical option, even in the world of politics. The way of violence and victory had already been tried, and it proved to be a disastrous failure. He believed that it was time to try the other way.

Muste had specific proposals in mind. He suggested, for example, that the United States assume responsibility for the building of a world government and that it invest the billions that it would normally devote to war in relief and rehabilitation. He proposed that no war guilt be assigned exclusively to one nation and that all nations, whether previously free or subject, be allowed to determine their own destinies. All people, he continued, should be assured of equitable access to markets and to essential raw materials. He also urged the United States to advance the cause of democracy by providing equality of opportunity for all within its own borders and by repudiating every form of racism. Finally, he lobbied for an immediate reduction in armaments.

Muste admitted that many Americans would call his proposals "fantastic" and "unrealistic." He countered by saying that it was only through negotiation with the enemy as an equal, a status which he believed the enemy had waged war to achieve, that real peace would be won. "Would Americans want to negotiate with a foreign power if that power held the upper hand?" he asked rhetorically. Neither would Germany and Japan. The time was right for mediation and negotiation. Besides, he believed that Americans understood—even felt deeply about—the futility of war. He charged leaders to act while the American people still had the spiritual energy needed to win a just peace.

Muste realized that he and his pacifist friends stood a good chance of losing the battle for peace. The possibility of such a loss, however, did not cause him to abandon his convictions. "Yes, though we be driven still further 'out of this world,' into seeming futility, confined to very simple living in small cooperative groups and for the rest giving ourselves to silence, meditation, prayer, discipline of the mind and spirit, we shall hold to The Way." That "way" was the development of the consciousness of the reality of spiritual things and the power of moral goodness.[38]

Thus, in success or failure, Muste finally rested his case not in politics but in religion. He appealed to the Inner Light, which would mediate direct knowledge of universal principles to the uncluttered, sensitive soul. He had faith in the power of love, which would ultimately triumph over hate and violence. The Inner Light and the power of love were not merely idealistic notions but real historical possibilities. "The point is that in a real sense conscience, the Inner Light, is the only guide among the complexities of life. What we know surely, and the only thing we can know, is that evil cannot produce good, violence can produce only violence, love is forever the only power that can conquer evil and establish good on earth."[39] On this fundamental level of religious conviction there were, in Muste's mind, no ambiguities, only absolutes. Every person had to choose between two alternatives: good or evil, love or hate, peace or violence. These choices applied to both means and ends, political policy and ethical ideal. Having seen the Inner Light, Muste decided for love, goodness, and peace, even if he had to stand alone, driven to the margins of history.

The Interventionists

New Circumstances

Most neutralists, to say nothing of interventionists, rejected Muste's absolute pacifism and, after Pearl Harbor, turned their attacks on their former pacifist allies. Before Pearl Harbor, however, neutralists and pacifists stood on common ground. Like the peculiar alliances formed in the America First Committee, the one bond uniting neutralists—the conviction that America had to stay out of the war—was strong enough to create a solid block of opposition to interventionists. They were absolutely committed to keeping America out of the war.

Surprisingly, most interventionists were, too. Some members of this party had only recently converted from pacifism. They wanted to show how their change of conviction squared with their former beliefs. Though confident that they were right, these interventionists nevertheless felt obliged to explain why they had turned about-face and were now leading the charge against their former allies. John Bennett, professor of theology at Union Seminary, New York, was one of many who came forward to defend his position. Contributing to the series of articles in the *Christian Century* that answered the question, If America is drawn into the war, can you, as a Christian, participate in it or support it?, Bennett admitted that he had never been an absolute pacifist and had previously opposed the war only because he believed that all modern warfare was destructive and futile. New circumstances had forced him to reconsider his position. "I can put the essential reason for this change of mind in a sentence. The fall of France and the immediate threat of a German victory opened my eyes to the fact that the alternative to successful resistance to Germany is the extension of the darkest political tyranny imaginable over the whole of Europe with the prospect that if Europe can be organized by Germany the whole world will be threatened by the Axis powers."[40]

J. H. Marion also explained why he had "changed his mind." Like Bennett, he too confessed that he had never been an absolute pacifist. He had embraced pacifism in the idealist atmosphere of the 1920s and 1930s. Hitler made him realize that pacifism was unrealistic. Pacifism, he intimated, might have helped to build a better world, had people been willing to try. "But today," he went on to argue, "with the world in flames the absolute pacifist as a political guide, we think, is like a man who, with his house afire, scorns the aid of the fire department and sits down to wring his hands because the house was not built fireproof in the first place. Some of us simply cannot follow that course."[41]

Bennett and Marion were members of a larger company of Christian leaders who joined together to urge interventionism. They expressed their convictions on the pages of a new religious journal, *Christianity and Crisis*. Henry Pitney Van Dusen was one of the founders of the journal. He had two basic reasons for his interventionist position. First, he argued that if Nazism was not resisted, it would soon consume Europe and other strategic parts of the world until the United States became an island in a sea of totalitarianism. Hitler's insatiable appetite for power thus created an intolerable problem of security for Americans because their nation would become increasingly isolated from Europe if Hitler accomplished his plans. Second, he predicted that a Nazi victory would strangle religious freedom. "Within a short time after Britain's capitulation, the Western hemisphere, possibly the North American continent, will be the last considerable area on the earth's surface where men and women will be permitted to gather for worship without police surveillance; where the elemental truths of Christian faith can be preached without imminent threat of concentration camp; where it will be permissible to pray for all nations and peoples, especially the needy and oppressed; where it will be legal to declare one's belief in all mankind as of one blood under the fatherhood of one God."[42] Other interventionists, like Edward L. Parsons, Lewis Mumford, and Lynn Harold Hough, expressed similar opinions on the pages of *Christianity and Crisis*. All of them turned against pacifism, arguing that it was shallow and politically naive.[43]

The intellectual leader of this circle of interventionists was Reinhold Niebuhr, who had emerged by this time as a ubiquitous and influential figure in the world of American religion. The presence of Niebuhr showed how wrong in at least one way the *Fortune* article was about the failure of the church. When the editorial argued that conditions in the American churches in 1940 were similar to those in 1914, it did not calculate the difference that one man, Reinhold Niebuhr, could make. His voice introduced a new element into the great debate. That was the notion of Christian realism.

Niebuhr had been a practical pacifist in the early 1930s but later changed his mind and challenged the ideology of pacifism and the politics of neutrality. Having been awakened to what he had come to believe were the dangers of pacifism, he turned against the pacifists' neutralist position, arguing that neutralists did not comprehend the threat that Hitler posed, nor appreciate the heritage that he threatened. Niebuhr changed his mind because he believed neutrality abandoned the very civilization that made it possible to hold to the pacifist point of view. "We believe the task of defending the rich inheritance of our civilization to be an imperative one, however much we might desire that our social system were more worthy of defense. We believe that the possibility of correcting its faults and extending its gains may be annulled for centuries if this external peril is not resolutely faced."[44]

Niebuhr alleged that the neutralists were dangerously mistaken. He marshaled three basic arguments. First, he contended that neutrality was bad politics because it would bring on America the very thing that neutralists wanted to avoid. Second, he proposed that it was bad ethics because it confused the absolute ethic of Jesus with the ambiguities of life in a sinful world. Third, he asserted that it was bad religion because it violated the heart of the Christian faith, the gospel.

Niebuhr's Political Argument

Niebuhr began with the political argument. He seemed to take great delight in observing that secular isolationists (often political conservatives) and religious pacifists (often political liberals) were of one mind on the single political issue of neutrality, however far apart they were in religious belief and social philosophy. Neutrality had created strange bedfellows: John Haynes Holmes, a liberal and a pacifist, had offered the invocation at a Lindbergh meeting; and the Ministers No War Committee had received funds from the America First Committee. It was peculiar that someone like Charles Clayton Morrison, a polemical Protestant if there ever was one, could agree so wholeheartedly with Francis Talbot, editor of the Jesuit weekly *America*, about the war. Niebuhr noted that neutralists did not have to agree on most moral and religious issues because they had one common concern—to keep America out of the war, which, according to Niebuhr, turned them into isolationists. That, in Niebuhr's mind, was bad politics.

He questioned the assumption that America was as safe from Nazism as neutralists believed. The world was becoming a community of nations, connected by complex systems of transportation, communication, and economics. It was no longer possible for the United States to insulate itself from the rest of the world. The Atlantic and Pacific Oceans could not provide the protection that America wanted or needed. There was thus no safety in isolationism. There could no more be an "America First" than there could be a "France First" or a "Belgium First." America was part of a shrinking world.

Niebuhr also attacked the idea that entry into the war would bring an end to democracy in America. He conceded that democracy in America would probably have to adapt itself to wartime conditions and that the president would undoubtedly accumulate more power. Yet he wondered whether democracy was worth preserving if it was certain that a war against totalitarianism abroad would necessarily lead to dictatorship at home. "For to say that democracy cannot resist tyranny without becoming totalitarian is to seal the doom of democracy. Any democratic civilization which believed such a dictum would have to yield to every demand of the dictators and would invite the dictators to make constantly fresh demands, in the certain knowledge that the democratic civilization which they were bent upon destroying was inhibited by fears and scruples from offering effective resistance."[45] Of course there were risks in war. But Niebuhr believed that there were times—the United States was surely in one of them—when the president had to assert his authority and the people perform their patriotic duty, although not at the price of sacrificing the freedom to question and criticize. That was the kind of flexibility and balance that the democratic system afforded.

If Niebuhr doubted the neutralists' low estimation of the strengths of democracy, he also objected to their low estimation of the weaknesses of Nazism. He could not quite comprehend how neutralists could seriously entertain the possibility of a negotiated peace. Of course Niebuhr wanted peace, as all Americans did. Yet he believed that it had to be a *just* peace, which meant that there had to be conditions attached to it. "The negotiators must come to the peace table as truly authorized spokesmen of the peoples whose fate is to be determined. They must be profoundly committed to the writing of a just, and therefore durable, peace. They must be men whose word can be trusted. The peace must guarantee not merely cessation of hostilities but also release from subjugation and restoration to liberty of those peoples who desired only peace, who committed no provocation to aggression, but who today endure slavery beneath the Nazi yoke. . . . None of those conditions is present."[46] Niebuhr asserted that the conditions existing in Europe in early 1941 would turn a "negotiated peace" into a Nazi victory. What would happen to Poland? Holland? Denmark? Would a negotiated peace bring justice to them? He argued that neutralists were blind to the realities of politics in a warring world, blind to the needs and rights of conquered nations, and blind to the perils of isolationism. In early 1940 Morrison had cited Holland and Denmark as worthy examples of the prudence and safety of neutrality. A year later Niebuhr did not hesitate to use them as examples of the folly—indeed, the impossibility—of neutrality. Would the United States be any safer than they were? Perhaps. But if so, he asked whether existence would be tolerable in a world where one nation was free and the rest were subject to totalitarian rule.

In Niebuhr's mind, the preferability of neutrality or interventionism could be reduced for the sake of argument to a matter of national interest, which was, according to Niebuhr, how all political decisions were made in the real world. What, he inquired, was America's national interest? How best could it be served and protected? Niebuhr contended that America's "ultimate peril" required armed intervention because he did not foresee a world in which Nazism and democracy could live together in peace. The nation's "immediate peril," however, was not quite so dire. Because democracies tended to decide national policy on the basis of immediate as opposed to long-range concerns, he urged the adoption of a moderate form of intervention, like the passage of the Lend-Lease Bill. Though morally dubious, it made good sense politically. "From the purely ethical point of view, it might be claimed that both our ultimate peril and our moral obligation for the preservation of western Christendom require us to give aid without reservations of any kind. But it must be recognized that the citizens of a nation do not sense an ultimate peril with the same urgency as an immediate one. The policies of nations must take this fact into account."[47]

At this point Niebuhr seemed willing—pacifists believed that he seemed too willing—to compromise ideals for the sake of practical gains. Such moral compromise made concessions to the popular will necessary and expedient. But if moral idealism was sacrificed that quickly, to what power could one appeal to overcome the inertia of the masses? It appeared to pacifists that Niebuhr's "realistic" politics undermined the Christian duty to make ethical decisions based on biblical ideals.

Niebuhr's Ethical Argument

Niebuhr himself did not believe that politics was the only, and not even the major, issue in the debate. In his mind *political* isolationists were more honest, though no less wrong, than *religious* pacifists. At least the political isolationists confined their arguments to the arena of politics and did not confuse political policy with ultimate moral concern. What bothered Niebuhr about the pacifists was how they tried to defend their position on moral grounds. Bad politics was bad enough. Bad ethics was probably worse.

Niebuhr was especially offended by the pacifists' dogmatic assertion, "There is nothing worse than war." Niebuhr believed that there was something worse than war, and that was tyranny. He contended that pacifist ethics were dangerously skewed at this point. "Tyranny is worse than war, for two reasons. First it is a 'cold war' which destroys life, liberty, and culture; secondly it must inevitably lead to war."[48] That pacifists did not see this weakness in their position puzzled and angered him. He set out to expose the fallacy of their thinking.

The basic error of pacifists, Niebuhr contended, was that they confused the absolute ethic of Jesus with the relative nature of human existence in a sinful world. The ethic of Jesus was uncompromising and ultimate. "Be perfect," Jesus said. "Resist not evil." "Be not anxious." "Love your enemies." Though "ultimately" normative, this ethic was "not immediately applicable to the task of securing justice in a sinful world."[49] Niebuhr asserted that life in this world is marred by ambiguity and sin. The absolute ethic of Jesus, "in which no concession is made to human sin," was set in sharp and ultimate conflict with "all relative political strategies which, assuming human sinfulness, seek to secure the highest measure of peace and justice among selfish and sinful men."[50]

Niebuhr argued that the vain attempt to make the ethic of Jesus the final, immediate, and practical standard for conduct in politics created insurmountable difficulties for pacifists, difficulties which could not be overcome. First, Niebuhr argued that the attempt itself was hypocritical because pacifists did not even try to live consistently with their own logic. They diluted Jesus' ethic by transmuting the absolute command of "non-resistance" into the relative principle of "non-violence" for the sake of political expediency, yet they would not concede that they had compromised Jesus' original intent. Even worse, they tried to make a distinction between material and spiritual uses of power to justify nonviolent coercion, as if "spiritual" coercion was a more worthy and less tainted expression of violence than "material" coercion. Niebuhr countered: "Life is not in conflict merely when it is reduced to physical proportions, and it does not transcend conflict when raised to spiritual proportions."[51] He went on to argue: "The whole effort to change the doctrine of non-resistance to one of non-violent resistance or to place the emphasis upon spiritual rather than physical resistance is nothing but the fruit of the confusion of liberal religion. There is no absolute line between physical and spiritual coercion, nor is there one between violent and non-violent resistance. There are tentative and pragmatic distinctions; but none of them can justify the assertion of their proponents that they have broken with the 'war system.' "[52]

Nonresistance, according to Niebuhr, was not the only command of Jesus that pacifists violated. Their inability to obey Jesus' absolute ethic cut a wider path than that. Sometimes they violated Jesus' commands by simply living in the real world. Even if pacifists did obey the command to "resist not your enemies" by the simple act of repudiating all forms of war, what simple act of denial could they perform to obey such commands as "have no anxiety" or "love your neighbor as yourself"? Niebuhr believed that the most saintly life contradicted these laws to some degree. Human existence by its very nature meant anxiety and competition, greed and suspicion, because humanity was sinful.

The absolute ethic of Jesus was, in Niebuhr's mind, both normative on one level and unlivable on another. The standards of Jesus' Kingdom could not therefore be transformed into "simple historical possibilities." There was no easy, direct connection between divine ethical principle and human experience, between the Kingdom of God and historical possibility. "The New Testament does not, in other words, envisage a simple triumph of good over evil in history. It sees human history involved in the contradictions of sin to the end. That is why it sees no simple resolution of the problem of history. It believes that the Kingdom of God will finally resolve the contradictions of history; but for it the Kingdom of God is no simple historical possibility. The grace of God for man and the Kingdom of God for history are both divine realities and not human possibilities."[53]

Not that the ethic of Jesus was entirely irrelevant to Christian behavior in a fallen world. Niebuhr believed that the ethic of Jesus was relevant to human experience in a fallen world in at least two ways. On the one hand, Jesus' ethic was useful for guiding conduct so that Christians, though living in a sinful world, could make distinctions between *relative* moral options— between good and better than, bad and worse than. It could enable Christians to make wise judgments in situations that did not seem to provide a perfect alternative but still required some kind of ethical decision. On the other hand, the ethic of love could function as a prophetic voice to expose all forms of evil, especially in those cases where evil was being done in the name of good. "The law of love therefore remains a principle of criticism over all forms of community in which elements of coercion and conflict destroy the highest type of fellowship."[54]

But there was another reason why Niebuhr was critical of the pacifist attempt to use the absolute ethic of Jesus as a practical standard for political policy. Niebuhr believed that the confusion between absolute and relative in pacifist thought put pacifists into a situation that made ethical conduct in an evil world impossible. The irony of the pacifist position was that in the name of perfection it prevented pacifists from doing what was merely good and right, though not perfect. For example, abhorrence of war kept pacifists from intervening on behalf of the needy. The church, Niebuhr declared, "is unable to help the needy for fear lest pity for the victims of tyranny imperil its precious neutrality. From every side one hears stories of churches and of church periodicals which will not allow the true story of Japanese aggression in China and of German tyranny in Europe to be presented fully, lest it arouse the 'war spirit.' . . . Thousands of Jewish-Christian German refugees look in vain for adequate help and relief from American Christians. . . . Thus the Christian love commandment is equated with blindness to the tragic realities of a warring world."[55]

According to Niebuhr, the absolutism and moralism of pacifists made them either self-righteous and pharisaical or indifferent and passive. Pacifists were unable or unwilling to make distinctions between relative degrees of right and wrong—between, for example, British imperialism (bad) and Nazi totalitarianism (worse). So they found themselves in the predicament of not being able to make moral choices at all. They were immobilized by their inability to reach perfection or by their unwillingness to risk becoming morally soiled in the dirty business of serving God in a fallen world where partial and tentative goods are the best that even the most saintly Christians can achieve. Pacifism, Niebuhr concluded, made Christianity unlivable in the real world. "The fact is that we might as well dispense with the Christian faith entirely if it is our conviction that we can act in history only if we are guiltless. This means that we must either prove our guiltlessness in order to be able to act; or refuse to act because we cannot achieve guiltlessness. Self-righteousness or inaction are the alternatives of secular moralism. If they are also the only alternatives of Christian moralism, one rightly suspects that Christian faith has become diluted with secular perspectives."[56]

Niebuhr translated this accusation into practical terms. He argued that repeal of the Neutrality Act was a morally defensible option because it enabled the United States to contribute weapons and supplies to help rescue a Europe that was teetering on the precipice of totalitarianism. Similarly, the

Neutrality Bill as it stood was a morally unacceptable option because it detached the United States from European affairs and deluded Americans into thinking that events in Europe were none of their business. Isolationism was irresponsible. "The man who shuts himself up in his house and refuses to go out on the village street because he doesn't like conditions in his neighborhood, is not a type that Americans admire. He is either a weak, timid soul, afraid of being contaminated by what is going on around him, or he is a moral prig who considers himself too good to associate with his disreputable neighbors. In either case he is a Pharisee."[57]

This quest for perfection implied that pacifists would choose tyranny over anarchy every time. Refusing to recognize the cloud of sin that hovers above all human relationships and social conflicts, pacifists would be forced by the logic of their position to decide that perfect pacifism was morally superior to imperfect resistance, though that resistance might be directed against an even more imperfect aggressor. Niebuhr considered it unconscionable that pacifists dealt with evil by trying to avoid it altogether. That made them passive accomplices to the spread of totalitarianism. True, Niebuhr admitted, tyranny was not war. In that sense pacifists were right, given the assumption that war is ultimate evil. Tyranny might be peace, but "it is a peace which has nothing to do with the peace of the Kingdom of God. It is a peace which results from one will establishing a complete dominion over other wills and reducing them to acquiescence."[58] The ability to make ambiguous but nevertheless unavoidable moral distinctions was lost among "Christian idealists who preach the law of love but forget that they, as well as all other men, are involved in the violation of that law; and who must eliminate all relative distinctions in history and praise the peace of tyranny as if it were nearer to the peace of the Kingdom of God than war."[59]

Niebuhr did not accept, then, the absolute distinction—a choice which pacifists tried to impose on interventionists—between war as evil and war as holy. He believed that there was a middle way, and that was the way of justice. This option was certainly more ambiguous, as fraught as it was with the possibilities of being morally wrong as well as morally right. But it was the only option that corresponded to actual human experience. "It is not possible to achieve this pure holiness; and yet we must act. The Christian acts with an uneasy conscience both because of the ambiguity of his cause and the impurity of his weapons. His conscience can be eased only as he is 'justified by faith,' and not by the achievement of holiness or by what is worse, the pretension of holiness."[60]

That Niebuhr neglected to mention the pacifist's positive and creative search for peace weakened his argument. He erred by making his opponents mere caricatures of what they really were, for pacifists of all kinds believed that neutrality was the better option in that it would put the U.S. government in a better position to negotiate peace in Europe. Pacifists believed that their point of view was morally responsible as well as politically realistic. Niebuhr also failed to acknowledge that they, too, understood the relativities of history and the messiness of making moral choices in a sinful world. They embraced pacifism not to reach perfection but to be faithful to Jesus, the Jesus of history who lived in the same sinful world in which they lived. Pacifists recognized the risks of their position and decided, considering the complexity of the problem, that it was better to be faithful to convictions and morally right than to be practical, relevant, and morally wrong. What good would victory be, they wondered, if the victors had compromised their convictions along the way?

Niebuhr's Religious Argument

Niebuhr's most biting criticism of pacifists emerged from his theology. Though Niebuhr tried to make his political argument stand on its own, he nevertheless grounded it in a set of theological assumptions. These assumptions were intended to expose the weakness of pacifist religion, which Niebuhr termed bad religion. Niebuhr argued that the Christian faith could not be reduced to a law of love, which he accused pacifists of doing. There was a tension that ran throughout the Christian faith between the divine mandate to love and human bondage to sin, between quest for perfection and awareness of guilt, between the power of righteousness and pardon for sin. In Niebuhr's mind, pacifists erred because they made Christianity into a simple religion of love and thus followed a "simple way out of the sinfulness of human history." They perverted Christianity because they underestimated the power of sin that made even the noblest and purest acts of love less than perfectly noble and pure.

Niebuhr believed that pacifist religion was a heresy. It was a modern version of renaissance humanism, which emphasized the goodness and perfectibility of humanity and expected inevitable progress in history. This secular religion deified humanity and absolutized history. Niebuhr presented the Christian faith as the alternative. "Christianity is a religion which measures the total dimension of human existence not only in terms of the final norm of human conduct, which is expressed in the law of love, but also in terms of the fact of sin. It recognizes that the same man who can become his true self only by striving infinitely for self-realization beyond himself is also inevitably involved in the sin of infinitely making his partial and narrow self the true end of existence."[61]

Niebuhr argued that the heart of the Christian faith was not law but gospel, not humanity's attempt to be like God but God's triumph on behalf of humanity. It was the gospel that resolved the intolerable tension between love and sin, perfection and guilt. The absolute nature of the Kingdom transcended historical progress and human possibility because it did for history and humanity what could not be done within the limits of finite experience. God acted in Jesus Christ to deliver humanity from the curse of striving for perfection and ending up with its opposite. God bridged the gap between what humanity knows it ought to be and what it really is. "The good news of the gospel is not the law that we ought to love one another. The good news of the gospel is that there is a resource of divine mercy which is able to overcome a contradiction within our own souls, which we cannot ourselves overcome."[62]

Niebuhr argued that the gospel thus gave to humanity the freedom to love and seek justice in a world of sin because these acts were released from the crushing burden of having to be perfect. The gospel freed humanity to be merely good instead of great. Thus the relativities of human experience were cut loose from having to conform to the absolutes of the Kingdom. The two were connected in the gospel, Niebuhr conceded, but they were not the same thing.

Niebuhr acknowledged that the church owed a debt to the witness of "historic pacifism." As long as pacifism was kept from being made a political program, it bore witness to the ultimate standard of the Kingdom and reminded the Christian community "that the relative norms of social justice, which justify both coercion and resistance to coercion, are not final norms, and that Christians are in constant peril of forgetting their relative and tentative character and of making them too completely normative."[63] Historic pacifism disavowed the political task and regarded the mystery of evil as beyond its power of solution. But Niebuhr thought otherwise of the political program of neutralists who, whether practical pacifists like Morrison or absolute pacifists like Muste, not only advocated a political program, which was mistaken enough in itself, but then also claimed moral and religious sanction for it.

Once again, Niebuhr did not acknowledge that it was the pacifists' recognition of the unfathomable depths of human and social sin that made them opt for pacifism. Contrary to Niebuhr's assumption, pacifists did not trust their own self-righteous use of violence any more than they trusted their enemy's. Niebuhr, furthermore, did not see that it was the pacifists' understanding of the power of the gospel that freed them to embrace their convictions. Redemption meant to pacifists that they no longer had to force history to take a certain course because God had already intervened in history. They could thus stop being managers of history and become witnesses to what God had done in Christ. They could dare to believe in pacifism because they believed that their religious convictions invited God to act within history to use their inadequate example as a force for good.

Niebuhr never came to the point of urging America to declare war on Germany. He recognized that political decisions had to be made on the basis of national interest, and he doubted whether the American people perceived the clear danger that Germany posed to the United States. The policy of aiding the allies provided a middle course of action. There was a chance, however slim, that England might be able to defeat Germany if the United States provided unlimited arms and supplies. Whatever the extent of America's intervention, Niebuhr admitted that the "negative" task of war, though necessary, did not guarantee that the world emerging afterwards would be better than the world that had existed beforehand. "We cannot, of course, be certain that a defeat of the Nazis will usher in a new order of international justice in Europe and the world. We do know what a Nazi victory would mean; and our first task must therefore be to prevent it."[64] Between contrition for the sins of the past and hope for the possibilities of the future stood the task of the immediate, and that was to win the war. As Niebuhr saw it, war was a risky, dangerous, and inescapable task. It looked toward a better future but did not ensure it.

Common Ground

There were significant differences between interventionists and neutralists, as this chapter has outlined. It would be a vain and hopeless task to force agreement where little if any existed. There was agreement, however, on at least one point: members of both sides were both critical of and loyal to America. Though interventionists like Niebuhr boasted that the United States had attained some of the highest achievements in Western civilization and was a far better alternative certainly than totalitarianism, he was not unaware of its weaknesses. America's achievements were spotty and partial. "In terms of obvious historical facts it is folly to call such a cause as the defense of western democratic civilization 'holy'—in the sense that it is unqualifiedly good. The achievements of western civilization are ambiguous and the weaknesses of western democracy are obvious. Some of these weaknesses helped to bring to birth the monstrous tyranny which we must now combat."[65] While American democracy was good, Niebuhr believed that it could be made better. While its standards of justice were sound, they could be implemented more equitably. Niebuhr refused to absolutize the goodness of American democracy, as clergy had done during the First World War, and then fight the war to impose American democracy on the rest of the world. He understood that American strengths could easily become crippling weaknesses, its partial righteousness turned into ugly self-righteousness. In early 1942 he charted out a course of action for the nation. Not surprisingly, that course of action maintained a tension.

> We cannot support the war with an easy conscience, but we will resist and refute the delusion that we might have had an easier conscience had we permitted the world to sink into slavery. We know of no political strategy which can do justice to our social responsibilities and give us a completely easy conscience. . . . We must resist tyranny and help to establish justice without hatred or bitterness. This can only be done if we avoid self-righteousness; for hatred is the fruit of a one-dimensional moral fervor. Moral fanatics understand the distinction between good and evil, between truth and falsehood, between democracy and tyranny; but they do not know the God in whose sight no man living is justified.[66]

Niebuhr assumed that the United States could live in this tension of confidence and humility, justice and repentance only if the church in America was strong, visionary, and active. The immediate purpose of the war—victory over Germany—was a horrible business, though necessary for the sake of Western civilization. During wartime Americans faced the danger of yielding to hate and revenge. After the war they would be tempted to desert Europe and isolate themselves from the postwar task of building a better world. The church had a mission both to help Americans fight the war successfully and to win a better peace afterwards. In the former case, the church's faith in a transcendent, just, and gracious God would enable Christians to support American interests without becoming hysterical and self-righteous. In the latter case, the church's vision of peace, its international loyalties, and its commitment to justice would provide needed resources for leaders in America to reach a just peace in the world. It was Niebuhr's belief in the gospel and commitment to the church that helped to make him a cautious interventionist.

Neutralists like Morrison tried to be both critical and loyal Americans, too. They opposed America's entry into the war because they did not want American democracy and civil liberties to be undermined, perhaps eventually destroyed, by the impact of war. They affirmed the strengths of America, but not without acknowledging the fragile and vulnerable nature of the American way of life. They were loyal in that they wanted to protect that way of life; but they were critical in that they recognized that the United States could, under the right conditions, go the way of totalitarianism. America was not above temptation, was not so strong that it could never be weakened, was not invulnerable to the encroachment of dictatorship. America, in short, was not secure enough in its freedom to dare to neglect the task of preserving it.

Thus if Niebuhr feared the threat of tyranny abroad, then Morrison feared it at home. If Niebuhr believed that the "anarchy" of war abroad would deliver the world from tyranny, then Morrison believed that the "anarchy" of liberty at home would prevent America from ever yielding to tyranny in the first place. If Niebuhr was committed to justice in Europe, then Morrison was committed to justice at home. However divided in the debate, both parties were passionately loyal to America, under the condition that America fulfill its historic mission. Both parties believed that a vital church was crucial in helping America rise to this task without becoming proud, self-righteous, and self-aggrandizing.

CHAPTER FIVE

THE BIG QUESTION

Justification or condemnation of war was not the only dilemma that confronted the church during the Second World War. An equally troubling dilemma involved justification or condemnation of God, or what is often called the problem of theodicy. The war forced Christians to ask troubling questions about faith. How is it possible to reconcile Christian faith with an evil such as war? How is it possible for Christians to reconcile the existence of a supposedly sovereign and loving God with blood and battle and death? How is it possible, in short, to reconcile the goodness of God with the badness of war?

Articles on theodicy were sprinkled throughout religious journals during the war. Not all were written by theologians. A surprising number came from the pens of common pastors and ordinary lay people who were as vexed by the problem of theodicy as the professionals. Their vexation revealed something of the magnitude of the problem. The existence of evil has always posed a perplexing problem for Christians who confess faith in a powerful, wise, and loving God. Periods of crisis have only exacerbated the problem. It was only natural for Christians to ask, "Why?"

They asked the question often. Typical of these articles were ones that carried such titles as: "Why Does God Allow War?" "The Sovereignty of God in a World at War." "How Could God Let a War Like This Go On?" "Could God Stop This War If He Wanted To?" The titles themselves—almost all of them in the form of a question—betrayed the turmoil of faith that the faithful experienced.

A Universal Theodicy

In general, these theodicies made two basic points: first, God is sovereign over evil, and second, God fulfills his purposes through evil. In most cases it mattered little when these theodicies were written and who wrote them, for they were simply contemporary expressions of an answer that Christians had been giving for centuries.[1] World War II was only the latest in a seemingly endless series of evils that Christians had to address from a religious point of view. The occasion was different, but the basic issues were the same.

Religious leaders pointed first to divine sovereignty, a theme they mentioned often during the war. Conservatives were particularly enamored with it. For example, Clarence Edward Macartney, well-known pastor of Pittsburgh's First Presbyterian Church, confessed that even in the calamity of war God was still in control of history. "To God there are no surprises, no accidents, no chances. All proceeds according to His Eternal Plan." He cited the crucifixion of Christ as the most profound example of God's mysterious control over the affairs of history. Though a great sin committed by evil men, the cross was used by God to accomplish his plan for history.[2] Joseph Taylor Britan, associate of the Friends of Israel Refugee Relief Committee, a fundamentalist organization, affirmed the same truth. He believed that nothing could happen, not even evil, without God allowing it. "We shall never have the right view of this world's agony and woe until we realize that God permits evil. He allows evil men to plan and execute evil. But in this permission He always retains control and uses the evil for the furthering of His own plans and His own glory."[3]

Still, an emphasis on God's sovereignty did not really answer the question, "Why does God allow war?" As Britan suggested, God's sovereignty had to have a purpose toward which it was moving, a reason behind why events on the stage of history were happening. That was the second theme that wartime theodicy addressed. God's sovereign purpose had both a negative side and a positive side. On the one hand, the war was a judgment on the sins of people and nations. What God had done to Israel before the time of Christ he was doing again. God was using a pagan nation to judge his people. "Do you not see the parallel between that time and this?" asked Culver Gordon, Chaplain at Fort Lawton, Washington. "The carelessness and the sinful indifference of the people of Israel, their love of pleasure, their unrighteousness in both private and public life, inevitably exposed them to the attack of their neighboring nation. The Chaldean invasion was the judgment of God, and yet note how it proceeded out of their own sin and folly. And it is upon a world of people indifferent to the claims of God that war has burst in our day. Germany and Japan have broken forth as a judgment upon sin, today as then. This war is a judgment of God upon us."

Typical of many during this period, Culver believed that because human beings were created to live in freedom, they had the option to pursue evil or good. They were free to act as they wished, but not free to determine the consequences of their actions, which would inevitably reflect the moral nature of the universe. God had made people free; he also held them accountable. God's standards were absolute. Relative degrees of justice reflected the necessities of making ambiguous decisions in the fallen world, but they had nothing to do with God's sovereign decrees. Americans could appeal to God to execute judgment against the totalitarian powers, but they would appeal in vain and at their own peril. If God's judgment began with Germany, why would it stop there? "God must proceed upon the principle of absolute justice. God cannot be moved by mere partisan or patriotic feeling. He must proceed upon eternal principles of right and wrong. And we may very well ask, If God is going to intervene in this present war on that basis, just where can He stop? It clearly would not be just to punish some unjust nations and not all unjust nations in this fashion."[4]

Yet Christian leaders wanted to see a positive purpose in the war, too. Though God would judge all nations, he would not judge them all in the same way. Though a fundamentalist leader like Joseph Britan could write that God would use pagan nations as tools to chastise Christian nations, he admitted in the end that God would eventually judge the pagan nations, too. Though every nation was guilty of godlessness, some nations were more guilty than others. Like most Christians writing during the war, Britan found himself having to make moral distinctions between relative degrees of right and wrong. "Fundamentally, therefore, the present war is not a war having its cause in economic injustice or in economic needs, but in the last analysis it is a war of godless despots against the Lord and His anointed Christ, a war against Christ's Church and the institutions of Christianity."[5]

Britan expressed the common opinion of his day. There was nearly universal agreement that the war had a significant purpose behind it, and America had a good reason to fight in it. It was not, like World War I, simply a war "to make the world safe for democracy" or a war to settle disputes between rival imperialisms. It was, as Reinhold Niebuhr argued in the first editorial of *Christianity and Crisis*, a war for civilization itself, that legacy of the past that had become the heritage of the Western nations. That civilization required preservation and development.[6] America was fighting the war, then, for nothing less than the future of civilization. Survival or destruction were the only two options.[7]

If civilization was at stake, then Christians in America had no other choice but to fight for it. War had sometimes become a necessity in the nation's past, and so it was again. Christians did not have to be afraid to fight for what was right. Asserted John W. Bradbury, editor of the Northern Baptist's *Watchman-Examiner*: "There will never be temperance and sobriety in this land of ours without fighting. There will never be freedom, security, and peace in the world without fighting. There never have been and there never will be any decent standards of morality and justice unless we go out and do battle for them. This is the type of world into which we are born. This will be our responsibility until we lay our armor down."[8]

John Mackay argued that the state had the right and duty to execute judgment on aggressor nations that violated the peace and freedom of their neighbors. "The United States of America cannot evade this responsibility under God, nor can it discharge it without deciding to gamble its very existence in the armed effort to break the yoke of Nazidom." This duty was both negative and risky. It was negative because America could accomplish at the most only the limited purpose of restraining demonic forces. It was risky because the just peace for which America was fighting was bound to be tainted by impure motives, self-righteousness, and lust for power. "For the painful truth is that man's best endeavours, even when he is justified in believing that God wills the actions which he undertakes, are always carried on with personally mixed motives and in a faltering and sinful way." Still, the largely negative purpose of war and the risk it entailed for the victors did not imply that Christians should stay out of war completely. "But that is no reason why, though conscious of his own guilt, he should not go forward in his faltering human way to make the world a worthier place for sons of God to live in, and closer in its principles to the principles of God's everlasting Kingdom."[9]

An American Theodicy

As Mackay's argument implied, many church leaders in America approached the problem of wartime theodicy from a distinctively American point of view. They asked how the war fit into and would further God's purpose *for America*. Mackay believed that America was responsible to fight in the war. Though the nation was guilty of sin, as many Christian leaders assumed, it was nevertheless summoned by God to resist tyranny and defend Western civilization from chaos and ruin. America was on the side of right. But how far on the side of right?

Inevitably Christian leaders in America wanted to give a religious interpretation of the war *for Americans* and *from an American perspective.* The question of theodicy could not remain general and abstract. It had to become specific and concrete. It could not simply be: Why does God allow war? It also had to be: What does God have in mind for America in this war? Two extreme answers were possible. On the one hand, Christian leaders could have argued in their theodicies that the war had no particular meaning for America. All people—Americans, Germans, Russians, Jews—were so evil that God had finally unleashed wrath upon the entire human race. On the other hand, they could have argued that the war had meaning only for Americans, whose destiny in history was special and significant. Totalitarianism was an evil that had to be destroyed; America was called upon to destroy that evil and build a better world upon the ruins. Thus religious leaders could have called the war either unholy or holy, an occasion for divine judgment on all nations, including America, or another manifestation of God's blessing on America.

It is clear that church leaders did *not* declare it a holy war. The evidence is overwhelming at this point. They recoiled from the idea and rejected it outright. Some called it just; none called it holy. "Let me repeat," declared John Mackay unequivocally. "There can never be any question of a 'holy war.' The fact that a given war may be justified as an unpleasant police operation to stave off anarchy and maintain enlightened human justice does not make it 'holy.' The fact that this war may be undertaken in the name of God and, as Karl Barth puts it, 'for the sake of Christ and Christian truth,' does not make it a holy war. For the attribute 'holy' cannot be applied to anything that is not directly related to the Kingdom of God, and war has nothing to do with the Kingdom of God as such."[10] Mackay's words represented the opinion of most Christian leaders. However crucial the outcome or significant the ideas over which the war was being fought, the war itself was not a holy one, and the church would have been wrong to declare it as such. The church had done that once before, during World War I, and later regretted it. The church would not do it again.

Still, religious leaders believed that America was special to God and had a unique role to play in history. Though guilty, it was not as guilty as the totalitarian powers. Though far from perfect, it had the potential to become good, even great. Though stained with the blood of the innocent, it still embodied certain principles of justice and freedom that made it "the last and best hope" on earth. If the churches were not going to declare—could not, in good conscience, declare—a holy war, then how could the churches invest the war with the kind of religious meaning that would speak directly to the American people? If the extremes were rejected—war as holy or futile, as meaningless for everyone or meaningful only for Americans, as God's judgment on all nations or God's blessing on America—could a middle way be found that would reflect biblical truth and still give meaning to Americans? How could theodicy keep God in heaven and still give a sense of purpose to the American people?

America's Failures and Heritage

America's Failures

The Second World War was a conflict of ideas. On that point everyone was agreed. Christian leaders drew sharp lines between totalitarianism and democracy, paganism and Christianity. They did not close their eyes to the ideological dimensions of the conflict. Still, church leaders were surprisingly harsh with America. They condemned the enemy's ideology, to be sure; but they also castigated their own nation, fearful lest it go the way of its opponents. Their God was a God of absolute truth; he did not surrender to the claims of relativity. Their God was a God of lofty ideals; he did not approve of the nation which had great ideals but failed to live up to them. Americans supposedly believed in such a truthful God and held such lofty, biblical ideals. On that score it stood on high ground. If America had a problem, it was that it possessed but did not live according to those ideals. It was falling short—far short—of its own blessed heritage.

Christian leaders were alarmed by America's betrayal of this heritage. Writing for the *Presbyterian*, the Reverend George Wells Arms of Brooklyn, New York, likened America to the people of Israel in Jeremiah's day who found comfort and security from false prophets who cried "Peace! Peace!" when there was no peace. "We have been boasting of our own self-sufficiency, that we are a great people, with all natural resources, bounded on the east by one ocean and on the west by another. . . . But men cannot establish peace. Only God can do that." Why, Arms asked, should God grant peace to a wicked nation? "Man has failed; civilization has failed; democracy has failed; Protestantism has failed. That is gloom and that is pessimism, and it is no more popular than the preaching of Jeremiah, but it is just as true." The "man" Arms had in mind was "civilized man," the man of the West who had inherited the achievements of the Renaissance and the Reformation. But the insidious influence of Modernism had perverted this glorious heritage and was driving the West to ruin. Germany was already lost. America and its allies were following close behind. America was guilty because its ideals had been undermined, its moral standards trampled under by countless injustices.[11]

Church leaders did not hesitate to catalogue America's sins. Severe criticism came from all quarters of the church, not only from neo-orthodox theologians, whose rediscovery of sin had made them adept at preaching jeremiads to America, but also from evangelicals, liberals, dispensationalists, and confessionalists. Church leaders in general seemed to be painfully aware of America's faults. Because they did not want America to follow Europe to destruction, they took it upon themselves to expose the nation's faults and reawaken it to its great ideals. America had a noble heritage. It needed to repent and return to it. Its greatest enemy was not totalitarianism abroad but compromise at home.

Some church leaders, like Edwin R. Errett, editor of the *Christian Standard*, a religious weekly representing the conservative, noncooperating wing of the Disciples, accused America of lacking discipline and neglecting its spiritual life. In 1940 Errett devoted an entire editorial to Hitler's accomplishments in Germany. Hitler had revitalized the economy, cleaned up Germany's moral filth, and given the nation a purpose. He had made Germany a disciplined nation. The price, Errett quickly interjected, was too high. The achievements of totalitarianism could never compensate for the evil it embodied.

Nevertheless, Germany's success underscored America's weakness. Americans put crosses in their churches but did not have a heart for God. They attended church every Sunday but did not live according to their convictions. They had the most advanced and just system of government in the world but did not take responsibility for it. According to Errett, the lesson was clear. "Unless we know what human liberty really is, unless we can discipline ourselves in some measure comparable to that imposed discipline, unless we can regain our devotion to the ideals of home and of unselfish sacrifice that belong to our better nature, we may find the hungry and disillusioned human spirit going over to the Nazis."[12]

Errett also asserted that America was so concerned about material things that it was failing to nurture its spiritual life. He pointed out that the real peril in the modern world was not totalitarianism but the cravings in people that made totalitarianism attractive. The rise of the dictatorial powers pointed to a deeper problem that resided in the human heart. Modern people were yearning for something. They were hungering for a life that was free from suffering, worry, deprivation, unemployment, and chaos. Totalitarianism gave them such a life, offering them the benefits of security and prosperity. Such bounty was the essence of its materialistic religion, which had proven itself to be successful enough to expose the inefficiency, poverty, and injustice of the democratic nations.

Of course totalitarianism exacted a price—human freedom. Sadly, it appeared to Errett that many were willing to pay it. "What we have, then, is a religion that offered power and speed and glory and unity and physical satisfactions in return for sacrifice of spiritual privileges, particularly those of liberty of thought and speech and art and religion." Unaware of this deeper issue in the war, Americans were vulnerable to the temptation of making their government do the same thing. Americans were making materialism their new religion. "The tragedy of the situation for Americans is that our own thinking is none too clear on the matter. We, too, have become involved in a world-wide movement 'to take the cash and let the credit go,' to yield up dearly bought privileges and safeguards to liberty if only the Government would give us physical benefits."[13]

Errett attacked political liberals in America because they were reinforcing this weakness in the American character by promising exactly what Americans were craving. They were thus leading the nation toward dictatorship. "These modern liberals are willing to ignore the weaknesses of unredeemed human character and, therefore, to let go of all the safeguards if only they may have the physical benefits of direct redistribution of wealth on guarantee of governmental care of all the citizens." In Errett's mind, liberals in America were as materialistic as totalitarian dictators insofar as they appealed only to America's material desires. They, too, were suffocating America's spiritual life, however well intentioned they were. But good intentions, Errett declared, were not enough. The American people thus had to make a choice: liberty or dictatorship. "Fundamentally we must face the question: Are we willing to sell the birthright of true liberty for the pottage of physical satisfactions?"[14]

Errett had already made up his mind. He preferred freedom. He realized, however, that Americans would have to revitalize neglected aspects of their heritage to be convinced of the superiority of this choice. Americans needed to wean themselves from their desire for material prosperity and renew their quest for spiritual depth.

Fundamentalists, like Will Houghton, president of the Moody Bible Institute, urged America to return to God, before it was too late. According to Houghton, it appeared that it already *was* too late. He cried: "We confess there are tears in our eyes and a sigh in our heart as we write this editorial. God pity America! It looks as if we are about to reap in tragedy for our sowing of unbelief. See the sad retrogression in these paragraphs. No Christ! No cross! No God! No Bible! And on every hand the fruit of unbelief in profanity and sensuality and sordid sin! O God, give America a spiritual awakening before it is too late!"[15] A revival was the only real solution. "This is the time," wrote Hyman J. Appelman, a fundamentalist and Hebrew Christian evangelist, "for all of God's people to come to the aid of their country. This is the time to strike the religious iron while it is blazing hot. This is the time for us who know and understand the Lord's dealings to call America back to God."[16] Fundamentalists believed that a revival of religion would enable Americans to comprehend the precious and fragile nature of their heritage of freedom and democracy and motivate them to defend it against both foreign and domestic foe.[17]

The same critical attitude toward America extended beyond the scope of conservative and fundamentalist leaders. Denis De Rougemont, a Frenchman writing for *Christianity and Crisis*, believed that Americans needed to become aware of the machinations of the devil himself, which he understood as the embodiment of evil in persons and systems. It was too easy, he argued, to assume the devil was active only in Germans. De Rougemont wanted them to know that the devil was alive and well in Americans, too. The problem of evil touched every human being because evil resided in the human heart. "It seems to me that the clearest lesson which emerges from European events is this: the sentimental hatred of the evil which is in others may blind to the evil which one bears in himself, and to the gravity of evil in general. The too easy condemnation of the wicked man on the opposite side may conceal and favor much inward complaisance towards that very wickedness." If Americans wanted to search for the devil, they would have to look no further than themselves. They would see him incarnated in the liberal intellectual who did not believe in the devil, or in the dynamic and optimistic playboy who could care less about the devil—whatever constituted popular images of the typical American. "We are all guilty in the measure in which we do not condemn and do not recognize in us too the mentality of the totalitarians, that is, the active and personal presence of the Demon in our passions, in our need for sensation, in our fear of responsibilities, in our civic inertia, in our ignorance of our neighbor, in our rejection finally of any absolute which transcends and which judges our 'vital' (as they always are) interests."[18]

In the opinion of these Christian leaders, God did not look favorably upon America. His standards were absolute, not relative. He viewed nations from the perspective of his perfect will; he used the Bible as the precise plumb line for judging people. If God measured America according to the lofty ideals of the Bible—ideals that, ironically, were embodied in America's heritage—then he would surely find fault with the nation. America had failed. Its first order of business was to rediscover those ideals.

America's Heritage

Yet these leaders also believed that America was different from its enemies. Though its ideals condemned it, they also made it unique. America was the only nation, as one Christian observed, that had been founded upon a noble idea. Church leaders were very careful, therefore, to affirm that America was clearly set apart from its opponents, even its allies, if judged according to its heritage. However sinful, America was summoned to reaffirm and defend that heritage, for the battle was not simply between rival armies but between rival ideas.

Countless articles in religious journals contrasted America's heritage with that of Nazi Germany, Communist Russia, and Fascist Italy. America's heritage, of course, always emerged as superior. Nazism exalted one race over others; Communism the party over the people; Fascism the state over the individual. All were foes of democracy and God. They used force and violence as the lever of progress. They were materialistic and greedy for power, full of revenge and bitterness, militaristic and dictatorial, haters of God, brazenly pagan and atheistic and idolatrous. They were "Satanic incarnations," only in different colors—red, black, and brown.[19]

These evil ideologies were founded upon philosophies of life that contradicted the Word of God. This was no more evident than in the comparison between Nazism's patron saint, Friederich Nietzsche, and America's great hero, Abraham Lincoln. According to Edward F. Schewe, Nietzsche was a militant atheist who deified the superman. He was heartless, cruel, and hungry for power. "Nietzsche thought pity a blunder, a weakness. He suggested that the unfit be removed and the path cleared for the strong. The common people were weeds and rubbish in his view. They were merely the background for the 'supermen.'" Nietzsche proclaimed that the will to power was "the driving force of all energy, ambition, and progress." Nietzsche was the seed of the Nazi harvest; Nazism was evil because Nietzsche's thought was corrupt. Nietzsche was to totalitarian Germany what Lincoln was to democratic America—its ideological patron. The differences between these two men revealed the stark contrasts between Nazi Germany and America. "Over against the pagan and inhuman philosophy of Nietzsche we put the social idealism and moral passion of Abraham Lincoln. Over against the Fuehrer of Nazism we put the unforgettable and ever potent personality of our own 'Great Commoner,' who believed in God and who also believed in man, white or black, and in man's equal manhood and even justice to all."[20]

Other Christian authors contrasted Hitler and Jesus, or the swastika and the cross. In an editorial in the *Banner*, H. J. Kuiper pitted the cross as symbol of Christianity against the swastika as symbol of Nazism. "The cross of our Lord is an eloquent witness to the unswerving justice of God. The swastika stands for the pernicious doctrine that might makes right—which means that there is no such thing as right. The cross stands for truth, for Christ was crucified because he bore witness to the truth; the swastika exalts lying if it can serve to promote the Nazi cause. The cross preaches love; the swastika is the banner of hate. The cross glorifies mercy; the swastika exalts cruelty, torture."[21] If the two systems of thought were that antithetical, it was imperative that America reaffirm its heritage and so find the resources necessary to win the war of ideas. It had to appropriate its ideals for the challenges that loomed ahead. The choice was clear enough.

It was not altogether clear, however, whether the American people were ready to make that choice. Which America would they believe in, contribute to, fight for? Would it be the America of materialism, modernism, indulgence, idolatry, laziness, and irreligion? Or the America of faith, freedom, democracy, goodwill, sacrifice, and godliness? The former America was not really America at all but a masquerade. The latter America was the true America, waiting to be rediscovered and renewed. It was this latter America that Christian leaders lauded. It was, according to Raphael Harwood Miller, editor of the *Christian-Evangelist*, the "other America" of lofty ideals, "the America of democracy, of free speech and press, of rights of conscience; the America which offers a haven of opportunity and hope; the America without aristocracy of birth and class; the America that recognizes worth and character above blood and race; the America that hates war and aggression; the America which would like to see peace and goodwill established in all the earth."[22]

God's Judgment and Purpose

Wartime theodicy also emphasized God's sovereign control of history and God's judgment of all nations. As ruler of history and lord of the nations, God was sovereign over all. Nothing could resist his will, nothing could withstand his power. Even Hitler was God's tool, war an instrument to accomplish his plans. He stood above all nations and peoples, who were "like dust on the scales" to him.

This belief in the transcendence of God created a theological problem for those who also believed in the freedom of humanity. Christian thinkers resolved this difficulty by affirming that, while God was sovereign, he nevertheless gave people freedom to make moral choices and that, while God was ruler of all nations, he intended nevertheless to show favor upon the nations that honored him. America was a good case in point. Christian theodicy thus allowed church leaders to affirm America's historical purpose without compromising their belief in God's transcendent power.

But God's sovereign judgment loomed so large in the minds of some Christian thinkers that their wartime theodicies tended to deny the possibility of human freedom altogether. They overlooked the significance of moral choice and the meaningfulness of human action in history. Their theodicies appeared to be amoral and historically pessimistic.

Two viewpoints in particular moved in this direction—the first was the theology of the dispensationalists, the second was the wartime theodicy of Charles Clayton Morrison, editor of the *Christian Century*. It would be difficult to miss the irony here. These two parties held very little in common. The dispensationalists were theological and political conservatives, Morrison a theological and political liberal who, like many other liberals under the influence of neo-orthodoxy, had rediscovered the significance of the transcendence of God in the 1930s after having affirmed the immanence of God in the decades before that. The dispensationalists, furthermore, articulated their theodicies early in the war—in 1939 and 1940. The timing itself mattered very little because their understanding of history emerged from their study of biblical prophecy. Their perspective changed only slightly in about 1941 when they came to the conclusion that the Axis powers would lose the war and the world would not come to an end because Hitler, Mussolini, and Stalin had not fulfilled the specific prophecies predicting the rise of the final Antichrist and the second coming of Christ. Morrison did not develop his theodicy until after Pearl Harbor because, in the period before America actually entered the war, he devoted all his energies to keeping it out. Finally, the dispensationalists mined the apocalyptic passages of Scripture to interpret the war; Morrison rejected their literalism in favor of metaphorical theology. Still, on one point they lined up on the same side: the sovereignty of God and the enormity of evil made human choice appear meaningless.

During the war the dispensationalists produced a huge literature on the European conflict, and they used biblical prophecy to interpret events in Europe. They were alarmed that other Christian leaders were not consulting their Bibles as faithfully as they were and were therefore speaking with little authority and even less accuracy about the war. Wilbur M. Smith, popular Bible teacher at Moody Bible Institute and a leading intellectual force among fundamentalists, denounced a report on war issued by the Federal Council of Churches because it did not refer once to what *Jesus* taught about war. It was sentimental and idealistic, not biblical. "Now, one would think that in a book compiled by a commission on Christian education there would be a sincere effort made to at least include the sentences on war which came from the lips of Christ; that when a council of Churches of Christ put out a large work dealing with quotations on peace and war, they would make it a point to include what Christ himself, the Head of the church, really said about war. . . . There is a price men must pay for ignoring our Lord's words, and that is a false hope for the cessation of war in this age."[23] What Christ actually taught, Smith propounded, was that war would flourish until Christ returned; and would, in fact, increase in frequency, intensity, and severity until the Second Coming. The repudiation of war was a fruitless gesture, then, because it contradicted the word of God.

"Wars and rumors of war" was one of the many signs that would precede the return of Christ, according to dispensationalists, who kept busy observing the "signs of the times" in order to predict when *the time* was drawing near. That it was drawing near was certain, although no one could actually know the precise day. That knowledge belonged only to God. Though dispensationalists could not identify the day or year, they were not hesitant to speculate about the conditions that would bring it closer. The *Sunday School Times* contained dozens of articles on biblical prophecy and the war, more than thirty of them written by Dr. Louis S. Bauman, a popular speaker at fundamentalist prophecy conferences. The November 1939 issue of the popular religious periodical contained a telling illustration symbolizing Bauman's approach to wartime theodicy. A half-burning city stood in the background. A Bible rested in the foreground, opened up and hollowed out. On it were written the words, "THE PROPHECIES OF SCRIPTURE." At the top of the picture two hands, labeled "HISTORY," were holding a large ladle, whose contents, called "WORLD EVENTS," were being poured into the Bible. The message was clear enough. The cataclysmic clashes of world empires could be understood only if one consulted the Bible and divined how they fulfilled biblical prophecy. They were signs that pointed to the end of time and confirmed the predictive accuracy of the Bible.

What were these signs? Bauman listed them: the revival of the Roman Empire, the clash of Germany and Russia, the apostasy of the church, the persecution of true Christians, the suffering of the Jews and their return to Palestine, the emergence of such "beasts" as Hitler and Stalin, the worldwide spread of Christianity. Many of these signs had already been fulfilled; others were yet to come. Bauman sensed that the time was ripe for their fulfillment. The imminence of two unfulfilled signs was particularly significant for Bauman. "The Synchronization of the Greatest War, Greatest Famine, Greatest Pestilence, and Greatest Earthquake of all time" was one; "The Engulfment of the Jews in a World-wide wave of Bitter Anti-semitism" was the other. Bauman was concerned that most Christians were not reading these signs as he was. "When signs stand out, as they do today, like mountain peaks— when God in his goodness is trying to warn a sinful world by every possible token that judgment impends—for men deliberately to close their eyes and their ears, and sneer at the warnings that the incarnate God himself gives them—can only fill one with disgust, if pity could leave room for disgust."[24]

Bauman conceded that he did not know—and did not have to know— whether or not World War II would bring an end to the world and usher in the return of Christ. Mussolini appeared to be the White Horseman who would revive the Roman Empire; Adolf Hitler appeared to be the Red Horseman mentioned in the book of Revelation. Only time would tell. And time eventually did tell. By 1941 it was clear that events in Europe were *not* fulfilling biblical prophecy in the way that dispensationalists had originally thought, though they were still, of course, fulfilling God's plan for history.

Fundamentalists thus began to explain why Hitler would eventually fail. For one, he had lifted up his hand against the Jews, the church, and God himself. For another, he did not meet the conditions that the Bible had laid down for the emergence of the Antichrist. Bauman believed that Adolf Hitler was a "dreamer" who was due for a "rude awakening." A satanic kingdom was eventually to arise within the "permissive will of God," but it would not, like Hitler's, have its center north of the Rhine or be a single kingdom with no influential allies. "It will be an allied kingdom, sponsored by ten sorely tried kings, who will seek to save themselves from some gigantic enemy power by the centralization of all their own power, armies and fleets, for 'one hour' in the hands of 'the beast'; and 'the beast' does not emerge from any Teutonic or Muscovite den."[25] Thus Hitler could not be the Antichrist. He would nevertheless conform to the inexorable prophetic laws of the Bible, whatever his role was to be. God had plotted history's course. It remained for Hitler to follow that course, used as God's unwitting tool. It remained for the church to trace that course through biblical prophecy and read the signs in anticipation of history's great climactic ending.

America did not appear to play a major role in the fundamentalists' scheme of history because the Bible said nothing about America. Bauman assigned a minor role to America insofar as it was Britain's ally and Britain occupied Palestine, which would be "desired by the nations." Only in that sense was America included in the specific prophecies of the end-times. John R. Rice, popular fundamentalist Bible teacher and writer, did not even concede that much. "I love America," he confessed. "I am for the American way of life, meaning our freedom, our individual enterprise, our 'horse-and-buggy' constitution, if it be that. But America must decline from her place of world eminence and world power. That is plainly foretold in the Bible. . . . Yet there are certain prophecies that specifically mention the whole world, including America, that show the outcome of world affairs. . . . America is to be subject to a dictator at Rome! That is the express declaration of the Word of God. Every nation in the world, including America, is to be subject to a dictator at Rome."[26] If anything, America could only expect chastisement and suffering because, like the rest of the nations, it was guilty of sinning against God. "If the God who rules the universe today is the God of Israel, then America can be purged of her murders and her crimes only by a bath of blood. And because of sin, God turned Jerusalem and Judah over to their enemies."[27] Or again: "Yet England and America are filled up with sinners, the same kind of sinners, individually, as fill the other nations of the world. We are one race, a warring, hating, covetous, uncontrolled race, beastly in wickedness and selfishness and godlessness."[28] In Rice's mind, the time was near, perilously near, for the end to come. Though he considered it wrong to predict the actual time of the end, he could not help but feel that the time was drawing close. The fulfillment of prophecy made him expectant. He believed that there was not a single prophecy yet to be fulfilled before Jesus came. "Already more has come to pass than I believed possible before the Savior should appear. I never dreamed that we would see the dictators arise as they are, the remaking of the map of Europe, the beginnings of the restored Roman empire. I thought surely these things must wait until after the rapture. I say not a single thing remains that is foretold to happen before Jesus comes."[29]

Dispensationalists built their view of history upon biblical prophecy. God was transcendent, the ruler of history. Christians could "read" history by studying the Bible, but they could do very little to influence it. Unlike the nations of Europe, America seemed to have a minor role in biblical prophecy. It stood on the margins of God's end-time plans. America could expect only judgment and chaos, especially as the end drew near.

Charles Clayton Morrison stood about as far apart from fundamentalists on matters of religion and war as any two Christians could. Rather than a fulfillment of Scripture, as fundamentalists thought, Morrison believed that war was a violation of everything Scripture taught. The violation was so great, in fact, that Morrison could see nothing redemptive in war. It was "judgment" and "hell," "tragedy" and "suffering." It was not simply a violation of morality; it was complete amorality. Morrison believed that up to Pearl Harbor America had a chance to act morally, to choose what was right, to seek peace. Pearl Harbor changed all that. It introduced what he called "a new situation" into the war. Relative rights and wrongs ceased to apply. "War signalizes the breakdown of the moral order itself and of every ethical standard known to civilization by which its character as right and wrong could be judged. When war becomes a fact, a concrete reality, it marks the end of all moralizing. The fate of the belligerents has been definitely given over to the arbitrament of sheer might, which is neither moral nor immoral, but amoral."[30] War was true tragedy because it stood outside the boundaries of morality. "Suffering and death and violence are a part of tragedy, but these are not the essence of it. The essence of tragedy lies in our human involvement in a situation from which there is no escape save by doing monstrous evil. It is not the suffering, but the moral predicament of the sufferer, that constitutes the tragedy. A tragic situation is one in which man has lost his freedom to choose between right and wrong. Yet he must act. But his act is determined for him by the iron law of necessity."[31]

Morrison called World War II an "unnecessary necessity" because, once in it, America could not get out; the nation was suddenly engulfed by an inescapable and inexorable reality. Before entering the war America had had the chance to stay out. The war did not have to happen. America could have chosen a different course. It had possessed the freedom to follow God and choose the way of peace. Belligerency changed everything. After Pearl Harbor America's only choice—no choice at all, really—was to fight, kill, win. Morrison called the war "hell" rather than "sin" because sin implied freedom of choice while hell implied no choice at all. America had sinned in 1940 and 1941 because it had not done everything it could to stop or stay out of the war. But in 1942 America plunged into hell because it began to pay for the consequences of its sin. "War is hell; and in hell conscience does not function according to the canons of right and wrong. It can project no course that is good and reject no course that is evil. . . . The only sin against which a soul in hell can bear witness is the sin that brought him there."[32] War was too vast, too cosmic, too total, too absolute to be called sin. It inverted and corrupted the social order that Morrison believed virtuous human beings had been striving to build. "In modern war the whole moral order of society is inverted and perverted. Total war means that civilization, whose normal orientation is toward human welfare and more abundant life, is now oriented toward destruction and death. . . . The lie becomes the truth; the truth, a lie. The press, the movie and the radio are converted from agencies of information and entertainment into agencies for the propaganda of hatred. Legislatures become rubber stamps of the commander in chief or the dictator."[33]

Morrison did not ultimately deny the reality of human freedom. But he did argue that the free choices made in the past created conditions in the present that would either expand freedom or limit freedom. The choices made one day, in other words, would become opportunities—or inexorables—the next day, depending upon whether or not they were good choices. America had sinned because the choices it had made before the war deprived it of freedom once it entered the war. World War II was the terrible penalty it had to pay. It symbolized that loss of freedom.

Both Morrison and the fundamentalists, however, did not go so far as to suggest that Americans had no freedom at all, no opportunity to do the will of God during the war. Though God was in his heaven, controlling history and punishing the nations, he nevertheless had a purpose in mind for America. Morrison found a way out of what appeared to be the absolutism of his position by making a distinction between America and the church in America. "It is a mistake to conclude that because we are inescapably caught in the torturous necessity of the war we are therefore doomed to total inaction. There is a wide area for moral activity for the Christian and the Christian community in wartime."[34] The church was still free to do the will of God, free to make use of American freedom, generosity, and democracy (concepts that Morrison would not discuss in his theodicy) to serve victims of war, to guard against hysteria, and to defend the rights of African Americans, Japanese Americans, and Jehovah's Witnesses.

The *Christian Century* did not hesitate to carry on a crusade for freedom and religion during the war. Though Morrison believed that the war was a tragic, hellish, unnecessary necessity, he did not abandon his biblical convictions once the war began. Though Morrison believed that God had turned his back on the America at war, he did not assume that God had rejected the nation altogether. The church was not at war, and the church was alive in America. Freedom and democracy were still operative in America, however threatened by Roosevelt's growing dictatorial powers, which was all the more reason why they had to be protected, preserved, and strengthened. Thus, if Morrison's God was absolutely transcendent in war, he was not so far removed from the world that he could not inspire Americans to do the will of God, nor so far removed that he could not charge people like Morrison to defend the America of democracy and religion, of freedom and justice. In fact, it was the "inexorable" of the war that made Morrison aware of just how much American freedom had to be defended, how special the American heritage was.

Dispensationalists did not appear to live consistently with the logic of their theodicy either. America had the historic destiny of contributing significantly to the fulfillment of one of the most important signs of the close of the age. It was charged with the responsibility to send missionaries around the world to preach the gospel until every nation had heard. Only then would the end come. "I am persuaded," declared H. A. Ironside, popular fundamentalist preacher and pastor of Moody Bible Church, "that what God is doing now is sending out the last call to the Gentiles in order to complete the bride of the Lamb and then He is coming to take His own to be with Himself." He acknowledged that Jewish missionaries would carry the gospel to the ends of the earth. Still, he wanted to impress upon his fellow fundamentalists the responsibility to publish the gospel to the people of their day while they were waiting for His return. "The heralds of the cross are fast publishing the gospel in all nations. Soon this witness-testimony will be completed. If it ends tonight, what about your soul? Then the door will be shut for guilty, apostate Christendom. Enter now while the day of grace is still here."[35] Fundamentalists tried to heed Ironside's exhortation. In the 1930s and 1940s they built an empire of Bible colleges, publishing houses, and missionary organizations to take advantage of American freedom and wealth, to get the message of the gospel out, and so to fulfill America's historic destiny. Their God was transcendent, the ruler of history and judge of all nations. Yet America still had a special role to play.

A tension thus ran through these two unusual examples of wartime theodicies. God was sovereign. He controlled history and judged the nations.

America could no more escape his judgment than Germany could. Yet America had a special destiny. Its heritage manifested the benevolent providence of God, its institutions reflected biblical principles, and its role in history fell just short of Israel's. Still, if these theodicies leaned in one direction, it was in the direction of divine transcendence, often at the expense of human freedom.

Two other writers tried to stress both divine sovereignty and human freedom, without compromising either one. They believed that God was using the Second World War to judge the nations, including America. Yet they also believed that America had a special role to play in God's plan for history. These two leaders, Edwin R. Errett and Reinhold Niebuhr, were an unlikely match. Errett was the editor of the *Christian Standard*, the voice of the conservative and noncooperating wing of the Disciples that would eventually separate to form the Independent Christian Churches and Churches of Christ in 1971. Niebuhr was the editor of *Christianity and Crisis* and professor at Union Seminary in New York City. Errett opposed the ecumenical movement, Niebuhr supported it. Errett was a separatist, Niebuhr inclusive. Yet both outlined theodicies that affirmed both the transcendence of God and the significance of America in God's plan for history.

Errett was not afraid to extol the virtues of the true America, the America that God could and would bless, as he already had in the past. It was the America that emphasized the value of the individual, that provided people with the opportunity to better themselves. It was the America of freedom— freedom of expression, of assembly, of speech, of protest, of religion. It was the America that did not dominate people but instead gave people the opportunity to participate in the affairs of government. It was the America that protected the rights of the minority from the rule of the majority. This America was essentially religious in nature. "It is significant that all these principles that go to make America get their real strength from the Christian emphasis upon the value of the individual soul. The Christian work of salvation and its consequences in the individual relationship with God upon the part of even the lowest in the scale of human culture inevitably eventuates in a community designed to protect the inalienable rights of the individual."[36] Religion was the soul of Errett's America. It was religion, therefore, that had to be protected from external and internal foes and cultivated in the lives of the American people.

America needed a vital Christianity and church more than Christianity and the church needed a vital America. America was the parasite, faith and church the host. The faith itself would last even if, or when, America collapsed. The nation was not central to God's plan for history; only its faith was, and that faith would survive no matter what happened to the nation. America was safe only if it provided hospitality to Christianity and the church, which of course its tradition of democracy and freedom had done in the past and would no doubt continue to do in the future. But even then America would not last forever. "Many of us believe that the greatest service that citizens of the United States can render is to preserve a representative government at peace even if all else collapses. But Christians need to be taught that that is not identical with Christianity. Even if the United States goes down, the kingdom of God will still live. And, despite handicaps it can still conquer."[37] Or again: "We do not have in mind that shallow sort of talk that goes so far as to say that the church depends upon democracy for its livelihood. That is, of course, not so. The church existed before democracy and will exist after it, if that is necessary. The church does not depend upon any state—much less upon any form of rule—for its authority or right to speak and live its message. It derives its origin and its authority from Jesus Christ Himself."[38]

Ambivalent, yes; it is hard to miss the "if that is necessary" in the paragraph. But prophetic, too, especially when one considers that Errett wrote the editorial in 1942. Errett believed that the church's primary duty in America was not to "improve" America by changing its institutions but to transform America by preaching the gospel. "The plan of God for the kingdom of heaven has a longer schedule, but a surer terminus. Instead of proposing to change the rules and thereby change the people, God proposes to create new people and thereby change the society."[39] Above all, Christians needed to keep America from becoming a victim of its own strength. They had to keep the nation humble. They had to help the nation be wary of thinking it could change the world and impose its own system of government on the rest of the world. "What right have we," Errett asked, "to dominate and dictate to all the rest of humanity?" "The greatest peril here, however, is not so much to us as to the cause of freedom itself; for if what professes to be a democracy should make itself hated because of its dictatorship of all the rest of the world, is not the inevitable result a transfer of the antagonism from the Americans to the thing for which the Americans stand; that is, democracy, or free government? In other words, we may very well succeed in making the world unsafe for democracy by our very zeal to rule the world in the interest of democracy." To preserve its heritage and live up to its ideals in a world at war, America had to surrender power, not usurp it; to live by example, not impose its system on the world. "Let us justify our faith in the principle and so champion the rights of all peoples to self-determination so as to make the world safe for self-government."[40]

Reinhold Niebuhr's perspective was complementary to Errett's, only more politically inclined. He contended that history was a process in which various nations and peoples emerged to fulfill a significant "mission" in the world. This "profundity of history," as Niebuhr called it, meant that "various nations and classes, various social groups and races are at various times placed in such a position that a special measure of the divine mission in history falls upon them." Niebuhr believed that God had chosen Britain and America for this task in such a fateful hour. Grace had determined by the "accidents" of special circumstances, by the fortunes of geography and climate, history and fate, by the convergence of ideas and institutions, that America and Britain would be perfectly situated to take the lead in history. "The democratic traditions of the Anglo-Saxon world are actually the potential basis of a just world order."

Niebuhr believed that there was peril as well as promise in this destiny. America would be tempted to think its special role was solely attributable to its own virtue instead of to divine grace. It would be tempted to become self-aggrandizing, to overlook its own weaknesses and deny its past and present sins and thus become self-righteous.

Even under ideal conditions, America stood no chance to fulfill its historical role with complete success. It nevertheless had an opportunity to fulfill it with partial success. That success depended upon the vitality of American Christianity and the strength of the American church. "But if this is to be accomplished, the Christian Church must understand its prophetic mission." America's destiny, then, could only be understood from a religious point of view and could only be fulfilled by drawing wisdom and strength from its religious heritage. "The position of the Anglo-Saxon peoples at the crucial and strategic point in the building of a world community is a fact of such tremendous significance that it can only be adequately comprehended in religious terms. It is a position of destiny and carries with it tremendous responsibilities. Without a religious sense of the meaning of destiny, such a position as Britain and America now hold is inevitably corrupted by pride and the lust of power. We may in fact be certain that this corruption will not be absent from our political life."

In Niebuhr's mind the church's role was central because it exercised influence in American culture and could provide a transcendent perspective to keep America from becoming proud and ambitious. America's heritage was embodied in a set of religious ideas. Its destiny depended upon the church's vision of divine mercy and justice. It was, therefore, the church's hour in America. The future of world civilization rested on its shoulders because it was called to be the prophetic conscience of the nation. "[T]he Christian faith is still in sufficiently close relation to the national life to encourage the hope that it will help to purify the nations for their mission; in both cases, however, the Christian forces are to some degree the salt that has lost its savour. If the nations should fail, therefore, the failure would be the consequence of the prior failure of the Christian Church."[41]

The theodicies of both Niebuhr and Errett reflected the thinking of many Christian leaders during the Second World War. Like most American church leaders, they did not proclaim it a holy war. God was too transcendent for that; God was lord of history and judge of the nations. God was active in history chastising the world for its refusal to acknowledge its finitude and God's greatness. America was not spared from this judgment, for it had failed to live up to its own ideals. It deserved and could expect God's wrath.

Yet America still occupied a special place in history. However far it fell short of its ideals, it nevertheless had a heritage that could be—and desperately needed to be—rediscovered and renewed. America, in fact, stood on the verge of fulfilling its historic and divine destiny. If it remained humble and contrite, the nation could rise to its full stature as a divine tool to secure peace and justice in the world. In the mind of most church leaders, it all depended upon the church, for America's historic destiny, like its great heritage, was grounded in the Christian faith. America would remain useful to God and secure in conflict only if its faith stayed strong. Wartime theodicy, then, moved beyond the general discussion of God's sovereignty and purpose to explain the meaning of the war *for America as God's special nation*. It affirmed America's chosenness, but not without certain reservations. America would continue to prosper under God's care and remain useful to God's purposes only if it resisted the temptation to become proud and ambitious.

CHAPTER SIX

CHRISTIAN FAITH & DEMOCRACY

World War II provided religious groups with an opportunity to reassert their influence in American society after suffering from what appeared to be a mainline "religious depression" in the 1920s and 1930s. Religious leaders saw the war as a catastrophe. Not only was the fragile peace of the world shattered, but alien ideologies were threatening to destroy Western—and Christian—values. Nations founded upon a Christian heritage became defenseless before a seemingly unconquerable power.

Religious leaders believed that if America and its allies had a chance of winning, they would need a power that transcended mere military might. That power was the Christian faith. Nothing less than the influence of Christianity was needed to fortify the very system of democracy and the ideal of freedom that the war in Europe and Asia was perilously close to destroying. Christian leaders believed that either totalitarianism or democracy would win. Atheism provided the foundation for the former, Christianity the latter.

Christian intellectuals argued democracy needed the Christian faith, not the other way around. Christianity was primary, democracy secondary, just as the church took precedence over the state. As Edwin R. Errett, editor of the *Christian Standard*, argued: "We do not have in mind that shallow sort of talk that goes so far as to say that the church depends upon democracy for its livelihood. That is, of course, not so. The church existed before democracy and will exist after it, if that is necessary. The church does not depend upon any state—much less upon any form of state—for its authority or right to speak and live its message. It derives its origin and its authority from Jesus Christ Himself."[1] It followed that the main concern of Christian leaders during the war was not the survival of democracy but the vitality of the Christian faith and the renewal of the church. When they discussed democracy, as they did often during the war, they usually affirmed its value in light of their deeper commitment to Christianity.

The Value of Democracy

There is no doubt that Christians in America favored democracy as a system of government. The religious press printed dozens of articles on the benefits of democracy. Christian writers argued that democracy protected people's freedom and provided them with the opportunity to use that freedom to improve their lot in life. As L. O. Hartman, editor of the independent Methodist weekly *Zion's Herald*, suggested, it contained a principle that allowed people the freedom to participate in the affairs of government and an "equality of opportunity" based on the integrity of the "human personality and the spirit of brotherhood."[2] Nathan R. Melhorn, chairman of the Commission of the League for Protestant Action, argued that the rule of the majority, which he considered the essence of democracy, demonstrated confidence in the people themselves.[3]

Democracy created a system that allowed people to use their freedom to make themselves and the world better. Francis P. Miller, who had coauthored *The Church against the World* in the 1930s, defined the system of democracy as "the form of government derived from the belief that the good of all persons should constitute the touchstone of public policy with that good determined by representatives chosen in free elections. . . . The representative form of government as we know it in the United States is based on the conviction that the person is the end of human society—not race or class or state but the person." The system created a government that was intended to be of, by, and for the people. The ballot, a representative assembly, a removable executive, an independent judiciary, and the Bill of Rights constituted the mechanics that made democracy work.[4]

The war only reinforced this appreciation of and commitment to democracy. In the face of external threat, Christian leaders appeared to close ranks in order to defend democracy and to use every possible occasion to point out its virtues. Some religious leaders were so enthusiastic, in fact, that they idealized democracy, either by treating it as if it were a religion or by making it an essential part of the Christian creed.

Several Unitarians, for example, advocated a point of view laid out by John Dewey, which stated that democracy should be viewed as a kind of religion in itself, because democracy embodied the best ideas that had been handed down through history. It symbolized the highest aspirations of humanity. Jacob Trapp suggested that democracy actually *was* a religion. "It has somehow come about, in more ways than I could begin to suggest, that democracy has become the most vital, the most crucial, the most forward-looking religion of our time. It has certain essential characteristics which I can think of only as religious." He claimed that democracy was a dream that was forever springing from the human spirit. It required faith in humanity, liberated people from old and new despotisms, and released creativity in human nature. It had great prophets and poets, an army of martyrs. It unified differing denominations, defended human rights, and undermined authoritarianism. "All these phenomena," he concluded, "are such as you would expect when a new and virile and dynamic religion emerges upon the historic scene." Democracy was the hope of humankind and the real religion of America.[5]

Others suggested that democracy be included in the Christian creed. John Paul Williams believed that preserving democracy was a religious job and a religious necessity. If American democracy was to survive—and Williams left no doubt concerning his own hope—then it was right and essential for Christians in America to make it a vital part of the creed of the churches. "If democracy were to become a part of the religion of the vast majority of Americans, those who are Catholics, or Protestants, or Jews would say of democracy that it is the will of God that men should live on democratic principles; and those whose conception of the nature of the universe does not include a belief in God would say of democracy that it is a part of the law of life; and that if man tries to defy this law, suffering will result no less surely than when he tries to defy the law of gravity or the laws of health." He concluded his argument with an appeal that anticipated the emergence of "civil religion" in the postwar period: "Let us make faith in democracy a part of all of the religions of the American people!"[6]

These enthusiastic endorsements were extreme because they failed to make a distinction between Christianity and democracy. The vast majority of Christian leaders were more circumspect. They preferred and defended democracy, and there was no shortage of laudations in their books, pamphlets, articles, and sermons. Still, in the minds of most religious leaders, democracy depended upon Christianity for its survival and success. The very existence of democracy pointed to the beneficent influence of Christian faith. There was little question in their minds that democracy was civilization's best political creation. Yet it could not stand alone, like a body without a soul. It needed a spirit that only Christianity could provide.[7] Writing for *Moody Monthly*, Harold L. Lundquist argued that it was only through the influence of Christian faith that "we find selfish, sinful men so transformed by the regenerating grace of God in Christ that they truly observe brotherly love, tolerance, submission to duly elected authority, consideration for others—all of which underlie democracy and make it possible."[8] As J. B. Hunley stated in the opening address of the Disciples Christian Action Conference, only the Christian faith could provide an indestructible "inner wall" that would preserve democracy and save America when "the outer wall" of military might collapsed. Only the Christian faith could nurture the kind of strong and independent "personality" that democracy needed to flourish.[9] Without Christianity, democracy could no more guarantee progress than humanism could get a person to heaven.[10]

Christian Influence

The Christian faith, then, was essential for the survival and success of democracy. Christian leaders stated four reasons why. First, Christianity emphasized the worth of the individual person. Speaking at the Congress on Education for Democracy at Carnegie Hall, conservative H. W. Prentis stated that "our American republic rests squarely on the religious doctrine of the sacredness of the individual, which all forms of collectivism—socialism, communism, fascism, naziism, and new liberalism—deny or tend to deny."[11] John W. Bradbury, editor of the *Watchman-Examiner*, a Northern Baptist publication, argued that it was the Christian faith that stressed the worth of each individual soul. "It is to Christ, the Saviour of men, we owe not only a high estimate of each human life, but also the respect with which the human will must be regarded. He seeks no conscripts, nor does he employ them. Every one of his gracious invitations to mankind reveals a reverence for human consent. He who has the right above all men to command, prefers to plead. The citizens of his kingdom are free to 'go in and out.'"[12]

Jesus himself ascribed worth to people and developed worth in them, thus affirming the sacredness of the human person.[13] "If America means anything at all," reasoned Francis Miller, "it means a society dedicated to the enhancement of the value of personal life. American destiny is related to the destiny of persons—all persons everywhere. That is our job. That is the task that we are being called upon to undertake in this fateful hour of human history."[14]

Second, Christianity provided Western civilization with the idea of liberty, which was founded upon this Christian view of human person hood. Roman Catholic philosopher Jacques Maritain believed that the rights of the person followed logically from the dignity of each person. "There are things which are owed to man because of the very fact that he is man. . . . The notion of right and the notion of moral obligation are correlative. They are both founded on the freedom proper to spiritual agents. If man is morally bound to the things which are necessary to the fulfillment of his destiny, obviously, then, he has the right to fulfil his destiny; and if he has the right to fulfil his destiny, he has the right to the things necessary for this purpose."[15] Catholic thinkers were convinced that the state itself was not and could never be the source of individual rights. "Once that is granted, once it is maintained that the State gives rights, it must also be granted that the State can take them away. But that would be the end of our democracy." The purpose of the state was to protect rights, not to take them away. The Christian faith was the source and guardian of those rights.[16]

The church was obligated, therefore, to defend liberty. Edwin Merrick Dodd believed that liberty was the essence of democracy and that Christianity was the source and defender of the idea. If democracy violated the principle of liberty, it would forfeit its right to call itself democracy and sever itself from Christianity.[17]

Third, the Christian view of human sinfulness sounded a note of caution about the ultimate reliability of human nature, thus making democracy a system that reflected a realistic perspective on what humans could achieve with power and how humans could abuse power. John Bennett of Union Seminary in New York City argued that Christianity provided a "spiritual basis" for democracy by engendering faith in the dignity of all people, but he also stressed that the Christian doctrine of "original sin" furnished "a basis for distrusting centers of privilege and power" and that the Christian belief in a transcendent God kept "all centers of power under criticism."[18] John Bradbury argued along the same lines. "At the heart of mankind there is sin. It is in the church and out of it. The one thing cursing this world and creating conditions which fill it with blood, cries, and tears is sin. And because it is in every man, there is no man among us who can deliver us from it. Even among our Christian best it is true that when they would do good, evil is present with them." He believed that the church was a failure in

America because it had neglected to emphasize the doctrine of sin and had therefore given the false impression that humanity could solve its problems through institutional change alone.[19]

Finally, Christianity contributed to democracy by cultivating a character in people that would enable them to use their liberty wisely and would keep them from being corrupted by the very liberty that the American way of life provided. Liberty could not discipline itself. It depended upon the Christian faith to do that. Norman Huffman, a professor at Wesleyan College, suggested that no form of government, not even democracy, could completely eliminate oppression and corruption. Only the character of the people could do that, and only Christianity could build true character. "I know of no other force which has been so successful in producing character of this sort in large masses of people and altruistic dedication of life in outstanding individuals. . . . It seeks to develop a live conscience favorable to decency, honesty and fair play. It calls for active hatred of evil in all forms. It develops a sense of brotherhood, based on the doctrine of the universal fatherhood of God. It instills into its followers a respect and reverence for human beings who are moral and eternal souls."[20] Oscar F. Blackwelder, a prominent Lutheran pastor in Washington, D.C., who later became pastor to President Truman, affirmed that Christian faith provided the "cement" that held society together and made possible a government controlled by the people. It developed people of "dependable character, capable of self-government, able to think not only technically but morally on public questions." He further declared that "Freedom does not rest upon law but upon men, for men make, obey, or break laws. Justice is not the foundation of society— men who do justly are that foundation. Men of great genius may be admired; men of great wealth may be envied; men of great power may be feared; only men of great character are trusted—for upon them democracy rests. Government of the people, by the people, and for the people will perish from the earth unless the average man has a larger degree of moral dependability. The church's greatest contribution to democracy is to produce men and women of character."[21]

True character would create discipline in the American people, and discipline was needed to hold in check the two great enemies of democracy— selfishness and individualism. "Democracy needs discipline," argued L. O. Hartman of *Zion's Herald.* "This is the lesson we need to learn from the enemies of democracy. No one can be truly free until he has achieved self-restraint, self-control, and self-sacrifice in the interest of a higher good." Where could Americans find the source of such discipline? It had to come from God, for its source was essentially spiritual.[22] Federal Council of Churches executive F. E. Johnson contended that America faced a much bigger crisis than the war. Democracy was deteriorating from within by the destructive influence of individualism. Again, democracy needed discipline to survive. Only Christianity could enable the American people to live together peacefully.[23]

Christian leaders were certain, then, that democracy depended upon vital Christianity as a plant needs rich soil, for democracy was rooted in the Christian faith. Though Christianity could thrive anywhere—democracy being only the preferred system—democracy itself would wilt and die without the continuing influence of Christian ideas. It was Christianity above democracy as ultimate truth, Christianity under democracy as spiritual foundation, Christianity alongside democracy as inspiration and strength that made these church leaders stress the importance of their faith for the future of America. On this point most church leaders were agreed.

What Kind of Christian Influence?

But not entirely. There was a great deal of discussion about what kind of Christian influence was necessary, which tradition of Christianity could provide the best foundation for democracy. With few exceptions, church leaders were quick to point out the weaknesses of their denominational and theological competitors and to prove that theirs was the only tradition upon which democracy could be built. Though not as intense as the "culture wars" of the 1980s and 1990s, this conflict among religious groups showed that religion in America was divided against itself in its very attempt to be united with democracy.

By the early 1940s some fundamentalists and mainline conservatives had begun to work cooperatively to reassert themselves into American culture as the guardians of the nation's true religious heritage. They formed such organizations as the National Association of Evangelicals (NAE) and Youth For Christ (YFC) to unify themselves, increase their numbers, and expand their influence. Though their creed was the same as separatist fundamentalists, their willingness to cooperate, their commitment to social service, and their desire for broader influence moved them toward the mainstream of American religion.

These "neo-evangelicals" asserted that mainline Protestantism provided a weak foundation for democracy because of its adherence to theological liberalism. It had accommodated itself to evolutionism and had compromised the authority of the Bible. Stated John Bradbury: "Many of the major denominations are unable to speak for Christianity with any sure or certain testimony, not even in some which are traditionally creedal or confessional. So enamored of the social gospel have these become that their testimony concerns itself with things for which they have little or no competency, while the primary task of pointing a sinful world to the Lamb of God who alone can take away its sin remains undone, if not scorned." If Protestantism, as Bradbury argued, made any progress during the liberal era, it had made such progress through the influence of "those denominations, churches, or groups of churches which have held most firmly to the traditional Christian faith."[24]

Harold Ockenga, pastor of Boston's Park St. Congregational Church and first president of the NAE, accused liberalism of destroying America because it had jettisoned the very principles upon which America was founded and its survival depended. America needed to return to evangelical faith, which Ockenga believed the fledgling National Association of Evangelicals best represented. Since liberal Christianity had forfeited its right to function as salt and light in America, evangelical Christians were the only ones who could fill the void of belief that existed. There were only two real alternatives: "heathendom," which promised sure destruction, or evangelical renewal. "We must recognize that we are standing at the crossroads and that there are only two ways that lie open before us. One is the road of the rescue of western civilization by a re-emphasis on and revival of evangelical Christianity. The other is a return to the Dark Ages of heathendom which powerful force is emerging in every phase of world life today."[25]

Roman Catholics tried to establish the supremacy of their faith, too, and for the same reason. They believed that it was the sturdiest foundation upon which to build a stable democracy. Their criticism was aimed at all Protestants, of course, and not simply at liberal Protestants. Writers for conservative Catholic publications like *America* and *Catholic Action* foresaw the decline and predicted the demise of Protestantism.[26] They assured the American people that Catholics were loyal Americans, and it was their Catholicism that made them loyal. When the results of a poll taken to determine the voting preference of Catholic college students was reported, Paul Blakely concluded that Catholics "would have the loyalty and the patriotism and the bravery that has always characterized Catholics in every war-crisis since 1776. Being Catholics, they are the best Americans."[27] They were the "best Americans" because Catholicism itself was the best religion of Western civilization. Argued W. E. Orchard for *America*: "To sum up, it needs to be made swiftly and widely known that Catholicism contains the only philosophy that makes sense of reason and gives purpose to life; that it has a mystical method which would save the modern mind from the burden of a falsely isolated personality and make accessible the heights of religious experience to all who sincerely seek them, with immense gains to character, health, and power; that it has social principles that would enable all men to live in reasonable security and work together in fruitful cooperation."[28]

Catholic leaders believed that they were in the best position to win world peace because the Catholic church was the only religious group that truly spanned the globe. The Catholic church also had a leader who represented God's supreme authority on earth. As the vicar of Christ and head of the universal church, the pope, above any political or religious leader, had the power and compassion to appeal to world leaders on behalf of peace and negotiate for that peace. "Instead of following the red gleam of war that leaps from part to part of Europe, the nations should rather turn toward the white beam of peace that shines from the tiny state of Vatican City. Instead of Leaders and Prime Ministers and Premiers watching the moves of one another and matching words, they should listen to the paternal advice and the spiritual appeal of the Pope."[29]

In the eyes of some Protestant leaders, however, Catholicism was one of democracy's greatest enemies. The war provided these Protestants with another occasion to launch new attacks upon Catholicism. Because the crisis of the war had exposed democracy's vulnerability, they feared that Catholics were poised to pounce on democracy while it was weak and destroy it. They believed that Catholicism was essentially totalitarian, the arch enemy of democracy and of its principle guardian, Protestantism. Southern Baptist M. P. Hunt of Louisville, Kentucky, for example, accused Catholics of being the modern-day counterparts of the Pharisees. "The Pharisees looked upon everybody who disagreed with them religiously as heretics, and believed that they should be crushed and destroyed. That in principle is the attitude assumed by official Roman Catholicism toward all who would worship God according to their own light and conscience apart from the Romanist dictation of what is required for acceptable worship."[30]

In the minds of many Protestants, the religious exclusivism of Catholicism exposed the real problem inherent in Catholic theology and polity. The Catholic church was propagandistic, opportunistic, and power hungry. According to a group of Christian leaders writing on Roman Catholic political activities in the *Churchman*, Catholicism was the enemy of science and progress, hospitable to fascism and antagonistic to Protestantism.[31] Louis

Adamic, a writer and activist for Yugoslavian interests in America, claimed that a Catholic strategy to dominate the world first developed during the Counter-Reformation was still in force around the world, including America, which was not aware of the enormous threat that Catholicism posed. The Counter-Reformation, he stated, "still continues, a movement whose wire-pulling high-pressure in Europe and the Americas has much to do with the war and will have more to do with the 'peace.' Its power in the U.S. today is such that a large number of key positions in and out of Government are filled by Catholic clergymen and laymen whose main outlook is Roman Catholic rather than traditionally American. At the same time, the general press and other organs of public expression are under what John Dewey called a 'virtual interdict,' banishing discussion of the Vatican's temporal policies, practices and aims." The one problem that loomed above all the others in the minds of Protestants was the Catholic conviction that "the only authentic Christianity is Catholicism, that the Catholic church is the repository and vehicle of the truth, that the duty of the Catholic Church is to spread the truth, no matter how, throughout the world. And it is—basically, in the long run—fanatically intolerant of everyone who questions this position. There is no doubt that the Catholic hierarchy here, as now constituted, is trying by every means, fair or foul, to impose the Roman Catholic outlook upon the state, and force conformity to Roman Catholic purposes by non-Catholics."[32]

Protestants pointed to the lack of religious freedom in officially Roman Catholic countries to substantiate their claim that Roman Catholicism was an enemy of democracy and thus of America. Protestants strongly objected to the Catholic policy that kept Protestant missionaries from entering Catholic countries. Denominational resolutions stated their concerns in the strongest language. The General Assembly of the Presbyterian Church in the United States, for example, adopted a statement at its May 1943 meeting that read: "At a time when the nations of North and South America are united for the defense of their fundamental freedoms, it is deplorable that the leaders of Roman Catholicism should be so far out of step as to propose the abandoning of this principle of religious liberty, for which men of both Americas are giving their lives."[33]

Protestant magazines carried dozens of editorials and articles on the subject of Catholic intolerance, of which Catholic Latin American policy was only the most blatant example. Two publications in particular—the *Churchman* and the *Protestant*—carried on a continual diatribe against the Roman Church in order to expose its real ambition, which, according to these publications, was nothing short of the destruction of democracy and eventual world domination. Many other Protestant publications and groups were also critical of Catholicism. They agreed with the editors of the *Churchman* and the *Protestant* that Catholic intolerance in Latin America was ultimately an ideological problem and represented a grave menace to America.[34] There were, of course, significant exceptions to this attack on Catholicism. Some Protestant leaders defended Catholics as good Americans and accused their Protestant brethren of launching another anti-Catholic crusade.[35]

Mainline Protestant leaders believed that Protestantism, contrary to Catholicism, embodied a superior expression of Christian faith. It was the true religion of democracy. Samuel McCrea Cavert, executive of the Federal Council of Churches, spoke for many when he outlined the distinctions of the Protestant heritage to show its spiritual genius and national usefulness. Protestantism, he said, insisted upon "the immediacy of man's relation with God," unmediated by moralism or sacramentalism. It held that the Scriptures provided the decisive norm of spiritual authority rather than tradition. It affirmed that there was a universal priesthood of believers rather than a hierarchical priesthood of the few, and it stressed the importance of religious freedom rather than churchly (Catholic) power. It honored common life and labor rather than purely religious vocations. Protestantism taught that the church was a community of people. Protestantism was "the custodian, in our modern world, of the principle of Christian individuality."[36]

But it was *liberal* Protestantism that these religious leaders had in mind. They believed that liberalism—the only truly modern and relevant religion—could save democracy. In defining "ultimate Protestantism," for example, Robert Whitaker contended that most biblical writers missed the whole point of Jesus' ministry. "Vastly more could be said on behalf of this supreme protestant of the ages who dared to make the Last Judgment itself an everlasting arbitrament on the side of the uttermost democracy. The 'accepted' are those who had lived the primacy of human need and human fellowship, the 'rejected,' those who had imagined that something else was religion." As Whitaker saw it, the predicament of modern Protestantism was "how to escape its age-long entanglements with outworn dogmas and conforming ecclesiasticisms."[37]

The Taylor Appointment

These conflicts simmered throughout the war. Religious leaders agreed on which system of government was the best, and they assumed that Christianity was the only sure foundation for democracy. They differed sharply, however, on which tradition within Christianity was best suited to ensure that democracy would succeed. Conservative and liberal Protestants skirmished with each other, as did Protestants and Catholics.

The skirmish between Protestants and Catholics threatened to turn into a war over one controversial issue. In December 1939 President Roosevelt appointed Myron Taylor, an Episcopalian, to be his personal representative at the Vatican. Roosevelt intended to use Taylor as a functional, though not official, ambassador to work with the papacy in negotiating a peace in Europe. The Protestant response was overwhelmingly negative. Scores of editorials and articles in religious magazines denounced the appointment, and many denominations passed resolutions condemning Roosevelt's action. For example, Northern Baptists stated: "That we affirm our historic Baptist position regarding the separation of Church and State and our unalterable opposition to any change in the American and Baptist view on this separation of Church and State; that we restate our conviction that no privileges should be given to one religious body that are not accorded to all; that we declare our irrevocable opposition to the establishment of diplomatic relations with any religious body whatsoever; and that we urge upon the President of the United States a reconsideration of the appointment at the earliest possible moment." Southern Baptists passed a similar resolution, as did leaders representing the National Lutheran Council.[38]

In a letter to the president, F. H. Knubel, president of the United Lutheran Church in America, reasoned that the one flaw in the president's plan was in assuming that the pope was God's servant to American national life. The inclusion of that one false premise was "unnecessary" because a representative from the American Catholic community could have been named instead to visit the president from time to time in order to discuss the prospect of world peace. It was also "un-American" since it gave "official recognition to a combination of church and state [the Vatican] which is contrary to American principles" and gave "pre-eminence to a minority of all the American people." It was "disruptive of American unity" and therefore out of harmony with the real cause of peace. Finally, it was "a cause of suspicion" that political influences from religious bodies were being drawn into American national life.[39] To most Protestants, the Taylor appointment violated the cardinal principle—the "Protestant principle"—of the separation of church and state.

Not all Protestants were so suspicious and critical. Some were grateful for any attempt to win peace in Europe. George A. Campbell, acting editor of the *Christian-Evangelist*, commended the president for his bold leadership, affirming that Roosevelt was wise in recognizing the importance of faith as a force for peace. "The churches," he said, "have a great stake—perhaps their future influence on civilization—in the outcome of today's wars. Too often they fail to do anything positive to further peace. Is it not time for all of us to take more risks for peace?"[40] Campbell cited a number of Protestant leaders and publications that approved of Roosevelt's decision—John Haynes Holmes, George A. Buttrick, Edgar DeWitt Jones, Ivan Lee Holt, the *Christian Advocate*, the *Messenger*, the *Christian Leader*. Campbell in turn criticized his Protestant friends who reacted to the appointment. He accused them of intolerance. He was concerned that a new wave of anti-Catholicism was about to surge in America. "We fear that anti-Catholicism is still so deeply ingrained in many Protestant leaders in the United States that they are blinded with passionate prejudice and unable to see that Mr. Roosevelt has taken a tremendous forward step by mobilizing the strength of religious forces in this country on behalf of peace. The possibility of a just peace is the basic issue in this matter."[41]

Catholics, of course, were quick to defend the appointment. Edward Skillin Jr., editor of the *Commonweal*, reasoned that Roosevelt's decision had nothing to do with church-state relations. Instead, it made good political sense, and it showed confidence in the moral power of Catholicism. "It is simply a fact that the unparalleled position of Catholicism as a unified, supranational religion, and hence as bearing a unique moral potential, has emerged today with unusual clearness."[42]

The Taylor appointment became a point of contention because more was at stake than the outcome of an abstract discussion about Christianity and democracy. Christian leaders recognized that abstract ideas have implications for concrete policies, such as how church and state are to function in a democratic society. The official Catholic position in America was outlined by John Ryan, Roman Catholic philosopher and ethicist. Ryan stated that the natural law gave rise to certain natural rights, which the state was responsible for protecting and preserving. It was the duty of the state to mediate between the conflicting claims of individuals for the sake of the just welfare of all. It was also the duty of the state to protect and advance the religious interests of the citizens, to assist in their education, especially moral education, to safeguard the liberty and health of the citizens, and to protect private property and provide citizens with an opportunity to obtain a livelihood.[43] Finally, it was the duty of the State to pass laws "against the spiritual and moral scandal produced by false and immoral preaching, teaching, and publication."[44] Ryan approved of democracy in America insofar as it preserved the freedom of religious minorities, of which Roman Catholics were the largest. But if Catholics ever became a majority, then they would be perfectly justified in making Catholicism the official religion of the country. The reason was simple enough—Catholicism embodied true Christianity. "Error has no rights," the official Catholic position read. Catholicism was the only true religion. As Louis Cardinal Billot wrote, "What the Pope denies is that the popular choice ever confers the rights of sovereignty in the sense of those who opposed Catholic doctrine."[45]

The "official" Catholic position made the Taylor appointment especially ominous to many Protestants because it seemed to move America slowly in the direction of Catholic domination. Protestants rejected such an establishment of religion. Methodists and Baptists in particular advocated the separation of church and state as the only sure defense against Catholic ambition. Samuel McCrea Cavert averred that all religious bodies in America be kept separate from and yet be treated equally by the federal government. No one church was to be favored above the others. "There was to be equal opportunity for all, special privilege for none. . . . Every religious group was to stand on its own feet, free and unhindered, depending for its influence on its own spiritual vitality, not on any external prestige or power conferred by the State."[46]

But Protestants themselves were hardly clear on what the separation of church and state really meant. Very few believed in *absolute* separation. After all, Christians in America did live in both spheres at once and therefore had the responsibility to bring their faith to bear on the state as well as on the church. The two spheres, as William Emch, a Lutheran, stated, were not opposed to each other. Ideally, they worked together in harmony, ran on parallel tracks, and even "supplemented" each other. The state was God's agency to enforce law and order, protect the rights of individuals, and ensure peace and justice. It had authority to hold check on sinful behavior. The church was God's agency to save humanity. The chief purpose of the church was to bear witness to its Savior and strive for the reconciliation of God and humanity. The state fulfilled its duty through education, law, and force; the church through spiritual truth and power. The state, furthermore, was obligated to serve the church by protecting its property and by preserving its freedom of worship, speech, and conscience. The church was required to serve the state by obeying the civil law and by providing moral support in all civic and national affairs—including "just" wars—that did not contradict the Word of God.[47]

This Lutheran position of "the two spheres," however, did not go far enough for some Protestants, not during such a crisis as World War II. They wanted to clarify exactly how the two spheres could work cooperatively for the preservation of civilization. One option was for each to strive for a common goal. William E. Gilroy, editor of *Advance*, a congregational publication, saw church and state in America drawing together in a common commitment to humanitarianism. "The evangelistic zeal which originally inspired the missionary endeavors of the church has been largely transmuted into a concern for human welfare. . . . Where once the state was merely a restraining force, it is becoming increasingly an agency of constructive activity." Very few people, he went on to say, were aware of the "consultative relationships" which had grown up between the church and the state.[48]

Another option was for the church to "christianize" the state. J. H. Bruinooge of the Christian Reformed Church suggested that the church could pray for the state and "preach righteousness and send her membership out into the world to mould public opinion in the direction of that which is good, noble, true, righteous and just." He also affirmed that the church could incorporate Christian ideas into legislative acts that would honor ultimate truth and morality and band together to vote Christians into public office. Bruinooge contended that true Christianity was destined to shape public life and influence the affairs of state. "We believe that an absolute separation of the church and the state is detrimental to the highest interests of both. The church needs the protection of the state to fulfil her calling to evangelize the world and the state needs especially the leaven of the gospel to remain virile and strong. An atheistic state means anarchy. Consequently, the state should not merely tolerate Christianity, but take an active interest in it." Christians, in turn, were to "make the state more Christian."[49]

No Interference!

Regardless of their conflicting approaches to church-state relations, Protestants and Catholics did believe that church involvement in the affairs of the state was both good and necessary. On that point there was agreement. Likewise, there was agreement that state interference in the affairs of the church was bad.

Church leaders were quick to react to any signs of such interference. Many observed with alarm the state's secular influence in all areas of life, like public education and benevolent enterprises. They cited examples of such secular encroachment throughout the war. As Talmage C. Johnson noted, the result was the "emergence of a state aware of only secular values and rooted in a pagan and materialistic culture."[50]

In the minds of some religious leaders there appeared to be ample evidence to support Johnson's contention. Raphael Harwood Miller, for example, criticized the policy of Colonel Early E. W. Duncan, commandant of the Air Corps at Lowry Field outside Denver, when he declared that Denver churches disagreeing with Roosevelt's foreign policy could be made "out of bounds" for military personnel. Miller claimed that Duncan's policy demonstrated that the state was attempting to make the church its own instrument. He countered: "Is it not the duty of the church to serve as one agency that reminds our people that the Germans are children of our God? Is it not our function to ameliorate, in so far as we can, the bitterness and the hatred which will well up like black torrents in so many hearts?"[51]

Ned B. Stonehouse of the *Presbyterian Guardian*, a publication of the Orthodox Presbyterian Church, was concerned about the state's growing power, too. He raised questions about two bills before the house that would limit free speech by making mailing of "defamatory and false statements" about members of any race or religion a criminal offense. Stonehouse believed that these bills threatened the freedom of the church to preach its own message without state interference.[52]

Two issues in particular, however, raised the ire of religious leaders in America. The first involved New York mayor La Guardia's attempt to dictate the content of the church's wartime message. In November 1941 La Guardia provided a patriotic sermon outline for ministers to use in bolstering national morale. The gesture seemed innocent enough, but the response was biting. Charles Clayton Morrison pounced on La Guardia. He told a reporter that La Guardia's act was "an unspeakable insult to the clergy of the United States. Hitler and Goebbels never went further. Totalitarianism is already here." Though religious leaders criticized Morrison for exaggerating the implications of La Guardia's action, many were nevertheless suspicious of La Guardia and concerned about what his action implied. "Both the propriety and the strategy of sending a canned sermon to the ministers are bad," announced E. J. Tanis, regular columnist for the *Banner*. "What right has the government to tell the Church what to preach?"[53] Edward W. Schramm, editor of the *Lutheran Standard*, wondered whether La Guardia's action would lead to further state entanglement in church affairs. "What disquiets us in this matter is that this may be a straw which shows which way the wind is blowing. . . . Are we about to fight totalitarianism with totalitarian methods?"[54]

The other cause for alarm was the government's policy of classifying preseminary students for the draft. The government would not give a deferment to pretheological students unless they declared themselves for the ministry early in their college careers, and even then local draft boards often assigned students a 1-A classification anyway unless they were in seminary or about to enter seminary. The government's policy seemed to favor those denominations that ordained ministers before they entered seminary or started training students for ministry before they started college. General Hershey, director of the selective service organization, tried to reassure denominational leaders that the draft boards would do everything they could to keep the ministry open to men of draft age. But Hershey did not seem to act consistently with these assurances. His policy changed often until, in the fall of 1944, he decided that only the students who had entered seminary before 1944 could be deferred from the draft. Church leaders like Henry Schultze of the Christian Reformed Church contended that the government's policy threatened the future ministry of the church, because it would inevitably reduce the number of men who could enter the ministry. He also observed that the policy appeared to favor those groups—Roman Catholics in particular—that seemed to be able to circumvent the law's requirements.[55]

So alarmed were Protestants that a group of denominational leaders met in Washington to draft a statement condemning the government's policy. The heads of twenty-five Protestant denominations, representing over 25 million members, signed the statement. These leaders argued that the churches, already burdened by having to provide chaplains for the armed forces from the ranks of active ministers, were burdened even more by having to compensate for a shortage of ministers. The real problem, they contended, was the government's decision to cancel the pretheological student deferment. The policy would weaken the ministry of the churches on the home front, and it would give unfair advantage to Roman Catholics, whose seminary training began far sooner than Protestant training.[56] Not all Protestants joined in the protest and some, like Reinhold Niebuhr, actually supported it.[57]

Conflicts among religious groups over issues like the Taylor appointment reveal something of the passion with which Christian leaders discussed the significance of the Christian faith in a democracy that appeared, in light of a world at war, to be fighting for its survival. They believed that democracy was the best system; they also believed that Christianity was the only sure foundation for that system. For the sake of democracy, then, the Christian faith had to be held high and the church protected from state interference so that it could spread that faith over America and the world.

But the conflicts also show that religious groups were in competition because each one—Fundamentalist, Neo-evangelical, liberal Protestant, Catholic—contended that the tradition it represented was the one best suited to help democracy survive and prosper. At issue, then, was the preservation of American democracy in a world that appeared so inhospitable to it. Most Christians in America assumed that democracy depended upon Christian faith. But *which* tradition within Christianity was another issue. The clash over which tradition *within* Christianity was best for a nation that desperately needed the influence of Christian faith explains why conflict among religious groups continued during a period when conflict on the home front was taboo. This tension between commitment to democracy and competition within the religious community did not end in 1945 but continued into the postwar period, contributing to the escalation of the "culture wars" of the 1980s and 1990s.

CHAPTER SEVEN

CHURCH & SOCIETY

The church's influence in society was as important in the minds of religious leaders as Christianity's role in a democracy. During World War II they urged their churches to contribute to the well-being of society. They believed that the survival and health of American society depended on the ministry of the church.

Christian leaders argued that America was at war largely because the church had failed to fulfill its religious duty. Many wondered what would happen to America, God's "almost-chosen" nation, if religious influence continued to decline. Frederick D. Kershner, a regular columnist for the *Christian-Evangelist*, lamented the "inconsequence" of the church because of its lack of leadership. Christian leaders, he said, spoke with feeble voices, and they often contradicted each other. Leadership in America was now coming from business and government, not from the church, which had abdicated its responsibility by default or internecine warfare. "Speaking broadly, nobody pays any attention to the church these days, because the church has nothing which commands attention."[1] Charles Clayton Morrison was critical of the church in America, too, because it had yielded to secular forces. "The gross fact that the Christian church has failed in its major and essential witness cannot be disputed. . . . The church has abdicated its spiritual independence and is now trailing along behind the politician, the businessman, the scientist, adjusting itself to their purposes and ideologies, and feeding their vanity by acting as chaplains and sanctifier of their temporal and relative interests."[2] Others complained that the church had surrendered its authority in America by neglecting its principal duty, which was essentially spiritual. It was ashamed of the gospel, too quick to accommodate to modern thought, reluctant to pray, and passive in the face of great suffering and confusion.[3]

These critical voices, however, were not willing to let the church absorb all the blame. They were also aware of more serious problems in American society. If the world had a problem, they argued, it was not the failure of the church but the failure of society to heed the church's message. Perhaps the church had compromised its mission in the past. Still, war was no time to belabor its shortcomings. If anything, the good news that it proclaimed was the only word that would bring lasting peace in the world. Declared Luther Stewart, editor of the *Christian Index*, a publication of the Colored Methodist Episcopal Church: "We refuse to acknowledge that the Church is primarily to blame for the situation that prevails among our race and in the world today. The Church has and does make its protest against war as being un-Christian. The Church does insist upon justice. . . . Powerful forces have been arrayed against the Church and have disregarded the teachings of the 'Lowly Nazarene.'"[4]

Christian leaders both criticized the church and defended the church; they were willing to admit failure and yet quick to accuse society of abandoning the faith. In one sense, the question of who or what was to blame missed the point. Far more important was the need to recognize that America now faced a crisis that mandated a return to Christian faith. The war thus provided the churches with an extraordinary opportunity to reaffirm the importance of the Christian message and the church's influence in American society.

A New Opportunity

The theme of "opportunity" surfaced everywhere in religious publications and denominational resolutions during the war. Edward Frantz, editor of the *Gospel Messenger*, wrote that the explosion of war in Europe had ushered in "the great hour for the church of Jesus Christ." As a representative of the peace church tradition, he interpreted "the great hour" as an occasion for the peace churches to witness against the folly of war.[5] Though holding very different convictions from Frantz, H. Norman Sibley, pastor of the University Heights Presbyterian Church of New York City, also believed that the war provided the churches with what he called "the Gospel's Opportunity." "The war is a manifestation of man's corporate failure and sinfulness. But it is also an opportunity for the Gospel to be known with power." The war revealed the true nature of humanity as fallen and needy. It forced a reassessment of ideals and led to a new realization of the fundamental place of religion in life.[6]

Denominational resolutions and reports reflected this same conviction. They affirmed that it was the church's hour. A crisis had arisen that only the church could meet. It was, according to the Committee on Social and Moral Welfare of the Presbyterian Church in the United States, "a time of unparalleled moral and spiritual danger but also of great and challenging opportunities for the Church."[7] The Social Service Commission of the Southern Baptist Convention stated in its 1942 report that the church could not escape its obligations to humankind but had to intensify its activities for the common good. "The Church now as never before must make America and the world conscious of the gospel truths of God's plan, man's welfare on earth. . . . War and its troubles give not a reason for retreat, but many reasons for offense. The truth that Christianity is basic to civilization is becoming more and more a conviction in the English speaking world, a matter of great encouragement at the moment."[8] The United Lutheran Church in America stated in its 1942 convention that the church was confronted with an "unparalleled opportunity" to mold the new age after "the pattern of the kingdom." The report, entitled "The Church and a World at War," charged Christians to seize the opportunity. "Great occasions call for great men. The plight of humanity today and the possibilities for the future call for great Christians and a more effective witness by the Church. Therefore, we summon our own people to a new and solemn dedication of themselves and all they have, of loyalty and love and life, for a renewed proclamation of Christ's Gospel, and a world-wide advance of His Church."[9]

Christian leaders did not want to be as unprepared for ministry as they had been during the First World War. Writing for *Advance*, Frederick L. Fagley argued that the churches had slumped during World War I largely because they were spiritually and morally unprepared for the conflict and thus vulnerable to manipulation and compromise. "To rebuild the life of society on the clear pattern of Christian teachings, in 1918, was a task for which the people were totally unprepared, and they permitted themselves to be grossly misled. The forces of a narrow nationalism, of selfishness and of greed, knew far better how to achieve their purpose than did those who were responsible for the realization of the moral idealism of Christianity, but who had neglected their full responsibility in order to serve the immediate needs."[10] Church leaders did not want the wartime pressures of patriotism to impede their distinctively religious work.

The War against Hate

Of all the blunders that the churches committed during the First World War, probably the most bitter to recall was the campaign of hate and hysteria that church leaders had conducted. Christian leaders made sure that it would not happen again. They challenged any and all expressions of hatred. Luther Stewart of the *Christian Index* announced, "The mission of the Church is not to excite its members to national hatred, but to lead them in worshipping and serving Him who loved all men, races and nations. In a world at war the Church can teach its members not to hate, but to pray for suffering men and women, even for enemies."[11] A statement adopted by the Federal Council of Churches Executive Committee on March 16, 1943 read: "We therefore deplore the public statements of certain citizens, in civilian and military life, urging that we should foster attitudes of hate among our people. . . . We recognize that never before in history has there been so widespread a provocation to hatred. . . . We call upon our fellow-Christians, while striving for right and justice, to reject all desire for vengeance; to seek God's forgiveness for any hatred we may harbor."[12]

Virtually every religious journal in America carried strong statements (in sermons, articles, editorials, denominational resolutions) declaring that hatred, vengeance, hysteria, and fanaticism were odious to God and a disgrace to the Christian faith. Even the titles of these pieces revealed the sentiments of denominational leaders: "To Conquer but Not to Hate"; "If We Hate, We Shall Fail"; "For Christians, Hatred Is 'Out'"; "Americans, Beware of Hatred!" The message was clear enough: however desperately Americans wanted to win the war, they would never win it, spiritually and morally, if they hated. The churches, then, became the self-appointed critics of America's attitude toward the enemy. Hatred was out and love was in. The churches hoped thereby to avoid repeating the mistakes of the past and to counter the hysterical propaganda that was pouring out of Washington and Hollywood.[13]

That Christians should not hate seemed obvious enough in theory, though difficult to put into practice. The church was responsible to pursue love instead of hatred. A simple reading of the Sermon of the Mount would allow for no other alternative. But could the church also choose to pursue victory over defeat? Could the church itself be at war?

The Church at War?

It was Charles Clayton Morrison who first raised the issue. Shortly after Pearl Harbor, the Federal Council of Churches (FCC) formed a commission to formulate Christian principles for the postwar peace. Morrison announced in no uncertain terms at the Delaware Conference (so named because the first conference was convened in Delaware, Ohio): "The Christian Church is not at war." He tried to press for its inclusion into the official document that the commission intended to publish out of the conference. He also wanted to force the participants to wrestle with the larger question of the church's role in the war. Morrison believed that the church should transcend the conflict and refuse to declare war on America's enemies. After prolonged debate in one of the working groups of the conference, the statement was finally included in the report. But since the inclusion would have violated the ordinance under which the Conference was to proceed, namely, that there should be "no controversial references to the war," the statement was eliminated by the steering committee.

Henry Pitney Van Dusen reported on the incident in *Christianity and Crisis*. He was one of many Christian leaders who rejected Morrison's declaration. Van Dusen believed that it was either misleading, meaningless, or irresponsible. It was misleading because it seemed to imply that some Christians were in fact claiming that the church was at war. That assumption, according to Van Dusen, was simply not true. It was meaningless because it seemed to be saying "The Christian church has not declared war" or "The Christian church is not waging war." These statements were simply too obvious to be called true. The church, after all, had not been directly engaged in military operations for centuries and was therefore involved in the conflict only insofar as Christians were citizens of the state as well as faithful communicants of the church. The statement, finally, was irresponsible because it implied that the church had no responsibility to the nations that were at war.[14]

Most Christians were in fact at war, even if the church, strictly speaking, was not, and they were also committed to victory. A few finally spoke up, issuing a statement in August 1942. Signed by such notables as Henry S. Coffin, Ivan Lee Holt, John A. Mackay, John R. Mott, Reinhold Niebuhr, and G. Bromley Oxnam, it affirmed that fundamental issues of religion and democracy were at stake in the war. The statement asserted that it was a war that the united nations had to win. Committed, as the signers of the statement were, to a free and just society and to equitable distribution of the world's resources, they believed that victory was essential if these aims were ever going to be reached. Though they abhorred war, desired peace, and admitted America's culpability, they were not ready to concede defeat or settle for a negotiated peace. The "aggressor nations" intended to conquer, subjugate, or destroy much of the world, including America's closest allies. The united nations could not tolerate this brutal goal and thus had to defeat the enemy. Such a formidable task necessitated the intervention of divine grace. "Confidently, therefore, and humbly we seek God's guidance and strength as we dedicate ourselves to the defeat of the aggressors now at large in the world and to the establishment of that world order to which Christians and men of good will in all lands aspire and for which the military victory of the United States has now become indispensable."[15]

Other Christian groups followed suit. The United Lutheran Church in America stated: "Therefore, we call upon our people in particular, and all Christian people in general, to dedicate themselves wholly, with every resource of heart and mind and conscience, to the defeat and destruction of this evil. We call upon our own people to give to our country the fullest measure of devotion and support, as the privilege and duty of Christian citizens."[16] The National Association of Evangelicals sent a message to President Roosevelt assuring him of their loyalty. Recognizing that the great ideas and institutions in America were the products of an evangelical influence, they declared their desire to renew faith in America, "to the end that our Nation may continue to occupy its exalted place among the nations of the world." "We, therefore, renew hereby our allegiance to and our prayers for those in authority over us, that guidance and wisdom from on High may be given to them in these days of perplexity, and that in the weighty duties of your high office and the important decisions to be made by Your Excellency from time to time, we give you the assurance of our prayers and to the end that our sacred privileges as free men may be preserved and the blessing of Almighty God rest upon our land."[17] As the Southern Baptists declared in 1942, the churches were called to be the great builder of morale in the nation. Only they could inspire the depth of patriotism that America needed.[18] These statements reflected the sentiments of most Christians.

Most, but not all. A small minority of Christians in America redoubled their efforts to oppose the war, even after Pearl Harbor. Two groups in particular played important roles; both were pacifist. The more radical of the two was associated with the Fellowship of Reconciliation and its official journal, *Fellowship*. They were led by such notable intellectuals as John

Haynes Holmes, pastor for over forty years of an independent (formerly Unitarian) church in New York City and a leader of the National Association for the Advancement of Colored People (NAACP) and the American Civil Liberties Union (ACLU), and A. J. Muste, a longtime labor activist and, beginning in 1940, executive director of the Fellowship of Reconciliation. Though dissociating themselves from those who planned to sabotage or obstruct America's war effort, they nevertheless refused to support the war. They believed that the United States was obligated at such a critical hour to confess its own guilt, commit itself to nonviolence, and strive for reconciliation between allies and enemies. In spite of war, they remained, as their declaration of purpose stated, "a group of men and women of many nations and races who recognize the unity of the world-wide human family and wish to explore the possibilities of love for discovering truth, dispelling antagonisms, and reconciling people, despite all differences in a friendly society."[19]

These pacifists practiced nonviolent resistance over nonresistance. One from their number, Nels F. S. Ferre, an ordained congregational minister and professor at Andover Seminary, believed that pacifists were called to be active and responsible citizens whose informed consciences would enable them to aid America at the deepest level of its needs and to do what Christ demanded, even if that required disobedience to the state. "[W]e see that the Christian [pacifist] is no rebellious misfit, but longs to cooperate constructively with his people. He has no self-righteousness, no fanatical devotion to moral principles to make of him a prig or a Pharisee. . . . But for this reason also the Christian must refuse to obey the State at whatever point he feels that his witness to God and his usefulness in changing the world are obscured and thwarted by conformity."[20]

As Vernon Nash stated in *Fellowship*, pacifists could not be passive in the face of evil. They had to act, but not in a way that exacerbated the very problem—violence—that needed to be overcome. "Submission or war are not the only alternatives. If they were, I would be unable to see any hopeful future for a humanity in possession of the destructive powers of a demi-god. Wrong can be opposed more effectively and more rationally by non-violent means than by pitting violence against violence. This has become increasingly true as life has become more integrated and more inter-dependent." Citing Gandhi, he affirmed that it was better to fight than to do nothing.[21] Following the lead of pacifists like Ferre, Nash, Muste, Holmes, and John Nevin Sayre, the younger generation of pacifists took this position of nonviolent resistance seriously. They refused to participate in Civilian Public Service camps and, when sent to jail, organized protests against what they believed were unjust prison policies.

The other group disavowing the war effort represented the peace churches—Friends, Brethren, and Mennonite. As pacifists, most refused to enlist in the military or to work in defense industry. Yet they also founded and administered Civilian Public Service camps for conscientious objectors. By operating these camps, they could simultaneously oppose war and yet serve the nation by doing work of "national importance." Rufus D. Bowman, a professor at Bethany Seminary in Chicago and a leader of the Brethren, and John Hershberger, a leading intellectual of the Mennonites, wrote frequently and passionately about the peace churches' responsibility to prove their patriotism without compromising their convictions. To them, the tradition of nonresistance was the best policy to follow.[22]

Still, whether opposed to the war or committed to winning the war, Christian leaders believed that the church's primary duty was not political and military but spiritual: to pray for God's grace, wisdom, and power, to lay a biblical foundation for a just peace, to love the enemy, to cultivate Christian character, to lead the nation to repentance, to insist that leaders use their power for the greater good of humankind. They urged the church to serve the needs of the nation in wartime and yet to transcend the conflict by being faithful to its Lord. A paragraph from the formative document *The Relation of the Church to the War in the Light of the Christian Faith* sums up how the church was supposed to function as an institution under the state and as a community above the state. It asserted that the church, whether in peace or in war, had to live in a tension. "On the one hand, members and constituent bodies of the Church are members also of civil communities and citizens of particular states that have emerged in history, and as such are obligated by the law of God to render loyal service aimed at promoting the welfare of their respective nations." Such was the church's patriotic duty. It was not, however, its only duty. "On the other hand, the Church being universal is not a subject of any state, nor a constituent body in any civil community. It is itself, in principle and to an increasing degree in actuality, an ecumenical community having members in all nations and owing direct allegiance to the God and Father of all mankind. Its proper service to civil life can be rendered only while its ultimate and direct obligation to proclaim the Kingdom of God is kept clear. Its service to the world must be a ministry, not a vassalage nor a partnership."[23]

Evangelism

Christian leaders tried to encourage the church to do its ministry during World War II in a way that reflected this tension. Two fields of ministry, both decidedly "religious," came to the fore and required special attention. Both fields of ministry grew out of their awareness that the world was facing a spiritual crisis. Religious leaders believed that the world needed to hear good news that only the church could preach and to experience a unity that only the church could create. Thus evangelism and church unity became important thrusts in the church's ministry during the war. These were the areas of service that helped the churches be patriotic without compromising integrity.

Many church leaders sensed a growing interest in religion among the American people. Though some conservatives, like R. B. Kuiper, an editor of the *Presbyterian Guardian* and professor of practical theology at Westminster Seminary, were wary of this "return to religion" and warned that it had to be measured against the standards of the Bible, it nevertheless appeared obvious that Americans were turning to God in record numbers. The churches wanted to be ready to ride the wave.[24]

Church leaders were certain that America needed a revival of Christian faith. Fundamentalists marched to a revivalistic cadence throughout the war. To them the war only reinforced a conviction that they already held. As one article stated, "For Preparedness Our Need Is Revivals and More Revivals." If America was going to be saved from the conflagration, it had to return to God. It was the church's duty to hold the gospel banner high.[25]

Fundamentalists thus made preparations for a forward thrust in evangelism. Leaders of the World's Christian Fundamentals Association affirmed that it had "come to the kingdom for such a time as this." The Lord had "raised up this movement and given it a vision and a program for this hour." Its leaders announced in the spring of 1940 that they were launching a major evangelistic crusade that would saturate the nation over the course of a year. Unlike previous campaigns, this crusade was going to engage, motivate, and train Christians for direct action. Its leaders planned to train and deploy one million "intercessors and evangelists." "We expect," wrote Paul W. Rood, president of the association, "to cover the entire nation during the year. Our desire is to gather the evangelicals of all denominations together to challenge them with God's call in this crisis. It is a call to prayer for a nation-wide revival." Rood planned that these conferences would also include evangelistic meetings in the evenings. "We shall use," Rood continued, "the printed page, the radio, the public platform, and every other means at our disposal in order to reach the nation."

Neo-evangelicals also sponsored evangelistic crusades during the war through the work of new organizations like Youth for Christ, Young Life, and the National Association of Evangelicals. They also organized "Christ for America" rallies in twenty-four cities, which featured evangelist Percy Crawford and track star Gil Dodds.[26] These movements prepared the way for the advance and growth of evangelical groups after the war.

Such evangelistic fervor was not the concern of evangelicals alone. Mainline Protestant churches were equally committed to evangelism, recognizing the signs of the times and the needs of the hour. Exhorting his own denomination to redouble its evangelistic efforts, D. R. Sharpe of the Northern Baptist Convention believed that the great hour of the church had arrived. Americans were ripe for conversion. "We call attention to the fact that there is now a renewal of interest in religion as the bulwark of democracy and the safeguard of our American way of life. Furthermore, there are evidences of a new interest in the church as the guardian of freedom and of civilization itself." Henry St. George Tucker, presiding bishop of the Protestant Episcopal Church, charged Episcopalians to take their role as evangelists seriously. "Today," he said, "we American Christians have a responsibility for witness, born of our Lord, greater than any Christians in history. Today the armies of our Lord must be put into action in a counter attack which will sweep from the field the forces which would destroy society. The order seems to me: Charge Forward!"[27]

Several mainline denominations did in fact start evangelistic campaigns and renewal movements during the war, like the Methodist's Campaign for a Million or the Northern Baptist's Christian Advance Program. Perhaps the most striking effort at evangelism originated in the Federal Council of Churches. In 1940 the FCC launched the National Christian Mission, an evangelistic campaign that blanketed twenty-two major cities in as many weeks. An average of thirty speakers appeared in each city, preaching from pulpit and platform to stir up the committed and to reach the unchurched for Christ, who was "the only adequate message for the world today." "The National Christian Mission humbly and yet boldly appropriates the name of Christ," the official explanation of the mission read. "Its holy cause centers in Christ. It knows no other Savior, acknowledges no other Lord and Master." The awful specter of a world at war made the mission timely. "In a world at war the National Christian Mission is thrust forth with a sense of immediacy and urgency. . . . Mankind is oppressed with perplexity and fear. Men are burdened with evils almost unsupportable and with problems apparently insoluble." Thus the mission sought "to recapture the fearless aggressiveness of the early Christian Church . . . to get Christianity into action." It was "a remobilization of our spiritual forces which the gravity of the hour" demanded. To prepare for the mission, leaders organized a World-Wide Fellowship of Prayer. The campaign was important because, as its theme declared, only "Christ is the Answer."[28]

Church Unity

Church unity was the other distinctively religious activity that captured the attention of the churches. It symbolized the church's commitment to world peace and harmony, and it became a priority for many Christian leaders during the war, as attested by the number of important cooperative organizations founded. The American Council of Christian Churches was begun in 1941, followed by the National Association of Evangelicals in 1942 and the National Council of Churches, which, though not officially organized until 1950, was nevertheless conceived of in the early 1940s. The formation of the World Council of Churches was also pushed forward by the war. As Stephen Neill and Ruth Rouse have stated, the flurry of ecumenical activity resulted from the impact of the war itself. "The German church struggle, and the emergence of the churches as the only powers able to exert an effective resistance, even to the point of martyrdom, to totalitarian aggression, brought the idea and the doctrine of the church again into the centre of the picture. It had become evident to many that a day had arrived in which the loosely organized efforts of men of goodwill were no longer adequate, and that nothing less than the intense and corporate loyalty of the churches as such to Jesus Christ could stand against the ruthless enemies of the mid-20th century."[29]

The need for church unity dominated discussion in the religious press and in denominational meetings. The reason was as simple to explain as it was difficult to apply. An intolerably divided world needed a unity that only spiritual forces could create. The church had to point the way and be the way. If the church failed, no other institution could ever hope to succeed. Henry Smith Leiper, American secretary of the World Council of Churches, believed that the primary responsibility of the church during the war was to become one in spirit. "They can oppose the atheism of force and the atheism of fear by manifesting the pre-eminent spiritual unity of Christendom through continuing fellowship and specific services both to nations at war and to nations still at peace."[30]

Commitment to church unity made 1939 very different from 1914. In 1914 there was nothing resembling an ecumenical church; in 1939 there was. "A wider and a deeper sense of fellowship has been born. In spite of national, racial and denominational frontiers the churches know today something of the Church, the Una Sancta, and experience some real measure of Christian communion which cannot be broken even by war."[31] The ecumenical movement thus provided the churches with an unimagined opportunity. "This reawakened creative faith in the fundamental unity of Christianity," stated Edward L. Parsons, "a unity which lives within all its diverse forms, opens the way to the most profound contribution which they can make to the new world."[32] What was true internationally was also true nationally. If unified, the church in America could help the nation to face the world crisis with one heart and mind. "The Christian church, which preaches the everlasting Gospel, can do more than any other single factor to unify our nation."[33]

Church leaders were eager to unify the Christian community but only under certain terms—terms, as it usually turned out, that reflected and reinforced the religious distinctions of each group, thus undermining the unity they sought to create. Conservative Roman Catholics, for example, affirmed that the global reach of their religion was the only sure foundation upon which the new world could be built. "When Nazism is finally destroyed," Francis X. Talbot, editor of *America*, declared, "when Fascism is uprooted, when Communism is totally effaced from the world, and when Catholicism is the spiritual bond between the nations, then we may look for the realization of the hopes of President Roosevelt and Prime Minister Churchill." Catholics were united under the authority of the pope, whose influence and power were critical to world peace.[34]

Mainline Protestants countered by urging exclusively "Protestant Fellowship." The FCC stated that the "genius of Protestantism" was its spirit of fellowship in freedom, which was possible to experience without altogether sacrificing freedom, as Catholics appeared to do. The "strategy of Protestantism" was its long-term plan to make the spirit of Protestantism dominant in every aspect of personal life and to create institutions that could nurture rather than undermine true community as, once again, Catholics did. It was essential for Protestants to propagate those beliefs. Sadly, they were hampered by their own disunity.[35]

Evangelicals were suspicious of both Catholics and liberal Protestants. They feared the Catholic church because in their minds it aimed to become the dominant religion in America, and they feared liberal Protestantism because it compromised the orthodox faith and planned to create an "international church."[36] Evangelicals realized that the time was long past for them to unite. Their unity was essential to changing the direction of the nation. "We must," announced William Ward Ayer to delegates at the first conference of the National Association of Evangelicals, "find a common meeting place for common purposes. There must be a hub in which the spokes of our several organizations can meet in order to make for firmness of purpose, service, and solidarity in testimony." Nothing short of America's survival was at stake. "It is not boasting to declare that evangelical Christianity has the America of our fathers to save. While our army and navy fight the enemy from without, we have the enemy at home to battle, and he is in some ways more dangerous than the enemy abroad. We unhesitatingly declare that evangelicals have the 'keys of the kingdom.' Millions of evangelical Christians, if they had a common voice and a common meeting place, would exercise under God an influence that would save American democracy."[37]

The Duties of Citizenship

Individual Christians had duties to perform as citizens that paralleled the church's mission in the larger society. The broad outline of these duties, which Christian leaders made clear, reflected something of a tension. They were committed to military victory but hesitated to make victory an end in itself. They stressed three duties in particular—sacrificial service, support of soldiers, and protection of conscientious objectors—that embodied this tension.

That responsible citizenship was important found clear expression in the writings, reports, and statements of religious groups. The Federal Council of Churches, for example, urged the churches to observe "I Am an American Day" on May 21, 1944. The council provided suggestions for the day's observance in the *Federal Council Bulletin* and urged ministers to make the duties and privileges of citizenship a religious concern. Samuel McCrea Cavert, general secretary of the FCC, hoped that the day would be "a time when older Americans can re-dedicate themselves to responsible and active citizenship, when ministers may reaffirm the spiritual values underlying American democracy and the moral duties by which man gains and keeps his freedom."[38]

Responsible citizenship excluded fanaticism. Several religious journals printed articles telling the story of Edith Cavell, whose memorial, standing on a busy London street, looked toward Trafalgar Square. A nurse during the First World War, Cavell was eventually executed by a German firing squad for being "merciful in a time of war." The words on her memorial echoed the wartime sentiments of many religious leaders—"Patriotism in not enough." The kind of patriotism that Christian leaders supported required sacrifice for the common good, protection of the weak, and honest criticism of the government.[39]

Christian citizenship required sacrificial service. Allegiance to America mandated action. Christian leaders believed that sacrifice was one way of honoring the people who had already made the ultimate sacrifice of dying to preserve the freedom of their fellow Americans. A statement adopted by the Federal Council of Churches Executive Committee in May 1942 read: "When other men are offering their lives we must at least offer our substance. Every Christian citizen should recognize a personal summons to give, on a truly sacrificial level, for the alleviation of the vast suffering arising from the war and for the maintenance of the great enterprises of mercy and relief which are now needed as never before." Christians, it went on to say, should count it a privilege to cooperate in rationing programs, to accept increased taxation, and to invest in government bonds.[40] Others echoed the same concern. For example, H. J. Kuiper, editor of the *Banner*, declared: "We can be patriots of a high order even though we do not fight with our armed forces. If we shun all selfish hoarding, refuse to profit financially by our country's peril, give sacrificially, help faithfully in the production of war material, or become 'blood-donors' to save the life of those wounded in battle, and do so, not under duress but voluntarily, we have the spirit of a true patriot."[41]

This spirit of sacrifice led many people (mostly men) into military service. A number of articles appearing in Protestant publications defended military service, arguing that it was not contrary to Christian discipleship. John W. Bradbury of the *Watchman-Examiner* considered military service a moral mandate. He was proud of the Christian youth serving their country by wearing a uniform. "[W]e hail this host of American youth, among whom are thousands of our Christian brothers, and we pray that the war they wage will end in victory, thus preserving freedom, justice, and the privileges of our faith for this and unborn generations."[42] Christian soldiers, as one writer put it, were as "conscientious" in their willingness to fight as pacifists were in their commitment to object. They lived according to conscience. Their convictions were right, so they deserved the church's support.[43]

But many leaders believed that conscientious objectors (COs) deserved the church's support as well, for they too lived according to conscience. Their conscience led them to object to a war that the vast majority of Americans supported. The pressure put on young men and women to join the military was enormous. The ten million plus Americans in uniform believed that they had good reasons for enlisting in the armed services. Their popularity and heroic service must have made COs feel conspicuous, even traitorous. They could have easily found themselves standing virtually alone, ignored or shunned by the vast majority of patriotic Christians.

Not every Christian group did support COs. Some conservatives contended that they were mistaken. They believed that COs failed to understand the Bible's teaching on the Christian's duty to government, for they exalted conscience above revealed truth. "It is to be remembered that man's conscience, even in matters relating to the law of the national government, is to be regulated, not by feelings or opinions, but by the authoritative Word of God." Conscience, then, did not deserve absolute protection, especially in wartime.[44]

But these critics represented the minority point of view. Most religious leaders wanted to protect the rights of COs. The occasion for such a defense arose in 1940 when the Burke-Wadsworth Conscription Bill was introduced on the floor of Congress. The first draft of the bill made little provision for COs. It provided that exemption from combatant service be allowed solely to members of "any well recognized religious sect whose creed . . . forbids members to participate in war in any form." Such criteria excluded all Christians except those who belonged to the historic peace churches. No method of procedure, no rules of evidence, no stated qualifications for the personnel of the tribunals were clearly set forth to protect CO rights. The first draft of the bill did not even improve the formula used by World War I draft boards.

But the churches had changed too much between the wars to make reversion to an old policy tolerable. Catholics and Protestants alike protested the bill. "Whatever one's view of pacifism," argued Edward Skillin of the *Commonweal*, "Christian pacifism, springing from deep religious and moral conviction, exists. To provide in such an insensitive way for safeguarding the human conscience is merely to show an utter contempt for the validity of the conscience which all religious men must deplore."[45]

Walter Van Kirk, executive secretary of the Department of International Justice and Goodwill, sent a letter of protest to President Roosevelt and Senator Morris Sheppard, chair of the Senate Military Affairs Committee. He advised Sheppard and his committee that all Christians, regardless of religious affiliation, should be given the right to exempt themselves from war, not simply those who belonged to the historic peace churches. He added that because most denominations in America had resolved to uphold the rights of COs, Sheppard's committee was "duty bound to take this fact into account in the legislation now being drafted." Referring to President Roosevelt's "Four Freedoms," Van Kirk pleaded that the committee respect freedom of religion, which was imperiled by the bill's provisions. He suggested that COs be given opportunities to serve their country in projects of national importance. After Van Kirk sent his letter to Roosevelt, Roswell P. Barnes, associate general secretary of the FCC, appeared personally before the House Committee on Military Affairs to testify on behalf of COs.[46]

Many religious groups followed the lead of the FCC. Soon after the Burke-Wadsworth Bill was sent to committee, a petition signed by hundreds of church leaders was sent to members of Congress. It read: "We desire to affirm our conviction that no action of government can abrogate or suspend our obligation as Christian ministers to counsel men in all circumstances to render obedience to conscience and resolutely to do the right as they see it. Therefore we must make it clear to our fellow-citizens, and in particular to conscientious objectors to war in any form that we stand ready to counsel and support in all ways within our power those who may be subjected to difficulty or persecution because they are unable conscientiously to cooperate in the operation of a conscription act."[47] The House of Bishops of the Protestant Episcopal Church sent a telegram to Van Kirk in support of his leadership, and they urged immediate consideration of the bill proposed by the FCC before the attorney general.[48]

At their 1940 convention Southern Baptists also took action on behalf of COs. Their defense of COs followed the traditional Baptist argument. They considered freedom of religion and the right to appeal to conscience an essential part of the American heritage, the original idea of which came from Baptists themselves. "A considerable number of members of churches of our Convention, through their interpretation of the moral teachings of Christ, have reached the position of conscientious objection to war that prohibits them from bearing arms. The Convention ought to accord them the right of their convictions as it accords to others the right to differ from them, and ought to protect them in that right to the extent of its ability."[49] The Northern Baptist Convention passed a similar resolution.[50]

Still, not all religious leaders agreed with the FCC. On the one hand, some argued that stricter measures be imposed on COs.[51] On the other hand, the historic peace churches lobbied for greater leniency and flexibility.

They suggested that civilians be given the power to review the cases of COs and to administer Civilian Public Service camps.[52] Clearly there was diversity of opinion. But in general the churches believed that COs deserved the same kind of support that soldiers received. They insisted that the government protect the rights of conscience from the pressures of a patriotism that moved in only one direction.

The churches were largely successful in their lobbying efforts. When the Burke-Wadsworth Bill was passed on September 15, 1940, it exempted COs from the military and allowed for alternative forms of service in Civilian Public Service camps. The historic peace churches funded and administered the camps, and they received some help, mostly financial, from other Protestant denominations.[53]

It is clear, then, that the churches served American society during the war. But they were not so preoccupied with that duty that they neglected other religious responsibilities. The churches were loyal to America; they tried to be more loyal to God. Thus, however committed to victory, they refused to become dominated by America's war effort. They had a vision that transcended the exigencies of a nation at war, a vision that affirmed the need for religious revival and church unity. Finally, though church leaders urged individual Christians to do their patriotic duty during the war, they still argued that patriotism was not enough unless it included compassion for the suffering, repentance for national sin, and support for COs. The war was important, but the kingdom of God was more important still.[54]

CHAPTER EIGHT

MINISTRY & MOBILIZATION

World War II was not merely a war of ideas. Christian leaders did more than discuss Christian perspectives on interventionism, theodicy, and democracy. They also encouraged their churches to initiate a wide variety of ministries to the millions of Americans who worked in defense industries or who joined the military. They recognized that the war provided opportunities to extend the church's influence and to apply the Christian message to meet practical needs. This commitment to wartime ministry transcended organization and ideology. It did not matter whether one was a Baptist, Presbyterian, or Mennonite, nor whether one was an interventionist or a pacifist. Virtually every religious group in America saw the war as an occasion for service.

Yet the wartime ministry of the churches manifested the same kind of cautious patriotism as wartime debate did. The churches wanted to serve a nation in need, and they did, but not at the expense of what Christian leaders identified as the church's independence and integrity. Even in ministry church leaders remained wary of fanaticism, vigilant against jingoism, and critical of a narrow conception of citizenship.

College Education

Like most other institutions, the churches felt an obligation to contribute to the war effort. So they offered what resources they had at their disposal.

One resource that proved valuable almost immediately after Pearl Harbor was the church-related college, which many denominational bodies made available to the military to help train men and women for work in the armed services. Both college and country benefited. Many colleges bolstered enrollments, which they desperately needed in order to stay open during the war, and the military was allowed to use existing educational institutions to train servicemen. The relationship was thus symbiotic.

The wartime prosperity of church-related colleges did not at first appear promising. Many professors left their teaching posts to make their academic expertise available to the war effort. Their absence forced the professors who stayed behind to carry overloads and to teach twelve months out of the year. The curriculum changed, too. Traditional liberal arts courses gave way to a disproportionately large number of courses in mathematics, engineering, nursing, and others useful for wartime service. The huge demand for servicemen and industrial workers caused a sharp decrease in enrollments. To accommodate those students who remained in college, colleges often relaxed their requirements for graduation and adjusted their schedules so that students could complete their education in less than three years.

Most colleges scrambled to adjust to these wartime conditions. They changed their curriculum to adapt to the nation's needs and worked cooperatively with the government to prepare students for wartime work. Shortly after Pearl Harbor 1,000 representatives from colleges across America gathered in Baltimore to discuss how education could serve America in wartime. Church-related colleges were well represented at the meeting. Like their secular counterparts, they lent their support to help America train its youth for war.

One program in particular had far-reaching impact. In 1942 and 1943 the armed services developed the A-12 program for the army and the V-12 program for the navy. These programs allowed the armed services to use the facilities of 485 colleges and universities across the country, 225 of which were church-related, to provide future officers with both broad, general education and specific, technical training. Students in the V-12 and A-12 programs joined the military before enrolling in college, and they wore uniforms and lived the regimented life of servicemen on campus. They took a minimum of four sixteen-week terms, completing about two-thirds of the work required for a bachelor's degree. The government paid all expenses. Students had to qualify for the program. They came from every conceivable background and did not have to hold religious beliefs to be accepted, nor were they required to participate in religious activities once on campus.

While military leaders did not assume control of colleges in the program, they certainly had some say about the curriculum. All the major denominations and sects in America participated in the program.

Doane, a congregational school in Nebraska, was one such college. Its president, Bryant Drake, commented that servicemen on his campus proved to be a disappointment. Though "a contingent of young supermen was expected, able to carry without difficulty the ambitious course outlined by the bureau of Navy Personnel," he discovered that the men of the unit were average college students at best. Far from being young patriots and idealists who joined the navy to fight for the Four Freedoms, they were, according to Drake, more interested in advancing their own careers and impressing others by wearing a uniform.[1]

But not all colleges evaluated the program so negatively. Hobart College, located in New York and oldest of the four colleges affiliated with the Episcopal Church, was also selected to participate in the V-12 program. Officials of the college considered participation a boon because it solved a severe financial problem, resulting from attenuated enrollments, and enabled the college to maintain its excellent facilities.[2] The University of Dubuque, a Presbyterian college in Iowa, was included in the program, too. Hermann S. Ficke, professor of English, gave it high marks and argued that it provided the church with an opportunity to address the spiritual needs of servicemen. "The Presbyterian churches have been alive to their opportunity," Ficke commented, "and the Presbyterian pastors have shown how the Gospel can influence the lives of young men." Ficke mentioned one other benefit as well. "It would be wrong not to mention the fact that one of the finest fruits of this educational venture has been the spirit of mutual understanding. There has been absolutely no friction between the adherents of the great Evangelical Churches and the Catholics and Latter Day Saints and the Pentecostal groups."[3] Most of the other large Protestant denominations, as well as the Roman Catholic Church, were also active in the programs.[4]

Leaders of church-related schools, however, were not supportive of the war effort to the extent that they were willing to compromise religious liberal arts education. They were concerned that the exigencies of war would undermine, even eradicate, the distinctions of church-related education. There appeared to be two points of contention. The first involved liberal education itself. Charles Clayton Morrison alleged that the V-12 program threatened the future of liberal arts, and he was not sure that it would be able to recover. He lamented:

The recent joint directive by the secretaries of war and the navy has given shocking wrench to the principles and conduct of institutions which have been relied on to train leaders for our democratic society. Henceforth, according to this order, for the duration of the conflict the army and the navy will prescribe the conditions under which all able-bodied men of eighteen and over will continue their education. They will define the curriculums our youth may study. For the army, at least, that course of study will include only subjects related directly to the prosecution of the war. Temporarily, liberal education is a casualty of war.[5]

Some Christian educators predicted that the elimination of the liberal arts curriculum would be fatal to American culture. Earl Moreland, president of Randolph-Macon College, believed that the liberal arts were indispensable to the preservation and development of Western civilization. While acknowledging that colleges were addressing the emergency brought on by the war, he argued that it was "unwise and unpatriotic" to overlook the distinctive contributions that liberal arts education had made to American civilization. "If we are to continue our way of life, we shall have to continue those agencies and institutions which have produced and maintained it. . . . The liberal arts program which serves as the foundation for all professional and graduate training, is not only distinctive to our system of education; it is indispensable to the continuity of our civilization in the days ahead."[6]

The second concern about the program was religious. It was not acceptable simply to train young men for war, nor merely to educate young people in philosophy, literature, and history. Education had to be Christian or it would fail. American society had always depended upon such education. Church leaders believed that the occasion of war was no time to sacrifice it. If anything, it was during such a time that Americans had to redouble their efforts to strengthen it. Wrote William Clayton Bower: "Religion is a phase of a people's total culture. It is, therefore, not the sole prerogative or responsibility of the church. It is a fundamental responsibility of society itself and of each of its constituent agencies. This seems to point in the direction of a clarification of functions and a cooperative sharing of responsibility on the part of the major institutions of society, especially the home, the school, and the church."[7] College education had to be Christian education. However zealous to carry out wartime obligations, colleges could not compromise their religious convictions. Argued Kenneth I. Brown of Denison University of Ohio: "A college may be doing a first-class job of intellectual training; it may be turning out potential leaders with quick, keen minds; but if life on that campus has not brought a quickening sense of divine presence—let me phrase it this way: no college dare claim the title Christian unless by the forces of campus life a student is daily tempted to the practice of the presence of God and to the practice of the brotherhood of man."[8]

Leaders of peace churches were also alarmed by the encroachment of the military on education in America. They wanted to preserve the distinctions of a curriculum that taught pacifist convictions and maintained the future vitality of "democratic education." Rufus D. Bowman, a professor at Bethany Biblical Seminary, a Brethren institution, averred that an education that was truly Christian emphasized the importance of the individual, of God, and of human welfare. Bowman was concerned about the steady erosion of those distinctions. "But much of the modern education in our day is leaving God out, and man out, and the church out, and democracy out. Yes, and moral standards are being left out. The smoking, the dancing, the loose moral standards, the young mothers today whose babies have unnamed fathers, the disintegration of home life, the militarization of the minds of youth, all speak of the necessity of protecting Brethren youth and of the necessity of Brethren colleges, which are creative centers for Brethren ideals. There is no other way to go."[9]

Rationing

The cooperation of church-related colleges was only one aspect of a much broader front of mobilization ministries. As Unitarian M. L. Wilson, assistant director of the Office of Defense, Health, and Welfare Services, announced to his fellow Unitarians, "There are no non-combatants." "Now," he said, "we are *all* in the war *all* the way, as President Roosevelt has so truly put it. People everywhere are asking what non-combatants can do to help win that war. . . . What the President really asked us to do was to resort to a new kind of thinking. He was not talking in figures of speech; he meant that today it is literally true that there *are* no non-combatants."[10]

Service was rendered, for example, by cooperating with the rationing program. Instituted by Roosevelt in 1942, it had perhaps the most universal impact on all Americans, including American Christians. Religious leaders exhorted church members to live simply and sacrificially. "Our normal, life-as-usual existence is being radically modified," wrote a news commentator in *America*. "We must, whether we like it or not, adopt ourselves to a slower, simpler and more sacrificial standard of living. We are in total war; civilians and soldiers alike."[11]

Unitarian George N. Marshall suggested that Christians—and pastors in particular—not take advantage of "immunities" from rationing, even for church work. Given an opportunity for service that they did not earn and deserve, pastors were to prove their patriotism by not availing themselves of the immunity. If anything, they were to protest against the policy of granting privileges to the churches.[12]

Though most Christian leaders did not agree with Marshall, they nevertheless advised pastors to use their liberal gasoline and tire allowances conscientiously. "Every automobile tire that any preacher owns is a challenge to him to spend that tire's usefulness in bolstering up the moral and spiritual courage of the people. Now, as never before, pastoral calling is of supreme importance."[13] The National Catholic Welfare Conference even formed a new committee, the Institutional Food Supply and Rationing Committee, to address the problems of rationing for charitable institutions. It worked closely with the Office of Price Administration to develop a sound policy.[14]

As the war went on, however, Americans seemed less willing to accept the regiment of rationing, especially when it no longer seemed necessary. Americans began to enjoy prosperity for the first time in over a decade, despite the suffering that people in Europe and Asia were still facing. This lack of sympathy for the world's misery bothered Reinhold Niebuhr. Americans, he noted, consumed an average of 3,300 calories a day, the French 1,900 calories, and the Greeks a mere 700 calories. "We are very rich in a poor world and very fat in a lean world." The comparative distance of America from the scenes of suffering only added to the problem of complacency. Niebuhr charged that it was the church's responsibility to urge the government and the American people to follow ever more stringent rationing regulations to fulfill their obligations to a starving world. "Only a very sensitive conscience and a vivid imagination can bridge the chasm between our abundance and the world's needs."[15]

Bonds

Cooperation with the rationing program was not the only field of service. Church leaders encouraged Christians to sacrifice in other ways, too. There were opportunities to give blood, to volunteer as "safety agents" in war industry, to save stamps, and to participate in civilian defense programs.[16] Christians could also buy defense bonds. "Here is, indeed," one commentator wrote for *America*, "a challenge to democratic efficiency. We urge our readers, accordingly, to invest as much of their incomes as possible in defense bonds. A Christian people should not have to be driven by Government decree to make sacrifices for the common good."[17]

Even leaders of the historic peace churches wanted the faithful to invest in bonds, though not defense bonds. They therefore worked out an agreement with the government to buy "civilian bonds" instead. A group representing the National Service Board for Religious Objectors, the organization responsible for advising the administration on policy involving conscientious objectors, negotiated with Henry Morgenthau, secretary of the U.S. Treasury, to set up an apparatus to administer the civilian bond program. Anyone was allowed to subscribe to a bond in the name of a charitable institution, which received the proceeds of the bond at its maturity. This program allowed members of peace churches to contribute from their abundance without forcing them to fund the war effort. It was a welcomed compromise.[18]

Critical Concerns

Church leaders, however, did not applaud all measures aimed at prosecuting the war more efficiently. They had their concerns, and the impact of industrial mobilization on American society was one of them. The churches gave tacit approval to industrial mobilization but nevertheless raised questions about its impact on society. However necessary, the prosecution of war could not proceed at the price of cherished American values.

Catholic leaders in particular remarked frequently and alarmingly about the ruinous effects of total mobilization. Edward Skillin Jr. of the *Commonweal* pointed out the irony that the government in America was becoming totalitarian in order to defeat totalitarianism.[19] Francis Talbot and Benjamin L. Masse of *America* also drew attention to the harmful policy of letting big business take nearly complete control of war production. Like Morrison of the *Christian Century*, they expressed concern over the future of small business, which was being squeezed out by the large corporations.[20] Talbot criticized both government and business for allowing big business to accumulate too much profit. "Business as usual," he cynically called it. Henry Taylor of the *Protestant Digest* declared that excess profits were "our domestic Munich" because wartime industrial demands allowed business to thrive, usually at the expense of labor.[21]

To hedge against the encroaching power of big business, Skillin advocated government-initiated decentralization of industry so that every region of the country could benefit from the business boom. He suggested: "The armament program should and can be utilized to encourage decentralization, a better distribution of the people in relation to one another and in relation to the natural resources of the country, their distribution, transportation and defense. At present this means first of all the building up of small and middle sized communities at the expense of the great metropolitan districts, and a general trend away from the Northeast to all the rest of the country."[22]

Francis Talbot also expressed concern about inflation, rising prices, and regressive taxes, the combination of which was punishing everyone but the rich. He suggested that the government protect the interests of the poor by taxing profits, putting a ceiling on prices and wages, and mandating rationing. "If we are to continue this war, and we must, three things seem inevitable. First, higher taxes; next a ceiling on prices, profits and wages; and third, strict rationing of all commodities. That system will not provide us with a feast, but it may, and probably will, secure for all of us a frugal meal."[23]

Both the *Commonweal* and *America* defended the rights of labor during the war, too. Writers from these publications recognized the advantages that management and big business would accrue in wartime, while labor lost ground. They were loyal to labor, but not uncritical. For example, they opposed the maneuvers of John Lewis and questioned the propriety of big strikes. Liberal Protestants also continued their support, but not, once again, without some reservations.

Big business and labor each had a responsibility to make sacrifices for the good of society. That duty extended to individual Americans as well, who were called to make similar sacrifices for the war effort. Every American had to bear part of the load. Francis Talbot, for example, believed that every American, rich and poor alike, had to practice thrift. "To tighten our belts, and to learn to get along with less, will help to provide against inflation, and help the Government to win the war." Victory, however, was not the only benefit that Americans could derive from a reduced standard of living. "Doing without" would also initiate Americans "into that stage of Christian living which embraces self-denial and mortification."[24]

Thus there were voices that raised questions about the way mobilization was proceeding. A few church leaders foresaw potential problems for small businesses, labor, and nonindustrialized regions of the country. They also wondered about the portentous growth of federal power and control. Though it may have been "business as usual" for industry, it was not for these few Christian leaders. They believed that mobilization should not proceed without some kind of attention given to its effects on society.

Mobility

The war precipitated an unprecedented social crisis in America. Millions of Americans were mobilized into action. They worked for defense industries, enlisted in the armed services, and volunteered for public service. Much of this activity forced them to uproot themselves from their familiar communities and move elsewhere. The churches recognized the magnitude of this problem, considered it an opportunity for ministry, and did their best to address the needs of civilian workers. They developed an impressive number of organizations and programs to minister to Americans in industry and to Americans on the move.

Church leaders were quick to recognize the needs and inform the churches. They called attention to the problems—and opportunities—of the rapid growth of war industry. Almost overnight "boom towns" sprang up in industrial centers across America to accommodate the huge influx of people who poured in to take jobs in factories. The populations in many of these cities doubled or trebled in a matter of months. Samuel McCrea Cavert of the Federal Council of Churches (FCC) noted the devastating consequences of such massive social disruption. "Families uprooted from their old homes and transplanted to new communities were without Christian fellowship, children of working mothers were uncared for, recreational facilities were lacking, organized vice quickly took root, juvenile delinquency showed a startling increase."[25]

Churches located in industrial communities were overwhelmed by the deluge of new people and the eruption of new problems. Church leaders "cried out" to their denominations for assistance—there were "headaches" in Dayton, Ohio, and "new challenges" in Mobile, Alabama, brought on, as was usually the case, by the sudden population explosion. Inadequate housing, lack of recreational facilities, limited day care programs, and family problems strained the already fragile stability of American society and drained the resources of local churches. Many of these local congregations tried to procure help from the outside.[26]

Organizing for Wartime Ministry

After Pearl Harbor churches and denominations developed organizations and programs to work in defense communities. The FCC led the way for most Protestant denominations. At the Conference on the Closer Relationship of General Interdenominational Agencies held at Atlantic City on December 9–11, 1941, leaders of the FCC invited interdenominational agencies to join them in setting up a comprehensive intercouncil agency for dealing with the wartime responsibility of the council's member churches. The new agency was called the Coordinating Committee for Wartime Service. At its first meeting participants decided that the necessary agencies for cooperative wartime service, like the General Commission on Army and Navy Chaplains (which later became independent), the Christian Commission for Camp and Defense Communities, and the Committee on the Conscientious Objector, though already in existence, needed to be united behind a comprehensive program.[27]

These agencies functioned almost exclusively to coordinate the work of member denominations, many of which had their own wartime commissions. For example, the National Lutheran Council operated as the primary agency for Lutheran churches (Missouri Synod being a notable exception). The council served as the umbrella organization for a number of wartime committees and projects, like the Lutheran Emergency Appeal campaign for "orphaned missions" and relief work, Lutheran Service Centers for servicemen in the camps, and Lutheran World Action, which supported orphaned missions and aided war refugees. The council also exercised control over the Armed Forces Services Commission, which processed and approved 800 chaplains from Lutheran churches and printed and distributed 400,000 copies of the *Army and Navy Service Book*, 10 million devotional tracts, and 80,000 copies of the monthly paper, *A Mighty Fortress*.[28] Other major denominations had similar organizations.[29]

Typical of the purpose of these organizations was the statement of goals from the Northern Presbyterian's War-Time Service Commission. "To render spiritual service to men in the armed forces in this country, on the high seas, or serving on distant and far-flung fronts; to provide for the spiritual welfare of men, women and children in congested war industry communities in the United States; and to help keep the spirit of Christianity alive in all corners of the globe by aid to the helpless, the suffering and the oppressed."[30] Other denominations retooled already existing agencies, like the Protestant Episcopal Church's Department of Christian Social Relations and the Department of Domestic Missions.[31] The Roman Catholic Church had its own agency, the National Catholic Community Service, founded in 1940 by the National Catholic Welfare Conference, to provide services to defense workers and men in uniform.[32]

Ministries in Defense Communities

The churches quickly launched projects in defense communities to address the problem of massive mobilization. The work proved to be difficult and frustrating. Willard M. Wickizer of the Disciples reported that Disciples churches located in defense communities were doing their best to meet the challenge. Their first priority was to attract displaced Disciples into their churches. Surprisingly, their efforts were being met with some resistance on the part of newcomers who did not want to identify with a Disciples' congregation; and they were not being helped much by the churches from which those displaced Disciples had come, many of which neglected to send the names of members who had moved to other cities.[33]

Still, the churches pressed forward to meet the needs. In Los Angeles, for example, the Church Federation, including over 400 churches, organized activities for children under the supervision of nearly 10,000 volunteers. Over 100,000 children were regularly enrolled, about one-half of whom came from homes in which the mother worked in a defense industry.[34]

Reporting from Vanport, Oregon, Jesse K. Griffiths, the War-Time Service Commission's representative on the United Church Ministry project, said that churches were succeeding in attracting newcomers to morning and evening worship. The United Church's Youth Fellowship, moreover, was organizing a variety of activities for the children of defense workers in the community. Griffiths himself was busy "day and night" making house calls and administering the Sabbath school program for children.[35]

In 1944 the Northern Baptist Convention instituted a service summer project, under the auspices of the Baptist Youth Fellowship. A team of five young people worked for six weeks at a new Baptist church near Willow Run, site of Henry Ford's huge bomber plant. They operated a vacation church school in the mornings and visited families in the afternoon.[36]

Through the War-Time Service Commission Northern Presbyterians started projects in 204 strategically located areas. These projects employed 158 people who worked with local churches to reach new residents in their communities and to adapt church programs to meet the emergency. Presbyterians remodeled old church buildings, erected new ones, or used a mobile ministry to create enough space to carry on their work. Sometimes industrial chaplains were hired to head up these projects.[37]

The Lutherans seemed particularly poised for action in this area of service. For example, the National Lutheran Council organized a special program for youth in defense communities. A staff of eighteen full-time pastors and thirty-six women, known as the Defense Area Visitors, supervised Scout Troops, Luther Leagues, Bible classes, and youth choirs for children in defense area housing projects. They even planned Youth Rally Services to reach Lutheran young people who had recently moved to defense communities. In Washington, D.C., over 300 young people attended the first one.[38] Lutherans also commissioned chaplains to work in defense communities. One of these chaplains, Orville E. Lueck, worked in Dundalk, Maryland, where he presided over worship services and organized other activities for the "new immigrant" of the 1940s.[39] The Missouri Synod was active in this field, too. By 1943 it had initiated projects in nearly 25 different industrial districts.[40]

The churches, then, began ministries in a variety of settings to address the needs brought on by wartime mobilization. In the face of actual human need, these churches were quick to respond. But when mobilization threatened traditional Christian convictions and institutions, as in the case of church-related college education, Christian leaders became less enthusiastic. They wanted the church to expand its influence, but not at the expense of cherished values. They cared deeply about the millions of people displaced by the massive mobilization of the Second World War. But they believed that only a church that looked at mobilization critically would be prepared to meet the needs of the millions of people on the move.

CHAPTER NINE

MINISTRY & THE MILITARY

The churches, as we have seen, mobilized people and resources to minister to millions of civilians working in defense industries. They also channeled their energy to meet the needs of the millions of men and women in uniform. By far the most visible of the ministries to servicemen and servicewomen was done through the work of military chaplains.

Long before the Second World War the churches had commissioned chaplains to serve in the armed forces. Passage of the Burke-Wadsworth Conscription Bill, however, meant that this traditional form of service was inadequate to meet the needs of the swelling military, which grew from an already large one million in 1941 to some ten million by 1945.

Christian leaders were aware of the problems that accompanied this unprecedented growth. "We are concerned," announced Aldis L. Webb of the Disciples. According to Webb, ready access to liquor, the popularity of gambling, the apathy of public officials, and the lack of privacy for soldiers created unhealthy conditions for these young men. They were forced into an environment that was inhospitable to Christian principles. "There is no escape from it, no release, no opportunity to dodge, and it soon gets more than tiresome."[1] Christian Reformed pastor J. H. Schaal also noted the intense scrutiny that Christian soldiers faced if they were serious about living out their Christian beliefs. It put them under intolerable pressure. But if they endured, Schaal added, these men would achieve a durable faith fit to last for a lifetime. "Advance he must, for the Christian life, regardless where it is lived, cannot remain static but will show either retrogression or progression."[2]

But there was serious question whether or not that faith would in fact endure. Church leaders pondered that question often during the war. Leaders did not agree on the correct answer. Some argued that interest in religion was on the rise because, as it was often said, "there are no atheists in foxholes." Others believed that it was on the decline. Whatever the thrust of the argument, they assumed that servicemen needed religious support, desperately so, and that the churches were responsible to provide it.[3]

Morale

Church leaders exhorted local churches and the families of servicemen to do everything they could to build morale and faith. Writing for the *Baptist Leader*, George S. Young suggested that local churches provide their soldiers with a good send-off, inform them of important church and community news, send useful gifts, and pray diligently for them.[4]

There were appeals everywhere to send the soldiers mail. "Morale is mail," declared Chaplain W. H. McKinney in his address at the International Convention of the Disciples of Christ. Commenting on his speech, editor Raphael Harwood Miller advised:

> Write cheerful, homey letters. Let him know you are taking your "share of hardness like a good soldier," on the home front. Strikes, demand for higher wages and income, complaint about taxes and about appeals for the national war fund, religious controversies, racial intolerance and party strife recorded in letters and papers sent to the boys at the front are acts of sabotage beyond the reach of law. . . . Letters which indicate the cooling of love and fidelity upon the part of brides left behind after a brief honeymoon, carelessness in associations while he is away, frivolous living while he faces life's ultimate tragedies, have disastrous results. They make wounds which no drugs can heal and put death in the heart of a living man.[5]

Church members and pastors did, in fact, write to their servicemen, regularly. In a survey of the Evangelical and Reformed churches conducted shortly after the war, 86 percent of the pastors responding to the survey reported that they periodically encouraged their congregation to correspond with servicemen, well over 60 percent sent them gifts and the weekly church bulletin, and nearly 60 percent wrote monthly letters. Correspondence was important because it built morale and kept servicemen in the faith.[6] The *Churchman* printed one such letter, sent just after a man's son went off to war.

> I will not worry about the future for you. You are in God's hands. I have committed you to His care and blessing. Therefore, I have accepted in faith the joy of being able to depend entirely upon His will and your cooperation with His will. You are with God and He is with you, whether you are here at home or at the battlefront. This is enough for me! I accept the future with a peace in my heart, confident that "all things work out for the best to those who love God, according to His purpose." Put yourself in His hands, Son. You trust me, your flesh and blood father. Remember, His love and care for you are greater than mine, because He is the Father Creator of us all! I am proud of you, Son! I know you will be a good soldier, for you are a good son.[7]

The churches also sent literature, which numbered into the millions of pieces. In 1944 alone the National Lutheran Council sent 4,240,000 tracts and devotionals, 188,500 *Service Prayer Books*, and 125,000 copies of the *Army and Navy Service Book*. Popular among the men and women in the service was the pocket calendar, which contained a brief prayer on one side. Soldiers also requested pamphlets and devotionals like "The Lord's Prayer," "My Faith," "Release from Worry," "Ready for Battle?" and "Arrow Prayers." Typical of the message of these pamphlets is the following paragraph taken from "I Need Not Walk Alone": "So many dear, familiar things I leave behind. . . . And yet, I do not walk alone into a strange and distant world. . . . The smile of courage on my mother's face is with me still. . . . My church remembers, too. High on a service flag I see a star, for me. . . . And in this moment there is born within my heart the sure, clear knowledge that even in uttermost parts God walks with me, all the way. . . . I have just said good-by to many things I love . . . and yet I do not walk alone. Thank God I need not walk alone."[8]

The churches were especially intent on sending Bibles. The fundamentalist Business Men's Council of the Pocket Testament League gained permission from the government to distribute New Testaments, free of charge, to servicemen. In 1944 the American Bible Society gave 400,000 Bibles, 1,800,000 New Testaments, and 1,500,000 Scripture portions to chaplains for distribution to servicemen. The religious press often carried inspirational stories telling how the Bible sustained the faith of servicemen in difficult circumstances. Sergeant John F. Bartek read aloud daily from a water-soaked

Bible to Captain Eddie Rickenbacker and the other survivors of a plane crash while they were helplessly adrift in the Pacific Ocean for three weeks. Their story inspired the navy and merchant marine to put a New Testament in a waterproof packet in every life raft. One soldier wrote about his appreciation for the Bible to the chief of chaplains: "We were under artillery fire and a church assembly was out of the question. But being quite a determined man, the chaplain solved this by sending a message together with several Testaments to the various foxholes. The message requested us to read several verses in the Testament, then pass the note and the book on to the next foxhole. We didn't go to church; the church that cold, windy Sunday came to us. In view of what lay in store for us the next week, I appreciate now those few verses from the Scriptures."[9]

The churches also sent religious magazines to servicemen. *Moody Monthly*, for example, had at least two pages of every issue devoted to the "men in service" and printed other inspirational articles for their spiritual encouragement. They sent out thousands of these magazines to men in camps and on the front lines.[10]

To gain firsthand knowledge of camp conditions and to encourage soldiers to remain faithful, prominent religious leaders sometimes visited servicemen at the camps and wrote about their experiences. These ambassadorial visits boosted morale among soldiers and comforted church members and families who wanted to let "their boys" know that they stood with them. Daniel A. Poling traveled to Europe and recorded his experiences in the popular *Christian Herald*, of which he was the editor. Cardinal Francis J. Spellman also went to the European front and wrote a book about his experiences.[11]

Christians prayed for servicemen, too. Harold Hafer has recorded that 95 percent of the pastors responding to his survey prayed regularly for servicemen in worship services. The World's Christian Fundamentals Association launched a movement to establish 10,000 Victory Prayer Meetings nationwide. Leaders of the association planned to have one or more groups in every community in America meet at least once a week for prayer. They were to make three requests: the salvation of servicemen, the safety of servicemen, and a national revival. Members of the First Baptist Church of Nashville started a program of continuous prayer for those in uniform. Begun on May 31, 1942, participants volunteered to pray at fifteen-minute intervals every day of the week, for the duration of the war. Nearly 1,000 people signed up for the program.[12]

Even the Brethren Church, whose official policy forbade military service, organized a committee to maintain contact with members who elected to join the military rather than to register as conscientious objectors. Members of the committee kept current records on these men, which numbered about 2,300 by the end of 1942. They prepared quarterly bulletins and carried on personal correspondence with some of the men, enlisted the help of 60 pastors to visit them in the camps, and asked missionaries on the field to provide hospitality to soldiers fighting in the Pacific theater.[13]

Many local churches also developed their own programs of ministry for servicemen. The First Christian Church of Orange, California, for example, presented each soldier with a New Testament and a box of stationary with his name and a picture of the church inscribed on it. Organizations of the church sent "care packages" to the servicemen. The minister of the church, Myron C. Cole, wrote bimonthly letters to the men, and he also contacted each man's chaplain to provide him with information about the soldier and to request that he send word after initial contact had been made. There were two purposes for this ministry, according to Cole. He explained: "First, we want the young men to know that the people of their church are interested in their welfare. They need to be reminded that the congregation of the home church is thinking of them and praying that the spirit of God might be in them. Our sons in the service must be remembered! Second, a few of the men have been lax in church attendance and interest, and it is felt that the continuous contact with them will rekindle their interest, bringing them home more anxious to serve and help in the program of the church."[14]

Some churches started programs to meet the needs of servicemen's wives, often left friendless and churchless because of frequent moves. Episcopalian wives were helped by the Woman's Auxiliary's Little Blue Boxes. Under its auspices Mrs. Roswell Blair, a navy churchwoman, founded a service committee of the United Thank Offering to form stronger ties between local churches and the wives of servicemen. She and her coworkers kept a file of names and notified Episcopalian churches of service wives who were moving to their community. By 1943 there were ten branch committees striving to include service wives in local churches. Initial contact with these women was made by bringing them a "box" of useful items.[15]

Ministry in Defense Camps

These ministries to servicemen demonstrated that the churches were ready to do their patriotic duty during the war. Few raised objections about these expressions of service. If anything, church leaders looked for every opportunity to meet the needs of servicemen. One of the most obvious and critical fields of service to soldiers was in defense camps. Church leaders were aware of the mass movement of these millions of men, and they initiated ministries in military camps to bring the church to them, because, in many cases, the soldiers could not get to church regularly. They were not oblivious to the magnitude of the challenge. "A year or so ago," wrote a Baptist church leader in early 1942, "the young men of America were doing about as they pleased. Today something like a million of them have been taken from their homes and sent to camp. That constitutes a major movement of the age—and a major challenge to the church."[16]

If the ministry of the church was ever needed, it was in these training camps. The churches moved quickly to organize for action. As early as May 1941 the Disciples recognized "the obligation of the church to follow these men wherever conscience or the circumstances of life may take them and to provide for them such moral and spiritual guidance as it can give." They responded to the need by initiating a program of ministry. They also supported the Christian Commission for Camp Communities, set up by the Home Mission Council and the Federal Council of the Churches (FCC), and they formed their own committee on Religious Service to Men in Camps. These committees worked with other church agencies to assist Disciples churches located in camp communities.[17]

The National Lutheran Council organized the Service Men's Division, which was headquartered in Minneapolis and directed by Nils M. Ylvisaker, a chaplain during the First World War and former president of the Chaplains' Association of the Army and Navy. The first fund-raising campaign in Lutheran churches was held on Mother's Day, 1941. The Service Men's Division had three goals: first, to serve Lutheran chaplains by providing literature and assistance; second, to assist local churches in their ministry to servicemen in camps; third, to establish centers in communities adjoining training camps where trainees could go for worship and recreation.

To meet that third goal, the National Lutheran Council established Lutheran Service Centers across the United States to provide hospitality, recreation, and spiritual nurture for Lutheran soldiers in training camps. These centers were overwhelmingly successful. Located at Lutheran churches, rented halls, or hotels near the camps, they provided refreshments, entertainment, and facilities where the soldiers could meet fellow soldiers and civilians living in the community. In 1943 alone close to two million servicemen visited these Lutheran centers. In the center in San Antonio, Texas, soldiers were able to meet in an auditorium for entertainment, use a gym for recreation, and sit in a lounge to eat and converse. Carl Lux, a Lutheran from Waco and "as Teutonic as a pretzel," joined the staff as athletic director. Lux had lifted weights and competed in gymnastics on the 1924 U.S. Olympic team. Servicemen by the hundreds signed up for his programs. The San Antonio center also printed maps for soldiers showing them where every Lutheran church in town was located. Many found their way to local Lutheran churches, where they were welcomed warmly and often given hospitality. One local family, the Henningsens, had up to seventeen Lutheran soldiers over for dinner every Sunday. The Center welcomed more than Lutherans. Six hundred Catholics registered at the center, with Baptists close behind. Even Muslims and Buddhists visited. Staff members from the center had contact with the families and pastors of the soldiers, and they responded to hundreds of seemingly insignificant needs, making soldiers feel like someone cared.[18]

The Northern Presbyterians started programs in the camps, too. By invitation of the Defense Service Council of the Southern Presbyterians, the Emergency Service Commission sent a group of about a dozen ministers each month into the South to work cooperatively with chaplains and local churches to serve Presbyterian soldiers from the Northern Church. The War-Time Service Commission, the umbrella organization for Northern Presbyterian wartime work, administered projects and programs in every conceivable field of wartime service, including, of course, defense camps. By May 1945 the commission had raised and distributed over $3,700,000 and had developed ministries in defense camps across America. One of its most effective was the founding of hospitality houses near thirteen military camps. The War-Time Service Commission also helped local churches meet the needs of the men in the camps. The First Church of Salt Lake City, for example, served soldiers a supper every Sunday evening and then held a worship service for them. On New Year's Day one thousand guests, many of them soldiers, gathered to observe the national day of prayer. From two o'clock in the afternoon to eight o'clock in the evening the church held a series of seven worship services; following worship, each group was served dinner.[19] Southern Presbyterians developed a similar program, under the able direction of Dan T. Caldwell.[20]

Evangelism was an important priority for at least some of the churches. Concerned about the one million plus Baptists in the armed services and the tens of thousands who had no personal faith and church home, the Home Mission Board of the Southern Baptist Convention initiated service projects in a number of camps, usually in the South.[21] Fundamentalists shared the same concern. The Philadelphia Fundamentalist Organization established the Morning Cheer Center for Service Men near Fort Dix. Supervised by Harry Rimmer and Samuel Coleman, the center was located in a large building which contained an auditorium, gymnasium, reception room with fireplace, game room, library, and a lounge. The center provided refreshments, Christian literature, and stationary. It also hosted gospel meetings every Wednesday and Sunday nights. On some days over 1,000 servicemen visited the center, and as many as 300 attended the gospel meetings. Fundamentalists like Rimmer believed that the war made the ministry of evangelism particularly important. Soldiers were eager to hear good news, and fundamentalists were ready to preach it.[22]

The National Catholic Community Service (NCCS) worked in defense camps, too, opening clubs in many cities to provide spiritual and social services to Catholics. They often served as a link between displaced Catholics and the home parish. In one case a frantic father called an NCCS club to say that his son, a young officer, had been honorably discharged by the army for a physical disability. His son was so crushed and distressed that he had locked himself in a hotel room and had gotten drunk. The father begged the director of the NCCS to see his son, help him overcome his bitter disappointment, and get him home safely. The director rushed to the hotel and, after a half hour of pleading, finally persuaded him to unlock the door. He spent six more hours with him until, sober and strengthened, the ex-soldier was able to board a train for home.[23]

The overwhelming challenge of meeting the needs of soldiers forced churches to work cooperatively. The most visible and successful example of this cooperation was the founding in November 1942 of the Service Men's Christian League under the inspiration and direction of Bishop Adna Wright Leonard and Daniel A. Poling. Representatives from over forty Protestant denominations in America worked together to organize the agency and develop its programs. Such nondenominational organizations as the Federal Council of Churches and the World's Christian Endeavor Union also supported it. The league was governed by an executive council of five high-ranking chaplains and twenty-five representatives from cooperating denominations. Likened to a local church's Sunday school and youth program, the league assisted the work of military chaplains, unified Protestants in the military, developed programs in evangelism, fellowship, and education, and helped servicemen maintain their church affiliation. Provision was also made for WAACs and WAVEs, called the Service Women's Christian League. To supply servicemen with a regular diet of Christian literature, the league published the *Link*, a monthly religious magazine.

The founding of the Service Men's Christian League reflected a Protestant concern about cooperation and unity. During the First World War there had been no organization formed to integrate the work of Protestant chaplains and to make Protestant services available to all men in the military. Protestant leaders did not want to be remiss again. Previous failure, however, was not their only concern. They were also alarmed by the power and influence of the Catholic Church, whose Holy Name Society ministered so effectively to Catholics in uniform.[24] The Service Men's Christian League was the Protestant's answer to that society.

Protestants and Catholics were not entirely opposed to working cooperatively. The interdenominational United Service Organization (USO), which provided recreational, social, and religious services for men and women in the military, gave them such an opportunity. Protestants, Catholics, and Jews were all represented in the USO. Protestants, in fact, had greater representation than Catholics and Jews because the YMCA, YWCA, and Salvation Army, all Protestant agencies, were three of the six member organizations (the others were the Traveler's Aid, Jewish Welfare Board, and National Catholic Community Service).

The work of the USO, however, did not mollify the fears and suspicions of some Protestants, who were carefully eyeing the growth of Catholic power in America. Ministry in the military provided yet another occasion for Protestant criticism of Catholic ambition. The war did not altogether ease the tension, at least not initially. In their minds, the USO represented another example of Catholic encroachment on Protestant America. These Protestants complained often of being underrepresented or misrepresented in the USO. At a conference of over a thousand ministers on the East Coast held at the First Presbyterian Church of Baltimore, Worth M. Tippy, executive secretary of the Washington Federation of Churches, and John W. Harms, executive secretary of the Council of Churches and Christian Education of Maryland and Delaware, issued a joint statement charging that the Protestant churches lacked adequate representation in the USO. "The Protestant churches as a corporate entity," the statement read, "are not included in the USO; nor have they delegated their ministries to any of the agencies in it." Though the Salvation Army was Protestant, Tippy and Harms argued that over the years it had become a denomination and a religious social service agency with its own methods and functions. They added that the

YMCA and YWCA were historically Protestant agencies that no longer identified with the official ecclesiastical life of Protestantism.

Apparently Protestants themselves were partly to blame, or so critics claimed. While the Protestant churches had contributed huge sums of money to the USO, they had not taken steps to participate more actively in USO activities. John W. Bradbury believed that Protestantism was thus losing ground to Catholicism and overlooking an opportunity for service in the war. "The Roman Catholic hierarchy is a centralized unit and as such is in a position of tremendous advantage of which it has not hesitated to make full use. Catholics have their own buildings and, in a very large number of cases, are in control of USO structures and programs. The same is true of the Jewish organization. They are centralized and are able to function easily." Bradbury suggested that each Protestant denomination appoint its own USO committee and that Protestant leaders gather in Washington to address the problem. He concluded: "The Christian churches of this country must abandon their aloofness from the military situation and immediately assume the responsibility that is theirs. The personnel of the armed forces are drawn from Protestant areas overwhelmingly, and for their churches to have no effective voice or leadership in the USO services is one of the most foolish and dangerous conditions we could ever have allowed to come about."[25]

Prodded by many denominational agencies and leaders, members of the Federal Council of Churches Christian Commission for Camp and Defense Communities launched an investigation of the problem. Members of the commission met with representatives of the YMCA for an "unhurried consultation" in April 1942 to discuss the situation. The consultation relieved the concerns of the Federal Council leaders. They decided to nominate representative church leaders to serve as members of the YMCA's Army and Navy Committee, which was responsible for the policy, program, and personnel of the YMCA in the USO. Further, they moved to have the national board of the YMCA include greater FCC participation in their field conferences for USO activities and to mandate that each USO-YMCA director make greater cooperation a specific responsibility. They suggested that though YMCA boards were composed almost entirely of the laity, the YMCA-operated USO clubs include representative ministers on their boards and allow local church federations to nominate those representatives. Finally, they affirmed the need for YMCA officials and Protestant leaders to collaborate in creating an effective program—a religious program in particular—for men in uniform. The YMCA, therefore, recognized "the primary responsibility of the churches for the spiritual care and guidance of the men."[26] After the meeting the FCC sent a report to its member churches. The controversy gradually dissipated and the work of the USO continued to unify religious groups in America in their service to the military.

This controversy over the work of the USO demonstrated that Protestants in particular did not readily devote themselves to wartime ministry at the expense of compromising their own identity as Protestants. Even during a war religious conflict continued because the churches were not willing to surrender ground for the sake of national unity and victory. The war, in fact, was interpreted as a battle to preserve the prominence of religion *in* America, not simply the religion *of* America.

Military Chaplains

Christian leaders believed that the churches could have the most effective ministry among servicemen through the work of chaplains. The churches, therefore, worked hard to recruit and assist chaplains during the Second World War. Nearly 10,000 served in the military sometime between 1939 and 1945. They ministered to men and women in the army, army air corps, navy, and air force. They were supervised by the official endorsing agencies of religious bodies in America—the Military Ordinariate of the Roman Catholic Church, the Jewish Welfare Board's Committee on Army and Navy Religious Activities, and the Federal Council of Churches General Commission on Army and Navy Chaplains. The General Commission became independent of the FCC in 1940, although it remained closely linked. Some denominations, like the Methodists and Southern Baptists, did not work directly with the General Commission. Instead, they set up their own committees and sent their endorsements directly to the army and navy.

The chief of chaplains, Major General William R. Arnold, a Roman Catholic, had official responsibility to work with these ecclesiastical endorsing agencies. Arnold designated the number of chaplains needed for duty, determined the denominational quotas based on the religious census of 1936, and administered the program. He also developed criteria for chaplain selection, and he organized the training of chaplains. During the Second World War chaplains were trained at the Chaplain School, first located at Fort Benjamin Harrison in Indiana, then at Harvard University, and finally at Fort Devens in Massachusetts. Sessions ran twenty-eight days, with 200 hours of instruction in such topics as military organization and law, graves registration, first aid, choir organization, venereal disease control, and personal counseling.

The chief of staff also called chaplain conferences and provided supervisory chaplains to assist chaplains on larger bases. A circular letter, the filing of reports, and staff visits helped to make the chaplains unit of the military, as General George C. Marshall said, "the best run group of the army."

Chaplains were primarily responsible for providing religious services to military personnel. Sunday worship was not the only religious service available. Chaplains proved themselves to be flexible and creative in the programs they offered. They emphasized daily devotions, organized premission services, attended briefings, and were present whenever servicemen were going to or returning from battle. They presided over worship services observing the religious year—lent, Holy Week, Passover. They sent letters home to the parents of Catholics indicating that their sons had taken communion. They also planned special religious activities for New Year's Day, Days of Prayers, Armistice Day, Mother's Day, and V-E and V-J Days. Special preaching missions were included in their duties.

Chaplains administered the sacraments, most frequently communion. Catholics had little trouble carrying out this responsibility, because communion was a part of the Mass. It created bigger problems for Protestants, inasmuch as Protestant communion services differed from each other both theologically and technically. Protestant chaplains resolved these problems by administering communion in a service separate from regular worship. Sometimes chaplains performed weddings, too, although military leaders frowned on wartime marriages, especially on the Pacific front. Funerals also fell under the responsibility of chaplains. The death of servicemen on American soil meant that chaplains would only have to officiate at a memorial service. Not so in Europe, Africa, or Asia, where chaplains were often required to arrange the entire funeral, including lining up the color guard, pallbearers, firing squad, and bugler. Though providing unusual opportunities for ministry, funerals nevertheless remained one of the grim duties of chaplains' wartime work.

Still, there was often a note of triumph in them. Daniel A. Poling, whose son, a chaplain, died in the sinking of the USS *Dorchester*, expressed this sentiment in a poem:

> They keep their rendezvous with death.
> So valiantly and soon;
> They pledge their youth and give their all
> And rest before their noon.

Now God will give them greater things,
　　And keep them by His side;
And, rested, they shall build new worlds,
　　Where death itself has died.

Upon hearing of a soldier's death, chaplains notified next of kin, usually through letters. Air force chaplains were even known on occasion to visit the sites of plane crashes to lead a memorial service. To protect servicemen from death, chaplains even blessed the instruments of war, like ships, guns, and planes.

Chaplains kept in constant contact with servicemen. It was learned in one survey, for example, that two chaplains had conducted over 1,000 personal interviews in just over a month and a half. Chaplains visited work areas, barracks, mess halls, clubs, hospitals, and guardhouses. A survey conducted in 1943 showed that chaplains averaged over fourteen such visits a month. Religious education was an important duty, too. Chaplains conducted Bible classes, prepared servicemen for church membership, counseled prospective priests, rabbis or ministers, lectured on such topics as sexual morality and citizenship, and organized recreational activities.

Chaplains were often forced into public relations work. Some were required to write articles for denominational journals, lecture to civilian communities on military life, and organize special meetings with community leaders of other countries. In addition, some of the chaplains in the Pacific theater of operations preached in native churches and visited orphanages, hospitals, leper colonies, and missionary outposts. After the war they distributed food and clothing, helped to rebuild hospitals, and assisted natives in constructing new churches.

The armed services backed the work of chaplains by providing the resources they needed to carry out their duties. As late as 1939 only 17 chapels had been built at posts or airfields in the entire history of the Army. All that changed during the Second World War. Chief of Chaplains Arnold collaborated with General Marshall to ensure that the construction of chapels would be included in the master plan of every base. Arnold suggested that small chapels be built for each regiment and that these chapels be appropriate and available to all faiths. In March 1941 Congress authorized the expenditure of over $14 million for the construction of 604 chapels, each to seat up to 600 men. That number increased until, by war's end, 1,532 chapels were in use. Servicemen themselves often helped in their construction, especially in foreign theaters. They used astonishing ingenuity to accomplish their projects. Chaplain Walter Osborne, for example, built a chapel at Cazes airport near Casablanca from scrap boxes. A German prisoner of war painted a religious mural for it, and Portuguese civilians donated a ship's bell and stained glass windows. Army and navy men built 150 chapels on islands in the South and Southwest Pacific, usually from native materials and in a native style.

The military apportioned chaplains with necessary equipment and supplies. For chapels they provided ecclesiastical appointments, such as brass baptismal bowl and candlesticks, as well as such religious articles or necessities as altar hangings, chaplain's Bible, communion sets with individual cups, sacramental wine, and certificates of marriage and baptism. They also made available a "chaplain's outfit" for use on the field.[27]

If chaplains had any doubts about their usefulness, they soon discovered that the overwhelming needs of servicemen—family troubles, the death of close friends, immorality, drunkenness, loneliness, fear—called for the kind of spiritual assistance that chaplains could provide. Chaplains proved to be very popular in the war, both to soldiers and to civilians. Their stories were told in film and in print. Typical of these stories was one told about Chaplain Herbert Rieke, who was stationed in North Africa. He was assigned to a group of pilots who were ordered to drop supplies from a base in Algiers to partisans in the mountains of southern France. As a rule, the missions were dangerous and often ended in failure and death. Chaplain Rieke flew on one such mission, claiming that "God hath not given us the spirit of fear, but of power and of love and of sound mind." The mission was successful, and the operations officer asked the chaplain to fly with other planes on which he claimed there was a "jinx."[28]

The most famous chaplain story, "The Silver Cord," was told about the heroic death of four chaplains—Clark Poling of the Reformed Church, George L. Fox, a Methodist, Alexander Goode, a Jewish rabbi, and John P. Washington, a Roman Catholic—on the USS *Dorchester*, a troopship. Torpedoed by a German submarine, the ship began to sink. Panic swept the deck. Life rafts went overboard; some men slid down the ropes, while others jumped. The four chaplains, however, remained on deck and quieted the men still stranded there. Then, as the deck was clearing, four young soldiers appeared, all without life belts. The four chaplains stopped the beltless men. After a short conversation the chaplains took off their life belts and gave them to the soldiers, who escaped over the side of the deck. The chaplains stayed behind. When there was no one left for them to help, the four chaplains knelt together in prayer. The life rafts drifted away, and the four of them, linked arm to arm, went down with the ship. That the four represented three different faith traditions in America—Protestant, Catholic, and Jewish—carried special meaning. "They were four strong men from the ends of the earth, as far apart theologically as the poles are apart. Yet among them ran that silver cord of the Spirit which binds true men of God together in that spiritual camaraderie which only they and God can ever understand." That the four were chaplains made their sacrifice poignantly spiritual. "Look at them there, all ye who are saying that Jesus Christ is dead! Look at them, ye who are asking so bitterly, 'Mankind is being crucified—and where is God?' Look at them, and lift your faces and lay hold upon the silver cord and know that hope did not die on Calvary, that there are still among us, as leaven from heaven, men made in the mold of the Christ."[29] The story of their death captured the attention of the nation. Later, it was commemorated in a special postage stamp.

Countless other chaplain stories, less sensational but no less inspirational, were written up in religious periodicals. For example, Chaplain Edwin L. Kirtley of the Disciples was awarded the Silver Star for heroic service on the Marshall Islands. During a battle Kirtley searched the front lines for groups of natives who were trapped in the crossfire, huddled helplessly in small blasted bomb shelters. Through a newly acquired knowledge of the native tongue, he was able to gain their confidence and lead them out of the battlefield to safety. He discovered later that many of the natives were Christians. After reaching safety, they held their first public worship since being conquered by the Japanese. Their pastor preached the sermon, "Jesus Christ has come back to us."[30]

Church leaders back home knew how influential the ministry of the chaplains was. Their ministry enabled the churches to demonstrate their patriotism to the nation, keep their own servicemen tied to the church, and expand their influence beyond the borders of their own denomination. The work of Catholic chaplains provided a special opportunity for the Catholic Church, which wanted to prove that it was truly American, and it enabled Protestants to unify their divided forces under a common purpose. Both Protestants and Catholics, then, benefited from this patriotic service.

The ministry of the chaplains was so important to church leaders that they actively recruited them, not leaving their calling to mere chance or providence. General Marshall had decided early on in the war to set a quota of 1 chaplain for every 1,000 troops. When the size of the armed services swelled to over 8 million in 1943, the churches had to recruit over 8,000 chaplains. Appeals surfaced everywhere. "Who will go for us?" asked the editor of the *Federal Council Bulletin* in 1943. At least 6,000 chaplains, he wrote, were already on active duty; 4,000 more were needed by the end of 1943. Of this number roughly two-thirds were supposed to come from Protestant groups. Though he recognized the difficulty of releasing so many pastors from churches, he declared that "it must be done" anyway. He appealed to the consciences of young ministers and the patriotic sentiments of congregations. "The younger pastors, who fall within the age limits for military service, cannot escape asking themselves whether they are right in remaining at home while so many of their youth are called to the hardship of war. . . . Congregations must also seriously reflect whether they are doing all they should to make it possible for their pastors to become chaplains." He wondered whether the church was alert to the opportunity.

> The whole Church needs to be more alert to the greatness of its opportunity in the chaplaincy. In the Army and Navy today are found millions of young men—and increasingly a large body of young women also—to whom the Church must minister. Some of them are its own sons and daughters—it must follow them with its spiritual nurture. Others are outside the Church, yet in their new situation they are more open to the Christian message: they are the greatest evangelistic challenge to the Church today. What the Church does or fails to do with reference to both of these groups will go far in determining its influence in the next generation.[31]

Following the lead of the FCC, virtually every religious body in America, with the exception of the historic peace churches, made appeals to the churches to recruit more chaplains. Two basic arguments were used: they had to fill their quota to stay competitive with other religious groups, and they had to recruit more chaplains to expand their influence among both servicemen and civilians.[32]

So important was this ministry that some Protestant leaders complained that the churches were neglecting this field of service. In a statement appearing in *Christianity and Crisis*, they suggested that the General Commission increase its budget, appoint religious leaders of national repute to devote more time to recruitment and oversight, and print more religious literature for the chaplains. Not surprisingly, the statement pointed out the advantages that Catholics had, making Protestant defects all the more glaring. Protestants, it stated, had to "make a more vigorous effort to overcome them."[33]

James Gordon Gilkey Jr. addressed a different problem. He charged Protestants to face up to the religious barrenness of Protestantism. While Catholics had daily Mass to remind the priest of his religious function as chaplain, the Protestant chaplain had no such reminders, except on Sunday. "Altogether too many Protestant ministers, having no daily religious duties, become so immersed in non-religious activities that only on Sundays is it apparent that they are ministers rather than social workers."[34]

The churches, then, proved their patriotic loyalty to the nation through these various forms of service to soldiers. Most religious groups in America came near to meeting their quotas for chaplains, and some exceeded those quotas (the one exception was the African American churches, which fell far short). The churches raised funds, provided a variety of programs for men and women in uniform, and reported frequently on the work of their chaplains to the faithful working on the home front. There is no question that the churches were committed to this ministry.

Controversies

Yet there were still areas of concern. Church leaders were not ready to subordinate their spiritual ministry to the control of the state. They wanted to maintain some kind of independence. At a meeting of Congregational chaplains from New England organized by Frederick L. Fagley, the official chaplain's representative of the Congregational Church, the chaplains agreed to a man that their work was essential but would only be effective if it transcended the immediate goals of the military. William E. Gilroy, the editor of *Advance*, attended the meeting. "An outstanding impression of the gathering," he reported, "was of the unanimity and intensity of the group in their abhorrence of war and in the primacy of their devotion to peace. They insisted that they were pacifists in the true sense in devoting themselves to the attainment of peace, though not accepting the position of non-resistance or conscientious objection." He continued: "Discussion showed an equal unanimity and insistence upon their essential status and the nature of their service as chaplains. When the question was asked, What is the chaplain's function? To win victory? To help build an efficient war machine? To act as morale officer? the protest was immediate, definite, and apparently unanimous that his primary task and duty was none of these but to meet spiritual needs, and the spiritual needs of individuals." On the problem of war itself, Gilroy reported that the chaplains "felt the discrepancy between ideals and realities and they were confronted with the dilemma that confronts every Christian in wartime, even though resort to war may be the only means of defending homes, lives and institution and of serving the cause of peace."[35] The chaplains at the conference seemed hesitant to move too far in the direction of uncritical support of the war machine.

This same caution surfaced more forcefully among the Disciples. Some expressed strong misgivings about the very idea of the military chaplaincy. They doubted whether it was possible to function as a military chaplain without also serving the military system. At their 1936 convention the Disciples resolved, by a sizable majority, that the International Convention request its United Christian Missionary Society "to withdraw our official representation from the Chaplaincy Commission of the Federal Council of Churches and abstain from further participation therein." It also requested the FCC "to sever its official connection with the war system by dissolving its chaplaincy commission." Finally, it resolved to ask the council "to provide a non-military ministry of religion to men in the armed services at the churches' own expense and under their own authority, without involving the Church of Christ in any alliance whatsoever with the state or the military system."[36]

Confusion followed the passing of the resolution. Chaplains from the Disciples were already serving in the military; it was unclear how they could receive endorsement from the church after the resolution was passed. They solved this problem by setting up their own committee that functioned independently from the denomination. They accused the convention of not faithfully representing the opinions of the majority of the churches. At the St. Louis convention in 1941 the issue came up again. Rather than being resolved, it became even more complicated. The chaplains found themselves subject to two committees—their own, which had been functioning already for five years, and the United Society's Department of Social Welfare, which appeared to be entirely unsympathetic with the work of military chaplains.

Debate over the confusing policy followed, showing once again that, though the churches supported wartime ministry, they were unwilling to make the church subservient to the military. Edwin R. Errett, editor of the *Christian Standard*, which spoke for the noncooperating wing of the Disciples, attacked the St. Louis arrangement. He argued that it was unfair to subordinate the chaplains to their unpatriotic "enemies" in the United Society.[37] Though W. E. Garrison, a Chicago professor and editor, agreed with Errett that the ministry of military chaplains was important, he nevertheless had reservations. He believed, for example, that Disciples should be watchful of any attempt on the part of the military to use chaplains to advance military plans. "It ought to be made clear that the function of chaplains is to carry religion to the soldiers and sailors, not to carry the message of the army and navy to the churches." He also recommended that the military arrangement under which rank, pay, and allowances were bestowed on ministers by the War Department be reconsidered and be replaced by a system that would "preserve the principle of voluntarism and separation of church and state in the army and navy as elsewhere in American life."[38] George A. Campbell, acting editor of the *Christian-Evangelist*, interpreted the problem as a matter of confusion over the proper division between church and state. "For the sake of the government itself," he wrote, "the chaplaincy ought to be under the jurisdiction of the churches. The separation of church and state is as important to liberal democracy as it is to Protestant Christianity." He advocated that the chaplaincy be operated exclusively as a religious service, for the sake of the church's "independence."[39]

The Disciples were not the only ones to raise questions about the chaplaincy. In 1940 the Box Butte presbytery overtured the General Assembly of the Presbyterian Church, United States of America, "to direct the Department of Social Education and Action to conduct a study of the Christian ministry to the armed forces of the United States, and to then report specific proposals by which the chaplaincy may be divested of military rank, dress and pay, that chaplains may be truly and wholly the servants of the Church."

The overture was voted down. Stewart M. Robinson, an opponent of the overture and editor of the *Presbyterian*, claimed that the chaplaincy did not make a minister the servant of the state any more than other forms of public service did. He nevertheless believed that chaplains should strive to make their ministry distinctively spiritual so that it be kept from becoming an appendage to the military establishment.[40] Thus even opponents of the overture had reservations about the role of chaplains. They were not willing to let the demands of patriotism turn the church into a tool of the military.

Edwards E. Elliott, pastor of St. Andrew's Orthodox Presbyterian Church, raised questions about the ease with which religious service in the military could undermine true Christian witness. "The function of a truly Christian chaplain may fully satisfy the Army and Navy, but the fact remains that, while the circles overlap, they do not center in the same point. Our idea of a chaplain's duties is not precisely the government's idea. Paternalism inevitably breeds control." In his mind, such control was already too evident. Religious distinctions were being erased and such essential Christian activities as evangelism were being neglected. "We are witnesses," he concluded, "to a break-down of the foundations of our civilization. . . . And our nation as a whole has no ears for this gospel. The armed forces are no exception."[41]

Church leaders saw signs of religious capitulation to wartime necessity. Once again, they wanted to serve the nation, but not at the expense of spiritual integrity. At least a few church leaders, therefore, refused to yield to the government's demand requiring that Christians treat the Sabbath like any other day. The Christian Reformed Church petitioned President Roosevelt to direct his attention to the flagrant violations of the Lord's Day that military and industrial defense work were forcing upon soldiers and civilians. "We are deeply persuaded that these men like all others, should if at all possible meet on the Lord's Day for public worship, in consideration of God's sovereign will and their own spiritual welfare." Though the resolution acknowledged that there were occasions when observance of the Lord's Day was impossible, it urged the president as commander in chief of the armed forces and as chief executive of the nation, "to discourage all Sunday work that is not strictly necessary, and, if need be, to prohibit it by express order or decree."[42] Writing for the *Presbyterian*, Chester M. Davis suggested that America could win the war militarily and still lose it spiritually if the Lord's Day was not protected.[43]

Other church leaders would not allow the military to silence their evangelistic voice. Southern Baptists protested the decision of the army to release Chaplain L. G. Gatlin, pastor of the First Baptist Church of Pulaski, Tennessee, who was discharged because, though upright in character and sincere in faith, he had been "extremely zealous" in his approach to evangelism, which was "considered unadapted to the military service." "His devotion to this type of activity," the text of Gatlin's official release read, "is and has been embarrassing and disquieting to his associates in the Navy; and he devotes himself to such activity to the exclusion of other important duties and services customarily performed by Chaplains and rightfully expected of them." In a sworn statement, Gatlin listed the "duties" he failed to perform: issue whiskey ration books, plan dances for men, teach servicemen the use of prophylactics, administer the sacrament of communion indiscriminately. Writing for the *Western Recorder*, John Huss was outraged. "Can a chaplain be over-zealous in evangelism? Dealing with men whose lives are in peril, is it not a travesty to dismiss a man because he ministers to a man's greatest necessity, namely: the want of his soul?"[44]

Some religious leaders challenged the policy of open communion, too. Again, the issue exposed a basic tension in the minds of some Christian leaders. They wanted the churches to serve the nation, but they did not want to sacrifice their own religious standards in the process. In 1941, for example, the General Synod of the Christian Reformed Church decided to ask the Commission on Army and Navy Chaplains "to petition the government to acknowledge our conviction in this matter [of close communion]," thereby implying that the government's insistence on open communion was a formidable barrier for ministers of the Christian Reformed Church to serve as chaplains in the armed services. Reaction to this synodic decision engendered strong debate in the *Banner* for several months at the end of 1942. Editor H. J. Kuiper received many letters urging the Christian Reformed Church to allow its ministers to serve open communion in the armed forces. One anonymous writer argued: "To bring the gospel to the men who defend our country in its darkest hour is *more important* than maintaining the rule on closed [sic] communion. I take the position that closed communion is normal and ideal, but that an open communion believingly participated in, administered by an orthodox man after a warning as to wrong participation, is not without validity, and can achieve legitimately the end for which communion was instituted."

But editor Kuiper countered by arguing, "to understand that the Church which has opened the communion table to all who feel in their hearts they have the right to partake of this sacrament has surrendered the right to exercise church discipline by barring some as well as admitting others to the Lord's table." Nor, he continued, was it hard to understand why close communion was valid even for administration of the sacrament outside of the organized church. "Even if the *church* would not be profaned by the administration of the sacraments to those who cannot be regarded as believers, *the sacrament itself would thereby be profaned*."[45] Kuiper believed that because chaplains could not exercise discipline in the military and could not protect the sacrament from being profaned, regardless of whether or not elders were present, they could not in good conscience serve as chaplains, unless, of course, they were allowed to administer close communion according to the policy of their denomination.[46]

These debates did not reflect the dominant sentiment of the churches. Still, they showed that at least some Christian leaders were not willing to support the allied cause unless they could also preserve the integrity and independence of their churches. Though the churches for the most part served the spiritual needs of men and women in uniform, a few of their leaders raised questions about how far such service should be allowed to go. Wartime ministry could not be allowed to run roughshod over the church and compromise the particular theological convictions of its many branches.

Church leaders maintained some measure of caution, then, even when they were busy carrying out the most popular of their wartime ministries. Service was acceptable, noble, and right, as long as it was spiritual and moral in nature. It had to serve the needs of a nation at war, yet somehow transcend the war itself.

CHAPTER TEN

CIVIL RIGHTS & THE WAR AT HOME

Americans have always held to the popular belief that their nation is the land of freedom and opportunity for all people. For millions of Americans during World War II, however, the experience of living in America contradicted this popular image. These Americans—Japanese Americans, African Americans, Jehovah's Witnesses, communists and fascists—were often the victims of prejudice, injustice, and persecution. Some lost the freedom to live as their fellow Americans did, others were pressured to fight for freedom and liberty abroad while being deprived of their rights at home, and still others were turned back in their quest for greater freedom in America. The war for freedom and democracy abroad imperiled liberty at home. The movement to secure freedom for all Americans, hardly popular with everyone in peacetime, became decidedly unpopular in wartime.

There were thus two wars in which America fought from 1939 to 1945—the war abroad and the war at home. Both wars challenged the churches to apply religious faith to life in society. The former forced the churches to define the true meaning of Christian patriotism, the latter to expand that meaning to include causes that some Americans considered unpatriotic. The war at home tested the churches' willingness to defend the rights and meet the needs of those Americans who, for the sake of victory abroad, were losing their battle for freedom at home. This domestic war gave the churches an opportunity to enlarge the idea of patriotism beyond what most of their fellow Americans would imagine or accept.

It is remarkable that the churches did anything at all to defend these forsaken Americans. They were pressured by the sheer force of events and the climate of the day to overlook problems at home for the sake of winning victory abroad. Civil liberties were not a popular cause during the war. It would have been understandable if the churches had simply allowed themselves to be carried along by popular sentiment. That they fought the war on the home front at all indicates that their definition of patriotism differed from the popular one of the day. It included a critical dimension because it stood for causes that were decidedly unpopular.

The leaders of the Federal Council of Churches (FCC) were aware of both wars right from the beginning. While opposed to totalitarianism and committed to its defeat, they did not hesitate to associate the exigencies of the war abroad with the necessity of fighting for civil liberties at home. They had objectives in mind that transcended mere military victory. These objectives were outlined in a statement adopted by the FCC in its biennial session on December 11, 1942: "(1) to maintain responsible freedom of thought, freedom of conscience, freedom of economic opportunity, freedom of worship and of religious life; (2) to establish for all men a system of justice based on law; (3) to develop a brotherhood of equal opportunity for all races; (4) to work for a political world-order which shall more fully express the unity of mankind as one family of God; (5) to educate youth in the understanding of Christian objectives and personal commitment to them." The statement went on to say that a united nations victory in the war abroad could not ensure that these "Christian goals" would be achieved.[1] These goals reinforced one argument that Christian leaders used frequently during the war: how can America fight for freedom abroad and deny it to people at home?

Japanese Americans

If there was a group in America during the Second World War that suffered irreparable loss, it was the Japanese Americans on the West coast. Numbering roughly 110,000, they were divided into three groups: the Issei, or immigrants born in Japan; the Nisei, or American-born, American-educated children of the Issei; and the Kibei, or American-born but Japanese-educated. The 40,000 Issei, though permanently excluded from citizenship and deprived of the opportunity to acquire agricultural and residential property by antialien land laws passed in the 1920s, had nevertheless permanently settled in America, where they desired to raise their children and where they prospered in retail and wholesale agricultural work on the West Coast. The 70,000 Nisei, predominantly teenagers and young adults, behaved in speech, dress, and manner like most other Americans. Only 9,000 of these, the Kibei, had taken at least three years of their education in Japan.

Long before Pearl Harbor these Japanese Americans had been subject to cruel and consistent discrimination, the victims of fear, prejudice, and jealously. Pearl Harbor only gave authorities and groups on the West coast an excuse to vent their hostility more aggressively. In early 1942 some 1,500 "enemy aliens," thought to have connections with Japan, were detained by the Department of Justice. The rest of the Japanese Americans were required to register, carry identification cards, and turn over all "contraband," such as cameras, radios, and firearms, to the civil authorities. They were forbidden to travel more than five miles from their homes and required to stay in their homes between eight o'clock in the evening and six o'clock in the morning. Japan's military successes only reinforced the suspicion. Rumors of sabotage in Hawaii and reports of submarine activity off the coast engendered a sense of panic. Citizens became increasingly fearful of an invasion that could be assisted from the inside by Japanese fifth columnists, and they voiced their concerns to Washington. At the same time antialien groups and unscrupulous agricultural competitors stepped up their pressure on the government to take action. Even such notables as journalist Walter Lippmann, California attorney general Earl Warren, and Lieutenant General John L. DeWitt, commanding general of the Western Defense Command in San Francisco, were caught up in the hysteria. Seven members of Congress from the Pacific Coast recommended "the immediate evacuation of all persons of Japanese lineage." DeWitt urged that a similar measure be taken and pressured the president to move quickly for the sake of national security.

On February 19, 1942, President Roosevelt signed Executive Order 9066, which gave the army authority to deal with the enemy alien problem as it wished. General DeWitt then designated the entire western half of California, Oregon, and Washington as a "military area" and announced that all persons of Japanese ancestry would be removed from that area "as a matter of military necessity." He explained that such removal was necessary because the Japanese constituted a "large, unassimilated, tightly-knit racial group bound to an enemy nation by strong ties of race, culture, custom, and religion." Because the Japanese had settled in an area vulnerable to attack—usually near vital shore installations and war plants—they were in a position of collaborating with the enemy by preparing for an invasion or sabotaging American industry.

DeWitt did not always act with noble motives. Though concerned about the safety of the West Coast, he also detested the Japanese. "A Jap is a Jap," he said. "It makes no difference whether he is an American citizen or not; he is still a Japanese. . . . The Japanese race is an enemy race and while many . . . have become 'Americanized,' the racial strains are undiluted. . . . Sabotage and espionage will make problems as long as he is allowed in this area." So convinced was he that the Japanese in America were saboteurs that he commented: "The very fact that no sabotage has taken place to date is a disturbing and confirming indication that such action will be taken."[2]

At first the evacuation was voluntary. Nisei and Kibei were instructed to move out of strategic areas on their own. About 5,000 complied. The request backfired, however, because DeWitt had not prepared the interior for this influx of unwanted Japanese. Consequently, some of them were turned back by Arizona border guards, who treated the Japanese like pieces of diseased fruit; others were greeted in Nevada by armed posses or held "on suspicion" by local peace officers. "No Japs wanted" signs appeared in many windows. On March 27, 1942, DeWitt called a halt to voluntary evacuation and ordered the army to force the Japanese to migrate from the coast. Surprisingly, there was no serious protest by the Japanese or anyone else. The Japanese were stunned and bewildered; nevertheless, they followed the principle of "realistic resignation." Many Nisei in particular believed that the future status of their American citizenship was at stake, so they resolved to prove their loyalty to America by cooperating with the order.

They had to dispose of their property quickly because they could take with them only what could be carried in their hands. Before the evacuation unscrupulous swindlers moved in like vultures on the helpless Japanese. They took advantage of the panic and badgered the Japanese to sell their property at ridiculously low prices. Furnishings valued at hundreds of dollars were purchased for only a few dollars. One woman sold the belongings of her family for $4,000, though their worth was over $25,000. Realtors threatened to report uncooperative Japanese to the FBI if they would not sell their land at reduced prices. Eventually the government itself had to step in to manage their property, businesses, and farms; but by then the losses were already staggering. By the end of the war it is estimated that the Japanese lost up to $350 million in income, property, and businesses.

To accommodate these homeless people, numbering some 110,000, the army constructed fifteen "assembly centers" at racetracks, fairgrounds, and livestock exhibition halls. Between March and June all citizens of Japanese ancestry on the West Coast were transferred to these centers, where they were kept under guard by military police. They had to endure frequent roll calls, wholesale vaccinations, censorship of mail, overcrowded conditions, and long lines. There were restrictions on the use of the Japanese language, on visitors, and on the ownership of such "contraband" as saws, safety razors, radios, liquor, cameras, and literature. To bring order out of the chaos, Roosevelt established the War Relocation Authority (WRA), which was given the responsibility to construct and manage ten "relocation centers" in seven states. By fall 1942 all 110,000 Japanese Americans had been transferred to these camps, where they remained until a program for resettlement was developed.[3]

Christian leaders and denominations responded immediately to the evacuation. Though occasionally sympathizing with the government's duty to protect America's national security, they did not support the policy of mass evacuation. Typical of their response was one given by W. E. Crouser, a Lutheran pastor in San Jose: "The action of the Federal Government has created considerable sentiment because of the principles and conditions involved. We have long believed that no American citizen could be deprived of life, liberty, and property without due process of law. For these Japanese evacuees there has been no hearing granted. The President of the United States has issued a proclamation giving the Secretary of War authority to prescribe military areas from which all persons may be excluded." Crouser questioned the government's decision but still respected military necessity and conduct. "No one questions the seriousness of the situation on the Pacific Coast nor the magnitude of the task of its defense. As far as we can see, the processes of the Army have been exceptionally kind and wholeheartedly sympathetic. The Army as we have contacted it, is composed of genuine gentlemen, kind, courteous, considerate, and very accessible." Crouser was thus ambivalent. "We are especially proud of our men in uniform; but we are also deeply touched by the sorrow and suffering and loss of our neighbors. We are also greatly pleased with the spirit of submission and trust in which these evacuees have met the emergency." Crouser felt the tug between the demands of patriotism and the mandates of justice, between love of country—"we are proud of our men in uniform"—and concern for people—"we are touched by the sorrow and suffering." He resolved the tension by making mild protest and then exhorting the churches to aid the Japanese.[4]

Marlin D. Farnum, a Northern Baptist, mentioned that of the 110,000 people evacuated, over 70,000 were American citizens whose rights had been suddenly stripped. Further, he noted that Germans and Italians had not been treated the same way, though recent immigrants of those nationalities were no more trustworthy than Japanese immigrants. He wondered, too, about the lapse of time between Pearl Harbor and the internment. He was also perplexed why people of Japanese descent living in Hawaii had not been evacuated, as they certainly would have posed a greater threat than those living on the coast. Farnum believed that the real cause for the evacuation was not the need for national security but the prejudice of people living on the West Coast. He quoted the managing secretary of the Salinas Vegetable Grower-Shipper Association to support this contention: "We're charged with wanting to get rid of the Japs for selfish reasons. We might as well be honest. We do. It's a question of whether the white man or the brown man lives on the Pacific Coast." Yet Farnum was ambivalent, too. His deep concern was mollified by "two other facts which must not be overlooked nor forgotten. One is the generally humane and kind way in which those charged with effecting the evacuation carried it out. The members of the military and the civilian directors exhibited an understanding and sympathy which at times was deeply moving. The second fact is that the Christian forces on the Coast rallied under the banner of Christ to minister to the evacuees. Along with other denominational groups, Caucasian Baptist churches and Home Mission agencies gave liberally of service and money to help those whose hearts were heavy and lonely."[5]

Denominational resolutions reflected similar moderation. In a statement approved at their 1942 convention, the Disciples acknowledged that it was the duty of government to take all necessary precautions to protect the country from betrayal and sabotage, and that in time of war nationals of one belligerent country residing in another could expect some restrictions upon their freedom. "But," it continued, "we hold that all steps taken for this purpose should be within the framework of the Constitution and should be based upon evidence of or strong presumption of guilt." The resolution thus recommended that hearings be set up to determine the loyalty of Japanese Americans, that the government enable Japanese Americans released from internment camps to reenter American society as quickly as possible, and that the government compensate innocent victims for losses sustained during internment. The Disciples stated that the internment of Japanese was not in harmony with past policies of the government but an unfortunate and unnecessary incident resulting from ill-considered action by reprehensible pressure groups. Though the considerate and humane treatment of the Japanese by the military and the cooperation on the part of the Japanese demonstrated goodwill on both sides, the liberties of the Japanese Americans had to be restored. Nothing less than the future of democracy was at stake. "We believe that the whole principle of democratic liberty as well as our future relations with Oriental peoples, is at stake in our treatment of the Japanese within our borders. We must demonstrate to peoples of enemy occupied, neutral, and colonial countries that we can maintain democratic liberties in wartime, and that we believe in them for others a well as for ourselves. . . . What we do in this situation will have a more important and far-reaching influence upon the colored peoples of the world than all the appeals we may make for confidence in the democratic cause in this world struggle."[6]

Methodists opposed the action, too. In 1942 the Southern California-Arizona Conference accused powerful interests, popular war hysteria, provincialism, and vigilantism of precipitating the crisis. The conference refused to join the movement of suspicion. "We deeply regret that the citizenship rights of many of them have been violated. We urge our church people to join in a positive movement to protect these people from threats of permanent loss of civil and economic rights. We seek with them for a new birth of freedom."[7]

Stronger statements were also forthcoming. Writing for the *Christian Century*, Galen Fisher, professor at the Pacific School of Religion and cofounder of the Committee on American Principles of Fair Play, declared that there was no reason why Americans should be afraid. The Japanese, he assured, had not sabotaged Hawaii, nor were they plotting to help the enemy invade the West Coast. The guilty party was not the Japanese at all but the American people, particularly reporters and "pseudo-patriotic bullies." Future treatment would be a test of America's justice and compassion. "For white Americans, it is a testing by fire of devotion to the letter and spirit of the federal Constitution, and of their ability to hold justice and national unity above antipathy toward persons of Japanese race. For white Christians, it is a challenge to demonstrate that Christian brotherhood transcends blood and skin color."[8] Joseph B. Hunter, special representative of the United Christian Missionary Society for ministry to Japanese evacuees, responded similarly: "The uprooting and transfer of almost one hundred thousand citizens without due process of law, without even declaring martial law, is the most severe blow which the Constitution and the Bill of Rights have suffered since they were written. The test of a democracy is its treatment of minorities, not in the fact that a majority rule."[9]

The religious press tried to put a human face on the evacuation and internment to expose something of the suffering involved. It carried many articles written by Christian Japanese Americans on the experience of being removed from familiar surroundings, stripped of their rights and belongings, and interned in strange, faraway places. These Japanese Christians testified that the Japanese in America were loyal to the country, eager to cooperate with the government, and ready to serve the nation in time of war. "A single basic attitude became evident," wrote Yoshitaka Takagi. "Everywhere, Japanese Americans expressed their loyalty to the United States and their eagerness to help defend America. In Hawaii, instinctively the Japanese fought and worked beside their brothers of other national origins. And it was in this spirit that the 110,000 Japanese Americans, both citizens and foreign-born, gladly cooperated with the authorities in their evacuation from the strategic West Coast military area to inland centers, despite great personal sacrifice." Takagi assured his fellow citizens that Japanese Americans identified with America in the conflict, not Japan, and once in the camps they initiated broad educational programs in American history, geography, and English. Though confused, Japanese Americans would prove that they were patriotic Americans devoted to allied victory.[10] His words proved true. Thousands of young Japanese American men enlisted in the army in 1943 and 1944. One regiment of Japanese Americans became one of the most decorated regiments of the war.

Churches continued to sympathize with Japanese Americans throughout the war. The religious press gave special attention to their living conditions, the religious atmosphere of the camps, the ministry of the churches among the Japanese Americans, and the problems of resettlement.[11] Christian leaders advocated that America's immigration and naturalization laws be made more inclusive and, therefore, more truly American.[12] The *Commonweal* provided extended coverage of the Supreme Court case *Korematsu v. United States of America*, which called into question the constitutionality of the internment.[13] The court ruled in favor of the Japanese in 1944, declaring the internment unlawful.

Individual Christians and scores of churches were also engaged in practical ministry to the Japanese Americans. This ministry began immediately after the evacuation and continued until they returned to their homes or were resettled into new communities. Though the churches failed to organize a unified protest against the evacuation during the first critical months of 1942, they did pull together to meet the practical and religious needs of the Japanese later on. It was that early failure to protest the government's policy, in fact, that reinforced their commitment to serve the Japanese Americans once evacuation began. Charles Clayton Morrison confronted the churches on this failure. "It is time that all the churches stir themselves to make plain to the nation the tragic mistake it is making. . . . The method is not democratic, is not in accord with American traditions, and is not right."[14] A newsletter from the American Friends Service Committee of northern California admitted: "In sending this letter we are keenly aware of our failure to mold public opinion sufficiently to save Japanese-Americans from their present serious predicament, but we crave your understanding help . . . that we become 'fellow-feelers with the afflicted.'"[15]

Still, some Christians and churches did what they could, even before the evacuation, to challenge popular sentiment, which was decidedly hostile. A few church leaders became advocates for the rights of Japanese Americans. Herbert Nicholson, former missionary to Japan and assistant pastor of the West Los Angeles Methodist Church, and Everett W. Thompson, pastor of the Japanese Methodist Church of Seattle, worked closely with Japanese congregations to allay their fear and panic. Galen Fisher, Thompson, and Floyd Schmoe of the American Friends Service Committee testified before the Tolan Committee, appointed to conduct hearings into the proposed evacuation. Their testimony was opposed ten to one by representatives of such groups as the American Legion and organized labor.

Other church leaders attempted to arouse the concerns of the churches after the evacuation began. Reverend Frank Herron Smith, chairman of the Seattle Council of Churches, wrote to religious leaders in the area urging them to organize committees in each church and to aid evacuees by holding their valuables. Many churches responded by offering to store furniture and protect property. On April 27 the *San Francisco Chronicle* printed a letter, signed by twenty-eight Protestant and Jewish clergy, promising assistance to Japanese Americans. Christians provided food during the evacuation and helped the Japanese pack. Herron Smith noted that "about the only friends standing by are the church people, and they have manifested a fine Christian spirit."

The churches were especially active in the camps. About half of the internees were Christians. They were assisted by their denominations in serving the needs of the Japanese. The churches sent Christmas presents, sponsored pastors and evangelists who traveled from one camp to another on speaking tours, organized Bible schools, and planned other special programs. The YMCA was also active in every one of the ten camps. Some individual Christians, like Herbert Nicholson, a Quaker, and Father Hugh

Lavery, a Catholic, spearheaded ministries in the camps on behalf of their supporting religious groups.

The problem of resettlement became a concern almost immediately after the Japanese entered the camps. Religious groups demanded immediate government action to restore the rights of citizenship and to resettle the Japanese. As early as April 29, 1942, church representatives sent a letter to President Roosevelt demanding that the government take steps to restore lost liberties. It was signed by Luther A. Weigle, president of the Federal Council of Churches, G. Pitt Beers, president of the Home Missions Council of North America, and Almon R. Pepper, chairman of the Commission on Aliens and Prisoners of War. On September 24, 1942, a strategic conference on resettlement was held in New York. Representatives of major Protestant denominations and organizations attended. They discussed the problems of resettlement with Thomas Holland and John Provinse of the WRA, who presented the government's plan. Two weeks later these same representatives met to determine a course of action for the churches. They decided to set up a committee, sponsored by the FCC and the Home Missions Council, to assist in resettlement. It was called the Committee on Resettlement of Japanese Americans. In addition to publishing pamphlets and a monthly newsletter, the "Resettlement Bulletin," the committee also channeled local church leaders into Citizens' Resettlement Committees to help find employment and housing for Japanese Americans.

The churches also participated in the National Japanese American Student Relocation Council, which enabled Japanese students to leave the internment camps to attend college, many of which were church related. Church groups in Colorado led the charge against an amendment that would have prohibited anyone of Japanese ancestry from owning land. The amendment was narrowly defeated. The Pacific Coast Committee for Fair Play, largely Christian in membership, called conferences to plan for the reintegration of the Japanese into their former communities, a task made particularly difficult by the widespread fear and prejudice that persisted even to the end of the war and beyond.

Some churches opened their doors to resettled Japanese Americans. The First Baptist Church of Chicago called a Japanese associate pastor, Jitsuo Morikawa. The Brethren and Friends started a hostel ministry to provide housing for Japanese Americans who were attempting to find jobs and housing in new communities. These hostels served more than 5,000 evacuees, in spite of the severe resistance that came from local communities.

Though hesitant to protest the government's policy, the churches were quick to meet the needs of interned and resettled Japanese Americans by organizing committees, participating in government programs, and launching special service projects. As Toru Matsumoto, a pastor in an internment camp, wrote: "The way the churches have risen above the hysteria of war and rendered services to the evacuee is a story of which Christians in America can be proud."[16] Matsumoto paid tribute to a ministry that many Americans, consumed by the wartime fever, considered unpatriotic. These Christians served the Japanese Americans precisely because they wanted to be patriotic. They believed that patriotism mandated a defense of those whose freedom was the hardest won and the easiest lost.

African Americans

Like the Japanese Americans, African Americans endured discrimination, humiliation, and segregation during the war. The gap between the ideals for which America was fighting and the reality that most African Americans experienced everyday created an ambivalence that made them keenly aware of their plight and eager to change it. The war was thus a turning point for African Americans. "The treatment accorded the Negro during the Second World War," wrote James Baldwin, "marks, for me, a turning point in the Negro's relation to America. To put it briefly, and somewhat too simply, a certain hope died, a certain respect for white Americans faded."[17] Writing during the period, Gunnar Myrdal predicted that the war would stimulate the protest. "There is bound to be a redefinition of the Negro's status in America as a result of this War."[18] Sociologist E. Franklin Frazier has stated that the war marked the point where "the negro was no longer willing to accept discrimination in employment and in housing without protest."[19] The war years could be considered the pivotal "forgotten years" of the civil rights movement.

They had reason enough to protest. The indignities they had to endure before the war increased during it. Discrimination in war industry was rampant. African Americans could only work as janitors in aircraft factories, in spite of the overwhelming need in that industry for employees. They were passed over in government-financed training programs to reduce the shortages of skilled workers. When the government ordered industry to reverse its discriminatory policies, the order was ignored. African Americans found little opportunity in the armed services, too, having been assigned a minor role and rigidly segregated. The navy only allowed them to serve in the "all-Negro messman's branch"; the marines and air corps excluded African Americans altogether; the army discouraged enlistment and assigned those who did enlist to four regular army "Negro" units. If they made it into the armed services, they rarely received promotions, were seldom sent into combat, and were assigned demeaning jobs. Though discrimination in industry caused greater suffering, discrimination in the armed services engendered greater humiliation. Herbert Garfinkel, a student of black protest during this period, has written that "in many respects, the discriminatory practices against Negroes which characterized the military programs . . . cut deeper into Negro feelings than did employment discrimination."[20]

African Americans were turned away from donating their blood and when, later in the war, they were allowed to give blood, the Red Cross segregated it from white blood. In the courts they were given harsh sentences if convicted, which, with white judge presiding and white jury deciding, was assured in nearly all cases. Many unions refused to enroll African Americans (the Congress of Industrial Organizations being the notable exception), and some unions went on strike when African Americans were hired for jobs that had traditionally belonged to whites.

African American intellectuals responded cynically to the outbreak of war in Europe. Many became isolationist, calling it a "white man's war." They remembered the previous war, which African Americans, led by W. E. B. Du Bois, overwhelmingly supported, "closing ranks" to subdue racial grievances to help win the war for democracy. The outcome of that war disillusioned African Americans and made them wary of throwing their support behind another crusade. They were aware of the obvious hypocrisy of defending democracy abroad while being deprived of it at home. The National Association for the Advancement of Colored People (NAACP) did not miss the irony. "*The Crisis* is sorry for brutality, blood, and death among the peoples of Europe, just as we were sorry for China and Ethiopia. But the hysterical cries of the preachers of democracy for Europe leave us cold. We want democracy in Alabama and Arkansas, in Mississippi and Michigan, in the District of Columbia—*in the Senate of the United States*." Wrote columnist George Schuyler, "Our war is not against Hitler in Europe, but against the Hitlers in America."[21]

By Pearl Harbor opinion had changed, but not entirely. African American leaders urged their following to fight the war abroad but not to neglect fighting the war at home. They wanted to win a victory in both theaters of operation. Thus African Americans used the war to advance their own quest for freedom. They tied their own demands to the principles over which the war was being fought, and they did not hesitate to point out the similarities between Hitler's and America's racist policies. America was just as much in need of deliverance from racism and violence as Europe was. Many African Americans sensed that they had reached a point of no return. There was a rise of militancy, an eagerness to protest, an inextinguishable desire for freedom and equality that surfaced during the war. World War II reminded them of what they were missing and made them want to secure for themselves what they were fighting to attain for others.

The March on Washington Movement (MOWM) represented the first major sign of militancy. It emerged out of the frustration of being discriminated against in the defense buildup. Agitation for a mass movement first surfaced after a group of African American leaders failed to win major concessions from President Roosevelt in September 1940. Various organizations, like the NAACP, the Committee for Participation of Negroes in the National Defense, and the Allied Committees on National Defense organized mass protests around the country. Helping to consolidate this protest, A. Philip Randolph wrote an article in early 1941 to point out the meager gains that African Americans had achieved in industry. He suggested that the power of indifference, wielded so effectively by the government, had to be met with the power of mass protest. Randolph called for 10,000 African Americans to march on Washington with the slogan, "We loyal Negro-American citizens demand the right to work and fight for our country."[22] The march was scheduled for July 1, 1941. The expected number of marchers was increased to 50,000 in June. Only President Roosevelt's executive order mandating an elimination of discrimination in war industries and establishing a Fair Employment Practices Commission (FEPC) satisfied Randolph enough to call off the protest. Roosevelt did not meet all their demands, but the FEPC was believed to be a step in the right direction.

The militancy of the MOWM had a rippling effect. The membership of the NAACP grew from a little over 50,000 members in 355 branches in 1940 to nearly 450,000 members in over 1,000 branches in 1946. African American journalists coined the phrase "the Double-V" campaign to provide a slogan for the two victories that African Americans wanted to win—one abroad, the other at home. Many white Americans were threatened by this militancy and thought that African Americans should subdue their grievances until after the war. Military leaders even restricted the selling of African American newspapers on bases because they thought the papers were too radical. Whites accused African Americans of being disloyal to America; they failed to realize that African Americans were protesting because they were not being given a chance to prove their loyalty.

Still, African American leaders persisted. In 1942 and 1943 they held a series of mass rallies around the country—in New York, Chicago, St. Louis—to demonstrate their strength and to voice their dissatisfaction. In December 1942 the MOWM announced that it was planning to use Gandhian civil disobedience tactics to break down racial segregation. When Paul McNutt, head of the War Manpower Commission, ordered FEPC to postpone a scheduled public hearing on discrimination of blacks in the railroads, African American leaders called a Save FEPC Conference in Washington and forced Roosevelt to reconstitute it.

This agitation across the nation showed that African Americans were angry. That anger exploded in the summer of 1943 when race riots erupted in several cities across America. The Detroit riot was the first (June 20, 1943) and worst. It started as a skirmish in an amusement park. Rumors of violence turned it into a major battle. Thirty-four people were killed, hundreds injured, and millions of dollars worth of property damage sustained. The army finally had to be called in to restore order. Suddenly Americans of all ethnic backgrounds and ideological stripes realized that the problem of racial prejudice and discrimination was desperate. Something had to be done, and African Americans were going to make sure something was done. As Richard M. Dalfiume writes: "The hypocrisy and paradox involved in fighting a world war for the four freedoms and against aggression by an enemy preaching a master race ideology, while at the same time upholding racial segregation and white supremacy, were too obvious. The war crisis provided American Negroes with a unique opportunity to point out, for all to see, the difference between the American creed and practice. The democratic ideology and rhetoric with which the war was fought stimulated a sense of hope and certainty in black Americans that the old race structure was destroyed forever."[23]

The religious press was aware of the problem. If it took a war to provide opportunities in American society for African Americans, what did that say about American society? The prospects did not encourage Christian leaders like William Stuart Nelson. The timing and the limitations of the modest gains African Americans had recently enjoyed, he argued, had portentous implications. As if standing on the first lowly peak of a great mountain range, African Americans had risen just enough during the war to see how far they still had to go to reach the heights where most other Americans stood. "It can be said that whatever his gains, if there be any, they will have been long overdue and that it is a mark of great shame that they should have been forced to wait upon a war."[24] Wrote Edwin R. Embree, president of the Julius Rosenwald Fund, "It is too late ever again to keep Negroes 'in their place.' If we wanted that, we should never have drawn them into war production nor called them to the tremendous education of the armed forces."[25]

Religious groups in America recognized the contradiction between the American creed and life as it really was, and they tried, however hesitatingly, to address themselves to it. Patriotism could never be allowed to justify trampling the rights of minority groups. The Christian Conference on Peace and War issued a statement that echoed these concerns. The basic argument repeated what many church leaders and groups were saying: America could not fight for freedom and democracy abroad if it did not defend those principles in its own national life. America's future leadership depended upon how well it lived according to the ideas for which it was fighting.[26]

Southern Presbyterians argued similarly in a resolution they passed in 1943. "It is constantly flung at us when we condemn the Nazi persecution of non-Aryans that we are ourselves guilty of racial prejudice and injustice in many forms in our own land. This is a time of supreme opportunity to rid ourselves of this menace to all things fine in our religion and in our national life. The Christian citizen will therefore combat with all earnestness and power racial prejudice against Negroes, anti-Semitism, and unsympathetic treatment of the Japanese in internment areas." These general principles were applied specifically to prejudice against African Americans in the south. "In the South we need to face this duty especially with reference to our Negro population. God hath made of one blood all nations of men that dwell upon the face of the earth. In America where so many different races and nationals have sought a home, we will use every opportunity for manifesting toward them a Christian spirit and seeking for them fair treatment and fine opportunities of life and development."[27] Northern Presbyterians made the same argument but urged a more radical solution: "We oppose any discrimination against the Negro in the military services and in opportunities for employment in, and training for, the defense industries."[28] In its message to the churches on interracial brotherhood, the FCC challenged the churches to strive as never before for "Christian fellowship among the races" as a countermeasure to the mindless racism that was encircling the globe. Though America had made some progress in this area, it was nevertheless clear that "every kind of race problem in the world" was found "in some form in the United States." It was the churches' duty to erase that mark against America.[29] Leaders from white and black religious groups met several times throughout the war to confer together about the problem of racism in America, brought to bold relief by the war itself.[30]

When church groups voiced their concerns during the war, their arguments reflected the same ones used by African Americans. America could not in good conscience fight for democracy abroad if it did not defend it at home. It could not tolerate the huge gap that existed between what America stood for and what America really was. The trajectory of that logic pushed many mainline religious groups toward becoming more militant after the war.[31]

The same argument appeared in the religious press, although the religious press was decidedly less temperate than the denominations for which it spoke, or to which it spoke. Writing for *Zion's Herald*, Guy Emery Shipler Jr. underscored the obvious contradiction between "fighting for democracy abroad but violating the rights of negroes at home." "It is obvious," he wrote, "that when a nation wars on tyrants because democracy has a mandate to respect and succor oppressed minorities in other countries, it cannot consistently violate the rights of one tenth of its own citizenry. . . . It could mean the loss of the war."[32] Added Judson J. McKim, "Or is it consistent to say that we are fighting for political and economic liberty when our own skirts are not entirely clean about the Negroes?"[33] Editor Edward Skillin Jr. of the *Commonweal* pointed at lynching in America as a fault that made the nation uncomfortably similar to Germany and Japan. "Who are we," he asked, "to reproach the nazis with their concentration camps for Jews if we ourselves can drag a Negro through the streets and then ignite him with gasoline, for the pleasure of a crowd of 300 acquiescent spectators?"[34] Writing for the *Christian Century*, African American writer and intellectual Benjamin E. Mays looked portentously into America's future if the nation did not solve its racial problem. "If America cannot see its way clear to move on this front, democracy in this country may be doomed even though we win the war." But if America did move on this front, he continued, America would earn the moral right to lead the world and democracy would have more than an even chance to survive.[35]

The religious press gave thorough coverage of the struggles of African Americans during the war. It usually sided with them when they were discriminated against and applauded their gains when government or business yielded to their demands. For example, religious periodicals reported on discrimination in the military, and some Christian leaders called for an end to it. Skillin of the *Commonweal* believed that segregation was perhaps the biggest problem the military faced because it produced a host of other evils. It undermined solidarity, guaranteed that whites would receive better quarters and facilities, and spread fear of "arming the Negroes, thus making them helpless and angry."[36]

Religious writers spoke forcefully in favor of a powerful, independent, and permanent FEPC. Leading clergy of the Protestant, Catholic, and Jewish faiths sent a letter to President Roosevelt asking him to reaffirm Executive Order 8802, forbidding race discrimination in war industry, to reconstitute the FEPC, to remove it from the jurisdiction of the War Manpower Commission, and to reschedule the hearings that director McNutt had postponed indefinitely.[37] In 1945 pressure again mounted to abolish the committee. Once again religious leaders spoke out in favor of a permanent FEPC. They considered it a necessity for strengthening democracy and establishing justice in America. Argued Richard J. Roche in *America*, "War does not change the basic principles of morality and justice."[38]

Church leaders deemed segregation in the churches intolerable and inexcusable. "Something is wrong," declared L. O. Hartman, editor of *Zion's Herald*. "Our sin against the Negro lies as a log across the path of Methodist progress. We shall never prosper until that obstacle is removed."[39] Many Methodists seemed to agree. Responding at least in part to the segregated conditions under which they met in Kansas City in 1944, they approved the following statement: "We look to the ultimate elimination of racial discrimination within the Methodist Church."[40] Hendon Harris, Southern Baptist missionary, presaged that the war was finally exposing the racial antagonisms that had been simmering around the world for a long time, even in America. "Let us make no mistake: this question is looming as a matter of international concern." It was a world problem, an American problem, and a Southern Baptist problem. "It is the profound conviction of this writer that Southern Baptists must implement their racial and Christian goodwill in such an official and clear-cut manner as that the negro will understand and all the world will understand that we propose to do something to meet the swiftly moving menace of mutual antagonism."[41]

African American church leaders joined the protest. They were as patriotic as other Americans during the war, exhorting church members to work and fight for victory abroad; but they were also critical of America, urging church members to be more vigilant of democracy at home. They complained of the treatment African Americans received throughout the nation, though they were helping to wage war to liberate people from tyranny and racism abroad. The irony and tragedy was too obvious to miss. Wrote J. W.

Brown, professor of history and economics at Paine College, "The time has come for the American Negroes to fight for the preservation and the extension of liberty and freedom, and at the same time contend for their constitutional rights."[42] James A. Bray, bishop of the Colored Methodist Episcopal Church, declared: "The same flag, the same institutions, the same government, income taxes and all, the same battles, the same laws, and we should have the same opportunities; anything less is rank, unmitigated injustice."[43] Bray was one of many black Christian leaders to agitate for change. They opposed the poll tax, pressured for more jobs in industry, and lobbied for fairer treatment in the military. Bray even appeared before both the national Republican and Democratic Committees to air the grievances of African Americans and to suggest possible courses of political action.[44]

African American church leaders voiced their concerns corporately, too. On February 17, 1942, the Fraternal Council of Negro Churches of America assembled in Washington to deliberate about the conditions under which African Americans had to live. They sent a message to President Roosevelt, which began by reminding the president that they were loyal Americans. "We pledge every spiritual and material resource at our command in support of our country in the ideals of freedom and democracy." But they also told the president that their loyalty to America compelled them to speak their minds about the status of African Americans in the nation. It was their patriotism that made them protest the erection of barriers that kept them from full participation in the affairs of the nation, including the war effort. Their exclusion from employment at war production factories and the practice of discrimination in the military injured all Americans, not just African Americans, and lowered the morale of the whole country, not just the African American minority. They concluded, "Negro Americans seek only the unhindered opportunity to make their full contribution to the defense of America, as is their right as loyal citizens."[45]

No one could accuse Protestants and Catholics of being too opposed to discrimination during the war. Still, what surfaced as particularly significant in the debate was the argument used. Time and again Christian leaders asked, "How can we dare fight for democracy abroad when we are systematically depriving a whole group of people from enjoying it at home?" That contradiction and oversight exposed a menacing hypocrisy in America. If democracy was worth fighting for abroad—and there was little doubt that it was—then it was worth preserving and extending at home. The churches began to feel this burden of national sin during the war and moved ever so slowly to act upon it.

Jehovah's Witnesses

Jehovah's Witnesses constituted a third group that suffered the loss of civil liberties during the war. They became conspicuous during the war because of the nature of their beliefs. As conscientious objectors who disavowed all wars except what they believed was going to be the last great war between God and his demonic enemies, they created problems for draft boards, which did not know exactly how to classify religious people who claimed to be objectors but were not absolute pacifists. Draft boards were not entirely sympathetic. Over 2,000 Witnesses ended up in prison during the war. Jehovah's Witnesses were also suspect because they were unwilling to salute the American flag, which they considered an idolatrous act. Finally, many Americans were offended by Jehovah's Witness recruitment tactics, which appeared intolerant and uncivil. For these reasons the group earned a bad reputation in American society. World War II created the setting that exacerbated an already strained situation and provided patriotic justification for continued prejudice.

Many Americans labeled Jehovah's Witnesses a social nuisance. In 1940 alone there were over 300 reported incidences of mob violence against them in forty-four states. In most cases violence erupted because Witnesses were accused of being unpatriotic Americans or, even worse, Nazi sympathizers. Albert Stroebel, a Jehovah's Witness from Flagstaff, Arizona, testified that, while visiting a friend, he was stopped by three men who asked, "Will you salute the American flag?" After he gave his negative reply, they tried to force him to give a salute anyway. He had a similar experience later that same day, this time at a service station. A mob gathered, shouting "Nazi spy!—Heil Hitler!—String him up!—Chop his head off!" Newspaper coverage did not always help their cause, either. On June 28, 1940 an editorial appeared in Jackson, Mississippi's *Daily News* which read: "Departure under pressure of a colony of 'Jehovah's Witnesses' camped on the Pocahontas Road just beyond the city limits was proper disposal of what threatened to become a serious situation. There is no room in Jackson or vicinity for any person who will not salute the American flag and openly says he will not fight for his country under any circumstances. . . . It so happens that sturdy citizens of Jackson don't believe in nonsense of that sort and will not tolerate its existence in or near this community."[46]

The Supreme Court also contributed to the problem. It made several rulings during the war that subjected Jehovah's Witnesses to even greater discrimination. In *Minersville School District* v. *Gobitis* (1939), the Supreme Court, in an eight to one vote, decided in favor of the school district, which had forbade Jehovah's Witness children from attending school because they had refused to salute the American flag. Felix Frankfurter wrote the majority opinion, arguing that national security and patriotic loyalty allowed the district to enforce such a discipline (the decision was reversed in 1942). In *Murdock* v. *Pennsylvania* (1942), the High Court ruled in favor of a municipality, which had demanded a license and charged a fee from vendors of religious literature in order to keep the Witnesses from distributing their literature in the community. In a five to four vote the majority reasoned that "the sole constitutional question considered is whether a non-discriminatory license fee, presumably appropriate in amount, may be imposed upon those activities." In one important case, however, the Supreme Court did rule in favor of the Jehovah's Witnesses. In *Cantwell* v. *Connecticut* (1940), the Supreme Court appealed to the "free exercise" clause to allow Witnesses to go door-to-door and play recordings which attacked organized religion and denounced Catholicism as demonic. The Cantwell case was significant because it marked the first time the Supreme Court applied the First Amendment to the states.

Still, in spite of—and perhaps because of—the popular opposition directed against the Jehovah's Witnesses, at least some members of the religious press came to their defense. L. O. Hartman, editor of *Zion's Herald*, accused the attackers of being more un-American than the Witnesses themselves, who had every right to live according to their religious conscience, regardless of how sharply it departed from the religious mainstream. "But if this is indeed free America, if we do love liberty as much as we profess to love it, the brutal attacks upon Jehovah's Witnesses are a sad commentary upon our high pretensions. The indulgence of mob violence, the fanning of fear and suspicion, the intolerance and persecution in connection with the drive against the Witnesses transgress the constitutional right of all American citizens to religious freedom."[47] Editor Skillin of the *Commonweal* conceded that the Jehovah's Witnesses could undermine the authority of the state, if they grew powerful enough. But he reasoned that it was precisely the protection of the rights of such marginal groups as the Witnesses that guaranteed the liberty of groups like the Roman Catholics, Methodists, or Baptists. If the state deprived the Witnesses of freedom of speech or conscience, what would prevent them from doing the same thing to other groups?[48]

Christian leaders reasoned that any form of compulsion, whether religious or patriotic, contradicted common sense as well as the constitution. It would have the opposite effect intended. Declared Paul Gia Russo: "The object of the flag is to generate love and attachment for the country it represents, but there is a psychological futility in compelling a child to salute it when that child believes it to be immoral. Under such circumstances the salute is an affront to the principles for which the flag stands; it produces precisely the opposite result to that intended."[49] Added Raphael Harwood Miller, editor of the *Christian-Evangelist*, "Compulsion by the state in matters of conscience will never make men good citizens or good Christians, and that can be said with equal truth of compulsion by the church."[50]

The timing of the problem made defense of Jehovah's Witness rights both urgent and weighty. Never before, declared William E. Gilroy, editor of *Advance*, had tolerance been as important as it was then. "We are not here discussing this matter of the relation of the individual to the State, but are pleading for that groundwork of spiritual tolerance between individuals and groups upon which there can be built the will to make freedom of thought and action in every sphere, including that of the State, as large as possible consistently with justice and the common welfare; in contrast with the spirit of intolerance which tends to make such freedom as limited as possible. The pertinence of this plea in the crucial times through which we are passing need hardly be stressed."[51] Roy L. Smith of the *Christian Advocate* reasoned that the Witnesses needed to be defended "for the sake of democracy's future," which could be imperiled even by zealous patriots who were attempting to protect it from domestic enemies.[52]

Some church leaders thought otherwise. John W. Bradbury of the *Watchman-Examiner* was concerned about the power of symbols. He affirmed that the flag itself symbolized the very freedoms behind which the Witnesses were hiding to protect themselves. A mandatory salute was right because such a gesture showed respect for the very principles for which the war was being fought. "The flag of our country is worthy to be saluted: Not because it is a piece of colored bunting or silk, not merely because it is the symbol of our patriotic pride, but because it is the token of our freedom under God, the sign of our voluntary national unity and democratic institutions, the emblem of religious liberty, and the guarantee of our inalienable human rights. We have no desire to vest it with unreasonable obligations. To do so would be to degrade it. But to respect it and to salute it for what it stands is the obligation resting upon every American citizen in the homeland and throughout the world."[53]

Communists and Fascists

The Dies Committee was already functioning when war broke out in Europe. The committee was originally called to investigate communist influence in America but eventually began to gather evidence against fascists, too, including such fascists and anti-Semites as Gerald Winrod and Gerald L. K. Smith. Its findings were published in 1940 in a book entitled *The Trojan Horse in America*. The work of the Dies Committee became a rallying point for groups that either favored or opposed the investigation of radical groups in America.

The Catholic weekly *America* gave strong support to the Dies Committee. Editor Francis Talbot was quick to attack communists whenever there was opportunity, which seemed to occur frequently. Talbot accused communists of threatening everything that the nation represented. He believed that the Dies Committee was therefore justified in investigating communist influence in America. "Since 1933," he stated, "Washington has been the Promised Land for Communists and fellow-travelers, and many obtained positions admirably adapted for spying." He accused these communists—the Dies Committee put the number at 3,000—of being agents for anarchy yet paid by the U.S. government. He wondered why the American people had become so tolerant. "The country may well ask why the Government has insisted upon keeping them in office but it should now demand that all be dismissed immediately, along with the officials who appointed them."[54] Talbot favored passage of the Hatch Act, which mandated exclusion from employment in the government of any who were members of political parties or organizations that advocated the overthrow of a constitutional form of government. "It is only the plainest common sense to bar from the house criminals who after robbing it propose to burn it down."[55] Talbot even suggested that the Hatch Act be amended to exclude anyone who had ever belonged to a Communist-controlled organization. "Until that amendment is made, communism has an unchecked opportunity to sap and to destroy."[56] Fundamentalists also threw their support behind the Dies Committee.[57]

The *Protestant* gravitated to the other extreme. It was antifascist, anti-Catholic, and procommunist, to such a degree that some early supporters, like Reinhold Niebuhr and Sherwood Eddy, whose names appeared on the masthead in 1939 and 1940, eventually withdrew their support. Kenneth Leslie, editor of the *Protestant*, used the periodical as a platform for attacking fascists and Catholics in America, like Father Coughlin. He also tried to defend the USSR in order to mollify American suspicion and fear, although such defense became unnecessary when America and the Soviet Union joined forces to defeat the Nazis. During those few years of partnership the American people lauded Russia's courage, although they never approved of communist ideology. Needless to say, Leslie was as critical of the early Dies Committee as Talbot was supportive.[58] The *Churchman* and the *Christian Register* reflected similar sentiments, although less radically, because the opinions expressed in articles and editorials were at least slightly tempered by their close association with religious groups that had long histories in America.

Liberals like Charles Clayton Morrison were wary of both fascists and communists. His criticism of the Dies Committee reflected the mainstream opinion of Protestantism in America. He based his argument on the need to defend civil liberties. The nation, he argued, had to preserve the civil liberties of all Americans, even when their point of view was unorthodox. "To us," Morrison wrote, "[the Dies Committee] bears an amazing resemblance to Europe's propaganda warfare, fought this time on the American front." Communists and fascists were entitled to the same civil liberties other Americans enjoyed. If they were dangerous enough to fight, they had to be engaged in the arena of debate, not in the hothouse of a paranoiac committee.[59] Eventually even *America* came around to that point of view. As early as 1940 Talbot raised questions about the tactics of the Dies Committee and objected to its seizure of Communist Party records in Philadelphia. He expressed his concern more forcefully in 1943. "It is in dealing with an unpopular minority that we must be most scrupulously careful of their rights; for they are our rights as well, and we tamper with them at our own peril."[60] With Morrison and most other religious leaders in America, he realized that to defeat opponents in America he could not deprive them of their civil liberties, for such a measure, undertaken to protect democracy in America, would surely undermine it. Liberty was only as good as the protection it afforded to those who departed most sharply from the majority point of view. This point of view differed from many political liberals, who used the law to restrain fascist groups in America. This "brown scare" returned to haunt these liberals during the McCarthy hearings in the early 1950s.[61]

The argument was everywhere the same, at least among the leaders of mainline churches. It was hypocritical to defend freedom abroad and not protect it at home. Allegiance to the allied cause could not allow Americans' to be blind to their own glaring weaknesses. Victory in Europe and Asia demanded that Americans strive to be worthy of it. That worthiness depended upon their willingness to defend the civil liberties of Americans who were, in the minds of the majority, unworthy of them. The threat of totalitarianism only strengthened the conviction that Americans had to preserve freedom in a world that was everywhere witnessing its destruction. As Roy L. Smith of the *Christian Advocate* argued, "To deny to human beings, made in the image of God, their fundamental human rights, because of prejudice and intolerance, is to become spiritual kinsmen of the Nazis and Japanese."[62]

Many religious leaders believed that America was one of the few places left on earth where freedom was still at the heart of its national identity. It was for this reason that freedom had to be made more than a slogan; it had to become a reality for all Americans, regardless of ethnicity, race, or religion. Thus America was fighting in two wars, one abroad, another at home. Christian leaders recoiled from the kind of shrill patriotism that glorified the one war and completely ignored the other. They believed that both wars were equally important.

Still, some expressed concern about freedom if it had no limits. They thought it important to define freedom before defending it. They were disturbed that freedom was becoming an absolute value, an end in itself. Catholic thinkers in particular were critical of Protestantism's attraction to and confidence in liberalism, which appeared to treat liberty as an ultimate good.[63] They argued that freedom would destroy itself if it lacked discipline. Discipline was necessary to protect freedom from exploitation and anarchy.[64]

Christian Reformed pastor G. A. Lyzenga believed that liberty of conscience, even in the service of God, had come to mean the freedom to preach any opinion without the possibility of censure. Lyzenga wondered about the integrity of a freedom that was not accountable to a final court of appeals and that was not subservient to absolute truth. "It may be well for each of us to study the Word more fully, and let our love of liberty be brought under the tutelage of the Scriptures in this age of doctrinal indifferentism. Give us liberty! But liberty as defined and circumscribed by God himself!"[65]

Fundamentalists, Evangelicals, and other conservatives were virtually silent on the issue of civil liberties. They made little or no mention of the plight of Japanese Americans, African Americans, Jehovah's Witnesses, communists, or fascists during the war. Why the silence? First, they believed that, because oppression was not fundamentally social or material but spiritual, true freedom could be found only in a relationship with Jesus Christ. Roosevelt's four freedoms were thus deceptive because they promised what was only in God's hands to deliver. The need of the hour—the need of every hour—was redemption through Jesus Christ.[66] Second, still functioning as a subculture in American religion, Fundamentalists were more interested in advancing their own cause rather than in upholding the rights of groups that fell outside their orbit of concern. Though wanting to be *the* religion of America, they were not yet willing or capable of embracing the diversity of needs, rights, and interests of the American people. Third, a few right-wing religious leaders with significant though waning influence actually embraced fascist ideology. If they were concerned about civil liberties, it was their own, but certainly not the civil liberties of such groups as the communists.

At this one point, then, theological tradition and cultural location contributed significantly to the way religious groups defined and expressed their patriotism during the war. On the one hand, church groups who conceived of themselves or were treated as "religious outsiders," like the Fundamentalists, tended to be less likely to defend the rights of those Americans whose already fragile status in society became even more threatened during the war (the one notable exception being the Catholic church). On the other hand, church leaders from the major Protestant churches assumed that they still represented the dominant religious tradition in America and therefore believed that they had an obligation to serve as guardians of the ideas and institutions upon which they believed the nation had been founded. As guardians, they wanted democracy to flourish everywhere and for everyone. So they strived for victory in the war at home as a corollary to their quest for victory in the war abroad.

CHAPTER ELEVEN

THE COST OF WAR

Statistics alone cannot adequately capture the real cost of war. They give the numbers but do not convey the experience of loss and pain. Christians across America read the statistics every week in their local newspaper or heard them over the radio. But they also experienced firsthand the profound loss in human life which those statistics reflected. Nearly everyone lost a loved one—a parent or son or friend or lover—to the war. They were thus forced to face the conflict between patriotism and protectiveness, pride and resentment, willing sacrifice and unanticipated grief.

The members of the First Reformed Church of Boyden, Iowa, sent over twenty of their "sons" into the armed services. To remind themselves of their absence and needs, they hung a large banner at the front of the sanctuary with blue stars sown on for every man in the military. In the narthex they had a plaque with the names of the soldiers inscribed in gold script. Every week they gathered to pray for these men. Occasionally they had special services—before D-Day, for example—to enlist divine support for America's cause.

Four of these soldiers did not return. Bob Kuiper died in the Pacific Theater. He left behind a sickly wife and two young sons. Upon hearing of his death, his family and friends gathered spontaneously at the church to pray and grieve. Church members acted immediately to support Kuiper's family. As in the case of the other three men who died during the war, Kuiper's blue star was replaced with a gold one. Those gold stars at the front of the church reminded the members of Boyden's First Reformed Church that sometimes patriotism demanded more from people than they had expected to give.

World War II surpassed all modern wars in the sheer cost of suffering and death. It was waged on an unprecedented, unimaginable scale. Billions of dollars were spent; tens of millions of lives were lost, including six million Jews in Nazi extermination camps; millions more were left homeless. It began with a blitzkrieg, became a conflagration under the shower of bombs dropped indiscriminately on cities in Europe and Asia, and ended with an atomic explosion that sent world history whirling in a new, frightening direction. Never before had the human race faced misery, chaos, and destruction on such a massive scale.

The churches felt the shock of war and trembled before its incalculable cost. Though committed to victory, they were not insensitive to the pain that the quest for victory left in its wake. Victory itself was not worth winning if America hardened its heart to the war's victims. It was obvious to many that Americans needed to gain perspective, for war could not become such an obsession that the allies would lose all concern for humanity. Americans also needed to have compassion, for war could not be waged without consideration given to its casualties. Finally, Americans needed to stand for justice, for war could not be allowed to make the state so powerful that peacetime liberties would become little more than a memory. The churches wanted the allies to win the war, but they also tried to mitigate the war's costs.

Social Disruption

The war did not disrupt American life in the same way it did European, for obvious reasons. Pearl Harbor was the closest target that the enemy's bombs hit. Americans had to endure black outs and rationing, but these measures were mere inconveniences, a far cry from the bombardment that London, Dresden, or Birmingham endured day after day. Still, Americans felt the pressure of war on the home front. Life could not proceed as normal. Millions of men and women had to leave their families, schools, jobs, and communities to become soldiers or to work in war industry. New opportunities exposed them to new temptations and created new problems.

The pressures of modern society already seemed to be undermining what was termed the "traditional" home. The war only accelerated the process. It separated families, forced people to live in transient communities that sprung up like mushrooms across America, and exposed children to "unwholesome excitements, anxieties, and hatreds."[1] Couples married quickly, and sometimes prematurely, to mitigate the fear and insecurity that often accompany long-term separation from loved ones. It was their way of creating stability in a world that everywhere seemed to be threatening it. Immorality and divorce were on the rise, because wartime conditions eroded the standards that in peace had usually supported conventional behavior.[2] Americans experimented with vices—sexual, recreational, consumptive—that they would have normally considered morally unacceptable, and the anonymity that resulted from social mobility made such experimentation more convenient and less noticeable.[3]

Among the many who sounded the alarm to the churches, E. J. Tanis of the Christian Reformed Church foresaw the long-term impact that the war was bound to have on the home. He questioned whether the church could counteract it. "The breakdown of the home will ultimately lead to the collapse of our western civilization. All the signs of the times indicate that we are moving in that direction."[4] He charged Christians not to neglect the home, even as their commitment to win the war put strains upon it. Victory abroad would be vain unless Americans protected the one institution that represented the American home front at its best. The home could not be made a casualty of the very war that was supposedly being fought to protect it. "The Christian home pervaded by faith and ideals is the best bulwark of freedom. It is the essential institution of democracy. In the homes of America Christianity must make its Verdun stand against the positive forces of evil now moving upon the church and democracy and the ways of free men."[5]

If the home was ever going to survive, it needed first to be recognized as the precious, fragile institution that it was. The American home could survive problems, such as wives and mothers working in war industry, if the American people continued to esteem it. Edward Skillin Jr. of the *Commonweal* argued: "If the home is honored for what it can and must do in the way of fostering the growth of the personality and balancing true social health, there is no irreparable injury done when a particular wife and mother must work in a munitions plant." The home could survive such a temporary strain if it was valued above all other institutions in America. The problem would come only if it were devalued. "But if the home is tolerated only, or thought of impatiently as that which keeps the wife and mother from war work, the amount of war work which she might do no longer signifies, for the soul of our society will already be lost."[6] While there were many ways to honor and strengthen the home, family worship was perhaps the best. After all, if Christianity did not thrive at home, where would it?[7]

Women were chiefly responsible for the home. Christian leaders believed that the American people could not allow war to drive or draw women away from their domestic duties. That seventeen million women were working in the labor force by 1943—many of these in jobs normally assigned to men—was cause for alarm in the minds of many Christian leaders. Though nearly everyone acknowledged the inevitability of this role change and a few even welcomed it,[8] most Christian leaders looked forward to the day when women would return to their homes and take up responsibilities that war had forced them to neglect.

It was assumed that men were obligated to provide for the material well-being of the home, a task for which they needed to be paid a living wage.[9] Women, in turn, had to live as models of humility, faith, service, and prayer. Indeed, women had access to the greatest power anyone could ever wield, in war or in peace. That was the power of prayer. As Lorna Zobel urged, "Let your heart serve with prayer. Bullets and bombs, planes and tanks are not enough. They will not win this war without the superior guidance of our Father in heaven. So pray often—this is the most important part you have as a Christian woman on the home front."[10] Their quiet suffering would surely speed their prayers heavenward.

> My heart goes out to you.
> Your load is heavier than you can seem to bear;
> And though a watching world still sees you smile,
> 'Tis well I know the ache that's hiding there the while.
> For all the smiles you wear cannot belie
> The fear and sadness in your eye.
>
> Be not afraid, dear heart.
> It is the very grief a million mothers know,
> But you know God, and so with steady beat,
> Your murmured prayers will march along beside your
>   soldier's feet.
> Come, dry your tears; your sobbing smother.
> You know God hears a praying mother.[11]

Signals came from everywhere that women's rightful place was in the home. That women were working in war industry to fulfill their patriotic duty was at least tolerable, if not praiseworthy. That women would leave these jobs and return home to make room for unemployed veterans was assumed. The conservative Catholic weekly *America* echoed the sentiments of many Christians when it questioned the propriety of women working at all. "Before we call on mothers, every man in a non-essential industry should be enrolled for farm or factory work. If that plan fails to get the needed workers, then we can work longer. Our strongest line, homes, must be protected at all hazards. If our homes are destroyed, what is left worth fighting for?"[12] Though women, "engaged in making the instruments of war," were performing "a necessary and laudable service," they were nevertheless "destined, by their very nature, primarily for the home."[13]

Conservatives in particular pressured American society to make sure women stayed at home or, if circumstances required them to leave, returned to where they belonged as soon as possible. This pressure was often conveyed in the most lofty and sentimental language. "No, superwoman is an abnormality, and so are womanless kitchens. Give us a normal mother in a normal American kitchen, making abnormally good pies and cookies—that picture is enduring. In all the chatter about the equality of women, one thing seems always overlooked. The question ought to be: are we the equals of our mothers?"[14] Thus, though women were pushed by government propaganda and wartime necessity into the work force, they were nudged by social convention and conservative religion to stay or to return home again. Both wartime service and domestic duty were imposed on them from without. Most wartime working women liked their jobs, wanted to remain in the workforce at war's end, and remembered the wartime years with longing. World War II thus provided another impetus to the feminist revolution. Still, it was only in the initial stages. The real revolution had to wait another twenty years.[15]

Healthy homes also depended upon strong marriages. These, too, appeared to be imperiled by the war. Considering the inevitability of military service and the possibility of death, young servicemen were prone to marry quickly and impulsively out of insecurity, loneliness, or fear. The women they left behind felt a similar burden. These hasty marriages and long separations made many marriages unstable, built, as they often were, on a hurried courtship, a passionate promise, and a few rich but ephemeral memories. Church leaders recognized the problem and wanted to protect the sanctity of marriage. They urged caution and encouraged the Christian community to support these fragile marriages. And of course they also performed many weddings.[16] In this matter, pastors seemed to understand the problem and erred, if at all, on the side of compassion.

They did not err on that side, however, in the case of "delinquent brides," who had made it a habit of marrying overseas-bound soldiers in succession, presumably to collect part of their pay check and, if they were killed, their life insurance policy, too. Church leaders considered such behavior morally reprehensible and condemned it.[17]

The Breakdown of Morals

The home had to be strong and secure for the sake of America's youth, who symbolized the nation's future. It was widely reported during the war— J. Edgar Hoover's voice was surely the most stentorian and authoritative— that lawlessness was sweeping America toward ruin, the war having broken down the moral boundaries within which Americans had lived for so long. The nation, then, had more to worry about than a foreign enemy; it also faced an internal foe that was threatening to destroy America from within. Nowhere was this more evident than in the problem of juvenile delinquency. Alarming statistics were mentioned often in the religious press. In less than a six months period, for example, incidences of juvenile delinquency increased 88 percent. In 1942 alone 17 percent more adolescent males under 21 were arrested for assault than the year before, 26 percent more for disorderly conduct, 30 percent more for drunkenness, 10 percent more for rape. Statistics for adolescent females were no better.

The solution to the problem was easy to discover but difficult to carry out. Church leaders believed that parents needed to establish order and practice discipline in the home. These tasks were made virtually impossible, however, because so many parents—mothers in particular—were working outside the home. Parents also needed to provide religious education for their children, both at home and at church. The need for more effective Christian education programs led many churches to participate in the Sunday school "Advance" movement. The literature promoting the program stated clearly that the shadow of war, falling over America's homes and churches, made it imperative for churches to redouble their efforts at revitalizing their Sunday school program and at organizing recreational activities to occupy young people's time, capture their interests, and develop their abilities.

The problem of juvenile delinquency also contributed to the wartime proliferation of youth movements, clubs, and organizations. Since youth no longer appeared to respect traditional authority, they needed to be exposed to new measures of control and nurture. The escalation of delinquency in America reminded church leaders that only the Christian faith, founded upon eternal truths and absolute values, could turn the tide away from lawlessness.[18]

Juvenile delinquency, however, was not the only, nor the worst, social problem that the Christian community had to address. Many Christian leaders carried on a virtual crusade against what they considered to be a more dangerous vice, the misuse of liquor among servicemen, who were not only drinking but gambling, carousing, and fornicating as well, with no thought given to the consequences of their immoral behavior. Christian leaders marshaled facts to back up their protest. In 1944 Americans spent $54 a year on liquor "for every man, woman, child and suckling infant in the country."[19] This expenditure drained the economy of money and manpower. Yet President Roosevelt approved of policies that allowed distillers and breweries to produce as much as they could. In 1944 that amounted to an increase of 50 million gallons above the 250 million already at hand. Though Americans had to endure the inconvenience of rationing and occasional shortages, the producers of alcohol could procure all the sugar they wanted and, in 1942, used 2,851,790,000 bushels of wheat, corn, barley, and rye in alcohol production. Church leaders accused Roosevelt of capitulating to the persistent pressure of distillers.[20] It all came down to a moral choice that the president had to make: would it be tires, food, and sugar, or whiskey?[21]

Many religious bodies told the president and the Congress to stop the madness. The United Lutheran Church declared to the president "its unalterable opposition to the evils of the liquor traffic, particularly as they relate to those in the armed services and in war industries, recognizing fully their dangerous and injurious effects upon the youth of our country, now removed from their homes," and urged Roosevelt "to take the most aggressive means at his disposal to protect them against these devastating evils."[22] The Disciples passed a similar resolution: "Be it therefore resolved, that the International Convention of the Disciples of Christ call upon the President and Congress, as well as our own Representatives and Senators, to forbid, or to pass such legislation as will forbid the manufacture, distribution, and sale of all alcoholic liquors, throughout the United States, except for medicinal, industrial, and scientific purposes, for the duration of the war."[23] The Southern Presbyterians followed suit, for they, too, wanted to protect servicemen "against the flood of liquor which has been loosed upon the land."[24] Baptists also attacked the liquor problem and lobbied the president and Congress "to support such legislation as will insure the elimination of the menace of intoxicating drink in and about military camps, from officer's clubs, on military posts, and from adjacent territory, with other vices associated therewith."[25]

The religious press, led by strong prohibitionists like the Baptists and

Methodists, launched an offense against liquor production, distribution, and consumption in America. Some called for a "second front" against alcohol to "defend the defenders" and "protect the conscripts" at their point of greatest vulnerability. The liquor traffic was labeled "Public Enemy Number 1" and "America's Protected Enemy."[26] "Liquor has defeated more men, more armies, more nations than any other cause. It does seem that the lessons that history records should serve as ample warning against this the greatest of all enemies."[27]

Senator Morris Sheppard introduced a bill in Congress that mandated the "complete prohibition of any and all sales of intoxicants of any alcoholic content at or within military camps" and gave the secretaries of War and Navy Departments the power to establish "dry zones" around any camp. Many church leaders endorsed the bill. James Cannon Jr., a Methodist bishop, declared that the bill had started the first major prohibitionist battle since the repeal in 1933. He acknowledged that the "liquor traffic" had the largest and best lobbyists ever organized in America. They were spending millions. The only hope for the cause of morality was the church, which could marshal the support of the masses. "The church is the only agency that can secure this protective legislation."[28] Charles Clayton Morrison used the liquor problem as an occasion to start another crusade for prohibition.[29] He was supported by many Baptists, Methodists, and Fundamentalists, but opposed by other Protestants and by Catholics, who favored regulation over prohibition. A writer in *America* warned, "We must be careful of anyone with a moral and political ax to grind."[30]

These religious leaders were aware of the government's policy of making military service as appealing as possible, even if that meant luring them into the military—or keeping them there—by providing entertainment and other diversions offensive to traditional American values. Church leaders wanted to build morale, too, but not at the expense of morality. In their minds, an appeal to patriotism as a justification for immorality was pushing patriotism too far.

War-Mindedness

War hands power over to the strong, aggressive, and militaristic, who are often not inclined to give that power up once the prospects of peace overtake the business of war. Christian leaders watched with sadness and alarm when the sons and daughters of America—over twelve million of them—submitted to the discipline and ruthlessness of military life. They also noted with concern the effects that the war machine was having on those working in industry.

The balance of power seemed to be shifting towards the war-minded. Christian leaders saw evidence of war-mindedness seemingly everywhere—in the widespread use of propaganda, in the president's accumulation of power, in the regimentation of life in America, in the persecution of minorities. They were worried about making the engines of war a driving force even in peacetime America.

Such war-mindedness appeared to be symbolized most dramatically when Congress began deliberating on the merits of postwar conscription, which required that every physically and mentally qualified male, on the day of his graduation from high school, fulfill one year of compulsory military service. Two bills mandating such compulsory service in peacetime—the May Bill and the Gurney-Wadsworth Bill—came under consideration in the Congress in late 1944. Two resolutions advocating an international agreement to eliminate compulsory military service—the Martin Resolution and the Ludlow Resolution—were deliberated on at the same time. Both the Military Affairs Committee and the Select Committee on Postwar Military Policy, better known as the Woodrum Committee, conducted hearings on these bills and resolutions.

Religious bodies were overwhelmingly opposed to peacetime conscription. Twenty-four of these groups, among them the Federal Council of Churches (FCC), National Catholic Welfare Conference (NCWC), Fraternal Council of Negro Churches, Peace Churches, Southern Baptist Convention, United Lutheran Church, and the Christian Reformed Church, passed resolutions against the measure. Many of these groups sent representatives to testify before congressional hearings. One observer commented on this groundswell of protest, "Never before in America have the forces of organized religion—Protestant, Catholic, Jewish—been as united on a single issue as they are on postwar training."[31] Only one religious group, Carl McIntire's American Council of Christian Churches, went on record endorsing postwar conscription.

The opposition groups warned that postwar conscription would threaten the peace and alter the tradition of a volunteer army that had served America well for nearly two hundred years.[32] A statement passed by the Federal Council of Churches Executive Committee declared that postwar conscription put military security ahead of a just and permanent peace. That was a violation of good international diplomacy, to say nothing of Christian principles. It was the peace itself that should determine policy on conscription.

"We are not here pronouncing judgment for or against conscription but we are pointing out that for the United States to change now its historic policy might be so interpreted as to prejudice the postwar settlement and jeopardize the possibility of achieving the kind of world order reflected in our government's war aims."[33]

The religious press also opposed the plan, almost universally. A few editors contended that peacetime conscription was necessary for America's national security and that it was not the ominous threat its opponents were intimating.[34] Several other periodicals tried to present both sides of the debate.[35] The overwhelming sentiment, however, was against the measure. Some registered their opposition mildly, as the FCC had, urging the Congress to table the bills for at least a year after the war was over. Argued Reinhold Niebuhr: "The men who will be trained in this decade are not likely to fight in a war of the future in any event. We therefore have a right to be slow in making our decision. It may be a good thing if we make the decision slowly, even though our tardiness is prompted by weariness and irresponsibility rather than a clear understanding of what is involved."[36]

Most objections were more forceful than Niebuhr's. It was charged, for example, that postwar conscription was contrary to American democracy, freedom, and tradition. Further, it was argued that the policy would prove to be a serious economic burden to a nation already staggering under an enormous weight of debt, that it would undermine rather than contribute to— as supporters of the bills claimed—the physical health, liberal education, and spiritual development of America's youth, and that it would hurt the chances of winning a lasting peace.[37] Far from ensuring national security, Christian leaders believed that it would surely threaten it. Rather than prepare America to defend itself against an aggressor, it would further weaken America, making it more vulnerable to attack.[38]

Two arguments against the measure surfaced most often. One challenged the authority of the state; the other stressed the authority of the church. Concerning the former, Raphael Harwood Miller of the *Christian-Evangelist* stated that "universal compulsory military training of her youth" was "repugnant to American traditions" because Americans knew that "militarism and free government and democratic ways of life" would not mix. He believed that Americans would not accept it because they valued "men above arms, and the goods of peace above the loot of conquest." He predicted that military prescription would inevitably lead to a "military-minded government with all the restraints which are inseparable from militarism."[39] Even conservatives like Ned Stonehouse, a professor of theology at Westminster

Seminary and a leader of the Orthodox Presbyterian Church, protested. He pointed out that the state in America already had too much power. Postwar conscription would surely engender "statism," which he defined as service to the state as an end in itself.[40]

War-mindedness, then, raised questions in the minds of church leaders about the growing power of the state and the diminishing influence of the church in America. If patriotism required that Christians put the protection of the state above the freedom of the church, the ability to wage war above the commitment to make peace, then church leaders wanted nothing to do with it. They advocated a patriotism that challenged war-mindedness and put limits on the state for the sake of higher causes, like world peace and spiritual renewal.

Mission Setbacks

The religious press paid close attention to the impact of Japanese aggression on denominational mission work in China even before World War II began. Presbyterians, Methodists, Lutherans, Baptists, and other religious groups commiserated with their fellow Christians in Asia when Japan bombed, overran, captured, or destroyed churches and mission stations. Many American missionaries had to be evacuated. Those who were unable or unwilling to get out were captured, forced to flee, or killed. America's missionary work in Asia was suddenly jeopardized, its commitment to the global church tested as it had never been before.

Reports about mission setbacks appeared regularly in religious periodicals and in official denominational minutes.[41] Searle Bates, former missionary in Asia and special consultant to the Foreign Missions Conference, notified the Disciples that missionaries had been detained in their homes, interned in camps, or evacuated. Eight hundred American missionaries, including 100 children, were being held in China, 450 in the Philippines, 80 in Japan, 28 in Korea, 58 in Indo-China. Native Christian leaders had to flee for their lives, thus depriving many churches of pastoral care when they most needed it. Destruction and suffering had accompanied the Japanese conquest. "The total war experience thus far," he stated, "is nothing short of revolution. Life is so radically affected for the Japanese, the Chinese, and other peoples in diverse fashions, that individually and socially, as citizens and as Christians, our brethren are living in a different world from that of 1937." The new situation in Asia demanded greater commitment from the church. "The Christian effort must be made more intense in durability, yet equally in flexible readiness to redirect its program toward greater effectiveness on swiftly altering scenes."[42]

Not all observers were as pessimistic. Methodist W. W. Reid suggested that the setbacks were not as bad as they seemed. The Methodist Church still girded the world and continued to press forward. The witness of Christ was still evident everywhere, especially through the work of missionaries and natives. "Their loyalty challenges American Methodists to carry on—yes, to increase their Christian service!"[43]

Observers speculated about the future of the fledgling churches in Asia, should these churches be required to forge ahead without any assistance from the West. These "orphaned missions" still needed financial and spiritual resources from America. The American churches could not let the war derail this important work.[44] Interned missionaries suffering in prison camps needed their support, too. Their sacrifices in life and their witness in death were held up as a lofty ideal for Christians in America.[45] Church leaders in Europe were also desperate for help, especially those who were trying to resist the Nazis.[46]

Concern for the status of missionary work around the world raised questions about the future of missions. Christian leaders asked if "foreign missions were finished and done for" and wondered what would be left after the war. The prospects appeared dim. Everywhere foreign aggressors were conquering territories where the missionary enterprise had been moving forward. Missionaries were being driven off or interned and mission stations and churches were being destroyed. America, in turn, was devoting its energy, might, and material resources to war, not to missions. Was there any hope in the face of such profound loss?

The war became a catalyst for the renewal of American missionary work, which had experienced a decline in most Protestant denominations between the wars. Christian leaders urged that the churches rekindle their efforts to carry on the missionary enterprise. The cost in mission setbacks thus motivated the churches to invest more in a new advance. The churches recruited new missionaries, called for bigger budgets, and recommended starting new programs. Charles Allen Clark, professor of practical theology at the Theological Seminary of the Presbyterian Church of Korea, considered it inconceivable that sincere Christians would question the importance of missions at such an hour. "To anyone who knows the nature of our Christian Gospel and the history of Missions, it seems incredible that any real Christian can be opposed to Missions." His knowledge of the past reminded him that Europe had become Christian through the work of missionaries, as America had. "There would be no Christian Church on earth if it had not been for missionary work."[47]

If there was ever a time for missionary zeal, it was during such a crisis as the war. "The need for missions is now—more than ever," stated Raphael Harwood Miller. "Think of what is before us. When the victory we pray for is won, we shall immediately need scores of new missionary families, ship-loads of relief supplies, millions of dollars of ready money, and spiritual interest on the part of church members to meet an unprecedented spiritual opportunity."[48] Christian leaders believed that the churches had to prepare for a new advance, to launch new programs, to give sacrificially to the cause of church expansion. The United Lutheran Church, for example, was not going to concede any ground, not even in Japan. "The Board of Foreign Missions, therefore, has not, nor does it intend to, nor dare it relinquish any one of our present mission fields—not even Japan. In God's time the present obstacles will be removed, and unprecedented opportunities will beckon to us and will require missionaries and money—many missionaries and much money."[49] Famous missionary leader E. Stanley Jones declared that it was not a time to pull back but a time to forge ahead. "The only way to meet the tragedy of this hour in the world is to decide to go through it and beyond it by planning a forward movement at the time of the deepest tragedy."[50] He acknowledged that perhaps it was a time for change, but not a time for retreat. The experiences of soldiers encountering native Christians in liberated areas of the Pacific only reminded church leaders of how fruitful the work of missions had been in the past and could be in the future.[51]

The churches had one mission opportunity, however, on their own soil. Once America entered the war thousands of prisoners of war (POWs) were brought to the United States and kept for the duration in POW camps. These prisoners were often viewed as America's enemy. Yet many churches supported ministries that treated them like friends. The wartime service committees of many religious groups in America appointed chaplains to work with German, Italian, and Japanese POWs. They collected Bibles, books, music, and other supplies for the prisoners, and they raised money to support the YMCA's War Prisoners Aid ministry to POWs abroad.[52]

Human Suffering

Church leaders in America recognized that the suffering that Americans experienced during the war fell far short of the extraordinary suffering that tens of millions of people in Europe and Asia faced day after day. They had heard enough about conditions abroad to know that needs around the world were incalculably great. Their knowledge provided a primary reason why some Christian leaders lamented the church's indifference in light of the needs. In a report filed in the *Federal Council Bulletin*, the churches were criticized for overlooking the overwhelming distress of people in Asia and Europe whose lives had been so disrupted and ruined by the war. For seven years, the report stated, appeals for aid had poured into America. Church leaders had formed new committees to address the needs, "but American Christians were slow, lazy, unresponsive." Though organized for action (eight agencies had been created to help the victims of war), the churches had not acted, at least at the level they could. Meanwhile, the carnage of war, the devastation in life and spirit kept mounting. "Men, women, and little children are in an agony of waiting to see whether the compassion of Christ can really break through the inattention and apathy of the members of His church."[53] Not that the churches were incapable of acting quickly and effectively. In fall 1942 the United Nations Relief and Rehabilitation Administration (UNRRA) initiated a clothing drive to help refugees in Europe survive the winter. Within six seeks the drive was completed, showing that "the churches can be mobilized on a large scale for specific action, and on short notice."[54]

Church leaders kept trumpeting the needs, hoping to stir the churches to action. Howard E. Kershner, chairman of the committee on Overseas Child Service Program and Operations of the Save the Children Federation, drew attention to the desperate plight of children in war-torn Europe. There were countless thousands of children in Europe without parents and without homes. They had been reduced to such severe suffering that "they roam about in gangs almost like wild animals, stealing, fighting, and foraging for food." Kershner continued: "One wonders if these desperate little ones, who have lived by their wits and by violence through the impressionable years, will ever become law-abiding, peaceable citizens. Guns and knives have been thrust into the hands of boys and girls of tender age, and they have been taught to work their will by force, by stealth, and by murder."[55] Many others echoed his concern. Merlin Neff could only hear the "heart-rending cry of the children," the moans of "little ones buried under the debris of bomb-shattered cities," and the wails of the "lost ones—lost children in a lost world!"[56] Millions were hungering for enough bread to survive another day, for adequate shelter to escape the cold and rain. Refugees were wandering throughout Europe and Asia. There were shortages in everything—food, clothing, medicine. Unless the American people rose to the occasion, these people would surely die.[57]

Christian groups organized for action. On January 9, 1939, fifty church leaders, among them Samuel McCrea Cavert of the FCC (and already secretary of the president's Advisory Committee on Political Refugees) and Rt. Rev. Edwin H. Hughes and Charles Mead, both bishops of the Methodist Episcopal Church, left a petition on behalf of German refugee children at the White House. It read: "The American people has made clear its reaction to the oppression of all minority groups, religious and racial, throughout Germany. It has been especially moved by the plight of the children. . . . Working within and under the laws of Congress, through special enactment if necessary, the nation can offer sanctuary to a part of these children by united expression of its will to help." The Federal Council of Churches Executive Committee lobbied the government to support Senator Robert F. Wagner's Child Refugee Bill, a piece of legislation that would allow 20,000 German refugee children to enter the United States in 1939 and 1940 without having first to fill out immigration papers or stay within the limits of immigration quotas. "In the extraordinary circumstances which have created the problem of Jewish and Christian refugees from Germany," the committee's statement read, "we feel that it is not enough to call upon other nations to help or to voice our protests but some such practical step as the one here contemplated is imperative and will do much to facilitate a larger approach to the problem of which it is but one part." Some of these leaders formed their own independent relief committees to broadcast the needs of Europe to the churches and to raise money. Included among them were such agencies as the American Committee for Christian Refugees, the Committee on Foreign Relief Appeals, and the Church Committee for Oversea Relief and Reconstruction.[58] Others endorsed the revised version of the "Hoover Plan" as a workable program for feeding Europe's starving millions.[59]

Virtually every major religious body organized relief committees and launched fund drives for relief work. The Catholics, for example, organized the NCWC War Relief Services and the Bishops' War Emergency and Relief Committee, which in 1943 collected nearly $1.3 million for world relief. Lutherans cooperated together to collect funds and initiate relief programs through Lutheran World Action, which distributed close to $5 million worth of food and clothing between 1939 and 1944. The National Association of Evangelicals organized its own War Relief Commission.[60] These committees communicated directly with pastors and local churches, making appeals, raising money, collecting clothing and other materials. They also set up programs that enabled local churches to sponsor refugees who were allowed to immigrate to the United States.

Denominational committees, in turn, funneled money, materials, and volunteers into agencies already working on the field or into large umbrella organizations that were started exclusively to coordinate the efforts of the many groups in America that wanted to help. The two largest coordinating agencies in America were the National War Fund, responsible for organizing one comprehensive fund raising campaign a year and for channeling the money raised to designated relief agencies, and the United Nations Relief and Rehabilitation Administration, which coordinated collection and distribution of such essentials as food and clothing. Four other agencies worked with the churches to help settle refugees in America: the American Friends Service Committee, the Committee for Catholic Refugees from Germany, the National Refugees Service, Inc., and the American Committee for Christian Refugees. Other agencies specialized in service abroad, like the Church Committee for China Relief, the Belgian Relief Committee, the Unitarian Service Committee, and the War Emergency Committee of the YMCA.

Yet the whole story cannot be told simply by explaining the work of organizations, for these organizations were staffed by thousands of ordinary people who labored tirelessly to relieve the blight of suffering that encircled the globe. These nameless heroes traveled extensively, built and staffed orphanages, distributed clothing, assisted refugees in the camps, fed the hungry, and shouldered the burdens of the war-weary.

Baptist missionary J. R. Saunders, for example, had served faithfully in China for 43 years. He postponed retirement in order to render volunteer service to the China Children's Fund. An expert in operating orphanages, he acted as a liaison between Baptist organizations in America and Christian orphanages in China that provided food, clothing, shelter, education, and vocational training for Chinese children. The orphanages were staffed by Chinese or American Christians. Saunder's years of experience in China made him aware of the needs of that vast country. He knew the people there and identified with their suffering. He wanted to prod American Christians to action. "Millions of children are left orphans and homeless," he cried. "In war, children always suffer most of all, and their needs are the most pathetic and urgent. More than seven and a half years of terrible war in China has brought about the worst suffering in the world's history."[61]

The National Association of Evangelical's War Relief Commission was one of many committees in America that worked with agencies overseas to relieve the suffering of the war's victims. In the spring of 1945 it appealed to local churches for clothing and within a few weeks received 27,500 pounds. It sent that clothing, under the auspices of the Friends of Belgium, to the Belgian Gospel Mission, which distributed the clothing to the needy of Liege, a city with 32,000 homeless. John C. Winston, director of the Belgian Gospel Mission, coordinated the project. Once again, his intimate knowledge of Belgium made him a worthy advocate for Belgium and a tireless catalyst for action in America.[62]

The Mennonite Central Committee directed relief projects in both Europe and Asia. Glen Miller directed the program in England. He was assisted by a number of coworkers who operated the London Center and a hostel for homeless children. In late 1944 he prepared his staff to move to Central Europe, where they coordinated relief efforts in countries that had only recently been opened to people from the West.[63]

Ralph Long and Paul G. Empie were the driving forces behind the organization and work of Lutheran World Action (LWA). Long had been the executive director of the National Lutheran Council since 1930. Empie, formerly founding pastor of Prince of Peace Lutheran Church in Philadelphia and director of an orphanage, became the director of LWA in 1944. Their energetic, efficient, and visionary leadership made LWA one of the premier movements in world relief. They started campaigns that collected nearly half a million dollars in 1941, three-quarters of a million in 1942, a million and a half in 1943 and again in 1944, over two million in 1945, and six million in 1946, the year in which Lutherans in America began in earnest to help rebuild the churches of Europe. Once again, Long and Empie were front-runners for relief, matching the resources of America to the needs of Europe.[64] These and countless other Christians led the churches into action.

This commitment to provide relief departed sharply from the many Americans who cared only about an American victory. Roosevelt was so singularly committed to the policy of winning the war that he tended to dismiss suggestions that America had an obligation to provide relief and assist refugees. He figured that the best way to help refugees was to defeat the enemy. Members of Congress, moreover, did little to help because of the anti-immigrant sentiment that lingered there from the 1920s. They also feared that an influx of refugees would flood America with undesirables or threaten its economic recovery. It is all the more remarkable, then, that the churches organized as quickly and efficiently as they did and that Christian leaders devoted themselves to a cause that so many Americans conveniently ignored.[65]

Their efforts, of course, were not as heroic as they could have been. Such efforts seldom are. Still, the concern of many Christians about the costs of war—war-mindedness, mission setbacks, and human suffering—indicate that at a time when the vast majority of Americans were weary of war and eager to return to ordinary life, there were at least some Christians whose vision of patriotism included caring for the victims of war and not simply doing everything they could to win the war.

CHAPTER TWELVE

SUFFERING BEYOND MEASURE

The suffering caused by World War II surpassed what the American people could ever have imagined at the time. Close to 300,000 Americans died in the war, which is bad enough in itself. But that number pales in comparison to the tens of millions who died in Europe, Africa, and Asia. The war was especially devastating because civilian casualties far exceeded military casualties. The war, in other words, did not stay conveniently confined to the battlefield. It destroyed countryside and city as well.

Yet nothing could prepare the American people for the shock of two epochal events that occurred during the war. One was the Holocaust; the other was the dropping of the atomic bomb. These two events caused a visceral reaction in the American people, and they cast a portentous shadow over America's future.

The Holocaust showed the American people how evil society could become. In this case they reacted with horror, incredulity, and shame. The use of the atomic bomb relieved many Americans at first because it brought the war against Japan to a speedy end. But it also sobered Americans because it exposed them to a power so great that total and immediate destruction of entire cities was suddenly possible. This was a power the changed the stakes of war forever and made peace all the more necessary.

Jewish Suffering

It appears that American Christians were well informed of the events leading up to the Holocaust. The religious press began to report on the persecution of the Jews in the 1930s. These reports continued unabated to the end of the war. Early on in the war many religious groups also went on record condemning anti-Semitism. In December 1940 the Federal Council of Churches (FCC) stated: "We express as Christians our sympathy with the Jewish people in this hour of calamity for so many of their group in Europe. We deplore the existence of anti-Semitism in America and declare our opposition to it because it is contrary to the spirit and teachings of Christ." The next September the Federal Council of Churches Executive Committee adopted another resolution. It read: "Even more strongly we condemn anti-Semitism as un-Christian. As Christians we gratefully acknowledge our ethical and spiritual indebtedness to the people of Israel. No true Christian can be anti-Semitic in thought, word or deed without being untrue to his own Christian inheritance." Also in 1941 a group of 170 Protestant ministers from New York City signed the "Manifesto to Our Brethren and Fellow Citizens of Jewish Race and Blood." Commiserating with Jews around the world, it stated: "We call upon our fellow citizens to remember that anti-Semitism is a threat to democracy and a denial of the fundamental principles upon which this nation is founded."

Many Protestant denominations also condemned anti-Semitism. The United Church of Christ issued a statement in 1940 arguing that anti-Semitism represented an attack on Christianity and Christianity's God, Scriptures, law, and prophets. Likewise, in 1944 United Lutherans exhorted their members to treat Jews as brethren, to defend their rights, and to pray for them. Northern Presbyterians issued a similar statement in 1943, Northern Baptists and Southern Presbyterians in 1944.[1]

Christian groups also castigated the racist policies of Germany and voiced their solidarity with European Jews. On December 14, 1939, Christian leaders joined others in organizing a mass meeting at Madison Square Garden to register protest against the treatment of Jews in Poland. Twenty thousand attended the rally. On December 11, 1942, the FCC affirmed the "Resolution on Anti-Semitism," which drew attention to the Nazi's plan to exterminate Jews. Acknowledging that the reports about Jewish extermination were in fact true, the resolution called for Christian sympathy, indignation, and action. It concluded: "The violence and inhumanity which nazi leaders have publicly avowed toward all Jews are apparently now coming to a climax in a virtual massacre. We are resolved to do our full part in establishing conditions in which such treatment of Jews shall end." On January 6, 1943, the heads of six Jewish organizations met in conference with official representatives of the FCC to discuss what the churches could do to assist Jews in Europe. Then on March 1, 1943, the Federal Council of Churches Executive Committee once again appealed to the governments of the United States and Great Britain "to consider offering financial assistance to Jewish refugees who have escaped to neutral countries from Naziheld territory, and the possible establishment of temporary places of asylum for those evacuated from Europe." In December 1943 eight Protestant leaders sent a Christmas appeal to Vice President Wallace, the Senate majority and minority leaders, and other members of Congress urging adoption of a resolution that proposed the creation of a special commission "to bring about the rescue of the surviving Jews of Europe."

The religious press was aware of the "Jewish problem," too, and provided regular coverage of the Nazi persecution of the Jews in Europe, thus holding up the horror before millions of American Christians. Some writers identified the visible problem as German brutality. But they argued that such brutality was the symptom of a deeper problem. That problem had to do with a blind spot in Western civilization. Ever since the Middle Ages the Jews had been persecuted by Christians; persecution had become endemic to the culture. It was a disease that had to be exposed and expunged, for the sake of democracy and Christianity. Though followers of different faiths, both Jews and Christians were nevertheless bound by common ties of religion and culture. Christians were indebted to Jews for much of their religious heritage and for the coming of their Messiah, the Jewish carpenter from Nazareth. Christians were therefore obligated to defend Jews. The genuineness of their Christian convictions hung in the balance until they acted. Anti-Semitism was anti-Christian. Thus Jacques Maritain argued that the attempt to justify racism on such a massive scale betrayed an overwhelming aversion to biblical revelation and Christianity. "[N]azi anti-Semitism is at bottom a furious aversion to the revelation of Sinai and the law of the Decalogue. It is above all . . . a supernatural fear and hate of Christianity and evangelical law. . . . It seeks to wipe the race of Christ from the face of the earth because it seeks to wipe Christ from human history, it takes vengeance on the Jews for the Messiah who issued from them, it humiliates and tortures the Jews, seeking to humiliate and torture their Messiah in their flesh; it is essentially a Christophobia."[2]

The churches supported efforts to rescue Jews in Europe. Many churches raised money for Jewish relief organizations like the Friends of Israel Refugee Relief Committee (which carried on vigorous advertising campaigns in such periodicals as the *Presbyterian Tribune*, the *Sunday School Times*, and *Moody Monthly*), the Fellowship of Reconciliation's Refugee Committee, the American Friends Service Committee, and the American Committee for Christian Refugees. Church leaders stressed the importance of fellowship and cooperation with Jews through such organizations as the National Conference of Christians and Jews.

These efforts, however, did little to arouse the conscience of the American public, including the Christian public. Sometimes they failed even to convince the American people that the reports were true in the first place. It was hard to believe that murder on such a massive scale was happening. Religious leaders themselves on occasion could hardly believe the reports, which they conveyed in a tone of absolute incredulity. Charles Clayton Morrison wondered if the reports were exaggerated or, worse, the product of propaganda aimed at inculcating hatred of the enemy, as the atrocity stories during the First World War had done.[3] It was inconceivable to him that over a million Jews could be murdered at one concentration camp. Yet gradually the horror began to sink in. It was Morrison's earlier disbelief that made the truth so shocking. He was forced to acknowledge a reality that he had earlier dismissed as fantasy. "We have found it hard to believe that the reports from the nazi concentration camps could be true. Almost desperately we have tried to think that they must be wildly exaggerated. Perhaps they were products of the fevered brains of prisoners who were out for revenge. Or perhaps they were just more atrocity-mongering, like the cadaver factory story of the last war. But such puny barricades cannot stand up against the terrible facts. . . . It will be a long, long time before our eyes will cease to see those pictures of naked corpses piled like firewood or of those mounds of carrion flesh and bones. . . . The thing is well-nigh incredible. But it happened."[4] Morrison recognized that the slaughter of millions revealed that humanity itself was standing on a precipice overlooking hell itself. Evil seemed to be on the verge of triumph. "In the nazis and beyond them we are looking into the very pit of hell which men disclose yawning within themselves when they reject the authority of the moral law, when they deny the sacredness of human personality, when they turn from the worship of the one true God to the worship of their own wills, their own states, their own lust for power. . . . The foul stench of the concentration camps should burden the Christian conscience until Christian men cannot rest."[5] Suddenly religious leaders looked out over a vast plain littered with millions of corpses, each mutilated and charred body a manifestation of the evil of the human heart. It was a terrifying sight to behold. As Arthur S. Maxwell, editor of *Signs of the Times*, sighed in disbelief, "So it was true."[6]

What kept the churches from doing more? No doubt part of the blame once again lies at the feet of President Roosevelt, who assumed that military victory was the solution to nearly every problem that Europe faced. Roosevelt simply overlooked alternative courses of action that might have speeded along the immigration of Jewish refugees or might have obstructed the Nazi's "final solution."[7] The State Department contributed to America's apathy by suppressing information about the death camps and opposing measures that might have interfered with Nazi plans. Its foreign service officers were not always willing to cooperate with such organizations as the American Friends Service Committee to find host countries for refugees, and its immigration policy actually became stricter after America entered the war.[8] The churches themselves were so concerned about the suffering of *Christians* in Europe that they neglected to intervene on behalf of the Jews. Like parents on a sinking ship who look out for their own first, American Christians responded instinctively—however reprehensible it appears now—to save their religious kinsmen. Thus Lutherans in America sought to help *Lutherans* in Germany and Denmark, Episcopalians in America *Anglicans* in England, Catholics in America fellow *Catholics* in Poland.

Anti-Semitism also lingered in the United States, though not as a powerful force. Though fascist and anti-Semitic leaders like Gerald Winrod and Gerald Smith were still active, their followings were dwindling and their fanaticism was considered odious to most Americans. The religious far right was vocal but small, and their fascism was hardly popular. For most Americans, including American Christians, anti-Semitism surfaced more in apathy than in hatred. They were more concerned about winning the war and getting soldiers home than in rescuing Jews in Europe.

Americans were also suspicious of the information they received from Europe, which sounded so horrible that it seemed unbelievable. Because they wanted to avoid the errors that were made during the First World War, they refused to believe the atrocity stories, resisted propagandist pressures to caricature and hate the enemy, and kept their passions under control.

When Christians did attempt to help Jews, either they tried to evangelize them, believing, as Fundamentalists did, that the greatest gift they could offer to Jews was the Gospel,[9] or they aimed at working cooperatively with Jewish organizations in America, which were often as slow to respond to the Nazi persecution of Jews in Europe as American Christians were. Also, though Fundamentalists were clearly the most interested in Jews because of their dispensational theology, they were also the most fatalistic because of their dispensational view of history. Their theology was the force behind both their concern and their apathy. Finally, many Christians expressed their sympathy for the Jews by endorsing the plan to make Palestine a Jewish state, which did nothing at the time to save Jews whose future in Palestine was imperiled by their immediate experience in Nazi concentration camps.[10] For these and other reasons, Christians in America did not act as compassionately on behalf of persecuted Jews as they could and should have.

Bombs and "The Bomb"

Every American soldier who died during World War II was a real human being whose life was sown into the fabric of friendships, homes, schools, clubs, and communities. The sudden and permanent absence of a soldier tore that fabric apart and exposed loved ones to pain, grief, regret, and doubt. The grim news usually came simply and impersonally—"The Secretary of War asks that I assure you of his deep sympathy in the loss . . ."—but lingered for so long afterwards. It put the patriotism of the grieving to an ultimate test.

Many of these grieving Americans were Christians, members of local churches. They were immediately surrounded by friends and pastors who cared deeply about them. Pastor Charles T. Holman was one who knew how to comfort his parishioners because he had to endure the loss of his own son. "[T]he hurt does not grow less," he wrote. "Indeed, as it penetrates, it seems to invade ever wider areas of both soul and body. The first shock is over, but the pain remains. . . . Religious faith is not a magic through which one gains special favors. But we are very sure that a life which is built like a house upon a rock will stand, no matter what storms—even the devastating floods of death itself—may beat against it."[11]

The instruments of death in World War II were devastatingly efficient in maiming, burning, and annihilating huge numbers of people, many of them civilians. It was the first war, in fact, in which the large-scale destruction of civilian property and the extinction of civilian populations became the preferred policy, on both sides of the conflict. Hitler began bombing London and other British cities in fall 1940 in order to force England to its knees. Tens of thousands of people died, yet the English people did not surrender. Churchill responded in kind two years later. The Americans eventually followed suit, in spite of Roosevelt's prewar promise that he would not destroy property and kill civilians indiscriminately. In the end, the obliteration of cities like Dresden, Hamburg, Berlin, Tokyo, and Hiroshima surpassed the destruction of allied cities like London. Millions of civilians died during the war. America was partly responsible for this bloody record.

The American people did not initially support the practice of large-scale bombing. Wars in Spain and China in the 1930s engendered an antipathy toward the destruction that bombing caused. Americans hated the violence, and the administration echoed their misgivings. In March 1938 Secretary of State Cordell Hull commented on the bombing of Barcelona, "No theory of war can justify such conduct. . . . I feel that I am speaking for the whole of the American people." On June 3, 1938, Undersecretary of State Sumner Welles issued a statement that condemned bombing and extended the moral embargo to nations that bombed civilian populations. Then, at the outbreak of war in Europe, President Roosevelt sent messages to all belligerents urging them to refrain from the "inhuman barbarism" of bombing civilian populations.

The war in Europe eventually changed public opinion in America. Bombing was bad only because it was *Axis* bombing. That ruthless policy made the American people want to punish the aggressor nations. Many did not hesitate to support bombing as a retaliatory measure. Some even advocated "saturation bombing," a policy that Great Britain began to follow in 1942. Saturation bombing was intended to disrupt communications, transportation, and services of enemy cities, create havoc in city centers, and break the will of the people. Fearful of public criticism in America, the military did not follow Britain's program in Europe, preferring instead to practice "precision bombing" of industrial and transportation centers.

By 1944 public opinion in America began to line up overwhelmingly behind any program, however brutal, that would defeat the enemy and shorten the war. As a result, military leaders also changed their strategy. Though German cities received the first blows of America's obliteration bombing, Japanese cities felt its full force. The air corps simply abandoned precision bombing and began to conduct massive incendiary raids against city centers in Japan. The public applauded, largely because of the racial bias against the Japanese that had been smoldering in America for decades and finally flared up during the war. As an editorial in *Time* read: "The ordinary unreasoning Jap is ignorant. Perhaps he is human. Nothing indicates it." Two years later, in 1945, *Time* called the great incendiary raid on Tokyo "a dream come true," which demonstrated that "properly kindled, Japanese cities will burn like autumn leaves."[12]

Like the general population, most American Christians supported the massive bombing of German and Japanese cities, and the churches for the most part remained silent on the issue. A small group of church leaders, however, protested the military strategy. Charles Clayton Morrison of the *Christian Century* spoke up first. Reacting to Doolittle's raid on Tokyo, he asked, "What of the people in those tinderbox houses? What of the simple old women . . . ? What of the children, perhaps clacking along the streets in their doll-like kimonos?" Morrison also questioned the reliability of "precision bombing." Still, he was too much bound by his own fatalistic theodicy to object strongly to indiscriminate bombing. He believed that once America entered the war, it had no choice left but to use the weapons dictated by the enemy. "It is all part of the hell of war. . . . we can only commit to the mercy of God those upon whom the bombs may fall, and those who release them toward a scarcely seen work, and not least of all those of us who have willed that they shall be released."[13] A year later Morrison challenged Oswald Garrison Villard's opposition to civilian bombing, which Morrison classified as one of the ugly inevitabilities of war. "It appalls us to say this, but it must be said: bombing, if it contributes to victory, is here to stay as long as war lasts. Those who merely raise the moral and humanitarian questions are talking in a vacuum."[14]

Not all Protestants were as ambivalent as Morrison, but neither were they as firm in their protests as pacifists were. The *Living Church* editor Clifford P. Morehouse, for example, raised certain questions about obliteration bombing. "Military operations directed against the civilian population as such would be a reduction of warfare to utter barbarism. . . . The only justification of any kind of military action is its relation to the destruction of the war power of the enemy." Morehouse, nevertheless, had confidence in America's military leaders, despite his concerns. "Like all specialists, they need to have their eyes raised from the immediate technical problems to the meaning of their techniques in human lives. . . . But in the last resort, we can only be confident that our military leaders will continue to do what any other American or Briton would do in their place—direct bombing attacks only at those objectives which have an important effect on the enemy's power to make war."[15]

Toward the end of the war E. J. Tanis, columnist for the *Banner*, a Christian Reformed Church weekly, advised that conditions of surrender, stated clearly to the Japanese, would quickly bring the war to an end, more quickly and less destructively than saturation bombing would, which he believed was morally reprehensible. "To this we would like to add that with our unrestricted bombing, which destroys vast agricultural and industrial areas, and wounds and kills thousands of helpless people, we are doing the very same thing that Germany did to other lands and to such cities as Warsaw and Rotterdam and London, and which we rightly condemned as ruthless and barbarous. We have it upon the testimony of men who have taken part in bombing expeditions that the wholesale and indiscriminate bombing of cities and civilian populations is not necessary to the winning of the war."[16]

Reinhold Niebuhr believed that the simple policy of "unconditional surrender" only put off the inevitable and, in the meantime, allowed American bombers to wreak havoc on Japan. Doubting the capacity of military leaders to think in moral and spiritual categories in matters pertaining to war, he suggested that their broad war strategy be subject to public scrutiny and discussion before it deteriorated to the point where complete destruction of the enemy was the only aim. "This is the more necessary because the military mind is inclined to disregard moral and political factors in strategy and it is therefore unsafe to give it a final moral and political authority in matters of this kind. . . . We have cause to be uneasy about the fact that our war strategy seems forced to place such great emphasis upon the physical destruction of the enemy, partly because we have no effective policy of political warfare."[17]

Catholic leaders were more critical still. The bombing raids on Hamburg, wrote one commentator in *America*, did not square with "God's law or the nobility of our cause."[18] Though total warfare had "enlarged the definition of military objectives and therewith the scope of attacks upon them," it had not nullified "the essential distinction between the military and the civilian." There were still "limits beyond which even total warfare may not morally go, and one of these is the indiscriminate bombing of entire cities, or ruthless attacks upon civilian areas."[19] Edward Skillin Jr. of the *Commonweal* called for a review of America's bombing policy. He suggested that conscientious Americans bring "air power under the control of and subordinate to the principles and the aims for which the United Nations are fighting in this war." He made several basic requests for a new strategy: that bombing be restricted to military objectives, that technology be developed to make bombing of military targets more precise, and that, regardless of what the enemy did, Americans not resort to saturation bombing.[20]

The strongest protest came from an article written by an Englishwoman, Vera Brittain. Published in *Fellowship* under the title "Massacre by Bombing," it launched a full-scale attack on the allied strategy of saturation bombing. A foreword was attached to her article, signed by such Protestant anti-war crusaders as George A. Buttrick, Harry E. Fosdick, John Haynes Holmes, E. Stanley Jones, Kenneth Scott Latourette, Clarence Pickett, Edwin McNeill Poteat, and Ernest F. Tittle. It affirmed the substance of Brittain's article and summoned the American people to repentance and resistance. "In some way it should be possible to apprise the public authorities of the grave and mounting anxiety of ordinary folk as they daily read the story of incessant bombing in Europe. In the meantime, Christian people should be moved to examine themselves concerning their participation in this carnival of death—even though they be thousands of miles away. Here surely there is a call to repentance."[21]

Though editorials in the *Christian Century* and the *Commonweal* supported Brittain's article, many religious leaders ignored it or condemned it. Evangelicals and Fundamentalists in particular cited it to expose what they considered a lack of patriotism among liberals. It gave them still another opportunity to show that they were better patriots. Harold J. Ockenga commented, "We protestants repudiate the unAmerican pacifism of Dr. Fosdick and associates." Carl McIntyre castigated the twenty-eight who had signed the foreword for their un-Americanism, pacifism, and pro-Fascism. "God has given us the weapons, let us use them."[22]

But could Americans use *all* weapons in good conscience? Church leaders were forced to answer that question soon enough when, in August 1945, President Truman ordered military leaders to drop a new weapon, the atomic bomb, on two cities in Japan—Hiroshima and Nagasaki. Christian leaders suddenly realized that the world was drawing perilously close to Armageddon. Some made a connection between obliteration bombing and the atomic bomb, arguing that approval of the former prepared the way for use of the latter. A statement on "The Use of the Atomic Bomb" written by representatives of the FCC read: "Our nation's leaders announced [the use of the atomic bomb] with satisfaction. We do not share this sentiment. We believe we have committed an atrocity of a new magnitude. . . . it violates every instinct of humanity. We have repeatedly voiced our condemnation of obliteration aerial bombing. . . . We cannot believe it was even essential to the defeat of Japan. Its reckless and irresponsible employment against an already virtually beaten foe will have to receive judgment before God and the conscience of humankind. It has our unmitigated condemnation."[23]

Church leaders perceived that a new day had dawned in world history. It was imperative that Christians seize the moment and strive to turn this overwhelming power toward serving the needs of humanity. But first they had to repent. "Now is the propitious time for the Church to issue her invitation to sinful men, to call them by name, to bring them in their awful condition before the presence of the Almighty, to present to them their only hope—the saving spirit of Jesus Christ. Let them crawl to the altar and, along with a prostrate ministry, acknowledge their cursed plight."[24] The American people had to make atomic power serve rather than destroy the human race. Such control required an effective international organization, to which all nations would have to surrender at least some of their sovereignty. Though the prospect of outlawing both the bomb and war was dubious, some level of cooperation was possible and, indeed, necessary.[25]

But international cooperation would have little salutary effect unless the churches themselves provided moral and spiritual leadership. Writing for *Christianity and Crisis*, Richard M. Fagley averred that only the church could adequately address the new situation that use of the atomic bomb had created. "The fate of the world, therefore, in a literal sense, depends upon the ability of the moral and religious forces, and above all, of the Christian churches, to call men effectively to repentance, worship, and service. The conversion of man, who, as Cousins puts it, 'has exalted change in everything but himself,' has suddenly become a life-and-death issue, not merely for individuals, but for the race. Beyond all other groups, our churches are confronted with the ultimatum of the atomic bomb, for they alone can provide a significant answer."[26] Only the gospel could turn the curse of the atom into a blessing. "Only through the redeeming power of our Lord's Gospel can the constructive promise of atomic power be realized. . . . In our ignorance and weakness, let us seek the help of Almighty God."[27]

It is always easier to condemn evil than to do good. Christians in America were well aware of Germany's hatred and persecution of the Jews. They read weekly news reports of the atrocities in their religious magazines. Christian leaders condemned the Nazis at almost every turn, and they appealed to the State Department to rescue Jews and channeled money to Jewish relief organizations. Likewise, Christian leaders raised questions about obliteration bombing, and many condemned the use of the atomic bomb.

But they were unable to marshal the kind of support that could have led to mass protest. The vast majority of Christians in America were too intent on bringing the war to an end, using whatever means were necessary. They were too eager to resume ordinary life, start families, and spend their savings, and they were too loyal to the allied cause and too weary of war to consider mass protest appropriate and necessary. Because nothing short of such protest would have changed government policy, nothing was done. In this case, as in many others throughout history, the prophetic words of the few were not enough to reverse the inertia of the many. Consequently, millions of people paid the ultimate price.

CHAPTER THIRTEEN

THE POSTWAR WORLD

The Holocaust and the bomb only reinforced what the memory of Versailles had already taught church leaders. Postwar planning was critical. In the twenty-five years between the two great wars, America had come of age. It was time now for the nation to play a major role in shaping world history. It was also time for Christians to make sure that the nation played that role according to Christian ideals.

Versailles was a bitter memory and a cogent reminder of what not to do. Yet it was not the only force that drove church leaders to involve themselves in shaping a stable and just postwar world. There were at least three others. The first was the lingering effect of internationalism, which had led church leaders to lobby for international cooperation in the 1920s and to advocate pacifism in the 1930s. Though these commitments suffered a series of setbacks just before and, of course, during the war, they were never quite withdrawn and abandoned. Protestant church leaders were not about to revert to isolationism, which had become anathema to them between the wars. While this internationalism divided them in the great debate, this same internationalism united both neutralists and interventionists in seeking a just postwar peace.

The second force was the influence of the ecumenical movement. Churches from around the world had already been working cooperatively together for years when, in the 1930s, many of them began to consider the possibility of organizing a World Council of Churches. The leaders of this movement formed strong bonds of friendship and began to envision what a united church could accomplish around the world. Far from undermining their plans, World War II caused these church leaders to press forward. They reasoned that, though the nations were divided, the churches could be—had to be—united. Though world leaders destroyed the nations, church leaders could restore them. The ecumenical movement, then, made Christians aware of their responsibility to serve the entire world, not simply their own nation.

The third force was the impact of realism on Christian political thought and policy. Christian realists like Reinhold Niebuhr believed that World War I exposed the political naïveté of many Christian leaders, who seemed to bounce all too easily from one extreme position to another. First they appeared to be blindly isolationist, then rabidly patriotic, and then uncritically internationalist. According to the realists, they had not yet become wise in the ways of politics.

In the 1920s and 1930s these Christian realists became more active politically, especially in such international movements as the Paris Pact, and they explored the ideas, sometimes even joined the parties, of the political left. With Reinhold Niebuhr as their de facto leader, church leaders prepared themselves to function in the world of wartime politics, to explore the complex relationship between Christianity and politics, and to conceive of specific political strategies on the basis of Christian principles. They were not going to let secular forces push them into another disastrous postwar settlement. Instead, they stood their ground and lobbied for a peace that honored Christian ideals without completely losing touch with the real world. Such realism surfaced in their willingness to acknowledge the need for collective security and the use of military power in the postwar peace settlement.

Not all Christian leaders, of course, held this point of view, Fundamentalists being one noteworthy example. Still, the critical mass of church leaders at least moved in this direction. They were patriotic because they were loyal to America—its ideals, system of government, and national security. Yet their patriotism was cautious because they were equally committed to world peace, international cooperation, and Christian faith. They were not unaware of America's interests, but neither were they blind to global needs. America's national sovereignty had to be limited for the sake of international security, America's dominant power in world politics used to protect the rights and security of all peoples, America's religious heritage revitalized for the sake of the nation and, indeed, the whole world.

Two concerns in particular preoccupied church leaders as they looked ahead: a just peace and a renewed church. Still, however hopeful, they did not approach the future naively. They were mindful of how quickly and easily the world could once again go wrong. An editorial in the *Watchman-Examiner* reflected the thinking of most Christian leaders. "Is it peace—now? Perhaps it is too early to say. The instability of world idealism and moral purpose makes us hesitate to draw a conclusion. We have no desire to foster suspicion. We must take some chances with unregenerate human nature. But we must henceforth take them with our eyes open and not with blinders of an insane optimism on, shutting out glaring, realistic facts." The greatest "fact" was the vain notion that humanity could live in peace without God. Thus, while Christians were obligated to pursue peace, they could not neglect their need to trust in God.[1]

But the sobriety of the editorial—typical of religious editorials in 1945—did not undermine the commitment religious leaders made to more practical and mundane matters, like welcoming home the veterans. However chastened by the conflict, they wanted to help the nation shift from waging war to living in peace. They wanted life to return to normal.

Peacetime Life

Eventually a society geared for war had to adjust once again to peace. Though applicable especially to industry, "reconversion" affected virtually every area of American life, including the return of some ten million servicemen. The churches wanted to prepare for their homecoming.

Veterans would not return home untouched and unscathed by war. Many had taken "detours from the path of righteousness" into drunkenness and sexual promiscuity, as one writer put it. Others had remained morally strong but were still lonely, eager for companionship and opportunity. Servicemen would return home having aged prematurely but not necessarily emotionally, socially, and spiritually. Chaplain Paul W. Burres, one of many chaplains whose ideas about the return of servicemen were printed on the pages of religious journals during the war, was particularly concerned about the spiritual impact of the war on soldiers. "After twenty-seven months overseas, experience with all types of soldiers, both service and frontline troops, I am forced to conclude that the net spiritual result of the war will be negative rather than positive. It is my observation that the number of those whose religious life has been stimulated by their war experiences is more than offset by those whose religious and moral living has lapsed or become vitiated by the low moral tone and religious indifference of military life."[2]

Other chaplains believed that veterans would be prone toward moodiness and depression, and they would probably feel like strangers in surroundings that had once been familiar. They also sensed that veterans would be impatient to get on with life and yet would be unable at times to make decisions and move forward. The cumulative effect of these needs presented the churches with an overwhelming challenge. Only a vital religious faith could make the churches sufficient for the task ahead. Chaplain Myndert M. Van Patten pleaded: "The man who has seen lands devastated, spirits crushed, hearts broken, minds demented, who has looked upon walking living skeletons, ghastly faces, and mangled bodies, needs an overpowering faith—a faith in God! He lived in a world of destruction and now he needs God, the great integrating force for all the worthful qualities within him which have been denied expression. Will the religion he finds at home increase his new-found faith in a supreme God?"[3]

These chaplains warned the churches not to make the same costly mistake they had made twenty-five years earlier—to censure war after the armistice with such severity that they also unwittingly alienated those who had participated in it. Daniel A. Poling recounted: "Following Versailles manufacturers who supplied military materials to the Government were branded as 'merchants of death'; soldiers were 'killers,' chaplains and the civilian clergy who supported them were caricatured in such best sellers as *Preachers Present Arms*. The chaplaincy itself was under heavy attack in many Protestant religious journals and a serious effort was made to withdraw church support if chaplains remained under Army and Navy regulations." Whatever their opinion about past and future wars, the churches were responsible to welcome servicemen home and help them adjust to postwar life. "Then let the Church set herself to meet the shock of the servicemen's return to civilian life, to meet it with the courage of a Christlike faith, to meet it with a strong hand of understanding and brotherliness. A hand that greets each man in his own right and without distinction."[4]

The government had already taken the lead. It had set up Separation Centers in communities across the nation. These centers discharged soldiers within 48 hours after arriving from abroad. At the centers servicemen attended orientation lectures about civilian life, received information on social security, insurance, pensions, medical care, and the GI Bill of Rights, and filled out special forms for discharge. They were also given Form 100, which contained information—skills learned, jobs performed, honors received, training undergone—useful for civilian employment interviews. The Veterans Administration initiated several programs—educational, vocational, medical—that trained veterans for civilian jobs or secured work for them. The government helped by giving five extra points to veterans and ten extra to disabled veterans on the civil service exam, mandated firms with government contracts to fill at least 10 percent of their work force with veterans, and promised to hire as many veterans as possible in its own employment. The United States Employment Service was also prepared to assist servicemen in finding jobs. The government, then, was obviously doing its duty. Still, church leaders declared that it was not enough. "The job of making Joe feel at home has just begun. The foundations have been laid but the big job of construction is still ahead. Where the government leaves off the church begins. The government can only go so far. From there it is obligated to leave the returning soldier to the church and to other civil organizations."[5]

The churches thus had an important role to play. Sergeant Virgil Henry recommended that local churches should welcome home veterans in a special service and then offer each soldier, married or single, a week's vacation. He also suggested that the church organize a long-range program of religious and educational activities designed to help veterans plan for the future.[6] William H. Poteat advised pastors to get special psychological training to help them address the emotional and social problems of returning servicemen.[7] Bishop Oliver J. Hart of the Episcopal Church suggested that churches become informed of local, state, and federal agencies that were organized to assist returning veterans. He also believed that churches were responsible for engaging veterans in active church membership, using them as teachers and officers.[8] Above all, the churches had to expose servicemen to vital faith. Veterans wanted and needed such faith, but they were inclined to doubt. To overcome that doubt, they needed to see faith in action. "Isn't it about time for a revival of true godliness, a time to put away sins and turn to God by faith? Isn't it time to revive the habit of prayer? Should not parents, relatives, friends of the boys in the services—all of us, in fact—give serious thought to our duty toward God and our fellow men?"[9]

Church leaders often gave supremely practical advice. Robert J. Wolfe warned church members preparing to welcome veterans home:

> Don't heroize. Too much of that sort of stuff is already done. . . . Say to those discharged from military duties that you missed them. Restore them to their former places in the family, community, and church. . . . Don't call on him in public (or even in private) to recount his harrowing deeds and exploits of warfare. Rather try to help him forget by

diverting his mind to channels of service that build. . . . Regard him as normal. If he's a cripple, don't stare at his handicaps, but aid him in developing his other faculties or arouse within him a desire to release hidden and undeveloped talents that he may possess. . . . Don't baby him, and don't do too much for him. Point out how he can help himself and thus become a contributing member of society, rather than a ward.[10]

Family members could help, too, by trying to understand the bitterness, desperation, and loneliness that their loved ones had experienced abroad. They could also show patience as veterans adjusted to life at home and allow them to be different from what they had been before.[11]

Many of the wartime service committees of the churches developed programs to assist veterans in their transition to peacetime life. For example, the Committee on Social Education and Action of the Presbyterian Church, United States of America, urged Presbyterian churches to provide resources to help returning veterans and to hold meetings for soldiers and families on adjustment to civilian life. It also encouraged churches to solicit the ideas of soldiers on how churches could welcome them home and to consider what was required of them all to be good citizens in postwar America.[12] The committee also published a monthly leaflet series, "Today and Tomorrow," to help veterans in the process of reentering civilian life.

Local churches started their own programs, too. The Third Baptist Church of St. Louis organized a HITS (Husbands in the Service) program for the wives of servicemen. The church formed a committee to plan programs for returning veterans. The committee decided to restore servicemen to membership and leadership in church organizations, to initiate a program of recreation for them, to enable them to complete their education.[13] The Glenshaw Community Presbyterian Church hired Clifford E. Davis, who had a doctorate in clinical psychology, to train teachers and youth leaders to help reintegrate servicemen into the church and to set up a program to meet their psychological needs. The church established four basic goals for this ministry: "1) To detect personality difficulties in young people before they break into overt behavior; 2) To give vocational guidance; 3) To offer psychological adjustments for wartime marriages among service men; 4) To aid in the change from war ideals to peace ideals."[14]

Catholics were also concerned about the reentry of their veterans. Catholic leaders tried to shape government policy to assist veterans in their adjustment to civilian life. Francis X. Talbot of *America* endorsed the GI Bill of Rights: "These men deserve well of us for their sacrifices, and democracy must do all it can in the future to give them those benefits of which aggressive totalitarianism has deprived them for the present."[15] Talbot, however, did not support legislation that gave preference to veterans in civil service jobs. He contended that it violated the rights of other Americans and was unfair to veterans, who wanted and needed to be treated like everyone else.[16] Ironically, Catholic support of the GI Bill enabled many Catholics to move from blue collar to white collar jobs. This shift, in turn, changed the face of American Catholicism. It became more middle-class, suburban, educated, and tolerant of other faiths.

In most cases veterans returned to their hometowns, where they hoped to resume their former way of life and to find meaningful employment. Christian leaders argued that for love of country and its soldiers, the churches had to make sure that servicemen were given opportunity to pick up where they left off—or better, to find jobs that made life better than it was before. Employment was the concern of most Americans, whose economic status, so prosperous during the war, was threatened by the peace. The question on everyone's mind was: would America slide into another depression? The sense of alarm was genuine, widespread, and reasonable. Millions of veterans were soon to return home, many of them looking for jobs. Meanwhile, industries employing millions of laborers were soon to stop production, because wartime demands were gradually subsiding. It was doubtful, then, whether America could continue the economic boom after the war.

Roman Catholics addressed the problem more than most other religious groups, largely because so many Roman Catholics were urban dwellers, union members, and common laborers. The Catholic church had also spelled out principles for economic policy in the past. These were used as a foundation for sketching out plans for the reconversion of industry. Writing for *America*, Joseph P. McMurray lobbied for full employment. Money itself, he reasoned, was not as important as work, which required training and opportunity. Full employment, in fact, was "the final test of democracy."[17] Harry Lorin Binsse supported abolition of settlement laws, extension of the social security program, and public works projects. Above all, he endorsed full employment, because he believed democracy was strongest when it protected economic and not simply political rights.[18]

Catholics argued that the other great enemy of reconversion, besides unemployment, was inflation, which eroded the ability of laborers to make a decent living. Richard L. Porter advocated strict control. "The worst part of the struggle against inflation always comes in the period of economic readjustment after the cessation of hostilities. Thus price inflation was worst after the armistice from 1918 to 1920. All inflation controls will have to remain in force at least two years after final V-Day if we are to avoid a re-occurrence of the evils which followed immediately after the end of the First World War. Indeed, in matters of capital inflation, new controls must be devised."[19]

The firm maintenance of such boundaries of "economic justice" required planning and cooperation. Industry was already reconverting to consumer production. New technology would make American life convenient and pleasant. Labor, too, was ready to contribute to the building of a stronger American economy. The success of the first few postwar years depended upon the vision of leaders who had to gain and maintain control of the economy.[20] "The problem involved in reconverting the American economy can be stated very simply: we must, on the one hand, give business every chance to begin large-scale production of peacetime goods as quickly as possible; on the other hand, we must maintain enough wartime controls to prevent speculative hoarding of materials and a runaway price inflation."[21]

The Peace

Church leaders believed that America had more than its own affairs to consider. Its patriotism had to transcend national interests, such as the reentry of veterans into civilian life. It had to lead Americans to consider the role America should play in world affairs. Church leaders were absolutely committed to making sure that the nation did not repeat history. Versailles was constantly on their minds. They believed that their own circumstances were perilously similar. If there was to be a lasting peace, it would not come from the top down, which had been tried once before and had failed. Peace would have to come from the people themselves, who could be—and had to be—mobilized and educated. Declared Union Seminary theologian Henry P. Van Dusen: "This suggests that the decisive role falls upon the people themselves. If it be true that the people cannot be trusted to outline a sound peace because of ignorance of manifold considerations, it is the lesson of history that statesmen cannot be trusted to make an enduring peace without pressure from the people."[22]

It was believed that Americans had to take more responsibility than other peoples because their country had been spared the ravages of war. If they withdrew into isolationism once again, the world would be no better off after the Second War than it had been after the First. As Raphael Harwood

Miller, editor of the *Christian-Evangelist*, argued, the pressure was on America. "The richest, freest, most powerful nation on earth, a land spared the physical scars of war, with its wealth of national resources and productive machinery intact; a country with its population (except for its fighting forces) still within its boundaries; its churches and schools and homes uninjured will be called upon to state its ideals and purposes to the representatives of nations which have suffered the worst that war can do and which long inexpressibly for peace and security. Will America also be the most just and honorable and cooperative in the day of her responsibility and opportunity?"[23] The will of the American people to pursue a just peace depended, in turn, upon the power of Christian ideas and the commitment of Christian leaders.

The churches did not wait until V-Day to begin planning for peace. They were engaged in the process even before America entered the war. Church leaders did not want to be caught by surprise again, so early on they devoted themselves to the task of securing a just peace. There was by no means universal agreement among church leaders, however, on what shape the postwar world was to take.

Pacifists favored a world government. Kirby Page believed that untrammeled freedom would lead only to the anarchy of individualism and nationalism, which he called the curse, as his socialist perspective informed him, of the American political and economic system. True freedom required sacrifice. "Freedom can be preserved only by voluntarily giving it up. Anarchistic liberty produces chaos and bondage. Government is essential to freedom, and government requires the relinquishment of liberty. Government is agreement, and agreement restricts liberty and thereby affords freedom." Freedom and law were not enemies but partners, for stronger government, in limiting freedom, would increase liberty. "Let him who runs read the message of history: freedom can be preserved only by voluntarily giving it up. Nations also must relinquish sovereignty in order that the peoples of the earth may be governed by agreement. The establishment of appropriate world government is necessary and that which is necessary is not impossible."[24]

Fellow pacifist A. J. Muste doubted whether the world would ever witness a righteous peace if the churches did not first deal with the real problem—war itself—and unequivocally renounce it. Only by adopting a pacifist position would the churches be able to usher in a true peace. According to pacifists, then, absolute opposition to war and establishment of a world government were two important pillars for the postwar peace.[25]

Pacifists believed that such a peace had to founded upon certain religious ideas. These included the universal sovereignty and Fatherhood of God, the unity of humanity in relation to God as creator and redeemer, the ecumenical nature of the church, and the Christian ethic of love. These would provide the platform for the implementation of such distinctively political ideas as limited national sovereignty, world government, international economic reconstruction, and social well-being.[26]

Conservatives could not have disagreed more. To them, a world government was a vain, deceptive solution because it overlooked the real problem—human sin. Sin could be conquered only by the power of the gospel, the church's most precious possession. The church was responsible to preach that gospel, not dictate the principles for a world government. Declared H. J. Kuiper in the *Banner*: "The Church can do nothing more than to preach the everlasting gospel of Jesus Christ in all its depth and in all its implications. Insofar as it has been remiss in this duty, because it has substituted a fast gospel of human worth and virtue for the true gospel of grace, it can make no greater contribution to the welfare of the world than to return to that gospel." In Kuiper's mind, the great enemy of world peace was Modernism. "If all those churches which are now weakened by Modernism should repent of their error and with a mighty voice proclaim the truth of God, they would be making a tremendously important contribution to the welfare of the post-war world."[27]

Elwyn N. Wilkinson, a Southern Baptist, contended that liberal peace proposals were spiritually bankrupt. Though acknowledging that liberals were correct in asserting that all people were members of the same family through creation, he was quick to add that such unity through creation did not embody a deeper unity, based on the work of Christ, that was available only to Christians. "All human beings are blood brothers because all come from one common source physically. But all are not spiritual brothers because all have not been born into God's family." Jesus had a program for rebuilding the world; he sent his disciples to preach the gospel. "Their commission was to preach the gospel, Christ crucified and Christ risen, that the souls of men might be renewed. They were to get people saved one by one, and when they were saved they were to teach them to practice all the things He had commanded them."[28]

Conservative Christians believed that true Christianity required commitment to certain spiritual essentials, such as basic Christian doctrines and duties. Seventh-Day Adventist writer and radio speaker Carlyle B. Haynes contended that churches that defined their role in political terms abandoned true Christianity. "It should be emphasized again and again that the Christian church has no commission to educate the world, to reform the world, or to civilize the world, and when it attempts to do so it is unfaithful to Christ and is abandoning its legitimate work. It has not been sent into the world to solve economic problems, nor to Christianize the social order, and certainly not to take part in governing the world. The church of Christ exists for one thing alone—to preach the gospel to every creature, nothing more, nothing less."[29]

John W. Bradbury of the *Watchman-Examiner* averred that the church's preoccupation with peace proposals betrayed a fundamental misunderstanding of the nature of the church. The church was essentially a spiritual force that could function best if it limited its ministry exclusively to spiritual matters. "The Church has no legitimate courts of justice, no armed force, no police power, no commercial or social economy, no disciplinary capacity over either secular affairs or men." It was not the responsibility of the church to seize temporal power of any kind. "Much of the impotence of Christianity can be traced to its ambition for temporal power." The ecumenical church in America erred because it had become subservient to the mammon of power, suffered from its involvement in diplomacy and politics, and deserted its fundamental spiritual calling.[30]

Fundamentalists were critical of liberal peace proposals for another reason. As premillennial dispensationalists, they were certain that biblical prophecy had already informed them of the future. Even before Pearl Harbor they knew that the Axis powers would lose. They also knew that conditions would grow worse in the world until the Antichrist appeared. One sure sign of the Antichrist's coming was the successful formation of a world government, which would arrogantly oppose the Almighty God and persecute his church. Like other experiments in world government—Babel being the most notable example—this final effort would fail, but not without shedding rivers of blood first. Christians, then, had to be wary, for any attempt to build a world government was tantamount to cooperating with the great Enemy.

They also had to be wise and so perceive the signs of the times, as one Fundamentalist writer, Erling C. Olsen, was trying to do. Years earlier he had wondered whether the unification of the world would happen in his lifetime. At the end of World War II he knew. "In those days it appeared to me that such amalgamation and unification of nations could hardly take place in my lifetime, but I have had to change my mind on that score. The wheels of God's purpose in the world seem to have speeded up at such a terrific pace that now such a thing seems not only possible in my lifetime, but highly probable. It might develop in the postwar world!" Only the gospel itself had the power to confront and resist this demonic strategy. "So on the authority of the Word of God, the Christian need have no apprehensions regarding the gospel of Jesus Christ in the postwar world. No government, no ecclesiastical body, no group of antagonists to the gospel will succeed in closing the door against the gospel of Jesus Christ."[31] Thus, while Fundamentalists eagerly anticipated the return of Christ, they recoiled from the historical forces that would bring that day nearer. They longed for Christ's return and history's end, yet they opposed world unity because, in their minds, it set the stage for the entrance of the Antichrist. They solved this dilemma by attending to the church's principal business, which was preaching the gospel.

Conservative Calvinists were actually in favor of a world government, as long as the principles upon which it was founded were truly Christian. These principles, according to John Murray, professor of Systematic Theology at Westminster Theological Seminary, had to be "supernatural" and "redemptive." "Christian order is order brought into existence by the deliverance from sin and evil wrought by redemption and regeneration. The principles and forces that must be at the basis and centre of Christian order in any of its forms must be the principles and forces of God's regenerative and sanctifying grace. Any idealism or reconstruction that proceeds upon a program that is congenial to fallen human nature or that is readily adjustable to the impulses and passions and principles of fallen human nature has denied the very genius of Christian order." It was not enough for Christians to attach a few amendments or corrections to secular proposals because that would not change the secular ideas, structures, and methods of the very institutions that needed radical transformation. The "Christian principle" of world order was radical because it was revolutionary. "It deals not by half-measures nor by indirection but by honest, thoroughgoing effectiveness with the reality of human sin and with the all-pervasive corruption it has brought in its train."[32] The advocates of this Calvinist perspective claimed to be committed to world order, but their appeal to "regeneration" made their ideas impractical, if not completely unacceptable, to other Americans who wanted world order but did not believe in Christianity.

Plans for Peace

Regardless of the ideological point of view, Christians across a wide continuum worked hard to apply Christian principles to the postwar peace.

Their concern put pressure on the government to consider the importance of ethics for postwar planning. They developed a culture of commitment to peace, even as Americans fought to win the war. One observer at the time noted the impressive impact Protestant church leaders had on postwar planning. Commented Winfred Ernest Garrison: "Religious opinion has had much to do with bringing into prominence the discussion of the peace and the reconstruction which must follow the war. A year ago, the dominant secular note was 'Win the war first.' Even the Atlantic Charter did not counterbalance this emphasis. But the churches were never content to win the war without thinking about what to do next. The nearer prospect of victory has reinforced this demand of the churches."[33]

Church leaders turned out scores of books and pamphlets on Christian principles for the peace.[34] Religious groups also formulated or endorsed declarations on world peace. On October 7, 1943, for example, 146 Protestant, Roman Catholic, and Orthodox Jewish leaders released a statement on the postwar world entitled, "Interfaith Declaration on World Peace." The heads of most major religious groups in America signed it, including Donald W. Richardson, moderator of the Southern Presbyterian Church; Rabbi Israel Goldstein, president of the Synagogue Council in America; and Edward Mooney, chairman of the administrative board of the National Catholic Welfare Conference. The statement affirmed the sovereignty of God, human dignity, and the rights of all people. It pressed for the adoption of a declaration of human rights and a comprehensive plan for the collective security of all people. It called for a just system that would ensure the rights of all people to economic livelihood, adequate education, cultural development, and political equality. The declaration also advocated the formation of an international organization that would enforce international law, assure collective security, reduce armaments, and control controversies. Finally, the statement defended the rights of the family.[35]

Denominational groups followed suit. The United Lutheran Church in America endorsed the Interfaith Declaration.[36] The General Assembly of the Presbyterian Church in the United States. passed a resolution with similar points.[37] Southern and Northern Baptists propounded their own peace proposals.[38] In 1944 Northern Presbyterians added to this avalanche of peace initiatives. They declared that victory in itself was not enough. "We cannot escape the fact that war, even when chosen for the highest end, is full of moral and spiritual dangers. It is possible to win the war, but to have so lost ourselves in its moral destructiveness that victory will be the beginning not of better but of worse things."[39] Then, in 1945, the general assembly outlined standards for a world organization. These standards included the importance of moral law, equality of rights and opportunities among the member nations, progressive reduction of national armaments, observance of human rights and fundamental freedoms by all nations. It also approved of measures for a just peace settlement: justice, economic well-being, territorial integrity and political stability, reeducation of enemy nations, and reconciliation.[40] The Disciples added one more element—the international protection of basic freedoms that were underwritten in the Atlantic Charter.[41]

Catholics passed their own peace proposals, including the Bishops' Statement on International Order, which approved of the Atlantic Charter, the rule of law in international affairs, the responsibility of strong nations to the weak, the need for a world court, and the innate rights of all humans.[42] Many of these points were based on Pope Pius XII's Six Conditions of a Just Peace, which affirmed the territorial integrity of all nations, the uniqueness and worth of all cultures, the need for economic cooperation, disarmament, cooperative institutions to maintain world order, and religious freedom.[43]

Some religious groups launched programs to engage church members in discussion of these peace proposals. The Methodist Church, for example, organized the Crusade for a New World Order (1943–44) under the direction of Bishop G. Bromley Oxnam. It was initiated to register the opinion of Methodists on the question of the participation of the United States in international cooperative ventures that were intended to preserve a just world order. A council of bishops first spent a week in Washington in early 1943 to confer with government leaders on their plans for the postwar world. By the middle of 1943 they had compiled this information, adding religious peace proposals to it, and they had decided how to introduce it to the larger Methodist body. The crusade was based on a threefold conviction: first, that religious forces in the nation had to become influential before the peace was made so that their contributions would be formative rather than reactionary; second, that Methodists had to become more globally concerned, because they belonged to a worldwide church; third, that Methodists had to press the government to cooperate in an international organization that would end war, establish world order and justice, and guarantee the freedom of the individual. The crusade platform stated:

> The peoples of the world must choose between international collaboration, in which lies the possibility of enduring peace; and isolationism, in which lies the certainty of continuing war.
>
> As Christians, we choose international collaboration and such in-

ternational organization as, in the judgment of experts, may be necessary to establish world law and order based upon justice and brotherhood. . . .

Jesus Christ is the Savior of the World.

The World is our Parish.

The crusade adopted a broad strategy for reaching as many church members as possible: mass meetings (nearly 200,000 attended), local parish services, house-to-house visitations, preparation and distribution of literature, letter campaigns, special programs of consecration and dedication, use of mass communication, and coordination of education, worship, and action. The crusade was extremely successful. Thousands of Methodist churches participated. Methodist publications provided wide coverage, and even secular magazines and newspapers reported its progress. Walter G. Muelder, a historian of Methodism, commented on its impact: "When American Protestantism in 1945 rallied behind the United Nations Conference in San Francisco, the moral and political voice of the United States had, in part at least, been shaped by the tremendous and brilliant Crusade for a New World Order."[44]

The Methodists were not alone. The Federal Council of Churches (FCC) Christian Mission on World Order took similar initiative. Its purpose was to bring the gospel to bear on world order and "to stimulate every church and community to inaugurate an effective program of study and action on the issues involved in Christian world order."[45] The Mission was intended to inform Christians, mobilize them to action, and develop community committees for world order. The Northern Presbyterian Church developed a similar program in 1944 when it launched its own World Order Movement.[46] Likewise, United Lutherans started the Christian Movement toward World Order.[47] These movements followed the strategy of the pioneering Methodist crusade, aiming their appeals at the Christian masses.

John Foster Dulles and the United Nations Organization

Yet none of these statements, strategies, programs, and crusades would have had the substance or impact without the FCC's creative and visionary initiative, and the person most directly responsible for the FCC's leadership in postwar planning was John Foster Dulles, a Presbyterian layman and an international lawyer. Dulles first became involved in exploring the relationship between Christianity and the postwar peace before the war actually began, as early as 1937. After attending the biennial meeting of the Institute of Intellectual Cooperation in Paris, a disappointing experience for Dulles because of the participants' nationalistic interests, Dulles went to the Oxford Conference for Life and Work. He was immediately impressed by the vision of the church leaders gathered there, for they had a conception of the church as a community that transcended the boundaries of any one nation. He gradually began to grasp the powerful impact that prophetic Christianity could have on international affairs and the value his own inherited religious beliefs held for political action.

From that moment on Dulles became increasingly involved in religious affairs, largely through the FCC. In 1939 he served as a delegate to the International Conference of Lay Experts and Ecumenical Leaders convened by the Provisional Committee of the World Council of Churches in Geneva. In 1940 he participated in the National Study Conference on the Churches and the International Situation, held in Philadelphia. Shortly thereafter Dulles was asked by the Department of International Justice and Goodwill to serve as chair of the Commission on the American Churches and the Peace and War Problem. In his capacity as chair of that committee, Walter Van Kirk appealed to Dulles to draft a unity statement that would give a Christian interpretation of the war without dividing the churches. Dulles presented his statement, "The American Churches and the International Situation," to the biennial meeting of the FCC held in Atlantic City. At that same meeting, Dulles was asked to chair a new FCC committee, the Commission to Study the Bases of a Just and Durable Peace. Dulles accepted, believing that it could play a major role in implementing the "Protestant principle of prophetic protest."

Dulles's leadership on the commission was masterful, his influence substantial. He met often with the commission's Committee of Direction, which comprised twenty members, and he was usually the one who drafted the statements and proposals that were sent to the members of the commission itself, which numbered between seventy and one hundred, among them such noteworthy leaders as Reinhold Niebuhr, John McNeill, Charles Clayton Morrison, John R. Mott, and Harry Emerson Fosdick. He was largely responsible for the two major documents that the commission produced: "Guiding Principles" and "Six Pillars of Peace."

Written in 1942, "Guiding Principles" advocated just administration of colonial governments, international control of military establishments, and assurance of certain personal liberties. It also affirmed America's special role in establishing the peace and the absolute centrality of the Christian message.[48] Dulles wrote "Six Pillars of Peace" in 1943. This document was circulated widely and quoted often in speeches, books, and articles. It stressed that the peace should provide for an international organization that would help the nations find agreement on national policies that had international implications. It also emphasized that the peace should provide for the autonomy of all subject people, establish procedures for controlling military establishments, and guarantee in principle, if not in practice, the right of individuals to religious and intellectual liberty.[49]

The publication of these documents was accompanied by three important conferences, all sponsored by the commission. The first met in Delaware, Ohio, March 3–5, 1942. Participants discussed and finally endorsed the commission's "Guiding Principles" document.[50] Dulles was pleased with the conference, as were many others, because in his mind it appeared to strike a balance between idealism and realism. The second conference was held in Princeton July 8–11, 1943. This "International Roundtable of Christian Leaders" was convened to enable Christian leaders from around the world to collaborate in promoting peace. Once again, representatives at the conference agreed on basic principles for the postwar peace as they were stated in "Six Pillars of Peace."[51] These first two conferences were significant in the minds of many Protestant leaders because they reflected a Christian "realist's" view of international affairs.

The third conference, held in Cleveland January 16–19, 1945, was called to discuss two important international meetings, Bretton Woods (New Hampshire, 1944) and Dumbarton Oaks (near Washington, D.C., 1944), at which the great powers had laid the foundation for stabilizing international currency, establishing an international bank for reconstruction and development, and clarifying principles for a system of postwar collective security. Once again, the Cleveland conference was important to its participants because it steered the churches in the direction of political realism.

Not surprisingly, Dulles's influence was substantial. He urged the conference to endorse the Dumbarton Oaks charter for a United Nations Organization (UNO) and to make suggestions for its improvement. The conference followed his lead. It stated: "We recommend that the churches support the Dumbarton Oaks proposals as an important step in the direction of world cooperation, but because we do not approve of them in their entirety as they now stand we urge the following measures for their improvement."[52] Those measures included a provision for passing amendments to the charter without a unanimous vote and a recommendation that international responsibility be taken to ensure autonomy of colonial and dependent areas. The conference also suggested that a special commission on human rights and fundamental freedom be formed as part of the organizational structure and that eventual universal membership be included in the organization's goals. Delegates also recommended that armaments be limited and that protection and defense of small nations be ensured.[53]

Informed by these principles, proposals, and strategies, religious leaders were equipped to evaluate proposals for the postwar peace emerging out of such important conferences as Dumbarton Oaks, Yalta, and San Francisco. The religious press in particular provided thorough, detailed, and balanced coverage of these conferences, and it offered many critiques.[54] With the exception of pacifists, who were disappointed that the conferences did not go far enough, and Fundamentalists, who dismissed them as vain and misdirected, most religious leaders responded to these secular proposals with cautious approval, affirming their strengths and urging amendments at their points of weakness.

From 1943 to 1945 Christian leaders expressed four basic concerns about the formation of an international organization. These concerns culminated in their evaluation of the UNO conference in San Francisco. These concerns were put in the form of positive suggestions. First, the preamble had to include the purposes set forth in the Atlantic Charter, so that the UNO would become an organization that served the cause of justice. Second, the general assembly had to have more authority to determine practical policy and the security council less authority to veto whatever its member nations, especially the Big Three (United States of America, Great Britain, and Russia), did not approve. Third, the constitution of the UNO had to be amendable by a two-thirds vote of the general assembly and not subsequently subject to the veto power of the security council. Fourth, to reduce the threat of armed conflict in the future, the UNO had to move toward disarmament, grant greater power to an international court of law, and make provision for military enforcement when international law was violated.

America's Enemies and Friends

Though church leaders tried to look beyond America's immediate interests to the problem of world order, they could not ignore the more vexatious and subtle problem of deciding upon a practical policy for dealing with individual nations, which were important players in the greater challenge of establishing a world order. The "Russia problem" appeared to be the most ominous. Russia had become America's wartime friend but remained in the minds of most Americans the nation's ideological enemy. Its role as an ally made Americans sympathetic, but its system of government, violation of human rights, domestic brutality, and global ambitions made Americans suspicious, even hostile. The tension between the two created ambivalence in the minds of many Christian leaders. They did not know what to say about a suffering ally whose leaders did not hesitate to exterminate millions of people.

While a few religious leaders (left-wing radicals like Kenneth Leslie, Harry F. Ward, Guy Emery Shipler, William Howard Melish, Robert Whitaker) defended Russia at every turn,[55] and others (Francis Talbot and John La Farge of *America*, for example) vehemently opposed Russia,[56] the mainstream of church leaders were cautious but tolerant, recognizing that, for the sake of a lasting peace, the United States had no choice but to cooperate with Russia.

The ambivalence was understandable. The Hitler-Stalin pact of 1939 provided evidence of Russia's untrustworthiness, making Americans suspicious. Later, when Germany invaded Russia, a sentiment of sympathy swept over America, mitigating that suspicion for awhile. Yet by the end of 1944 the sentiment had dissipated. Russia was not satisfied with the mere liberation of territory under Nazi control; it wanted to conquer territory. Stalin's belligerence at Yalta only reinforced the fear that Russia was eager to expand its own influence, even if it came at the expense of nations that had already suffered under the Nazis.

Church leaders tried to face the problem squarely. They attempted to understand Russian motivation and urged a policy of restraint.[57] They hoped that, in time, Russian leaders would change their minds. Wrote Edward Skillin Jr. of the *Commonweal*: "The mentality of these men will remain a suspicious mentality, because they have been taught and forced to be suspicious, but it may be a mentality in which suspicion is not the trigger to set off the gun, but merely a reasonable prudence and check. If this be true, the most difficult years are those which lie immediately ahead of us; we can reasonably expect, one day, only the tension usual between great powers with overlapping circles of interest."[58]

Russia's treatment of Poland only exacerbated the problem. Poland, in fact, became the testing ground—and battle ground—of Russian-American relations. No one trusted Russia, but neither did anyone want a Third World War. America had two basic options: oppose Stalin and risk war, or trust Stalin and sacrifice Poland. Though the American government appeared to remain relatively neutral, religious opinion swung to Poland's side. Though realism seemed prudent, church leaders considered it tragic that Poland had to be sacrificed. At least one religious writer accused America of betraying an innocent people. Declared R. H. Markham: "We should not be foolish perfectionists and we shall have to accept practical arrangements which we don't like, but let us quit humiliating ourselves by calling wrong right, slavery freedom, and the subjugation of an ally the basis of international justice. Let's get clear in mind. If we still have to keep some of our neighbors in slums, let us not call those slums beautiful architecture or a paradise for little people. Let's recognize them as slums, and with all our might keep on trying to clean them up."[59]

Russia's strategy of occupying and controlling liberated territory sobered many Christians in America, especially conservative Christians. The loathing and fear that they had of totalitarianism, directed for so many years against the Nazis in Germany, was transferred to the Communists in Russia after the war. The revulsion was the same, but the object toward which it was directed changed. They saw what Nazi totalitarianism had done. They had reason to believe that Russian totalitarianism would be no better. Many believed in retrospect that America had allowed the Nazis to go too far before challenging them, with catastrophic consequences. They did not want to let that happen again. Liberal Christians were less suspicious of the Russians, though hardly trusting either. They were convinced that good-will, understanding, and diplomacy would provide a better way of dealing with Russia than hostility, accusation, and brinkmanship. They were intent on building a new world order that would—and had to—include Russia.

Church leaders were no less concerned about the fate of Germany and Japan. Germany attracted more attention than Japan because its religious and cultural heritage was similar to America's. American Christians watched the German church closely throughout the war. They wondered what compromises the church had made, how faithful it had remained, and what it would do after the war to recover its integrity and heal the nation. They were of course disappointed by the failure of German Christians to resist Hitler, but they were encouraged by those few—Martin Niemoeller and Dietrich Bonhoeffer, for example—who had stood their ground. In any case, Christian leaders in America wanted to reestablish ties as quickly as possible and to rebuild the churches there.[60] Germany's destruction gave American Christians—Lutherans in particular—a chance to pay their debts to a people who had helped to establish the church in America so many years before.

"One hundred years ago," stated Arnold H. Jahr, "the Lutherans of the world looked to Germany as the center of Lutheran World Action." By 1945 the situation had been reversed. "Those whose forefathers were concerned about the Lutherans in America now look to the descendents of those American Lutherans and have a right to expect them to be concerned about the Lutherans in Europe as well as those in other portions of the world."[61]

Christian leaders believed that Germany had to be reeducated, the success of which depended upon the power of the gospel to engender repentance and faith. Charles Clayton Morrison struggled because he recognized the need for reeducation and yet admitted that, left to itself, such reeducation would fall short of its goal. Germany needed more than education to have its reeducation succeed. "Education cannot make contact with the soul of Germany at its deepest level. . . . It can humiliate Germany; it can break her will; it can subdue her to an external conformity. But it cannot redeem her, because it cannot induce repentance; and it cannot establish self-respect. Only the Christian gospel can induce repentance in the German people."[62]

Christian leaders believed that Germany was a guilty nation. The Federal Council of Churches Commission on a Just and Durable Peace advocated just punishment, but it also urged moderation. The commission set forth four principles: the allies were not to be vindictive, Germany was not to be dismembered, the forces within Germany favoring freedom and cooperation had to be supported, and Germany was to be assisted in its economic recovery.[63]

Church leaders were similarly concerned about the church in Japan, although less informed and optimistic. Once again, they stressed the appropriateness of restrained reparations.[64] In both cases, Christians in America had to learn how to forgive the enemy, although that did not eradicate the necessity of punishing war criminals and exacting moderate war reparations.[65] What Christians in America had to avoid was hate, vengeance, and fear, lest they repeat the tragic mistakes of Versailles. National self-interest, in other words, had to be made subservient to international concern, tempered by the spirit of forgiveness, inspired by a vision of peace and cooperation.

The Church

Church leaders did not believe that a political solution was in itself sufficient to effect lasting peace in the world. While they did not neglect the political sphere of influence, they took special care to strengthen the church and spread its unique message of hope and salvation. Once again, patriotism appeared to be subordinate to specifically religious concerns. Christian leaders believed that the justice and permanence of the postwar peace depended ultimately upon the church and its faith. They were convinced that the world needed Christianity as never before. That conviction became stronger as they looked ahead to the coming peace. It was the church's hour, and Christian leaders meant to make the most of it.

One word kept appearing over and over in the religious literature—"opportunity." Christian leaders believed that the war had exposed people to violence, destruction, and unmitigated evil. Now the world stood at a crossroads. It was time for the church to challenge the world to consider the claims of Christianity, the only religion that could provide hope to face the future unafraid and wisdom to understand such a tragic hour.

Reinhold Niebuhr was keenly aware of the church's opportunity. "Such a time would seem to be the strategic moment for the reaffirmation of the Christian faith in terms which will regain the loyalty of the multitudes and re-establish it as the source of spiritual sanity and health." He contended that people found themselves in the contradictory position of advancing in technical knowledge yet destroying civilization, of knowing the necessity yet facing the impossibility of creating a world community. "Where but in the Christian faith do we find history so interpreted that the achievements are understood as a partial fulfillment of the meaning of our existence but where it is also understood that there is no final fulfillment of life except in the 'forgiveness of sins, the resurrection of the body and life everlasting'?"[66] Niebuhr believed that Christianity was perfectly suited to address the postwar needs of humanity. Only Christianity could explain the paradox of humanity's greatness and misery; only Christianity could enable self-interested people to become unselfish; only Christianity could give a spiritually incisive and yet politically practical answer to the world's profound questions. The churches had an unprecedented opportunity, then, to usher the world into a period of justice and peace. Wrote Lawrence S. Price, a Lutheran pastor: "None of this will come to pass until we add to the formalities of our religion—our church edifices, our worship services, our ecclesiastical organizations, our nominal Christianity—the power of an aroused, concerned, and consecrated spirit. Christianity will have no power until it has power through you. It is an appalling responsibility we carry. The future of the Church of Christ rests in our hands."[67]

Church-Related Colleges

Christian leaders believed that it was imperative to protect the church's independence and assert its influence at war's end. This concern had concrete implications. For example, Christian leaders wanted to make sure that their church-related colleges resumed their former mission and became subject, once again, to the control of the church. They were aware of the damage that the war had inflicted on Christian colleges and purposed to recover their colleges' former strength. Confessed Raphael Harwood Miller, editor of the *Christian-Evangelist*: "The war has done serious damage to liberal arts colleges and particularly to church-related colleges. Moreover liberal and Christian education in America now faces the threat that all education in the future will be directed for government purposes. The present tendency to separate from the church colleges which had Christian foundation is a backward step toward solely secular education." Church-related colleges had been useful in America's past because they had trained people in the Christian faith and for democratic leadership. According to Miller, the relationship between liberal education and political and religious freedom was fundamental. Christian college education now stood at a crossroads in American history. "The kind of nation and world we shall have after victory in war will depend on whether our colleges turn out robots, trained and subdued to obedience as subjects of totalitarian states, or free men who think and initiate and build for a democratic and Christian society."[68]

The college's principal duty was to teach a way of life that confronted secularism and naturalism, ideologies that had been embodied so frighteningly in Nazism and, even with Germany's defeat, still threatened the world. Every nation, not simply Germany, desperately needed reeducation. Public righteousness could not be maintained without personal religion. "The gilt has peeled off the dry rot of paganism in our modern society and revealed its contempt for the value of the human soul, its worship of wealth and power, its will to exploit the weak and its dependence on armed might to keep ambitious states in position to dominate the world. Re-education not only for Germany but for all nations will be the order after the war."[69]

Such education had to be moral and spiritual. To accomplish that purpose, church-related colleges had to build an educational system that in its assumptions validated a religious view of life and exposed students to the Christian faith.[70] "The college which seeks to be religious," declared Clarence P. Sheed of the Yale Divinity School, "will make it evident to students that religion is inseparable from higher education."[71] Henry Schultze of Calvin College explored the implications of such an education. He believed that a distinctively Christian education was necessary to fulfill such worthy goals as commitment to good values, preparation for a balanced life, international goodwill, and development of character. The realization of these grandiose plans, concluded Schultze, "lies beyond the competency of any school uncongenial to Christian education."[72]

Church-related colleges had to plan for a flood of discharged servicemen at the end of the war. The government's GI Bill of Rights had suddenly made college education affordable to millions of veterans. The government had made it possible; now church-related colleges had to make it worthwhile. Colleges could not return to "business-as-usual" because enrollments would be too great and the needs of veterans too distinctive. Veterans would be more savvy and complex than traditional college students. Colleges, in fact, could not inculcate dogma, as they had done before the war, because soldiers, fighting shoulder to shoulder with people of all faiths, had discovered the meaninglessness of denominational divisions. Colleges could not force religion on them at all because veterans had developed enough maturity during the war to make up their own minds about matters of faith and would resent and resist indoctrination.[73]

Evangelism and Missions

Two other tasks summoned the churches to action. The first was evangelism. In "A Call to the Churches" the FCC declared: "The time is at hand for evangelical Christianity to launch a movement to win America for Jesus Christ, our Lord and Savior. He alone can give us new life, and save us from self-destruction. He is inevitable and altogether sufficient."[74] In addition to evangelism, Christian leaders were also aware of the need to forge ahead in world reconstruction and world missions.[75]

Religious bodies across America took these responsibilities seriously. Virtually every one of them formulated ambitious plans for church renewal, evangelism, world relief, and missions. Methodists led the way with their Crusade for Christ, a four-year program launched in 1945 to continue the momentum of the Crusade for a New World Order, to raise $25 million for postwar relief and reconstruction, to begin a nationwide evangelistic campaign, and to reverse dwindling enrollments in Sunday school. Methodist leaders expected the crusade to be "the greatest forward movement for Methodism in modern times."[76]

Lutherans organized for action, too. On February 8, 1944, one hundred representatives from the official boards, departments, and organizations of the American Lutheran Church gathered in Columbus, Ohio, to discuss the prospects of a renewed emphasis on evangelism. Participants committed themselves to unite all agencies within the church behind a program of evangelism.[77] American Lutheran leaders also met with officials of the emerging World Council to lay the groundwork for a campaign to help rebuild devastated churches and to relieve suffering in Europe. Lutheran World Action later collected $10 million in two years for that very purpose.[78]

Lutherans did not neglect missions, either. Abdel Ross Wentz, president of the United Lutheran Board of Foreign Missions, introduced the Forward Movement in Missions to the churches. He announced: "The United Lutheran Church seems to be about to renew her youth. There are many indications that the agencies of the Church are preparing to attack their work with new vigor and aggressiveness. The mighty achievements of physical force in wartime will have their parallel in noble undertakings and loftier attainments for the Kingdom of God." Wentz believed that the churches needed spiritual renewal, just as the world needed material relief. Though both were important, Wentz was particularly concerned about the former, which motivated him to stress world missions. He had high expectations. "A great and effectual field will soon be opened before us, a field with opportunities hitherto unmatched in all our history. Already the stream of recruits has begun to flow into the ranks of foreign missionaries. Surely funds will not be lacking."[79] Lutheran groups in America also inched toward formal union, due in part to their successful cooperation in such wartime agencies as the National Lutheran Council, Lutheran World Action, and Lutheran Service Centers.[80]

Baptists were also busy preparing to move forward. Baptist leaders affirmed the distinctiveness of their Baptist heritage, believing that it offered the greatest religious hope for the world. They were not embarrassed to recruit converts to Baptist churches and to the Baptist understanding of Christianity. They also exhorted Baptists to rekindle their passion for souls and to embrace a more militant form of Christian faith. "We believe that the world is getting a little weary of formal, dead Christianity. . . . The cry for a religious revival which goes up from all parts of the land is due to a sense of futility in religious things. Some people would like God to do again what he has done before. We may be sure it will never take place until religious men and women are willing to be impassioned with the love of God."[81] Sensing, as J. H. Rushbrooke, president of the Baptist World Alliance, did, that they had a world responsibility, Baptists in America started to plan for a postwar advance. Northern Baptists developed an eleven-point program of rehabilitation, which would require at least $10 million. The program included a specific plan for postwar evangelism in America. Southern Baptists initiated their own Centennial Crusade, hoping to win "a million new souls for Christ." The Committee on Preparation for Post-War Missions was also appointed to recruit new missionaries and extend the church's reach in old and new fields of service.[82] Disciples, Congregationalists, Episcopalians, Presbyterians, Catholics, Fundamentalists, Neo-evangelicals were also active in planning similar programs in evangelism and missions.[83] All of these initiatives showed evidence of renewed vitality in the churches. The war created the opportunities, and the churches planned to take advantage.

But tensions among the churches remained. The first tension surfaced in the practice of evangelism. Church leaders tended to conceive of evangelism in terms that advanced the interests of their own particular church body, often at the expense of others. The gospel, in other words, always had a label of ownership on it—Baptist, Methodist, Fundamentalist, Protestant, Catholic. The churches thus never really propagated the "simple gospel." They did not evangelize with complete denominational disinterest. They propagated a distinctive version of the gospel—their own gospel; and they labored for the growth of a particular church—their own church. Commitment to evangelism often gave way to competition for unchurched people. This tension of universal church mission and particular church interest became an important theme in postwar American religion.

The second tension involved the churches' commitment to cooperation. Church leaders were inclined to define that cooperation in terms that served the interests of their own church body. They strived for a unity of Lutherans over against other Protestants, of Fundamentalists over against liberal Protestants, of Protestants over against Catholics. There is no doubt that pressure for unity was strong. The war reminded them that Christians had an obligation to work together to heal the world's wounds. Cooperation would give them greater authority. Yet the pressure for separation was strong, too. If the world did in fact need Christianity, as most church leaders believed, it had to be a particular expression of Christianity. It had to be the religion of Baptists, Evangelicals, Lutherans, or Catholics. Many American Christians were willing to cooperate together only if the integrity of their religious traditions was kept intact. However cooperative, then, many of these religious groups were also exclusive. This tension of cooperation and exclusion became another dominant issue in the religious world after 1945.[84]

The church's failure during World War I and the church's opportunity during World War II spurred the churches to action. Christian leaders started to discuss the postwar peace even before Pearl Harbor, and they launched ambitious programs in church cooperation, evangelism, and missions as the war drew to a close. They believed that the future of world civilization depended on the gospel and the church's ministry. Unlike twenty-five years earlier, this time the churches did not appear to be caught by surprise.

CHAPTER FOURTEEN

THE PROSPECTS OF A CAUTIOUS PATRIOTISM

A cautious patriotism characterized the basic attitude of the churches during the Second World War, as I have tried to prove in this book. Such caution surfaced during the initial debate about intervention and continued through the discussions about the postwar peace. Christian leaders in particular did not want to surrender to the pressure of a narrow, fanatical patriotism. Though victory was the immediate goal, it was never considered to be the final goal. The bitter memory of World War I and Versailles, as well as the lingering influence of pacifism from the 1930s, kept many Christians from jingoism. Commitment to the ecumenical movement and an independent, vital church reinforced their convictions. The Holocaust and the atomic bomb reminded church leaders of the evil and destruction that nations were capable of unleashing on the world. The anxiety and uncertainty they felt as they looked to the future only added to their sobriety. Christians were convinced that the world desperately needed their influence.

The war awakened the churches to what many leaders identified as the major challenge of the hour—to be *in* the world but not *of* the world. That the churches were *patriotic* cannot be questioned. They helped to mobilize America for war. They served soldiers and civilians. They strived for victory, as most Americans did. That the churches were *cautious* seems above question, too. Christian leaders in particular defended civil liberties, planned for the postwar peace, stressed the foundational role that Christian faith had to play in a democracy, and showed the important contribution that the church could make to society. They tried to be prophetic even as they were pastoral. They maintained an international perspective even as they addressed national concerns. They wanted to be faithful to Christian convictions even as they functioned as good citizens in a nation in crisis.

Harry Emerson Fosdick

If anyone represented the perspective of a cautious patriotism, it was surely Harry Emerson Fosdick, pastor of the famous Riverside Church in New York City. Fosdick remembered World War I with a feeling of horror and shame because, as Abrams's *Preachers Present Arms* reminded readers in the 1930s, he had enthusiastically supported allied victory during the war with little thought given to larger Christian concerns. After the Great War he turned to pacifism and remained a pacifist for the rest of his life. He promised himself that he would never compromise his Christian convictions again. He kept that promise during the Second World War. Yet he was no dreamy idealist who lived according to lofty convictions while the rest of the world floundered in confusion. He was a man of the world, a man for the world. Sunday after Sunday he had to face his parishioners—pacifists and interventionists, conscientious objectors and soldiers, homemakers and warmakers—and make sense out of human experience from an eternal perspective. He had to help them live in the world but not be of the world.

Fosdick pondered the problem of the war well before America entered it. He wanted to avoid two extremes—unsympathetic detachment and uncritical involvement. He was profoundly loyal to America, but he was also committed to the Christian faith. He hoped for a favorable outcome to the war, yet he did not want to confuse patriotism and discipleship. He finally devised a solution to his dilemma. During such a crisis he believed that Christians had to "live under tension" in the two contradictory worlds in which they found themselves. "This present world, war-torn and terrible, denies everything that Christ taught and stood for. Cruel and brutal, so that we can hardly credit, though we see it, its insane iniquity, it is, as it were, an incarnate anti-Christ; and in this world, part and parcel of its grim necessities, we must live. Yet we are Christians, too. Not altogether in vain did Jesus teach in Galilee and die on Calvary. We have seen in him and in some who have resembled him visions of a way of life—lovely, elevating, challenging—that found in us response, so that the best in us has risen up to follow him."[1] If only Christians could live in one world or the other, Fosdick lamented, then they would be free of the crushing burden of living under the tension. But in Fosdick's mind, such escape was impossible. Disciples of Jesus Christ were "doomed to the tension of living in two worlds at once"—"the actual and the possible, the visible and the invisible, the temporal and eternal, the shaken and the unshaken."

Fosdick believed that Christians must live under tension for the sake of both the future and the present, to help the world return to sanity and peace at war's end, and to keep it sane and peaceful even while madness seemed to rule. "The function of the church of Christ is to keep alive and alight this realm of spiritual judgment and guidance, so that even amid the storm of war we may not lose those faiths and values on which man's hope at last depends."[2] Such was the delicate and difficult responsibility of being Christian in a warring world.

The Last Good War

Many now call the Second World War the "last good war" in which America fought. Such a war made it easy for the churches to defer to Uncle Sam and serve with utter devotion—and in good conscience—the cause of saving Western civilization. America, it was assumed at the time, had not provoked the enemy; America had not invaded peaceful nations; America had not poisoned an entire people with hate and greed; America had not systematically exterminated millions of people. Clearly America was innocent; Germany and Japan guilty. Moreover, America faced an enemy with unprecedented power and wealth. It had to commit its total energies to the war effort. Every citizen's contribution and loyalty was necessary. The Second World War, then, was not a war for the few but for the many. It was not a war for the ambivalent but for the committed. It mandated a purity of patriotic devotion that the nation had never witnessed and needed before.

It was also a war in which it was difficult to be both patriotic and prophetic. In the minds of most Americans, the purpose for which it was being fought was as simple as the war effort itself was total. This was not a war of subtle distinctions and fine shades of meaning. America was good; the enemy was bad. Common sense was sufficient enough to come to that conclusion. It was thus the kind of war that clearly divided the loyalists from the traitors, the patriots from the critics. World War II, in short, made fanatical patriotism easy and measured opposition difficult. It would appear that the war left little room for anyone to "live in the tension."

Yet that is exactly—and surprisingly—what we observe in the churches, and especially among Christian leaders. Everywhere there was ambivalence, struggle, caution. The churches were committed to the allied cause—they sent their sons and daughters to war, commissioned their chaplains, worked in industry, invested in war bonds, defended the superiority of democracy, and prayed for victory. But they were concerned about other causes, too— the rights of persecuted minorities in America, the needs of the victims of war, the settlement of a just and durable peace, and especially the independence, integrity, and mission of the church. Christian belief was more fundamental than democracy, the church's ministry more important than national need, biblical principles more absolute than America's interests. The Christian faith did not undermine loyalty to the nation, but it did transcend it. The churches thus lived in the tension of a cautious patriotism.

Prospects and Limits

The church's response to American involvement in World War II tells another chapter in the long and complex history of church-state relations in the United States. The "cautious patriotism" of the churches during the war presents itself as a potential model for how the church should cooperate with the state during a major national crisis, as World War II surely was. Is it a worthy model, one the Christian community should imitate? I would answer that it is a worthy model, yet serious attention must be paid to two issues that surfaced in the United States during and after the war, and partly as the result of the church's response to the war.

The Significance of the Past

The first issue centers on the way Christian leaders understood and appropriated their recent past in light of the conflict of the war itself. How people interpret the past influences the way they set a course for the future. That was true for Christians who lived in America during World War II, whose past included a European heritage that made Christians especially sympathetic with the plight Europe was facing, as well as an experience of a previous war that made them determined to avoid committing the same error again.

The vast majority of Americans were quite naturally concerned about the plight of the people from whose stock they had come. Europe was the source of both lineage and faith for most Americans. Europe had sent millions of its own to America. It had given birth to Christian faith in America, and it had nurtured that faith for nearly two hundred years. If America was the child that came of age during World War II, then Europe was the ailing mother who needed help from the child she had raised. This bond of blood and faith engendered a spirit of loyalty and concern in American Christians which extended not only to England but also to Germany, the nation that had caused so much destruction and suffering.

This connection to the European past had consequences for the way in which Christians in America responded to their two major enemies. They showed far more sympathy to Germany than they did to Japan. Not that their sentiments for Germany were entirely positive. There was more than enough hatred of Germany and everything for which it stood. Still, there was a qualitative difference between how Christians, especially Christian leaders, responded to Germany and how they responded to Japan. Writer after writer agonized on the pages of religious journals to understand how Germany, of all nations, could have changed so dramatically and turned into something so evil. Christians were shocked, sobered, and grieved that the land of Luther and Bach had become the land of Hitler and Himmler. They wondered why Germany's Christian heritage had failed, what had gone wrong, and how it could be restored. What happened to Germany surprised them; what happened to Japan did not.

Thus, when Germany was caricatured by the religious press during the war, the cartoons portrayed *Hitler* as the personification of evil. When Japan was caricatured, the cartoons portrayed an *ordinary Japanese citizen*, implying that the Japanese *as a race* were wicked and perverse. Christians in America did not turn against German Americans or Italian Americans during the war. But many did turn against Japanese Americans, sending tens of thousands to internment camps. The religious press could never quite believe that the Nazis were capable of exterminating millions of Jews until reports and photographs from American soldiers forced them to think otherwise. The religious press rarely expressed incredulity when they heard reports of Japanese atrocities. The Japanese, in short, never received the attention from religious leaders that Germany did and, when they did receive attention, it was almost always vicious and racist. The Christian response to Germany's capitulation to evil was ambivalent; the response to Japan's was not. The Christian response to Germany was sympathetic; the response to Japan was decidedly hostile.

How church leaders remembered World War I also influenced their response to World War II. Christian leaders were determined not to fail in the same way they believed they had failed during the Great War, a war that evoked bitter memories of shrill voices condemning the enemy, of a failure to pursue peace and justice after the war, and of the pressure of propaganda. They would not allow themselves to be duped again. This fear of repeating history made Christian leaders cautious and critical when war broke out once again in Europe. It caused them to question the popular opinion that Hitler was a monster and Germany was evil. It made them stubbornly neutralist up to Pearl Harbor and suspicious when stories began leaking out of Germany that millions of Jews were being murdered. It made them eager to begin planning for the peace before the war was even close to ending. How Christian leaders responded to World War II can only be understood, then, in light of their experience of World War I. They did not want to fail so miserably again. They did not want to repeat history.

But in the 1950s and 1960s the same could be said about the way they remembered and reacted to their experience of the Second World War. America's late entry into the war and slow response to German atrocities— both reactions to World War I—allowed totalitarianism to gobble up Europe and millions to die unnecessarily, even though it cast America as a hero who, arriving late on the scene, rescued the world from total destruction. America's early entry into the Cold War and strong opposition to communism— both reactions to World War II—turned America into what many nations called a global policeman and international bully, even though it also helped in the long run to destroy communism in the former Soviet Union and liberate Eastern Europe from Soviet domination. The fear of another futile war made many Christian leaders neutralists and pacifists in the 1930s; the fear of totalitarianism made them militarists and interventionists in the 1950s. In either case, how Christians responded to a national crisis was based in part on how they read their own past, especially past failures. The Christian interpretation of the past played a key role in shaping the nation's future.

Christianity and Democracy

The other issue revolves around the relationship between Christianity and democracy in America. During World War II many religious leaders argued that Christianity was the only foundation upon which democracy could be built. Only a thriving Christianity would make democracy prosperous. These leaders thus identified themselves as the religious guardians of the nation's heritage. They laid claim to America as their own. Because they believed that America's future depended upon the Christian faith, they felt obligated as the leaders of the church to take responsibility for America—to shape its values, determine its priorities, purge its sins, and set a course for its future. Such was their duty as people who represented the very faith upon which the nation was established. There were exceptions, of course, especially among the Peace Churches and among outsider groups like the Jehovah's Witnesses, but not enough to counter the trend.

This determination to exercise Christian influence was so great among mainstream religious groups that it engendered a preoccupation with the affairs of the nation, even at the expense of the church's unique and independent mission. The church's identity, in other words, became attached to the nation's destiny. Many Christians invested so much of their energy into the nation's well-being that their investment seemed to compromise the church's biblical identity as a people set apart, living as "strangers, sojourners, and aliens" on earth. In short, America's future became an obsession of the church.

This preoccupation with America's destiny created conflicts and divisions in the church. The culture wars of today reflect an unhealthy degree of competition among religious groups that continue to fight over which group has the right to shape America's values and plot a course for its future. These groups share the same Bible, the same apostolic heritage, the same basic creeds, the same history. Their conflict is not doctrinal, as it used to be. Churches are no longer fighting very much over the correct way to interpret the Lord's Supper or the Atonement. It is not concern about theology that drives the debate; it is concern about politics and economics, about private ethics and public policy. It is not disagreements over the proper configuration of ecclesiastical structures that cause conflict; it is disagreements over how to shape American society. Religious groups seem determined to dominate America. The churches are literally waging war for America's soul.

Perhaps it is time to raise questions about the goal itself. Should the success of America be the church's primary goal? Perhaps the assumption itself—that America is still God's almost-chosen nation, the modern counterpart to ancient Israel, a light to all nations, the last and best hope for the world—should be challenged. Perhaps the church's identity is more spiritual than close identification with America would allow, its moral vision more demanding, its mission more global, its separateness more fundamental to its own identity. Perhaps the church's calling is not to save America but to transcend it, just as it is called to transcend all times, places, and circumstances for the sake of its greater loyalty to the Kingdom of God.

NOTES

ABBREVIATIONS OF RELIGIOUS PERIODICALS

AD	Advance
AM	America
BA	Banner
BR	Baptist and Reflector
BL	Baptist Leader
CAN	Catholic Action
CA	Christian Advocate
CC	Christian Century
CE	Christian-Evangelist
CHD	Christian Herald
CI	Christian Index
CAC	Christianity and Crisis
CR	Christian Register
CS	Christian Standard
CH	Churchman
CWE	Commonweal
FCB	Federal Council Bulletin
FS	Fellowship
GM	Gospel Messenger
LC	Living Church
LU	Lutheran
LS	Lutheran Standard
LW	Lutheran Witness
MN	Mennonite
MM	Moody Monthly
PRES	Presbyterian
PG	Presbyterian Guardian
PS	Presbyterian Survey
PT	Presbyterian Tribune
PR	Protestant Digest (Protestant)
RR	Radical Religion
ST	Signs of the Times

SA	Social Action
SST	Sunday School Times
UEA	United Evangelical Action
WE	Watchman-Examiner
WR	Western Recorder
ZH	Zion's Herald

CHAPTER ONE

1. Reinhold Niebuhr, "The Crisis," *CAC* 1 (February 10, 1941): 1–2. For other essays on this crisis in Western civilization, see the Right Reverend William T. Manning, "American Christians in the World Crisis," *LC* 101 (October 18, 1939): 11–12; Harold Ockenga, "Christ for America," *UEA* 2 (May 4, 1943): 1–4.

2. "The Church in Crisis," statement issued by the Council of Bishops, the Methodist Church, *CA* 117 (January 1, 1942): 6–7.

3. Christopher Dawson, "The Threat to the West," *CWE* 31 (February 2, 1940): 117–18.

4. L. O. Hartman, "While It Is Day, *ZH* 120 (March 18, 1942): 248.

5. "The Church—and a World at War," statement of the Louisville Convention of the United Lutheran Church in America, *Minutes of the Thirteenth Biennial Convention* (1942), 143.

6. John A. Mackay, "Yet Not Consumed," *PRES* 112 (February 5, 1942): 3–4.

7. See, for example, Rufus W. Weaver, "The World Crisis and Religious Liberty," *BR* 105 (October 19, 1939): 5; Robert B. Day, "Liberal Religion in a Time of Crisis," *CR* 118 (October 19, 1939): 603; "Building an Ecumenical Church," editorial, *FCB* 26 (March, 1943): 3; statement of the Board of Foreign Missions of the United Lutheran Church in America, *LU* 24 (July 22, 1942): 6.

8. Mackay, "Yet Not Consumed," 4.

9. L. O. Hartman, "While It Is Day," 248.

10. Nathan R. Melhorn, "On the Way Out," *LU* 26 (June 28, 1944): 3.

11. "Crisis of Christianity," statement issued by the board of the National Catholic Welfare Conference, *CAN* 23 (December 1941): 3–6.

12. Dawson, "Threat to the West."

13. Manning, "American Christians."

14. Mackay, *Heritage and Destiny*, 1, 102.

15. Bainton, *Christian Attitudes toward War and Peace*, 221.

16. Abrams, "Churches and the Clergy," 110.

17. G. Elson Ruff, "The Year 1943 in the Churches," *LS* 102 (January 1, 1944): 4–5.

18. Theodore C. Hume, "The Local Church and the War," *CAC* 2 (April 20, 1942): 3–6.

19. Horton, *Can Christianity Save Civilization?* 19.

CHAPTER TWO

1. The following articles and books provided useful information for this first section of the chapter: Abrams, "Churches and the Clergy"; Johnson, "Impact of the War on Religion"; Bainton, "Churches and War"; Miller, *American Protestantism*; Meyer, *Protestant Search for Political Realism*.

2. Miller, *American Protestantism*, 326–27.

3. Ibid., 327.

4. Bainton, "Churches and War," 36.

5. Ibid., 35.

6. Miller, *American Protestantism*, 340.

7. Ibid.

8. Ibid., 341.

9. Editorial, *Fortune* 21 (January 1940): 26–27.

10. *Time*, August 17, 1942.

CHAPTER THREE

1. "Resolutions on Social Issues," *CE* 77 (November 9, 1939): 1213–15.

2. "Resolutions Approved by the Convention," *CE* 79 (May 22, 1941): 616–618.

3. Ibid.

4. "A Message to the Churches," *CE* 79 (May 15, 1941): 578.

5. "The Churches and a Just and Durable Peace," editorial, *CE* 80 (August 13, 1942): 886.

6. Raphael Harwood Miller, "Peace, Peace When There Is No (Ap)Pease," *CE* 79 (December 11, 1941): 1383. For other Miller editorials in *CE* that underscore the same kind of ambivalence, see "There Is Yet Time," 77 (August 31, 1939): 899; "America and Europe's War," 77 (September 7, 1939): 931; "No Peace-Time Conscription," 78 (June 13, 1940): 635; "Implications for America in the Destroyer Deal," 78 (September 12, 1940): 947; "Not by Arms Alone!" 78 (July 18, 1940): 755; "Why Not Cooperate in Peace?" 79 (March 13, 1941): 317.

7. Muelder, *Methodism and Society*, 157.

8. "Statement of Commission on World Peace," *ZH* 118 (December 25, 1940): 1260.

9. Lynn Harold Hough, "The Pacifist Heresy," *ZH* 119 (March 12, 1941): 243.

10. L. R. Templin, "The Heresy of Judgment," *ZH* 119 (March 26, 1941): 297.

11. "Maintain the Christian Spirit," editorial, *ZH* 117 (October 4, 1939).

12. Roy L. Smith, "Twenty-five Years from Now," *CA* 116 (February 20, 1941): 229.

13. Smith, "A Negotiated Peace," *CA* 116 (June 12, 1941): 760.

14. Smith, "The Logic of War," *CA* 116 (July 10, 1941): 890.

15. Smith, "The Only Solution," *CA* 116 (January 9, 1941): 37.

16. "The Church in Crisis," statement issued by the Council of Bishops, the Methodist Church, *CA* 117 (January 1, 1942): 7.

17. Muelder, *Methodism and Society*, 184–85.

18. "The Catholic Church and National Defense," *CAN* 22 (August 1940): 4–5; "Crisis of Christianity," statement issued by the board of the National Catholic Welfare Conference, *CAN* 23 (December 1941): 8–11.

19. "Nationalism and the Present Crisis," editorial, *CAN* 22 (July 1940): 13.

20. The Right Reverend Monsignor Michael J. Ready, "Conscription vs. Voluntary Enlistment," *CAN* 22 (August 1940): 11–12.

21. "Holy Father and President Roosevelt Collaborate for World Peace," *CAN* 22 (January 1940): 5.

22. McNeal, *American Catholic Peace Movement*, 81–121.

23. For examples of the debate, see Jacques Maritain, "Just War," *CWE* 31 (December 22, 1939): 199–200; John Kelly, "Reply to Jacques Maritain," *CWE* 31 (December 29, 1939): 221; Robert L. Grims, "How Humane This War?" *CWE* 32 (July 19, 1940): 263; William M. Agar, "Can We Justify Neutrality?" *CWE* 33 (November 22, 1940): 179.

24. "Conclusions and Agreement," editorial, *CWE* 32 (June 21, 1940): 177.

25. "Peace Is the Object," editorial, *CWE* 33 (November 22, 1940).

26. "Steps to a Loyal Opposition," editorial, *CWE* 35 (October 24, 1941): 3.

27. "Against Peace Time Conscription," editorial, *CWE* 32 (August 23, 1940): 357.

28. "How the U.S. Can Intervene," editorial, *CWE* 31 (March 1, 1940): 393.

29. "The War," editorial, *CWE* 35 (December 19, 1941): 211.

30. Francis X. Talbot, "Comment," *AM* 61 (September 16, 1939): 530.

31. On lend-lease see the following editorials in *AM*: 64 (January 15, 1941): 422, and 64 (February 14, 1941): 507. See also John La Farge, S.J., "Church in the New Order," *AM* 64 (March 1, 1941): 654. On conscription, see the following editorials in *AM*: 63 (August 3, 1940): 462, and 63 (August 10, 1940): 491.

32. Brooke Hilary Stewart, "We Save Europe? Yes, but How?" *AM* 63 (April 27, 1940): 62.

33. John P. Delaney, "We Fight in Their War? Why?" *AM* 62 (October 14, 1939): 6.

34. Hilaire Belloc, "Poland, the Bastion of Our Civilization," *AM* 62 (October 28, 1939): 63; "Remember Poland," editorial, *AM* 62 (February 10, 1940): 491.

35. Francis X. Talbot, "Hatred for None," *AM* 63 (June 1, 1940): 210.

36. Talbot, "FDR Consistent in Foreign Policy," *AM* 65 (April 12, 1941): 2.

37. Talbot, "War and Conscience," *AM* 66 (December 27, 1941): 322.

38. Talbot, "Our Sure Refuge," *AM* 66 (January 10, 1942): 378.

39. "War, Peace and Pacifism: A Testimony," *BA* 74 (November 2, 1939): 1028–29.

40. R. B. Kuiper, "Things That Destroy Nations—and Churches," *BA* 75 (July 19, 1940): 680–82.

41. H. J. Kuiper, "The Sin of Our Military Unpreparedness," *BA* 77 (March 13, 1942): 244.

42. Kuiper, "Conscription," *BA* 75 (August 16, 1940): 749.

43. Kuiper, "The Attitude of Our Churches toward the Present European War," *BA* 74 (October 5, 1939): 916.

44. Kuiper, "We Favor a Foreign Policy of Morality, Not Neutrality," *BA* 75 (October 25, 1940): 988.

45. Kuiper, "No Right to Go to War!" *BA* 76 (January 31, 1941): 100.

46. E. J. Tanis, "The World Today," *BA* 76 (December 19, 1941): 1180.

47. "Peace in Our Time," statement issued by the National Lutheran Council, *LS* 97 (November 4, 1939): 4.

48. *Minutes of the Biennial Convention of the United Lutheran Church* (1942), 145.

49. *Minutes, General Council of the Congregational and Christian Churches* (1940), 43–45.

50. *Annual of the Northern Baptist Convention* (1940), 353; (1941), 225–26.

51. *Minutes of the General Assembly of the Presbyterian Church in the United States of America* (1940), 180; (1941), 184.

52. Peachey, *Mennonite Statements on Peace and Social Concerns*, 119.

53. Ibid., 130.

54. *Annual of the Southern Baptist Convention* (1941), 167; and (1940), 87, 96.

55. *Annual of the Southern Baptist Convention* (1941), 99.

CHAPTER FOUR

1. For the perspectives, politics, organizations, and strategies of the two parties, see French, *Common Sense Neutrality*; Jonas, *Isolationism in America*, who argues that isolationism was advocated by five very distinct groups representing different points of view; Stenehjem, *An American First*; Johnson, *Battle against Isolation*; Langer and Gleason, *Challenge to Isolation*.

2. For a discussion of how the perspective of "Christian realism" uses religion in ethical argument, see Hudnut-Beumler, "American Churches and U.S. Interventionism"; Lovin, "Reason, Relativism, and Christian Realism"; Outka and Reeder, *Prospects for a Common Morality*.

3. Francis X. Talbot, "War Clouds," *AM* 61 (May 6, 1939): 75.

4. Harold E. Fey, "Save Neutrality, Save Peace!" *CC* 56 (October 11, 1939): 1234–36.

5. Charles Clayton Morrison, "What Hinders Peace," *CC* 56 (October 18, 1939): 1263–65.

6. Morrison, "What Can America Do for Peace?" *CC* 57 (May 15, 1940): 630–32.

7. Morrison, "The Search for a Lasting Peace," *CC* 58 (February 19, 1941): 248–50.

8. Francis X. Talbot, "No Hatred," *AM* 62 (March 16, 1940): 630.

9. Charles Clayton Morrison, "Mr. Hoover," *CC* 58 (October 29, 1941): 1326–28.

10. Morrison, "War for Europe," *CC* 57 (November 26, 1940): 1470–71.

11. Morrison, "Mr. Churchill and the U.S.," *CC* 59 (March 3, 1942): 272–74.

12. Francis X. Talbot, "No Recovery through War," *AM* 61 (April 22, 1939): 36.

13. Talbot, "Bolshevism Emerges," *AM* 66 (September 6, 1941): 602. See also "More Concern about Aiding Russia," *AM* 66 (August 16, 1941): 506.

14. John Haynes Holmes, "If America Is Drawn in the War," *CC* 57 (December 11, 1940): 1546–48.

15. Francis X. Talbot, "Our One Defense," *AM* 63 (August 3, 1940): 462.

16. Harry Emerson Fosdick, "If America Is Drawn into the War," *CC* 58 (January 22, 1941): 115–18.

17. George M. Gibson, "The Flight of Moral Leadership," *CC* 58 (June 25, 1941): 829–30.

18. Talbot, "No Recovery through War," 36.

19. Talbot, "The Land That All Forget," *AM* 63 (June 1, 1940): 210.

20. Talbot, "The Still Subsisting War," *AM* 62 (January 6, 1940): 350.

21. Harold E. Fey, "Defense or Despotism," *CC* 57 (January 24, 1940): 110–13.

22. Charles Clayton Morrison, "No Third Term!" *CC* 57 (October 16, 1940): 1270–73.

23. Francis X. Talbot, "Twelve Years, Too Much," *AM* 61 (June 24, 1939): 253.

24. "Foreign Policy in the Campaign," editorial, *CC* 57 (October 23, 1940): 1302–4.

25. Oswald Garrison Villard, "Who Rules America?" *CC* 58 (July 23, 1941): 933–34, and "Let Congress Keep Control," *CC* 58 (August 13, 1941): 1005–6.

26. Francis X. Talbot, "Clear-Headed Vision," *AM* 61 (June 24, 1939): 252.

27. Charles Clayton Morrison, "Defending Democracy," *CC* 57 (June 5, 1940): 726–27.

28. Morrison, "No Free Speech for Freedom's Foes?" *CC* 57 (September 4, 1940): 1068.

29. William Hubben, "If Conscription Comes," *CC* 57 (August 14, 1940): 994–95.

30. Francis X. Talbot, "The Gains of War," *AM* 61 (May 6, 1939): 86.

31. Paul L. Blakely, S.J., "All Will Be Lost by War," *AM* 63 (June 29, 1940): 317.

32. E. T. Buehrer, "Wall Street's War Babies," *CC* 57 (June 26, 1940): 822–24.

33. Paul L. Blakely, S.J., "The Old War Propaganda and the Streamline Model," *AM* 62 (October 14, 1939): 4–5.

34. Nels F. S. Ferre, "The Non-Conformist Conscience," *CC* 58 (April 30, 1941): 586–87.

35. A. J. Muste, *War Is the Enemy*.

36. Ibid., 18.

37. Ibid., 19.

38. Ibid., 35.

39. Ibid., 20.

40. John C. Bennett, "If America Is Drawn into the War," *CC* 57 (December 4, 1940): 1506–8.

41. J. H. Marion Jr., "If America Is Drawn into the War," *CC* 58 (July 16, 1941): 908–10.

42. Henry Pitney Van Dusen, "If America Is Drawn into the War," *CC* 58 (January 29, 1941): 146–48.

43. For examples of other interventionist views, see Lynn Harold Hough, "Defending Justice Despite Our Injustice," *CAC* 1 (April 21, 1941): 4–6; Lewis Mumford, "The Aftermath of Utopianism," *CAC* 1 (March 24, 1941): 2–6; Edward L. Parsons, "Just Wars and Holy Wars," *CAC* 1 (March 10, 1941): 3–5.

44. Reinhold Niebuhr, "The Christian Faith and the World Crisis," *CAC* 1 (February 10, 1941): 4–6.

45. Niebuhr, "Pacifism and America First," *CAC* 1 (June 16, 1941): 2–5.

46. Niebuhr, "The Mirage of Mediation," *CAC* 1 (July 28, 1941): 1–2.

47. Niebuhr, "The Lend-Lease Bill," *CAC* 1 (February 10, 1941): 2.

48. Niebuhr, "Tyranny and War," *RR* 4 (Fall 1939): 8–9.

49. Niebuhr, *Christianity and Power Politics*, 9.

50. Ibid., 11.

51. Niebuhr, "Politics and the Christian Ethic," *RR* 5 (Spring 1940): 24.

52. Ibid., 27.

53. Niebuhr, *Christianity and Power Politics*, 20–21.

54. Ibid., 22.

55. Ibid., 33–34.

56. Ibid., 29–30.

57. Niebuhr, "Repeal the Neutrality Act!" *CAC* 1 (October 20, 1941): 1–2.

58. Niebuhr, *Christianity and Power Politics*, 16.

59. Ibid., 17.

60. Niebuhr, "Just or Holy?" *CAC* 1 (November 3, 1941): 1–2.

61. Niebuhr, *Christianity and Power Politics*, 2.

62. Ibid.

63. Ibid., 5.

64. Niebuhr, "The Christian Faith and the World Crisis," *CAC* 1 (February 10, 1941): 4–6.

65. Niebuhr, "Just or Holy?" 1–2.

66. Niebuhr, "Our Responsibilities in 1942," *CAC* 1 (January 24, 1942): 1–2.

CHAPTER FIVE

1. Reinhold Niebuhr, "The Christian Perspective on the World Crisis," *CAC* 4 (May 1, 1944): 2–5.

2. Clarence Edward Macartney, "Those Things Which Cannot Be Shaken," *PRES* 109 (October 1939): 3, 6.

3. Joseph Taylor Britan, "God in a World at War," *MM* 43 (May 1944): 500–501. See also H. J. Kuiper, "Hitler My Servant," *BA* 76 (January 3, 1941): 7; Thomas R. Birch, "War and God's Sovereignty," *PG* 9 (February 10, 1940): 41.

4. A. Culver Gordon, "Why Doesn't God Stop This War?" *PG* 12 (January 10, 1943): 1–2.

5. Britan, "God in a World at War," 500–501.

6. Reinhold Niebuhr, "The Crisis," *CAC* 1 (February 10, 1941): 1–2. See also John W. Bradbury, "What Are We to Defend?" *WE* 29 (December 11, 1941): 1264–65; "In the Face of the World's Crisis: A Manifesto by European Catholics Sojourning in America," *CWE* 36 (August 21, 1942): 415–20.

7. Sterling W. Brown, "Christians and Patriots," *CE* 79 (July 3, 1941): 779–80.

8. John W. Bradbury, "Why We Must Fight," *WE* 31 (January 14, 1943): 33–34.

9. John A. Mackay, "God and the Decisions of History," *CAC* 1 (December 1, 1941): 2–5.

10. Ibid.

11. George Wells Arms, "The Bible and the War," *PRES* 110 (July 18, 1940): 3, 7–8. See also Lou G. Findley, "Can Any Good Come Out of War?" *PRES* 114 (January 13, 1944): 5.

12. Edwin R. Errett, "The Deepest Peril in the Present Crisis," *CS* 75 (September 14, 1940): 903.

13. Errett, "Let Us Not Deceive Ourselves," *CS* 75 (May 18, 1940): 471.

14. Errett, "Liberals or Libertarians," *CS* 75 (June 29, 1940): 615. For a fundamentalist voice on America's vulnerability, see Dan Gilbert, "The Antichrist Advance in America," *MM* 40 (May 1940): 473–74; Edward Hughes Pruden, "Do We Deserve Victory?" *WE* 31 (January 14, 1943): 36–37.

15. Will H. Houghton, "What Is Wrong with America?" *MM* 41 (November 1940): 123.

16. Hyman J. Appelman, "America's First Line of Defense," *MM* 43 (July 1943): 615–16.

17. Samuel J. Allen, "God Save America!" *PG* 10 (October 25, 1941): 99.

18. Denis De Rougemont, "On the Devil and Politics," *CAC* 1 (June 2, 1941): 2–5.

19. Morris Gordin, "The Christian Answer to Communism and Fascism," *MM* 40 (December 1939): 181–82. See also Walter C. Erdman, "The Lie," *MM* 40 (December 1939): 183–84; Harold Paul Sloan, "How Hitler Happened," *CA* 116 (July 3, 1941): 867–68; J. H. Bruinooge, "Conflicting Views of Life," *BA* 79 (November 3, 1944): 1040; Sheen, *Philosophies at War*.

20. Edward F. Schewe, "Nietzsche and Nazism: Seed and Harvest," *CA* 118 (June 24, 1943): 776–77.

21. H. J. Kuiper, "The Crooked Cross," *BA* 78 (May 14, 1943): 460.

22. Raphael Harwood Miller, "God Bless America," *CE* 80 (January 8, 1942): 27–28. See

also Joseph C. Todd, "God in the World Today," *CE* 79 (January 30, 1941): 158–59; Edwin R. Errett, "Here Is the Real Issue," *CS* 75 (October 26, 1940): 1087; A. V. Havens, "Christianity and the Ideologies," *CE* 79 (October 23, 1941): 1190–91.

23. Wilbur M. Smith, "What Christ Actually Taught about War," *MM* 42 (June 1942): 586–87.

24. Louis S. Bauman, "What the End of the Age Must Be Very Near," *SST* 82 (February 3, 1940): 89–90.

25. Bauman, "Europe's Triumvirate of Beasts," *SST* 82 (July 20, 1940): 579–80.

26. Rice, *World-Wide War*, 26–27.

27. Ibid., 22–23.

28. Ibid., 60.

29. Ibid., 119–20.

30. Morrison, *The Christian and the War*, 20.

31. Ibid., 22–23.

32. Ibid., 53.

33. Ibid., 54–55.

34. Ibid., 128. For a thorough critique of Morrison's theodicy, see Reinhold Niebuhr and Charles Clayton Morrison, "The Christian and the War," *CC* 59 (December 23, 1942): 1589–93; Albert Edward Day, "Metaphors and War," *CC* 59 (March 18, 1942): 352–54.

35. Ironside, *Lamp of Prophecy*, 159.

36. Edwin R. Errett, "What Is America?" *CS* 76 (June 28, 1941): 671.

37. Errett, "The Gates of Hades Shall Not Prevail," *CS* 74 (September 30, 1939): 935.

38. Errett, "If the Church Believes in Democracy," *CS* 77 (March 14, 1942): 242.

39. Errett, "God's Purpose—but Whose Method?" *CS* 77 (February 28, 1942): 195.

40. Errett, "Pax Americana?" *CS* 77 (July 4, 1942): 653.

41. Reinhold Niebuhr, "Anglo-Saxon Destiny and Responsibility," *CAC* 3 (October 4, 1943): 2–4.

CHAPTER SIX

1. Edwin R. Errett, "If the Church Believes in Democracy," *CS* 77 (March 14, 1942): 3.

2. L. O. Hartman, "Democracy—July 4, 1940," *ZH* 118 (July 3, 1940): 632.

3. Nathan R. Melhorn, "The American Way of Government," *LU* 22 (November 8, 1939): 8. See also Ned B. Stonehouse, "On Being a Christian in a Democracy," *PG* 10 (April 25, 1941): 119; Curtis W. Reese, "Presuppositions of Democracy," *CR* 121 (July 1942): 244–45.

4. Francis P. Miller, "Relation of the Christian Faith to Democracy," *CAC* 2 (February 23, 1942): 3–6.

5. Jacob Trapp, "Democracy as a Modern Religion," *CR* 121 (July 1942): 238–40.

6. John Paul Williams, "Faith in Democracy—A Religious Faith," *CA* 117 (April 16, 1942): 460.

7. Allen J. Miller, "Can Christianity Save Civilization?" *CH* 155 (January 15, 1941): 11–12.

8. Harold L. Lundquist, "Can Democracy Survive without Christianity?" *MM* 42 (July 1941): 629.

9. J. B. Hunley, "Building the Inner Wall," *CS* 76 (July 26, 1941): 5–6; Daniel S. Robinson, "Christianity and Democracy," *CS* 75 (November 9, 1940): 5–6.

10. Frederick Lee, "The Day of Disillusionment," *ST* 70 (July 20, 1943): 8–9.

11. H. W. Prentis Jr., "A Republic—If We Can Keep It," *MM* 40 (November 1939): 124–25.

12. John W. Bradbury, "Christianity and Democracy," *WE* 28 (November 21, 1940): 1217.

13. John S. Nollen, "Religion Undergirding Democracy," *AD* 132 (March 1, 1940): 100.

14. Francis P. Miller, "Relation of the Christian Faith to Democracy," *CAC* 2 (February 23, 1942): 3–6.

15. Maritain, *Christianity and Democracy*, 37–38, and *The Rights of Man*, 145.

16. "Bulwarks of Democracy—Freedom of Faith," statement issued by the Study Club Committee of the National Catholic Welfare Conference, *CAN* 23 (September 1941): 11–14.

17. Edwin Merrick Dodd, "The Civil Liberties of Americans," *CR* 120 (March 1, 1941): 91–93. See also William E. Sweet, "Religion the Bulwark of Democracy," *AD* 133 (January 1, 1941): 4; Willard Johnson, "History Shall Not Repeat Itself," *CE* 82 (February 16, 1944): 163–64; Warren Brown, "Democracy and the Aspirations of Minority Groups," *CE* 78 (February 1, 1940): 145–46; "Nation-Wide Conference on Religious Liberty," *CS* 75 (July 27, 1940): 7, 24.

18. John C. Bennett, "The Spiritual Basis of Democracy," *AD* 135 (May 1, 1943): 194–95.

19. John W. Bradbury, "Wherein We Have Failed," *WE* 29 (January 2, 1941): 8–9.

20. Norman Huffman, "Christianity and Democracy," *CA* 118 (October 28, 1943): 1355.

21. Oscar F. Blackwelder, "The Church Holds the Key," *LS* 98 (June 29, 1940): 3–5.

22. L. O. Hartman, "Tragic Fault—Lack of Discipline," *ZH* 118 (August 14, 1940): 775.

23. F. E. Johnson, "Democracy and Discipline," *CAC* 3 (December 13, 1943): 1–2. See also A. V. Havens, "That Democracy Shall Not Perish," *CE* 80 (June 25, 1942): 698–700.

24. John W. Bradbury, "Clarification for Confusion," *WE* 32 (February 3, 1944): 104–5; Victor I. Masters, "Disintegrating Liberalism at Work in American Christendom," *WR* 116 (January 1, 1942): 7.

25. Harold J. Ockenga, "Christ for America," *UEA* 2 (May 4, 1943): 1.

26. Leslie Rumble, "Are American Catholics Growing Soft and Satisfied?" *AM* 64 (January 4, 1941): 342.

27. Paul L. Blakely, "A Father's Letter That Will Live," *AM* 68 (November 21, 1942): 178; "What Would They Vote This Autumn?" *AM* 63 (September 21, 1940): 658.

28. W. E. Orchard, "The Church in the States Enjoys a Great Advantage," *AM* 63 (July 13, 1940): 368.

29. Francis X. Talbot, "When All Men Cry Papal Intervention," *AM* 61 (July 22, 1939): 348; "Holy Father and President Roosevelt Collaborate for World Peace," *CAN* 22 (January 1940): 5.

30. M. P. Hunt, "The Catholics' Position on Civil and Religious Liberty," *WR* 114 (May 23, 1940): 3.

31. "Roman Catholic Political Activities," *CH* 157 (March 15, 1943): 7–8.

32. Louis Adamic, "Are We Becoming a Catholic State?" *CH* 158 (November 15, 1944): 6–7. See also John W. Bradbury, "The Right to Be Protestant," *WE* 33 (July 19, 1945): 696–97.

33. Reprinted in *PR* 4 (June–July 1943): 51. The Federal Council of Churches (FCC) also adopted the Cleveland Declaration on December 11, 1942. It protested Catholic policy in Latin America. At the same time, the Roman Church in America accused Protestants of intolerance. "Every effort made to rob them [Ibero-Americans] of their Catholic religion or to ridicule it or to offer them a substitute for it is deeply resented by

the people of those countries and by America Catholics." See *PR* 4 (December–January 1943): 8.

34. For example, *CH* carried such articles as W. Stanley Rycroft, "Religious Liberty in Latin America," 158 (December 15, 1944): 11; Thos. F. Opie, "Catholicism and the Rest of Us," 159 (September 1, 1945): 10–11; Lawrence Fernsworth, "The Heresy of 'Christian Democracy,'" 157 (March 15, 1943): 11; A Chaplain at the Front, "Our Deluded Protestants," 159 (July 1945): 14. Editorials included "Roman Catholics and 'Intolerance,'" 157 (January 1, 1943): 4; "Should We Print the Truth?" 155 (October 15, 1941): 3. *PR* printed such articles as Kenneth Leslie, "The Strange Predicament of Our Democracy," 3 (August–September 1941): 5; Denis De Rougemont, "The War's Religious 'Grand Strategy,'" 4 (April–May 1942): 9; Lawrence Fernsworth, "The Catholic Church and America," 3 (August–September 1940): 12; S. R. Herbert, "Father Coughlin Is a Catholic," 3 (August–September 1940): 34. It also carried such editorials as "Papal 'Democracy,'" 6 (February 1945): 3. See also C. B. Gohdes, "The Past Illumines the Future," *LS* 98 (May 18, 1940): 6–7; W. L. Emmerson, "Can Rome Survive?" *ST* 71 (July 4, 1944): 10–11; "No Religious Monopoly!" *ST* 70 (January 19, 1943): 4–5; W. Stanley Rycroft, "Toward a New Day in Latin America," *ZH* 120 (July 15, 1942): 678–79; Raphael Harwood Miller, "Has the Vatican Gone Democratic?" *CE* 83 (January 10, 1945): 28.

35. Benson Y. Landis, "Protestants and Catholics," *CWE* 43 (July 27, 1945): 356–58. Several Protestants suggested that Protestants, however sharp their opposition to Catholicism, had things to learn from it. See Myles D. Blanchard, "Concerning Rome," *AD* 137 (May 1945): 13–14; John Scotford, "Catholics and Protestants," *AD* 137 (March 1945): 3–4.

36. Samuel McCrea Cavert, "Our Protestant Heritage," *FCB* 27 (October 1944): 7–9.

37. Robert Whitaker, "The Ultimate Protestantism," *PR* 4 (December–January 1943): 25–30.

38. *Annual of the Northern Baptist Convention* (1940), 349. See also *Annual of the Southern Baptist Convention* (1940), 24; "Official Relations Opposed: National Lutheran Council Addresses Resolution to President Roosevelt," *LU* 22 (February 21, 1940): 8–9.

39. Letter to President Roosevelt from F. H. Knubel, reprinted as "Against Vatican Relationship," *LU* 22 (January 10, 1940): 6. Knubel's argument was echoed throughout the Protestant press. See, for example, Edwin H. Rian, "The Papacy and Peace," *PG* 9 (February 25, 1940): 59; Ned B. Stonehouse, "The President, the Pope and Protestantism," *PG* 9 (January 25, 1940): 25; Theodore Graebner, "The American Envoy to the Pope," *LW* 59 (January 9, 1940): 4; Edward W. Schramm, "We Must Speak Out," *LS* 98 (January 13, 1940): 5, "Why We Protest," *LS* 98 (May 18, 1940): 3, and "Adding Insult to Injury," *LS* 98 (April 20, 1940): 7 (which criticized George Buttrick of the FCC for mitigating the problem); Arthur S. Maxwell, "Vigilant Protestants," *ST* 67 (February 6, 1940): 3. These are a few representative examples. *CC* also contained many editorials on the Vatican appointment. Editor Charles Clayton Morrison was convinced that it signified a serious breach of church-state separation.

40. George A. Campbell, "The Appointment to the Vatican," *CE* 78 (January 25, 1940): 103.

41. Campbell, "Anti-Catholicism and the Vatican Envoy," *CE* 78 (March 28, 1940): 377.

42. Edward Skillin Jr., "The Appointment to the Vatican," *CWE* 31 (March 22, 1940): 461.

43. Boland and Ryan, *Catholic Principles of Politics*, 27, 104.

44. Ibid., 131.

45. Ibid., 67.

46. Samuel McCrea Cavert, "Separation of Church and State: Why It Matters," *FCB* 23 (May 1940): 3–5.

47. William Emch, "Church and State," *LS* 100 (July 4, 1942): 6–7. See also Paul H. Krauss, "An Important Interpretation," *LU* 23 (August 28, 1940): 10–11.

48. William E. Gilroy, "Church and State Draw Together," *AD* 136 (July 1944): 3.

49. J. H. Bruinooge, "God and Caesar," *BA* 79 (March 10 and 17, 1944): 224 and 248.

50. Talmage C. Johnson, "Do Baptists Want a Secular State?" *WE* 30 (February 26, 1942): 204–5. See also Dame Christabel Pankhurst, "Christ and Caesar," *SST* 83 (June 7, 1941): 461.

51. Raphael Harwood Miller, "The Church's Freedom in War-Time," *CE* 79 (November 13, 1941): 1267–68.

52. Ned B. Stonehouse, "A New Threat to Freedom," *PG* 13 (May 21, 1944): 158–59.

53. E. J. Tanis, "The World Today," *BA* 76 (November 21, 1941): 1087.

54. Edward W. Schramm, "On Receiving a 'Canned Sermon,'" *LS* 99 (December 6, 1941): 7.

55. Henry Schultze, "Selective Service and the Pre-Seminary Students," *BA* 77 (July 24, 1942): 672.

56. "Discrimination Protest," *LU* 27 (May 17, 1944): 9. See also John C. Hirschler, "Recruiting the Training Ministers in War," *CE* 80 (October 1, 1942): 1074–75.

57. Editorial notes, *CAC* 4 (May 15, 1944): 2. See also Conrad Henry Moehlman, "Protestant Cowardice," *PR* 4 (August–September 1942): 14.

CHAPTER SEVEN

1. Frederick D. Kershner, "The Inconsequence of the Church," *CE* 79 (October 9, 1941): 114.

2. Charles Clayton Morrison, quoted in Frederick Lee, "Unready for the Crisis," *ST* 68 (January 21, 1941): 6–7.

3. "The Failure of Christians," editorial, *MM* 40 (November 1939): 115; "Why Churches Are Impotent," editorial, *WE* 31 (November 25, 1943): 1126–27; Oliver J. Caldwell, "The Passive American Church," *ZH* 121 (March 10, 1943): 229; William Henry Dilts, "What Guidance Can the Church Give Now?" *PRES* 112 (December 24, 1942): 3.

4. Luther Stewart, "Appraisal of the Church," *CI* 72 (May 29, 1941): 2. See also "If We Fail," editorial, *CS* 76 (September 13, 1941): 3; "Now That We Are at War," *CE* 79 (March 27, 1941): 367; "Blaming the Church," editorial, *WE* 29 (July 31, 1941): 809; "What's Right with the Churches?" editorial, *FCB* 27 (June 1944): 7.

5. Edward Frantz, "The Great Hour for the Church," *GM* 90 (October 25, 1941): 3.

6. H. Norman Sibley, "The War as the Gospel's Opportunity," *CAC* 3 (August 9, 1943): 4–5.

7. "The Christian Church in a World at War," report of the Permanent Committee on Social and Moral Welfare, *Minutes of the General Assembly of the Presbyterian Church in the United States* (1942), 134–38.

8. "Report of the Social Service Commission of the Southern Baptist Convention," *Annual of the Southern Baptist Convention* (1942), 91–92.

9. "The Church and a World at War," *Minutes of the Thirteenth Biennial Convention of the United Lutheran Church* (1942), 145–46.

10. Frederick L. Fagley, "Keeping the Churches on Even Keel," *AD* 134 (March 1, 1942): 100–101.

11. Luther Stewart, "The Church in a World at War," *CI* 73 (January 8, 1942): 2.

12. "Hatred in Wartime," statement adopted by the Federal Council's Executive Committee on March 16, 1943, *FCB* 26 (April 1943): 6.

13. On hatred and hysteria, see, "To Conquer but Not to Hate," editorial, *CE* 80 (March 5, 1942): 264; "If We Hate, We Shall Fail," editorial, *CWE* 37 (January 29, 1943): 365; Raymond M. Hudson, "For Christians, Hatred Is 'Out,'" *ZH* 120 (April 29, 1942): 389; Robert Rieser, "Anglo-Saxon Destiny: Americans, Beware of Hatred!" *CH* 159 (September 1, 1945): 9; "War and Hate," editorial, *PG* 11 (July 15, 1942): 199; L. Lofton Hudson, "To Hate or Not to Hate," *BR* 108 (June 18, 1942): 4; W. A. Smart, "Can We War without Hate?" *CA* 118 (August 19, 1943): 6–7. For denominational pronouncements, see *Minutes of the Thirteenth Biennial Convention of the United Lutheran Church* (1942), 145.

14. Henry Pitney Van Dusen, "Is the Church at War?" *CAC* 2 (April 6, 1942): 2–3. For other critiques of Morrison, see "The Church at War," editorial, *LC* 104 (March 18, 1942): 16–17; "Is the Church at War?" editorial, *WE* 30 (April 16, 1942): 367–68; "Is the Church at War?" editorial, *AD* 134 (May 1, 1942): 204–5. For Morrison's defense, see "Is the Church Aloof?" editorial, *CC* 59 (October 14, 1942): 1246–49; "War and the Crisis of Faith," editorial, *CC* 59 (November 25, 1942): 1446–48; "Recruiting the Churches," editorial, *CC* 59 (January 7, 1942): 8–10.

15. The statement was widely reprinted in the Protestant press. See, for example, "Christians for Victory," *LC* 104 (August 23, 1942): 8; "This War Must Be Won," *AD* 134 (September 1, 1942): 395. Articles on the issue also appeared about the same time. Egbert W. Smith, for example, declared: "Prayer, repentance, and now, again, such a time as this is a time for UTMOST EFFORT to win this war of liberation." Egbert W. Smith, "The Duty of the War," *PS* 32 (November, 1942): 506–8. Other groups made similar statements. See "Victory and Peace: A Statement by the Archbishops and Bishops of the United States," *CAN* 24 (December 1942): 8–9; "Win the War!" *LC* 104 (September 20, 1942): 12–13. Some denominations supported the allied cause but struggled over whether or not they should advocate outright victory. See F. Ernest Johnson, "Denominational Pronouncements on the War," *CAC* 4 (August 7, 1944): 6–8.

16. "The Church—and a World at War," *Minutes of the Thirteenth Biennial Convention of the United Lutheran Church* (1942), 145.

17. "To the President of the United States," *UEA* 4 (May 1944): 2.

18. *Annual of the Southern Baptist Convention* (1942), 94.

19. "The Course before Us: Statement of F.O.R. Executive Committee Issued on December 10, 1941," *FS* 8 (January 1942): 2.

20. Nels F. S. Ferre, "Christianity and Compromise," *FS* 8 (April 1942): 53–55.

21. Vernon Nash, "Pacifism Is Resistance," *FS* 6 (November 1940): 137–39. See also Laurance Housman, "Unconditional Surrender," *FS* 9 (September 1943): 155; A. J. Muste, "As the War Rolls On," *FS* 9 (September 1943): 156–57. For the story of nonviolent

resistance of pacifists in Civilian Public Service (CPS) camps, see Peck, *We Who Would Not Kill.*

22. Rufus D. Bowman wrote for *GM*, a Brethren publication, during the war. Guy Franklin Hershberger represented the Mennonite tradition. See, for example, his *Mennonite Church in the Second World War.* One of the big problems that these churches had to address was the number of their draft-age men who compromised peace church policy and entered the military. See "Why Mennonite Boys Choose Military Service," *MN* 60 (July 31, 1945): 5. See also Forrest Weller, "The Positive Side of Nonresistance," *GM* 90 (January 11, 1941): 5–7.

23. *The Relation of the Church to the War in the Light of the Christian Faith* (1942), 59–60. Reports of denominational commissions tended to reflect the same dialectic. See Donald H. Stewart, "The Church and the War," *CAC* 2 (June 29, 1942): 4–6; "The Defense of America," editorial, *WE* 29 (June 26, 1941): 686; "The Church in a Time of War," editorial, *PG* 9 (May 25, 1940): 151.

24. R. B. Kuiper, "The Word of God and the Present Return to Religion," *PG* 12 (February 11, 1943): 43–45. On the need for revival in the mainline churches, see "Has the Tide Turned?" *LS* 101 (July 17, 1943): 6–7. Citing statistics of church attendance among mainline Protestants, the article showed that the churches desperately needed to turn around. Not everyone agreed, however, that the war was causing a revival of religion. See, for example, "Is the War Filling the Churches?" *LC* 104 (April 19, 1942): 12–13.

25. "For Preparedness Our Need Is Revivals and More Revivals," editorial, *WR* 114 (July 4, 1940): 8; "Our Need of Repentance, Revival and Evangelism," editorial, *WR* 116 (January 8, 1942): 7; "Three Alternatives before the Country," *BR* 107 (February 27, 1941): 3; Harold L. Lundquist, "Can America Be Saved?" *MM* 40 (November 1939): 120–22; Will H. Houghton, "America's Spiritual Responsibility in the War and After," *MM* 44 (October 1943): 69–70.

26. Paul W. Rood, "A Nation-Wide Crusade," *SST* 82 (January 13, 1940): 28; Horace F. Dean, "Christ for America," *SST* 85 (May 1, 1943): 351–52. *UEA* reported on crusades in virtually every issue. See "Christ for America," *UEA* 5 (March 19, 1945): 2.

27. D. R. Sharpe, "Northern Baptists, Awake!" *WE* 29 (May 22, 1941): 557. See also Aaron N. Meckel, "A Plea for a More Vigorous Evangelism," *AD* 135 (February 1, 1943): 54–55.

28. The campaign was first mentioned in January 1940 and then reported on monthly over the next year. "The National Christian Mission: Its Purpose," *FCB* 23 (January 1940): 7–8.

29. Rouse and Neill, *History of the Ecumenical Movement,* 595. See also Ludlow, "International Protestant Community in the Second World War," 311–62.

30. Henry Smith Leiper, "World-Wide Community—Myth or Reality?" *PS* 31 (July 1941): 294–96.

31. "The Ecumenical Church in Time of War," editorial, *FCB* 22 (November 1939): 3.

32. Edward L. Parsons, "Church Unity and World Unity," *CAC* 3 (May 31, 1943): 1–2.

33. Edward W. Schramm, "The Nation's Great Unifier," *LS* 98 (November 23, 1940): 3.

34. "Comment," *AM* 65 (August 23, 1941): 534; Francis X. Talbot, "At Sea," *AM* 65 (August 23, 1941): 546.

35. "Protestant Fellowship," *FCB* 27 (March 1944): 8.

36. "The Universal Church," *SST* 82 (September 7, 1940): 697–98; "The Federal Council and Internationalism," *UEA* 2 (February 1943): 1.

37. William Ward Ayer, "Evangelical Christianity Endangered by Its Fragmentized Condition," *WE* 30 (May 14, 1942): 484–85.

38. "Churches Asked to Observe Citizenship Day," *FCB* 27 (May 1944): 10.

39. "Patriotism Is Not Enough," editorial, *CE* 80 (January 1, 1942): 3. See also Edwin O. Kennedy, "Christian Patriotism," *PT* 57 (June 1941): 16–17; Frank Glenn Lankard, "Thank God I Am an American," *CA* 119 (October 12, 1944): 1278–79.

40. "Some Responsibilities of Christian Citizens," *FCB* 25 (June 1942): 9.

41. H. J. Kuiper, "Are We Patriots?" *BA* 77 (February 13, 1942): 148.

42. John W. Bradbury, "Christian Patriotism," *WE* 30 (June 25, 1942): 632–33. See also Carlyle B. Haynes, "Can a Soldier Be a Christian?" *ST* 70 (June 1, 1943): 7; William L. Pettingill, "Should a Christian Go to War?" *SST* 84 (January 10, 1942): 19–20.

43. Desmond Morse-Boycott, "May a Christian Fight?" *LC* 102 (July 10, 1940): 5. See also Bob Shuler, "In Defense of the Conscientious Soldier," *CA* 116 (February 13, 1941): 210; Lofton Hudson, "Should a Christian Fight?" *BR* 108 (May 28, 1942): 7.

44. H. J. Kuiper, "The Conscientious Objector," *BA* 75 (December 13, 1940): 1156; "Conscientious Objectors," *PG* 9 (September 25, 1940): 73–74.

45. Edward Skillin Jr., "Consciences and Conscription," *CWE* 32 (July 19, 1940): 258.

46. "The Council and the Conscientious Objector to War," *FCB* 23 (September 1940): 6.

47. "Pastors Affirm Right of Conscience in Face of Conscription," *FS* 6 (September 1940): 110.

48. *Journal of the General Convention of the Protestant Episcopal Church* (1940), 57.

49. *Annual of the Southern Baptist Convention* (1940), 37.

50. *Annual of the Northern Baptist Convention* (1940), 349.

51. See, for example, "Registry of Conscientious Objectors," editorial, *WE* 28 (May 16, 1940): 538; Byron L. Johnson, "Baptists Should Support Their COs," and John Bunyon Smith, "The Convention Should Not Support COs," *WE* 29 (May 22, 1941): 552–53; "What Is Conscience?" editorial, *LU* 22 (January 24, 1940): 15; Paul J. Kirsch, "An Important Interpretation," *LU* 22 (September 18, 1940): 22–23.

52. On the involvement of representatives of the historic peace churches in the Burke-Wadsworth debate, see Eller, *Conscientious Objectors and the Second World War*; Keim and Stoltzfus, *Politics of Conscience*; Sibley and Jacob, *Conscription and Conscience*; Brock, *Twentieth-Century Pacifism*; Hershberger, *Mennonite Church in the Second World War*. For an example of opposition to CPS camps, see Oswald Garrison Villard, "No Compulsory Work Camps," *FS* 7 (February 1941): 24–25.

53. The journals of the historic peace churches carried articles and reports on COs and CPS camps nearly every week. For the story of CPS camps, see Hershberger, *Mennonite Church in the Second World War*; Gingerich, *Service for Peace*; *Introduction to Friends Civilian Public Service*. For mainline support of or opposition to CPS camps, see "The Council and the Conscientious Objector to War," *FCB* 23 (September 1940): 6–7; George N. Reeves, "When C.O.s Go to Camp," *CE* 79 (October 2, 1941); 1118–19; "A Clear-Cut Resolution," editorial, *LS* 100 (November 12, 1942): 6–7; "Resolutions of the Board of Social Missions," *LU* 27 (November 1, 1944): 24–25; "The Churches and Conscientious Objectors," *FCB* 24 (December 1941): 8.

54. "The Christian Church in a World at War," *Minutes of the General Assembly of the Presbyterian Church in the United States* (1942).

CHAPTER EIGHT

1. Bryant Drake, "The Colleges and Its Service Men," *AD* 136 (April 1944): 15.

2. "The Services and Our Colleges," editorial, *CH* 157 (May 15, 1943): 4.

3. Hermann S. Ficke, "Religion in V-12," *PRES* 114 (April 20, 1944): 6.

4. For an example of Lutheran participation, see Gould Wickey, "War Comes to the Campus," *LU* 25 (May 12, 1943): 8–9.

5. Charles Clayton Morrison, "Education—A War Casualty," *CC* 60 (January 6, 1943): 6–7.

6. J. Earl Moreland, "War Comes to the Campus," *CA* 118 (April 29, 1943): 518–19.

7. William Clayton Bower, "Religion on Released Time," *CC* 58 (August 6, 1941): 980–81.

8. Kenneth I. Brown, "Church-Related Colleges and the Crisis," *WE* 30 (January 22, 1942): 82.

9. Rufus D. Bowman, "The Brethren Colleges and the War Emergency," *GM* 92 (September 18, 1943): 5–6.

10. M. L. Wilson, "There Are No Non-Combatants," *CR* 121 (June 1942): 190.

11. "Comment," *AM* 67 (May 23, 1942): 170.

12. George N. Marshall, "Earning Our Priorities," *CR* 122 (July 1943): 249.

13. "Tires and Preachers," editorial, *CA* 117 (January 29, 1942): 131. See also James W. Fifield Jr., "Thin Tires," *AD* 134 (July 1, 1942): 295.

14. "Our Catholic Common Interests," *CAN* 25 (April 1943): 3–4.

15. Reinhold Niebuhr, "I Was Hungry," *CAC* 5 (April 2, 1945): 6.

16. Charles C. Hartung, "She Gave Her Blood," *CA* 118 (January 14, 1943): 44; Opal Gooden, "Is This Waste Necessary?" *CH* 158 (July 1, 1944): 9; "War Savings Stamp Campaign Goes Forward," *CAN* 25 (August 1943): 14; James M. Landis, "The Church in Civilian Defense," *CR* 121 (December 1942): 425.

17. "Comment," *AM* 66 (January 17, 1942): 394.

18. "A Letter from the Office of the Secretary of the Treasury of the U.S.," *MN* 57 (May 5, 1942): 7; Melvin Gingerich, "War Bonds," *MN* 57 (May 26, 1942): 1; "The Civilian Bond Purchase Plan," *MN* 57 (July 21, 1942): 1–4. See also Hershberger, *Mennonite Church in the Second World War*; Gingerich, *Service for Peace*.

19. Edward Skillin Jr., "Total Mobilization," *CWE* 36 (May 22, 1942): 101.

20. Benjamin L. Masse, "Congress Moves to Help War-Stricken Small Business," *AM* 66 (April 4, 1942): 712; Francis X. Talbot, "Threat to Enterprise," *AM* 68 (February 6, 1943): 490. See also Charles Clayton Morrison, "War Profiteering Not Yet Checked," *CC* 60 (October 13, 1943): 1157, and "Small Business Is in Imminent Danger," *CC* 59 (July 22, 1942): 900–901; "The Plight of Small Business," editorial, *CWE* 41 (October 27, 1944): 28.

21. Francis X. Talbot, "Business as Usual," *AM* 66 (April 4, 1942): 715; Henry Taylor, "Our Domestic Munich," *PR* 3 (June–July 1940): 59–65.

22. Edward Skillin Jr., "Social Effects of Arms Billions," *CWE* 32 (September 20, 1940): 438–39.

23.Francis X. Talbot, "More and Higher Taxes," *AM* 66 (March 21, 1942): 651, and "Taxes and Inflation," *AM* 67 (May 23, 1942): 183.

24. Talbot, "Thrift, Thrift!" *AM* 67 (June 6, 1942): 239.

25. Samuel McCrea Cavert, "Cooperation of the Churches in Wartime," *CAC* 3 (December 13, 1943): 8.

26. "The Church Cries Out," *LW* 62 (March 2, 1943): 70; Carl Driscoll, "Headaches in Ohio," *LU* 25 (January 20, 1943): 10; Ansley C. Moore, "The Industrial Defense Worker—Mobile's Challenge," *PS* 32 (September 1942): 392–93, 396; "Mrs. Defense Worker Speaks," *PS* 33 (March 1943): 115–17.; William J. Hazel, "The Church in the Defense Areas," *PRES* 112 (January 15, 1942): 607.

27. "Plans for Wartime Service," *FCB* 25 (February 1942): 8.

28. Nelson, *Lutheranism in North America*, 125; Wentz, *A Basic History of Lutheranism*, 299; *Minutes of the Biennial Convention of the United Lutheran Church* (1940–42) gives information on these agencies, too. *LU* and *LS* also included many reports on their organization and work.

29. For information on the War-Time Service Commission, see *Minutes of the General Assembly of the Presbyterian Church in the United States of America* (1940–45). *PRES* also carried articles on the commission. For information on the Defense Service Council, see *Minutes of the General Assembly of the Presbyterian Church in the United States of America* (1940–45). *PS* also contained reports on the work of the council. For a thorough study of the wartime work of the Evangelical and Reformed Churches, see Hafer, "Evangelical and Reformed Churches." For information on the Disciples' Committee on War Services, see *CE* and *CS* for reports and articles.

30. "The Presbyterian War-Time Service Commission," *PRES* 112 (August 27, 1942): 8.

31. For the wartime work of the Protestant Episcopal Church, see *Journal of the General Convention of the Protestant Episcopal Church* (1940, 1943). *LC* and *CH* also included articles, editorials, and reports on the church's wartime work.

32. *CAN* carried many reports on the work of National Catholic Community Service (NCCS). For a thorough exploration of the NCCS, see Lynn, *The National Catholic Community Service*.

33. Willard M. Wickizer, "The Church and Industrial Centers," *CE* 80 (May 7, 1942): 511; H. G. Haney, "Religious Work in Defense Centers," *CE* 80 (January 15, 1942): 63.

34. Samuel McCrea Cavert, "Cooperation of the Churches in Wartime," *CAC* 3 (December 13, 1943): 8–11.

35. "War-Time Service Department," *PRES* 113 (December 2, 1943): 11.

36. Marguerite Winters, "A Service Summer at Willow Run," *BL* 7 (May 1945): 38.

37. *Minutes of the General Assembly of the Presbyterian Church in the United States of America* (1944), 173–74.

38. H. Conrad Hoyer, "In War Industry Centers," *LU* 27 (April 4, 1945): 12.

39. Orville E. Lueck, "The Lutheran Church Pioneers Again," *LS* 101 (June 26, 1943): 4, and "On the Field with a Defense Area Chaplain," *LS* 101 (July 17, 1943): 4.

40. "Where Our Church Is Serving Workers in War Industries," *LW* 62 (March 30, 1943): 108.

1. Aldis L. Webb, "We Are Concerned," *CS* 76 (July 26, 1941): 2. By the same writer, see also "What about the Army Morale?" *CS* 76 (September 13, 1941): 7, and "Greatest Mass Movement in Nation's History," *CS* 76 (April 19, 1941): 7. For a Missouri Synod perspective, read L. W. Meinzen, "The Special Spiritual Needs of Men in Service," *LW* 60 (April 29, 1941): 148.

2. J. H. Schaal, "Life in the Army," *BA* 76 (November 21, 1941): 1088.

3. For opinions on the vitality of religion in the armed services, or lack of, see "Foxhole Religion," *CAC* 4 (March 6, 1944): 5–6. In a letter to the editor Chaplain Kenneth L. Ames took issue with the "Foxhole" article; see *CAC* 4 (May 29, 1944): 8. For other perspectives on religion in the military, check Charles William Phillips, "Are Soldiers Religious?" *LC* 106 (February 6, 1944): 10; Frederick W. Vogell, "Are Service Men Turning toward Christ?" *ZH* 122 (July 19, 1944): 450; Percy M. Hickcox, "Church Attendance in the Army," *ZH* 120 (January 7, 1942): 2.

4. George S. Young, "The Church's Ministry to Men in the Armed Forces," *BL* 4 (November, 1942): 10.

5. Raphael Harwood Miller, "Morale Is Mail," *CE* 82 (November 8, 1944): 1071. See also Harlan M. Frost, "The Home Church and the Soldier," *ZH* 120 (July 1, 1942): 630–31; W. Stuart Anderson, "The Home Front and Our Men in the Service," *LU* 26 (November 11, 1943): 8; Charles W. Kelley, "Helping with Letters," *ZH* 120 (June 24, 1942): 598.

6. Hafer,"Evangelical and Reformed Churches."

7. "Dear Son—," *CH* 157 (May 1, 1943): 13.

8. Ruth Curby, "They Do Not Walk Alone," *LU* 27 (March 28, 1945): 24–25.

9. F. M. Paist, "New Testaments for Servicemen," *SST* 84 (January 25, 1942): 70; "The Bible on the Battlefront," *SST* 86 (November 11, 1944): 814.

10. "Onward Christian Soldiers!" *MM* 42 (April 1942): 512.

11. Spellman, *No Greater Love*; Daniel A. Poling, "Heaven's Highway, Troubled Earth," *CHD* 68 (June 1945): 13.

12. Paul W. Rood, "A Statement to Fundamentalists," *SST* 84 (April 25, 1942): 331–33; "Baptists Inaugurate Continuous Prayer for Men in U.S. Service," *BR* 108 (June 11, 1942): 1.

13. Merlin C. Shull, "Ministry to Men in Military Camps," *GM* 91 (November 28, 1942): 15.

14. Myron C. Cole, "How One Church Helps Soldiers," *CE* 80 (April 9, 1942): 398–99. For other examples of the local church's ministry to their servicemen, see "These Churches Build Morale," *CS* 77 (November 28, 1942): 1; Hafer, "Evangelical and Reformed Churches"; George Farrand Taylor, "With Their Boys at the Front," *CH* 156 (November 1, 1942): 12.

15. Harriet K. Neal, "Service Wives," *LC* 105 (May 9, 1943): 8.

16. "A Million in Arms," *BL* 3 (January 1942): 11–14. See also G. Pitt Beers, "Service in Areas of Military Camps," *WE* 29 (February 20, 1941): 179.

17. "Resolutions," *CE* 79 (May 22, 1941): 617.

18. The Lutheran Press often reported on the ministry of the Service Men's Division, especially on its Lutheran Service Centers. See, for example, "We Will Not Fail Them,"

LU 23 (April 16, 1941): 2; "Lutheran Service Centers Help Thousands," LS 100 (April 18, 1942): 11; Nils M. Ylvisaker, "Service Commission Expands Program," LS 101 (June 12, 1943): 8; Walter H. Hellman, "The Lutheran Church Goes to War," LS 101 (January 30, 1943): 4–6; Carl Soldberg, "Where Sixteen Stand By," LU 24 (April 22, 1942): 5.

19. A. H. Kleffman and Walter L. Whallon, "Presbyterians at Camp Croft," PRES 112 (February 12, 1942): 3; "With Our Soldiers and Sailors," PRES 113 (February 25, 1943): 11; Harry L. Bowlby, "Answering the Call!" PRES 112 (June 11, 1942): 6–7; Minutes of the General Assembly of the Presbyterian Church in the United States of America (1945), 78, 112.

20. "The Defense Service Council," PS 31 (August 1941): 346–47; "The Local Church Can Help the Defense Service Council," PS 31 (October 1941): 443–45; B. R. Lacy Jr., "The Defense Service Council," PS 32 (April 1942): 148–49; Dan T. Caldwell, "Our Church and Our Service Men," PS 33 (April 1943): 147–49; Annie Tail Jenkins, "Visiting the Defense Service Council," PS 34 (April 1944): 135–37.

21. J. B. Lawrence, "Work in Camps and Communities," BR 107 (July 17, 1941): 6; Norris Gilliam, "Special Offering for Defense Program," BR 108 (January 1, 1942): 5.

22. Philip E. Howard Jr., "The Morning Cheer Center for Service Men at Fort Dix," SST 84 (April 25, 1942): 327–28, 332.

23. "A New Job for NCCS," CAN 25 (July 1943): 8; "Aid in Defense Program Pledged by U.S. Bishops," CAN 23 (January 1941): 7.

24. "A Needed Organization," editorial, WE 30 (December 3, 1942): 1185; Adna W. Leonard, "The Service Men's Christian League," CA 118 (January 7, 1943): 6; Dan T. Caldwell, "The Service Men's Christian League," PS 33 (May 1943): 206–8.

25. John W. Bradbury, "Protestant Representation in USO," WE 30 (April 23, 1942): 391.

26. "The Churches, the USO, and the YMCA," FCB 25 (June 1942): 6, 7; "The Churches, the YMCA, and USO," FCB 26 (May 1943): 5. For reports on the work of USO in Protestant publications, see Clarence W. Hall, "Off Lonesome Street," CA 117 (July 16, 1942): 902–3, 922; Kathryn Wolf, "Servicemen Befriended by the USO," CH 156 (November 15, 1942): 12–13.

27. There is a vast literature on the chaplaincy during the Second World War. For histories of the chaplaincy see Bowman and Caldwell, They Answered the Call; Cross, Soldiers of God; Drury, History of the Chaplain Corps; Gushwa, Best and Worst of Times; Honeywell, Chaplains of the U.S. Army; Jorgensen, Service of Chaplains; Crosby, Battlefield Chaplains; Thompson, American Army Chaplaincy. The religious press provided thorough coverage of the work of the chaplains, too. See, for example, "The Work for Service Men," LC 105 (October 10, 1943): 25–29; "The Army and Navy Commission," editorial, LC 104 (November 8, 1942): 12–14; A. W. Leonard, "Methodism's Commission on Chaplains," CA 116 (September 18, 1941): 1211; P. W. Bloomquist, "The Holy Communion Goes to War," CH 158 (January 15, 1944): 13; William A. Gamble, "What the Army Chaplains Are Doing," CH 155 (March 1, 1941): 13; Elizabeth McCracken, "Triptychs for Servicemen," LC 106 (January 30, 1944): 13; Joy A. Bonwit, "The Religious Program of the Army," CE 79 (June 5, 1941): 682; Aldis L. Webb, "What Does an Army Chaplain Do?" CS 76 (May 10, 1941): 2.

28. Jorgensen, Service of Chaplains, 275.

29. "The Silver Cord," CHD 66 (June 1943): 21.

30. "Disciples in the Service," CE 82 (August 9, 1944): 770. For other inspirational or

informational reports of chaplain work, see Howard Rushmore, "The Chaplain Goest Ashore," *CHD* 67 (August 1944): 15–17, 63; Harry Boer, "Tarawa: A Chaplain Reminisces," *BA* 79 (May 19, 1944): 464; E. Lynne Wade, "Sovereign Grace in the South Pacific," *PG* 13 (February 10, 1944): 1; Anne Miller, "A Chaplain Speaks," *BL* 6 (May 1944): 12–13; "Where Men Meet the Grim Reaper," *WR* 119 (January 18, 1945): 11–12.

31. "Who Will Go for Us?—The Church and the Chaplains," *FCB* 26 (May 1943): 4–5.

32. For examples of these appeals, see J. M. VandeKieff, "The Urgent Call for Chaplains," *BA* 77 (February 13, 1942): 158–59; "Chaplains," editorial, *PRES* 110 (June 20, 1940): 4; Alfred Carpenter, "Call for More Chaplains," *BR* 108 (September 10, 1942): 4; "Increased Interest Needed in Army and Navy Chaplains," *WR* 115 (February 20, 1941): 8; Herbert A. Allenby, "Why Be an Army Chaplain?" *AD* 135 (February 1, 1943): 69; Percy M. Hickox, "Too Little, Too Late," *ZH* 120 (April 15, 1942): 338; "N.A.E. Requested for More Chaplains," *UEA* 6 (May 2, 1945): 12; Carroll C. Roberts, "Call for Chaplains," *CS* 77 (January 24, 1942): 17.

33. "The Church and the Chaplains," statement printed in *CAC* 3 (November 1, 1943): 1. It was signed by such notables as John C. Bennett, Henry Sloan Coffin, Sherwood Eddy, Douglas Horton, Lynn Harold Hough, Henry Smith Leiper, Francis J. McConnell, John A. Mackay, John R. Mott, Reinhold Niebuhr, Justin Wroe Nixon, and Henry P. Van Dusen. Niebuhr mentioned the problem again in another editorial, "The Church's Support of the Chaplains," *CAC* 4 (March 6, 1944): 3.

34. James Gordon Gilkey Jr., "The Church and the Chaplaincy," *CAC* 4 (November 27, 1944): 3–5.

35. William E. Gilroy, "Churches and Chaplains," *AD* 134 (May 1, 1942): 208–9.

36. "Should the International Convention Reconsider Its Chaplaincy Action?" *CE* 79 (April 24, 1941): 498.

37. Edwin R. Errett, "What Happened to Chaplains at St. Louis," *CS* 76 (May 24, 1941): 7, and "We Can Learn from Our Shame," *CS* 77 (August 1, 1942): 3–4.

38. W. E. Garrison, "The Convention and the Chaplaincy," *CE* 79 (April 24, 1941): 498.

39. George A. Campbell, "Disciples and the Chaplaincy," *CE* 79 (February 13, 1941): 207.

40. Stewart M. Robinson, "The Box Butte Overture," *PRES* 110 (March 14, 1940): 6.

41. Edwards E. Elliott, "Re-Thinking the Chaplaincy," *PG* 13 (July 15, 1944): 202–3.

42. "Synod at Work," *BA* 77 (August 14, 1942): 716.

43. Chester M. Davis, "Are We Losing the War on the Spiritual Front?" *PRES* 112 (April 2, 1942): 7.

44. John E. Huss, "Can a Chaplain Be Over-zealous in Evangelism?" *WR* 118 (August 24, 1944): 5–6. See also Karl H. Moore, "Baptist Navy Chaplains," *WR* 118 (August 24, 1944): 5.

45. H. J. Kuiper, "Should the Christian Reformed Chaplain Administer Open Communion?" *BA* 77 (October 2, 1942): 876–77.

46. Kuiper, "The Chaplaincy Question," *BA* 77 (November 6, 1942): 996–97.

CHAPTER TEN

1. "The Issues at Stake in the War," statement adopted by the Federal Council of Churches, *FCB* 26 (January 1943): 10–11.

2. General John L. DeWitt, quoted in Barnhart, Matson, and Ten Broek, *Prejudice, War, and the Constitution*, 327.

3. Sources on Japanese Americans include Okihiro, "Religion and Resistance"; Matsumoto, *Beyond Prejudice*; Arrington, "Price of Prejudice"; Bosworth, *America's Concentration Camps*; Uchida, *Desert Exile*; Girdner and Loftis, *The Great Betrayal*; Daniels, Kitano, and Taylor, *Japanese Americans*; Daniels, *Decision to Relocate the Japanese Americans*; Daniels, *Prisoners without Trial*.

4. W. E. Crouser, "California and the Japanese," *LU* 25 (June 24, 1942): 6.

5. Marlin D. Farnum, "Northern Baptists and America's Greatest Mass Migration," *WE* 30 (July 9, 1942): 684–85. See also "Native Born," editorial, *CWE* 35 (April 10, 1942): 603; "Native Born II," editorial, *CWE* 35 (April 17, 1942): 635. For other responses, see "Japanese Americans Evacuated," *LU* 25 (August 26, 1942): 14; "The Alien Citizen," editorial, *CA* 117 (March 19, 1942): 356; Galen Fisher, "The Japanese Evacuation," *LC* 104 (April 12, 1942): 10–11. *AM* affirmed the government's treatment but encouraged rapid and just assimilation.

6. "Resolutions Approved by the Convention," *CE* 80 (August 13, 1942): 886.

7. Statement, Southern California-Arizona Conference, quoted in Muelder, *Methodism and Society*, 198. Northern Baptists passed a similar resolution. See *Annual of the Northern Baptist Convention* (1944), 266–67. So did the Northern Presbyterians. See *Minutes of the General Assembly of the Presbyterian Church in the United States of America* (1942).

8. Galen M. Fisher, "Our Japanese Refugees," *CC* 59 (April 1, 1942): 424–26.

9. Joseph B. Hunter, "Christians and Japanese Evacuation," *CE* 80 (June 4, 1942): 616–17. For other examples of strong opposition, see "A Blot on Our Record," editorial, *CAC* 2 (April 20, 1942): 1–2; Floyd Schmoe, "America's Protective Custody," *FS* 8 (July 1942): 111–13; Caleb Foote, "Democracy in Detention," *FS* 8 (December 1942): 205–7.

10. Yoshitaka Takagi, "Japanese Americans and Democracy," *CR* 122 (March 1943): 90. For other such accounts, see "Four Interviews," *CWE* 39 (March 10, 1944): 511–13; Dave Tatsuno, "As I See It," *PT* 57 (July 1942): 11; Daisuke Kitagawa, "An Open Letter," *LC* 104 (April 19, 1942): 14–15; Yoichi Matsuda, "Grateful Enemy," *CA* 118 (May 20, 1943): 8; Sarah Elisabeth Evans, "We Will Love Both Friend and Foe," *ZH* 120 (October 28, 1942): 1038–39; "Look at It through Their Eyes," *FS* 8 (August 1942): 134–35.

11. "Types of Americanism," *FCB* 27 (February 1944): 4; W. Maxfield Garrott, "Southern Baptists and Japanese Americans," *WR* 118 (January 13, 1944): 4–5; Charlotte B. DeForest, "Worship in Manzanar," *AD* 137 (January 1945): 14; Elmer L. Shirrell, "Check and Double Check," *CA* 118 (August 5, 1943): 966–67.

12. Frank D. Campbell, "Interracial Cooperation," *ZH* 120 (September 9, 1942): 862.

13. "In the Supreme Court," *CWE* 39 (March 10, 1944): 520.

14. Charles Clayton Morrison, "Justice for the Evacuees," *CC* 59 (June 10, 1942): 750–52.

15. Newsletter, American Friends Service Committee, quoted in Sandra C. Taylor, "'Fellow-Feelers with the Afflicted': The Christian Churches and the Relocation of the Japanese during World War II," 125.

16. Matsumoto, introduction to *Beyond Prejudice*. For other accounts of ministry, see Suzuki, *Ministry in the Assembly and Relocation Centers*; Daniels, Taylor, and Kitano, *Japanese Americans*. For reports on the work of individual denominations, see William

Lindsay Young, "Cool Heads for Hot Times," *CE* 80 (November 5, 1942): 1202–4; Owen Still, "Our Own Neglected Fields," *CS* 80 (June 23, 1945): 4; Marjorie E. Moore, "What Is a 'Japanese Relocation Center'?" *PS* 33 (June 1943): 266–69; E. Stanley Jones, "The Christian Church and the Japanese-Americans," *LC* 105 (March 28, 1943): 10–11. On the churches' involvement in resettlement, see "Resettle Japanese Evacuees," *FCB* 25 (September 1942): 5; "Japanese-Americans to Be Resettled," *FCB* 25 (October 1942): 13; Daisuke Kitagawa, "Resettlement of Japanese-Americans," *LC* 106 (April 30, 1944): 19; Vere Loper, "California Welcomes the Nisei," *AD* 137 (June 1945): 6–7; Joseph B. Hunter, "Problems of Relocation," *FS* 10 (September 1944): 156–57; Kenneth C. Hendricks, "Righting a Great Wrong," *CE* 83 (March 7, 1945): 236.

17. James Baldwin, quoted in Dalfiume, " 'Forgotten Years' of the Negro Revolution," 299.

18. Myrdal, *An American Dilemma*, 2:756, 997.

19. Dalfiume, " 'Forgotten Years' of the Negro Revolution," 299.

20. Garfinkel, *When Negroes March*, 20.

21. George Schuyler, quoted in ibid., 302.

22. Garfinkel, *When Negroes March*, 305.

23. Ibid., 310.

24. William Stuart Nelson, "Balance Sheet of the Negro in America," *CAC* 4 (March 20, 1944): 3–5.

25. Edwin R. Embree, "Negro Gains in Wartime," *AD* 137 (February 1945): 5–8. For other accounts of "Negro gains" in wartime, see Oswald Garrison Villard, "The Negro's Great Gains," *CC* 59 (November 4, 1942): 1351–52.

26. "A Program for Action," *CR* 122 (February 1943): 44.

27. *Minutes of the General Assembly of the Presbyterian Church in the United States* (1943).

28. *Minutes of the General Assembly of the Presbyterian Church in the United States of America* (1941), 164.

29. "Interracial Brotherhood and the World Crisis," *FCB* 24 (February 1941): 6.

30. "Leaders Confer on Race Problems," *FCB* 25 (May 1942): 8.

31. Orser, "Racial Attitudes in War," 337–53. Orser argues that the war pushed the churches, however slightly, toward greater racial concern and more radical action. "The years of the war had indeed brought new challenges to racial attitudes: the greater attention to racial injustice in denominational pronouncements and the church press, both South and North, was dramatic testimony to that fact, particularly in comparison to their general neglect of the issue in the pre-war years" (353).

32. Guy Emery Shipler Jr., "A Dangerous Inconsistency," *ZH* 120 (February 4, 1942): 98.

33. Judson J. McKim, "Prejudice—The Enemy of Peace," *ZH* 123 (March 7, 1945): 147.

34. Edwin Skillin Jr., "Motes and Beams," *CWE* 35 (February 6, 1942): 379.

35. Benjamin E. Mays, "Negroes and the Will to Justice," *CC* 59 (October 28, 1942): 1316. For other articles on the plight of African Americans during the war, see "It Is Our Problem, Too," editorial, *AD* 134 (October 1, 1942): 443; Ira De A. Reid, "This War and That Negro," *CAC* 2 (July 13, 1942): 2–6; Donald G. Lothrop, "Racism versus Americanism," *CR* 121 (February 1942): 46–47; Laurens H. Seelye, "The Race Issue and Victory," *AD* 135 (April 1, 1943): 160–61; "The Major Question of Minorities," editorial, *CE* 80 (September 17, 1942): 1015; "Color Line in Peace and War," editorial, *CE* 80 (February 5, 1942): 160.

36. Edward Skillin Jr., "More Houston 'Martyrs'?" *CWE* 34 (September, 19, 1941): 509. See also his "Negroes in the Armed Services," *CWE* 40 (July 14, 1944): 291–92, and "The Racial Front," *CWE* 35 (January 23, 1942): 332–33.

37. "Protest," *CH* 157 (February 15, 1943): 16. See also George Higgins, "Catholics and the FEPC Case," *CAN* 26 (January 1944): 6–7, 21; "Further Abandonment of the Four Freedoms," editorial, *CWE* 37 (January 29, 1943): 363–64.

38. Richard J. Roche, "FEPC—A Challenge to Democracy," *AM* 73 (April 14, 1945): 29. See also "Tell the President You Back Him on FEPC," *ZH* 123 (June 13, 1945): 324; Kenneth C. Walker, "For a Permanent FEPC," *CR* 124 (August 1945): 292.

39. L. O. Hartman, "Tongue-Tied," *ZH* 120 (April 1, 1942): 295.

40. Quoted in "Now It Is History," editorial, *ZH* 122 (May 17, 1944): 311.

41. Hendon M. Harris, "Fostering Racial Goodwill," *WR* 116 (December 10, 1942): 3–4.

42. J. W. Brown, "The Negro in This War," *CI* 73 (October 15, 1942): 11–12.

43. "Mammoth Race Relations Day Program Held by Chicagoans," *CI* 72 (February 20, 1941): 5.

44. "Anti-Poll Tax Bill," *CI* 74 (June 3, 1943): 3; "Democracy Here First," *CI* 73 (October 22, 1942): 3; "Special Resolutions on the Negro and National Defense," *CI* 72 (May 15, 1941): 9; Albert L. Dunlap, "Negro and American Democracy in an Ever-Changing World of Today," *CI* 72 (May 8, 1941): 6–7; William B. Barton, "Racial War or Racial Brotherhood—Which?" *CI* 73 (June 18, 1942): 7; "Negro Pilots?" editorial, *CI* 72 (April 10, 1941): 2; "Bishop J. A. Bray Speaks before National Republican Committee," *CI* 75 (June 29, 1944): 5; "Bishop Bray before the Democratic Platform Committee," *CI* 72 (August 3, 1941): 2–3.

45. "Negro Leaders Address the President," *FCB* 25 (April 1942): 7–8.

46. Quoted in L. O. Hartman, "Respect for the Flag," *ZH* 119 (January 29, 1941): 103–4.

47. L. O. Hartman, "Respect for the Flag," 103–4.

48. Edward Skillin Jr., "Liberty Is Liberty," *CWE* 36 (June 26, 1942): 221.

49. Paul Gia Russo, "A Victory for Jehovah's Witnesses," *PR* 3 (May 1940: 22.

50. Raphael Harwood Miller, "Unity or Uniformity," *CE* 80 (June 25, 1942): 691.

51. William E. Gilroy, "Spiritual Tolerance a Primary Need," *AD* 132 (September 1, 1940): 394–95.

52. Roy L. Smith, "A Momentous Decision," *CA* 117 (June 25, 1942): 804–5. For other defenses of the Jehovah's Witnesses, see Edwin Merrick Dodd Jr., "The Civil Liberties of Americans," *CR* 120 (February 15 and March 1, 1941): 67 and 91; Julius F. Seebach, "In the World's Eye," *LU* 22 (June 26, 1940): 5; "The Flag Salute Case," editorial, *CC* 57 (June 19, 1940): 791–92.

53. John W. Bradbury, "Saluting the American Flag," *WE* 28 (June 27, 1940): 712–13.

54. Francis X. Talbot, "Reds in Office," *AM* 61 (October 7, 1939): 613. See also his "Lame Ducks and Reds," *AM* 61 (September 9, 1939): 516.

55. Talbot, "Bar the Door," *AM* 62 (November 18, 1939): 154.

56. Talbot, "Aid for Communism," *AM* 66 (March 14, 1942): 630.

57. "The War Is Not Over," editorial, *MM* 40 (April 1940): 416.

58. See Roy, *Communism and the Churches*, 281. *PR* carried scores of articles on fascism, Catholicism, Russia, and communism during the war.

59. Charles Clayton Morrison, "On the Dies Committee's Propaganda Front," *CC* 56 (September 20, 1939): 1125.

60. Francis X. Talbot, "The Communist's Rights," *AM* 63 (April 20, 1940): 42; "Who Are Communists?" editorial, *AM* 70 (December 11, 1943): 267.

61. Ribuffo, *Old Christian Right*.

62. Roy L. Smith, "The Tarantula," *CA* 119 (August 17, 1944): 1012–13. See also "Civil Liberties in Wartime," editorial, *CAC* 2 (February 23, 1942): 1–2.

63. "Eternal Vigilantes," editorial, *CWE* 40 (July 25, 1944): 316.

64. Roger Caillois, "The Paradox of Freedom," *CWE* 40 (August 4, 1944): 366–69.

65. G. A. Lyzenga, "Liberty of Conscience," *BA* 79 (October 20, 1944): 992.

66. W. R. White, "The False Freedom," *MM* 42 (February 1942): 340–41.

CHAPTER ELEVEN

1. "A Wartime Priority," *LS* 101 (May 1, 1943): 2.

2. H. C. Brearly, "War and the Family," *CE* 80 (April 30, 1942): 480–81.

3. Seward Hiltner, "What Is War Doing to Civilians?" *CAC* 5 (February 19, 1945): 3–5.

4. E. J. Tanis, "Women in War Work," *BA* 79 (February 25, 1944): 175.

5. "The Holy Family," editorial, *CE* 82 (December 20, 1944): 1215. For other expressions of alarm, see C. F. Hafermann, "A Job and a Home," *LS* 103 (January 13, 1945): 6–7; "Divorce—A National Menace," *LS* 101 (May 1, 1943): 5; Elmer G. Homrighausen, "Build Homes—Even in Babylon," *PT* 59 (July 1944): 9–10; Evelyn Millis Duvall, "Conversing Family Life in Wartime," *PS* 33 (November 1943): 499; "Guard the Home!" editorial, *BA* 78 (March 26, 1943): 292–93; H. Conrad Hoyer, "200,000 Lutherans on the Move," *LS* 101 (May 15, 1943): 4–5; Ethel B. Wickey, "An Approaching Blackout," *LU* 25 (September 29, 1943): 8–9.

6. Edward Skillin Jr., "Women and the War Effort," *CWE* 36 (May 29, 1942): 125. See also Lester L. Raush, "Indispensable Unit—the Family," *ZH* 119 (July 23, 1941): 671–92.

7. W. J. Goos, "The Church in Thy House?" *LU* 25 (December 16, 1942): 8–9; J. J. Steigenga, "Our Family Life in War Time," *BA* 77 (May 14, 1942): 463.

8. "Give Women Their Rights," editorial, *CH* 159 (September 1, 1945): 4–5; "The American Woman's Primer," *SA* 9 (September 15, 1943): 12.

9. "When Married Women Work," editorial, *CWE* 31 (February 9, 1940): 334–35.

10. Lorna Zobel, "The Christian Home Front," *LW* 63 (February 15, 1944): 56–57.

11. Helen Kuiper Noordewier, "War-Mother," *BA* 77 (May 15, 1942): 463.

12. "Homes," editorial, *AM* 68 (November 14, 1942): 155.

13. "Classic Nonsense," editorial, *AM* 68 (December 12, 1942): 266.

14. "More on Women's Equality," comment, *AM* 69 (July 24, 1943): 423. See also Martin S. Sommer, "The Place of Women," *LW* 60 (November 11, 1941): 384; Mrs. Theodore D. Wedel, "The Church Woman's Postwar Job," *CA* 119 (November 16, 1944): 1436–37; "Motherhood Is a Vocation," editorial, *CS* 77 (May 9, 1942): 3.

15. In the past ten years scholars have debated the degree to which the wartime experience of women contributed to the feminist revolution of the 1960s and 1970s. Though women did flood the workforce during the war, often doing jobs traditionally assigned to men, received greater pay than they had before, and continued to work after the war ended, they did not necessarily experience the "liberation" that some feminists had hoped. Toward the end of the war they received a great deal of pressure to make

room for returning veterans in the workforce, to marry, settle down, have children, move to suburbia, and to return to traditional female jobs. Perhaps they never forgot those years of independence and opportunity and, though realizing that such freedom would never be theirs again, sowed the seeds of expectation and longing in their daughters. In the 1950s, however, the "feminine mystique" held sway over millions of women in America. See Anderson, *Wartime Women*; Campbell, *Women at War with America*; Hartmann, *The Home Front and Beyond*; Rupp, *Mobilizing Women for War*; Chafe, *Women and Equality*; Olga Gruhzit-Hoyt, *They Also Served*; Weatherhead, *American Women and World War II*; Wise and Wise, *A Mouthful of Rivets*.

16. Cyrus E. Albertson, "Too Many Weddings?" *CA* 118 (June 24, 1943): 778–79; Vere V. Loper, "War Marriages—Wise or Otherwise," *AD* 135 (July 1943): 11; Walter John Marx, "What about Marriage?" *CWE* 36 (July 10, 1942): 270–72; C. F. Hafermann, "Hasty Marriages in Wartime," *LS* 100 (June 13, 1942): 2–3.

17. "Thousands Being Trapped," *LW* 62 (November 23, 1943): 385; "Delinquent Brides," *CE* 82 (October 25, 1944): 1021.

18. "Juvenile Delinquency—An Ugly Situation," editorial, *LW* 62 (August 31, 1943): 287; August C. Brustat, "The Challenge of the 17,000,000," *LW* 62 (November 23, 1943): 389; F. W. Godtfring, "Juvenile Delinquency," *WE* 32 (April 13, 1944): 349–50; Mrs. W. H. Moody, "The Juvenile Problem and Its Solution," *WR* 118 (January 13, 1944): 3; John Edgar Hoover, "Crime Challenges the Churches," *BR* 111 (January 18, 1945): 6; Robert L. Atwell, "Baptismal Vows and Juvenile Delinquency," *PG* 13 (August 15, 1944): 229–30; "Juvenile Delinquency," editorial, *BA* 79 (January 21, 1944): 52; "Growing Juvenile Delinquency," editorial, *CWE* 39 (October 22, 1943): 4. See also *Minutes of the General Assembly of the Presbyterian Church in the United States of America* (1944), 233–35; *Annual of the Northern Baptist Convention* (1945), 274; "An Internal Foe," editorial, *ZH* 119 (April 23, 1941): 391; Orville C. Jones, "Juvenile Delinquency and the Church," *AD* 136 (July, 1944): 15.

19. "Americans Spend More Than Ever for Liquor," editorial, *CC* 62 (February 7, 1945): 164. For an excellent study of changes in wartime moral behavior, see Costello, *Virtue under Fire*.

20. "A Day of Shame," editorial, *CE* 82 (August 16, 1944): 783; "This Would Help Win the War," *LS* 100 (May 23, 1942): 6.

21. J. Raymond Schmidt, "Tires and Food,—or Whiskey?" *SST* 86 (August 5, 1944): 549.

22. "Recommendations," *LU* 26 (October 28, 1943): 18.

23. "Resolutions," *CE* 80 (August 13, 1942): 888.

24. *Minutes of the General Assembly of the Presbyterian Church in the United States* (1943), 143.

25. *Annual of the Northern Baptist Convention* (1945), 273. Southern Baptists passed a similar resolution. See *Annual of the Southern Baptist Convention* (1944), 135.

26. Clarence W. Hall, "Now for the Second Front!" *CA* 117 (June 25, 1942): 808–9; "Defend the Defenders," *CA* 116 (March 13, 1941): 326; Henry M. Johnson, "Liquor a Prime Cause of War and Defeat," *WR* 116 (January 15, 1942): 10; "Protecting Our Conscripts," editorial, *ZH* 118 (October 16, 1940): 991; Elmer E. Helms, "The War and General Booze," *CA* 117 (May 28, 1942): 686; James Cannon Jr., "First Major Battle since 1933," *ZH* 119 (October 15, 1941): 929; George E. Health, "America's Protected Enemy," *ZH* 119 (April 30,

1941): 418–19; Clinton N. Howard, "Dry Facts vs. Wet Fallacy," *WE* 32 (May 4, 1944): 428–29; "Drink and Our Fighting Forces," editorial, *WE* 31 (January 28, 1943): 81; J. Raymond Schmidt, "Administration Backs Whiskey over Food," *WR* 118 (September 7, 1944): 3; E. J. Tanis, "Liquor Imperils Our Army," *BA* 77 (February 20, 1942): 175; "The Liquor Problem," *FCB* 26 (March 1943): 5.

27. Henry M. Johnson, "Liquor a Prime Cause of War and Defeat," *WR* 116 (January 15, 1942): 10.

28. James Cannon Jr., "First Major Battle since 1933," 929. See also "Defend the Defenders," *CA* 116 (March 13, 1941): 326; Jacob Simpson Payton, "Wake Up America," *CA* 116 (November 20, 1941): 14; "The Sheppard Anti-Liquor Bill," *PRES* 112 (January 22, 1942): 4.

29. Charles Clayton Morrison, "Call on President to Order Wartime Prohibition," *CC* 59 (June 10, 1942): 747.

30. "Comment," *AM* 67 (July 18, 1942): 395; "Surrender to Suds," editorial, *AM* 65 (August 9, 1941): 490; "Common Sense Liquor Regulation," editorial, *CH* 157 (January 1, 1943): 4; "Facing Facts about Prohibition," editorial, *AD* 134 (April 1, 1942): 157–58; "Protestantism and Prohibition," *LC* 104 (July 12, 1942): 8.

31. "Compulsory Military Training," *SA* 11 (September 15, 1945): 29.

32. "Resolutions," *CE* 82 (November 29, 1944): 1155.

33. "Council Action on Postwar Military Training," *FCB* 27 (December 1944): 10.

34. "A Synod Speaks on War," editorial, *BA* 79 (May 5, 1944): 412; "Postwar Compulsory Military Training," editorial, *LW* 63 (November 21, 1944): 376–77; "Universal Military Training," editorial, *LC* 107 (June 17, 1945): 18.

35. Lieutenant Colonel Harold W. Kent, "Universal Military Training? Yes," *CA* 120 (June 28, 1945): 758–60; Ernest Freemont Tittle, "No," *CA* 120 (June 28, 1945): 760–61; Ernest Martin Hopkins, "For Peacetime Conscription," and Bryant Drake, "Against Peacetime Conscription," *AD* 137 (September 1945): 6–9; J. B. Weatherspoon, "Attention Southern Baptists!" and Jon J. Wicker Jr., "Weatherspoon Wrong," *WR* 119 (May 10, 1945): 3–4; Edwin B. Goodell Jr. and Lawrence G. Brooks, "Peacetime Military Conscription," *CR* 124 (February 1945): 64–65.

36. Reinhold Niebuhr, "Editorial Notes," *CAC* 5 (November 25, 1945): 2. See also "This Can Wait," editorial, *CA* 119 (November 30, 1944): 1476–77; Allan P. Farrell, "Compulsory Peacetime Military Training?" *AM* 71 (September 9, 1944): 551. For reaction from the religious press, see Eldon Burke, "Peacetime Conscription," *GM* 94 (January 6, 1945): 9; "That Word, Compulsory!" editorial, *CE* 83 (July 25, 1945): 711; "The Churches and Peacetime Conscription," *CE* 82 (December 6, 1944): 1168; "Peacetime Conscription," *MN* 59 (October 17 and December 5, 1944): 3; Leona Krehbiel, "Peacetime Military Conscription," *MN* 60 (April 17, 1945): 1–2; Harrop A. Freeman and Ruth S. Freeman, "International Abolition of Conscription," *FS* 11 (June, 1945): 108–9; Harrop A. Freeman, "Peacetime Conscription Unconstitutional," *FS* 11 (January 1945): 3; John M. Swomley Jr., "Should Patriotism Be Compulsory?" *ZH* 123 (March 7, 1945): 148–49; Charles A. Ellwood, "Permanent Conscription?" *CA* 119 (October 26, 1944): 11; C. Franklin Koch, "Conscription," *LU* 27 (June 20, 1945): 27; Julius Seebach, "Drafting," *LU* 27 (December 20, 1944): 6–7; Richard R. Wood, "Questions about Conscription," *LS* 102 (July 29, 1944): 9; "Shall Conscription Be Permanent?" editorial, *WE* 32 (November 30, 1944): 1161; "Universal Military Training," editorial, *WE* 33 (January 11, 1945): 32–33; "Presbyterians Combat

Peacetime Conscription Now," editorial, *PT* 60 (February 1945): 6; E. J. Tanis, "Peacetime Conscription," *BA* 80 (August 17, 1945): 751; "The Issue of Peacetime Conscription," editorial, *CWE* 41 (December 15, 1944): 219; John C. Bennett, "Peace-Time Conscription," *CAC* 4 (December 11, 1944): 1.

37. Frank L. Wright, "The Case against Conscription," *MN* 60 (March 13, 1945): 7–8. The article first appeared in *CC*. Harrop A. Freeman also contended that peacetime conscription was unconstitutional.

38. Alexander Stewart, "They Say—But Who Is Right?" *ZH* 123 (January 24, 1945): 51–53.

39. Raphael Harwood Miller, "Training for War or Peace, Which?" *CE* 83 (April 18, 1945): 372.

40. Ned B. Stonehouse, "Universal Military Training," *PG* 14 (February 25, 1945): 57–58.

41. For examples of these reports, see Alexander Paul, "China Crisis," *CE* 82 (October 18, 1944): 1009; "The Present Position of the Church in Japan and Korea," *CS* 76 (March 22, 1941): 5–6; "Flashlights from our Missionaries Interned in the Philippines," *GM* 94 (August 25, 1945): 11–12; "The Missionaries in War Zones," *GM* 91 (March 28, 1942): 18; Ralph E. Diffendorfer, "Missions in a World at War," *ZH* 120 (March 4, 1942): 203; "Situation Critical," *LU* 27 (October 4, 1944): 16–17; Edwin Moll, "Our Missions in Wartime," *LU* 26 (January 19, 1944): 6; "War Affects Eastern Mission Work," *LU* 23 (December 18, 1940): 2; "These Also Are Ours," *LU* 23 (October 23, 1940): 16–17; O. H. Schmidt, "What about Our Foreign Missions at the Present Time?" *LW* 61 (March 31, 1942): 20–21; Harold E. Fey, "What War Is Doing to Missions," *CE* 78 (April 4, 1940): 375–76; George A. Hudson, "A World Crisis and Missions—the Challenge from China," *PS* 35 (September, 1945): 293–95. For reports in minutes of denominational meetings, see *Minutes of the General Assembly of the Presbyterian Church in the United States of America* (1942), 218; *Annual of the Southern Baptist Convention* (1942), 171.

42. Searle Bates, "Missions in the Far Eastern War," *CE* 80 (March 5, 1942): 268–69.

43. W. W. Reed, "Methodists Witness Still Girds the World!" *ZH* 120 (November 23, 1942): 1134.

44. "Orphaned Missions," *LC* 103 (May 14, 1941): 6; "Orphaned Missions—Current and Post-War," *FCB* 27 (May 1944): 11.

45. Lorenz A. Buuck, "Missionary Life in a Japanese Concentration Camp," *LW* 62 (January 19, 1943): 24.

46. Henry Smith Leiper, "Churches on the Continent Resist the Nazis," *PS* 31 (December 1941): 532; Martin et al., *Christian Counter-Attack*.

47. Charles Allen Clark, "Are Foreign Missions Finished and Done For?" *PRES* 112 (September 17, 1942): 5–7.

48. Raphael Harwood Miller, "Is Not the Day of Foreign Missions Past?" editorial, *WE* 30 (May 14, 1942): 479–80.

49. Edwin Moll, "This Crisis Time in Foreign Missions," *LU* 24 (July 22, 1942): 6–7.

50. E. Stanley Jones, "The Cross and the Crisis in Missions," *CA* 117 (March 5, 1942): 301.

51. Edwin L. Kirtley, "Liberating the Marshall Islanders," *AD* 137 (January 1945): 4; Van Dusen, *What Is the Church Doing?*

52. See, for example, "Chaplains for Prisoners of War," *FCB* 24 (February 1941): 9;

Paul C. Empie, "Through Barbed Wire," *LU* 27 (March 21, 1945): 8; "For Prisoners of War," *LU* 26 (December 8, 1943): 2; "Prisoners of War," *LC* 104 (October 25, 1942): 12; Tracy Strong, "Combating Barbed-Wire Sickness," *CA* 118 (August 12, 1943): 1006–7; O. K. Armstrong, "Good Will toward Men," *CHD* 66 (December 1943): 15; John Barwick, "Prisoners of War," *GM* 92 (November 27, 1943): 13; Jean Hallack, "I Was in Prison and Ye Came unto Me," *ZH* 123 (July 11, 1945): 435; Bert H. David, "We Took Prisoners," *CA* 119 (June 1, 1944): 670–71.

53. "The American Churches and Relief," *FCB* 24 (September 1941): 12.

54. "What the Clothing Collection Proved," *FCB* 27 (December 1944): 4.

55. Howard E. Kershner, "What of the Children of War-torn Europe?" *CA* 120 (June 14, 1945): 10–11.

56. Merlin L. Neff, "War and the Children," *ST* 71 (March 21, 1944): 4–5.

57. "Humanity Hungers," editorial, *CE* 80 (December 31, 1942): 1394; "Refugees," *CA* 116 (January 23, 1941): 112–13; "While the World Bleeds," *CA* 116 (August 28, 1941): 1114.

58. Snoek, *The Grey Book*, 7; "The Problem of Child Refugees," editorial, *CWE* 32 (July 19, 1940): 258–59; "Opening the Way for the Children," editorial, *CWE* 32 (July 26, 1940): 278. For the whole story, see Wyman, *Paper Walls*, and Genizi, *American Apathy*.

59. Some Christian leaders, including representatives from the FCC and the editorial board of *CAC*, opposed the earlier Hoover plan of 1941 because it appeared to make it too easy for food aid to fall into the hands of the enemy, who would use it for their own troops. These same leaders endorsed the 1943 plan because, in the intervening years, it was shown that food aid would go directly to those who needed it. The critical need also mandated immediate action. See Henry P. Van Dusen, "Food for Europe?" *CAC* 1 (April 4, 1941): 3–6; "Food as War Strategy," editorial, *WE* 29 (March 20, 1941): 272–73; "Mr. Hoover," editorial, *CC* 58 (October 29, 1941): 1326–28; Henry P. Van Dusen, "Relief for Our Starving Allies," *CAC* 3 (February 8, 1943): 6–8.

60. Denominational magazines and the minutes of denominational meetings contain a great deal of information on these committees and the work they did. For a few examples, see *Annual of the Northern Baptist Convention* (1941), 217, and (1944), 76, 231; *Minutes of the General Assembly of the Presbyterian Church in the United States* (1942). See also *LC* 105 (May 9, 1943); William T. Pearcy, "Why Complete the Emergency Million," *CE* 80 (April 23, 1942): 458; "Relief and Rehabilitation," *CAN* 26 (January 1944): 8–10; Paul Dearing, "We Won't Let Them Down!" *CAN* 26 (March 1944): 5, 21–22; "Lutheran World Action and You," *LU* 27 (May 2, 1945): 8–9; "Again the People Have Given," *LU* 27 (November 22, 1944): 23.

61. J. R. Saunders, "Mercy toward Chinese Orphans," *WE* 33 (March 8, 1945): 226–27.

62. John C. Winston, "Bundles for Belgium," *SST* 87 (June 16, 1945): 465.

63. *Mennonite Yearbook* (1945), 11.

64. Nelson, *Lutheranism in North America*, 127–30.

65. For detailed information on these agencies and committees, see James M. Speers, "The Challenge of the Hour," *PR* 3 (February 1940): 30; Leslie Bates Moss, "Prescription for a New World," *PS* 33 (August 1943): 351–53; Elizabeth G. Whiting, "The Modern Exodus," *SA* 6 (March 15, 1940): 31; Morton, *Development and Structure of the War Relief Agencies*; Seymour, *Design for Giving*.

CHAPTER TWELVE

1. Snoek, *The Grey Book*.

2. Jacques Maritain, "Racist Law and the True Meaning of Racism," *CWE* 38 (June 4, 1943): 181–88. See also "The Tragedy of the Jew Today," *SST* 86 (September 30, 1944): 689; Dorothy Moulton Mayer, "Blessed Are the Meek," *CH* 157 (April 1, 1943): 14–15; John Van Beek, "The Wandering Jew," *BA* 78 (March 12, 1943): 246; Willard Johnson, "Guilty Until Proven Innocent," *CA* 116 (October 16, 1941): 1340–41; Allan Anderson, "The Future of the Jews," *ST* 72 (May 15, 1945): 4–5; Hyman Appelman, "The Hated Jew," *SST* 83 (November 1, 1941): 875–77; "The Plight of the Jews," editorial, *CE* 78 (October 3, 1940): 1032; Fred Kendal, "Why Does God Allow Hitler to Torture the Jews," *MM* 44 (October 1943): 72–73; Sterling W. Brown, "Christians and the Jewish Problem," *CE* 82 (February 16, 1944): 164–65.

3. Charles Clayton Morrison, "Biggest Atrocity Story Breaks in Poland," *CC* 61 (September 13, 1944): 1045.

4. Morrison, "Gazing in the Pit," *CC* 62 (May 9, 1945): 575–76.

5. Ibid.

6. Arthur S. Maxwell, "So It Was True," *ST* 72 (May 22, 1945): 3. For other reports on the atrocities, see "Looking behind the Atrocities," editorial, *CE* 83 (May 16, 1945): 468; "Atrocity Stories," editorial, *MN* 60 (June 3, 1945): 3–4; Alfred Hassler, "Atrocity Stories—1944," *FS* 10 (March 1944): 38–39; "Master Race," editorial, *ZH* 123 (May 23, 1945): 326–27; "A Word about Atrocities," editorial, *LS* 103 (June 2, 1945): 3; "German Atrocities—and Hate," editorial, *PT* 60 (July 1945): 5; "The Mystery of Man's Cruelty," editorial, *BA* 80 (June 22, 1945): 580.

7. Maurice Levin, "Holy Week for Jew and Christian," *CH* 158 (April 1, 1944): 13; Robert A. Ashworth, "Christians and Jews," *WE* 32 (April 6, 1944): 323.

8. For the accounts of American apathy toward Jews in Europe, see Ross, *So It Was True*; Wyman, *Abandonment of the Jews* and *Paper Walls*; Friedman, *No Haven for the Oppressed*; Genizi, *American Apathy*; Davie, *Refugees in America*.

9. On Jewish evangelism, see J. Van Beek, "Our Jewish Problem," *BA* 77 (January 30, 1942): 102; John Stuart Conning, "Stricken Jewry Is Calling to God," *PS* 32 (December 1942): 533–34; Ned B. Stonehouse, "The Challenge of Jewish Missions," *PG* 12 (November 25, 1943): 323–24; Morris Gordin, "The Challenge of Jewish Evangelization," *WE* 29 (March 20, 1941): 276–77; Laurence T. Beers, "Baptists and Jews," *WE* 32 (January 13, 1944): 36–37; Chaplain C. Umhau Wolf, "To the Jew First," *LS* 100 (July 4, 1942): 5; Stover, *Plight of the Jews*.

10. On Palestine, see Howard Boniwell Warren, "Can We Be Christian to the Jews?" *ZH* 123 (May 2, 1945): 277; Sol Vail, "A Three-Point Program for Turbulent Palestine," *CR* 124 (September 1945): 334–35; Rabbi Milton Steinberg, "Palestine and the Problem of European Jewry," *AD* 134 (June 1, 1942): 262–63; Ira Eisenstein, "The Problem of Jewish Homelessness," *ZH* 120 (May 13, 1942): 443; Allan Anderson, "Will the Jews Take Over Palestine?" *ST* 72 (May 22, 1945): 6; George T. B. Davis, "Why Are the Jews Returning to Palestine?" *SST* 86 (June 17, 1944): 435. There was of course by no means universal support for the formation of a Jewish state in Palestine. See, for example, "Palestine and the Jews," editorial, *LU* 27 (July 18, 1945): 13. Esther Yolles Feldblum argues that the

Catholic press in America opposed a Jewish state for three reasons: 1) Interlinking the refugee problem with Palestine mitigated the *Christian* refugee problem in Europe; 2) Jewish control of the "Holy Land" would secularize and modernize it; 3) Jews in Palestine would spread the influence and threat of communism. See *The American Catholic Press and the Jewish State.*

11. Charles T. Holman, "When the Dreaded Message Comes," *CHD* 68 (May 1945): 18.

12. Quoted in Hopkins, "Bombing and the American Conscience," 451–73.

13. Charles Clayton Morrison, "Bombers over Tokyo," *CC* 59 (April 29, 1942): 550.

14. Morrison, "Bombing Civilians," *CC* 60 (April 21, 1943): 478–79.

15. Clifford P. Morehouse, "Obliteration Bombing," *LC* 106 (March 26, 1944): 13–14.

16. E. J. Tanis, "The World Today," *BA* 80 (July 20, 1945): 679.

17. Reinhold Niebuhr, "Is the Bombing Necessary?" *CAC* 4 (April 3, 1944): 1–2.

18. "Bombing Raids on Hamburg," *AM* 69 (August 14, 1943): 505.

19. "Bombing of Berlin," *AM* 70 (December 4, 1943): 227.

20. Edward Skillin Jr., "Responsibility," *CWE* 38 (September 10, 1943): 505.

21. Vera Brittain, "Massacre by Bombing," *FS* 10 (March 1944).

22. Harold J. Ockenga and Carl McIntyre, quoted in Hopkins, "Bombing and the American Conscience," 467–68. Daniel A. Poling attacked "the 28," too; see his "Let Christian Leaders Beware!" *CHD* 67 (May 1944): 13.

23. E. Kendall Scouten, "The Bomb's Blast: A Call to Repentance," *CA* 120 (September 6, 1945): 1016.

24. Ibid.

25. Reinhold Niebuhr, "The Atomic Issue," *CAC* 5 (October 15, 1945): 5–7. See also "War," editorial, *LC* 107 (August 19, 1945): 8, 9; A. J. Muste, "The Atomic Bomb and the American Dream," *FS* 11 (October 1945): 167–70; "Can Men Harness Basic Power?" editorial, *SST* 87 (August 25, 1945): 645–46; L. C. Kreider, "The Atomic Age," *MN* 60 (August 28, 1945): 1–2; "The Moral Aspects of Atomic Bombing," editorial, *BA* 80 (August 17, 1945): 748; "Charter and Bombs," editorial, *CE* 83 (August 22, 1945): 807.

26. Richard M. Fagley, "The Atomic Bomb and the Crisis of Man," *CAC* 5 (October 1, 1945): 5–6.

27. "Statement on Control of the Atomic Bomb," *FCB* 28 (October 1945): 6. In 1946 the FCC appointed a commission to study the moral and spiritual implications of the atomic bomb. The report was issued as *Atomic Warfare and the Christian Faith.*

CHAPTER THIRTEEN

1. "The War's End," editorial, *WE* 33 (August 30, 1945): 840–41.

2. Chaplain Paul W. Burres, "We Who Return," *CA* 120 (June 28, 1945): 754–55.

3. Chaplain Myndert M. Van Patten, "The Returning Veteran and His Religion," *PRES* 115 (July 26, 1945): 3. For the needs of returning servicemen, see also Chaplain Earl D. Weed, "War Changes Men's Inner Lives," *AD* 136 (September 1944): 14–15; Chaplain Herbert Moehlman, "How Will They Return?" *LU* 26 (October 27, 1943): 6–7; Captain Edward K. Rogers, "When They Come Home," *LU* 27 (July 4, 1945): 8–9; "How Soldiers View Religion," *LU* 27 (August 22, 1945): 8–9; Arch Soutar, "Home-Coming Isn't Easy," *LS* 103 (April 28, 1945): 4–5.

4. Daniel A. Poling, "Day of Judgment for the Protestant Church," *CHD* 68 (March 1945): 12.

5. Chaplain Donald R. Brownell, "Make Joe Feel at Home," *AD* 136 (December 1944): 11–13.

6. Sergeant Virgil Henry, "Converting Soldiers into Civilians," *CA* 119 (December 28, 1944): 596–97.

7. William H. Poteat, "Jobs to Be Done by the Church," *SA* 10 (March 1944): 30; "What Can Churches Do for Returning Service Men?" editorial, *WE* 32 (February 24, 1944): 176–77.

8. The Right Reverend Oliver J. Hart, "The Church and the Returning Soldiers," *LC* 106 (May 21, 1944): 10–11.

9. "When the Boys Come Home Again," *ST* 71 (May 30, 1944): 8–9.

10. Robert J. Wolfe, "When They Are Again at Home," *LU* 26 (July 5, 1944): 6–7. For more practical advice, see Clarence L. Nystrom, "How to Act toward the Wounded," *LS* 102 (May 27, 1944): 3; Russell L. Dicks, "When You Talk to Veterans," *CA* 120 (June 14, 1945): 6–7.

11. "Help That Returning Soldier!" editorial, *ZH* 122 (August 2, 1944): 487.

12. *Minutes of the General Assembly of The Presbyterian Church in the United States of America* (1944): 228–29.

13. Oscar P. Campbell, "The Return of Servicemen," *BL* 6 (October 1944): 6, 8.

14. "A Job Well Done," *SA* 10 (March 1944): 33.

15. Francis X. Talbot, "The G.I. Bill of Rights," *AM* 71 (April 8, 1944): 16.

16. Talbot, "Starnes-Scrugham Act," *AM* 71 (July 29, 1944): 435.

17. Joseph P. McMurray, "Full Employment: The Postwar Promise," *AM* 71 (July 15, 1944): 388, and *AM* 71 (July 22, 1944): 409; McMurray, "Full Employment: The Postwar Scene," *AM* 71 (August 19, 1944): 491.

18. Harry Lorin Binsse, "There Must Be Jobs," *CWE* 40 (May 5, 1944): 54–57.

19. Richard L. Porter, "Inflation on the Land," *AM* 73 (August 4, 1945): 349.

20. Edward Skillin Jr., "Postwar Life of Riley?" *CWE* 38 (September 10, 1943): 506–9.

21. "Reconversion Program," *AM* 73 (September 1, 1945): 425. See also Martin C. Kyne, "The Problem of Our American Society," *CWE* 41 (November 3, 1944): 54–57.

22. Henry P. Van Dusen, "Twenty-five Years," *CAC* 3 (November 15, 1943): 1–2.

23. Raphael Harwood Miller, "No Second Versailles," *CE* 83 (April 11, 1945): 347.

24. Kirby Page, "Toward World Government," *CE* 80 (September 17, 1942): 1019–20.

25. A. J. Muste, "A Just and Durable Peace," *FS* 8 (April 1942): 62.

26. "Four Affirmations of Christian Faith," *SA* 8 (June 15, 1942): 20.

27. H. J. Kuiper, "What Can the Church Do for the Post-War World?" *BA* 79 (July 1, 1944): 676.

28. Elwyn N. Wilkinson, "Rebuilding a Broken Post-War World," *WR* 118 (January 27, 1944): 3. See also "Winning the Peace," editorial, *MN* 58 (February 2, 1943): 1–2; "The Bases of a Just and Durable Peace," editorial, *BR* 108 (March 26, 1942): 3.

29. Carlyle B. Haynes, "The Churches Plan for Peace," *ST* 71 (January 25, 1944): 6–7.

30. John W. Bradbury, "The Limitations of the Church in Meeting the Problems of World Peace," *WE* 31 (June 24, 1943): 598–99. See also "The Church and a Just Peace," editorial, *CS* 77 (March 21, 1942): 5.

31. Erling C. Olsen, "The Gospel in the Postwar World," *MM* 45 (February 1945): 321–23. See also Chester E. Tulga, "It Was One World," *MM* 45 (October 1944): 65–67; Roy L. Aldrich, "A Just and Enduring Peace," *MM* 44 (July 1944): 603–4, 644; Perry F. Haines, "The Place of the Church in the Post-War World," *MM* 44 (November 1943): 130; Stephen E. Slocum, "God at the Peace Table," *SST* 86 (November 4, 1944): 789; Arthur S. Maxwell, "These Tumultuous Times," *ST* 71 (June 6, 1944): 2; "The Times of the End," *ST* 71 (June 6, 1944): 8–9; Arthur S. Maxwell, "Prophecy Marvelously Vindicated," *ST* 71 (November 7, 1944): 2–3.

32. John Murray, "The Christian World Order," *PG* 12 (October 10, 1943): 273. See also "Bases of a Just and Durable Peace," editorial, *BA* 77 (April 24, 1942): 388–89, which critiques the FCC's Guiding Principles for a Just and Durable Peace.

33. Winfred Ernest Garrison, "The Year in Religion," *CE* 82 (January 12, 1944): 31–32.

34. Walter W. Van Kirk, "What Kind of Peace?" *CC* 59 (February 4, 1942): 139–41. Sperry, *Religion in the Postwar World*; McConnell, *A Basis for the Peace*; Barnes, *A Christian Imperative*; Leber, *The Church Must Win!*; Paton, *Church and the New Order*; Gray, *Postwar Strategy of Religion*; F. Ernest Johnson, *Religion and the World Order*.

35. "Interfaith Declaration on World Peace," *FCB* 26 (November 1943): 7. Roy L. Smith commented in a 1945 editorial that mainline Protestants, Jews, and Catholics agreed on the fundamentals of a peace proposal. See "Agreement on Fundamentals," editorial, *CA* 120 (May 3, 1945): 507–8.

36. *Minutes of the Fourteenth Biennial Convention of the United Lutheran Church* (1944), 346.

37. *Minutes of the General Assembly of the Presbyterian Church in the United States* (1944), 148.

38. "Southern Baptists and World Peace," *Annual of the Southern Baptist Convention* (1944), 149; *Annual of the Northern Baptist Convention* (1944), 269.

39. *Minutes of the General Assembly of the Presbyterian Church in the Untied States of America* (1944), 225.

40. Ibid., 198.

41. "Resolutions," *CE* 82 (November 29, 1944): 1156.

42. "Bishops Assembled Issue Statement on International Order," *CAN* 26 (December 1944): 3–5.

43. "Pius XII Envisions New World Order," *CAN* 24 (February 1942): 6–8.

44. Muelder, *Methodism and Society*, 186.

45. "The Christian Mission on World Order," *FCB* 26 (September 1943): 6; "The Christian Mission on World Order," *FCB* 26 (November 1943): 9.

46. *Minutes of the General Assembly of the Presbyterian Church in the United States of America* (1945), 195.

47. O. F. Nolde, "A Christian Movement toward World Order," *LU* 25 (September 29, 1943): 6–7; "A Christian Movement toward World Order," *LU* 26 (October 6, 1943): 6–7.

48. Toulouse, *Transformation of John Foster Dulles*, 66–67. I have borrowed extensively in this section on Dulles from Toulouse's excellent book. See also *A Righteous Faith for a Just and Durable Peace* for essays by Dulles and other members of the commission.

49. Muelder, *Methodism and Society*, 188.

50. McConnell, *A Basis for the Peace*. The book is a collection of the major addresses of the conference.

51. "Princeton International Roundtable," *FCB* 26 (September 1943): 7.

52. Toulouse, *Transformation of John Foster Dulles*, 81.

53. "Cleveland Conference on a Just and Durable Peace," *FCB* 28 (February 1945): 6–8.

54. For a few examples of such critiques, see "Report from San Francisco," editorial, *CAC* 5 (June 11, 1945): 1–3; "Appeal to San Francisco Conference," *FS* 11 (May 1945): 93–94; Paul Comly French, "Is Dumbarton Oaks the Way to Peace?" *GM* 94 (January 13, 1945): 4–6; Vernon H. Holloway, "Christian Responsibilities and American Power," *SA* 11 (April 15, 1945): 13–24; Emery Reeves, "Will San Francisco Bring Peace?" *CH* 159 (July 1945): 7; "The Charter of the United Nations," editorial, *WE* 33 (July 26, 1945): 720–21; "The Purposes of the Charter," *WE* 33 (August 2, 1945): 744–45; "Membership—General Assembly and Security Council," *WE* 33 (August 9, 1945): 768–69; "International Court of Justice," *WE* 33 (August 23, 1945): 816–17; "One View of Dumbarton Oaks" and "Another View of Dumbarton Oaks," *PT* 60 (January 1945): 4–5; A. J. Muste, "Dumbarton Oaks and the Churchman," *PT* 60 (March 1945): 15; John Paul Jones, "The Churchmen Understand," *PT* 60 (May 1945): 12–13; Edward Skillin Jr., "Yalta," *CWE* 41 (February 23, 1945): 459; "How the Dumbarton Oaks Proposal Should Be Revised," editorial, *CWE* 41 (April 6, 1945): 603; Henry S. Villard, "The Meaning of Dumbarton Oaks," *CR* 124 (April 1945): 125–27; "Homer P. Rainey," "The Significance of Yalta," "The Yalta Agreement," and "Questions and Answers," *CR* 124 (April 1945): 127–35; "Stones from a Glass House," editorial, *CAC* 4 (October 16, 1944): 1–2; "Our Part in the San Francisco Conferences," *FCB* 28 (May 1945): 3–4; "No Evangelical Voice at San Francisco," *UEA* 6 (May 19, 1945): 3.

55. William Howard Melish, "Can We Be Good Samaritans?" *CH* 157 (January 15, 1943): 6; "Religion and Anti-Soviet Propaganda," *CH* 157 (June 15, 1943): 15; "A New Day for Religion in Russia," *CH* 157 (October 1, 1943): 7; "The Four Freedoms and the Russians," *CH* 158 (January 15, 1944): 7; Robert Whitaker, "The Soviets Don't Fear Religion," *PR* 4 (August–September 1942): 30; Harry F. Ward, "Protestants and the anti-Soviet Front," *PR* 4 (December–January 1942): 62; Kenneth Leslie, "Stalin, Architect of Peace," *PR* 5 (March 1944): 1–3.

56. "Peace Imperiled," editorial, *AM* 72 (December 23, 1944): 230; John La Farge, "Russia Challenges the Allied Conscience," *AM* 73 (June 9, 1945): 191.

57. "We Are in Peril," *CAC* 3 (October 18, 1943): 2; Waldemar Gurian, "The Soviet Union," *CWE* 42 (June 29, 1945): 244; "On Russian Relations," editorial, *CWE* 42 (May 18, 1945): 100; "The Russian Record," editorial, *CWE* 40 (September 22, 1944): 531; "Be Fair to Russia," editorial, *ZH* 121 (March 17, 1943): 247; A. J. Muste, "The Spiritual Menace of Russian Communism," *FS* 10 (June, 1944): 103.; "The Fact of Russia," editorial, *CC* 60 (December 8, 1943): 1430–32.

58. Edward Skillin Jr., "Russia II," *CWE* 41 (October 20, 1944): 3.

59. R. H. Markham, "Our Political Immorality," *CC* 62 (January 31, 1945): 140–41.

60. Chaplain Earl L. Stainbrook, "A Chaplain Views the Evangelical Church in Germany," *LS* 103 (August 11, 1945): 8–9; Prince Hubertus zu Loewenstein, "The Role of Religion in Postwar Germany," *LS* 101 (October 23, 1943): 3; P. O. Bersell, "Germany's Religious Status Baffling," *LU* 27 (June 27, 1945: 22; A. J. Warnhuis, "Help for German

Churches?" *AD* 137 (September 1945): 30; Henry Smith Leiper, "Ten Years of Religion under Hitler," *LS* 101 (June 19, 1943): 4–5; "Tested and Not Found Wanting," *LS* 101 (July 24, 1943): 8; "German Churches Not Paganized," *LU* 26 (May 10, 1944): 7.

61. Arnold H. Jahr, "A Chance to Pay Our Debts," *LS* 101 (June 26, 1943): 2.

62. Charles Clayton Morrison, "Germany's Regeneration," *CC* 62 (June 13, 1945): 702–4.

63. "The Peace Settlement in Europe with Special Reference to Germany," *CAC* 4 (June 26, 1944): 6–7. See also "A Statement on Germany," *LS* 102 (October 14, 1944): 4–5; P. O. Bersell, "What Shall We Do with Germany?" *LS* 103 (June 30, 1945): 4–5.

64. "A Statement on Our Policy toward Japan," *CAC* 5 (June 25, 1945): 6; "Statement on Post-War Policy towards Japan," *CAC* 4 (July 10, 1944): 5–6; "World Settlement and Japan—A Statement," *FS* 11 (January 1945): 6–7; Guy Emery Shipler Jr., "What of Christianity in Japan?" *LS* 100 (February 14, 1942): 6.

65. Edward W. Stinson, "Christian Forgiveness," *PT* 60 (November 1944): 15–16; "Neither Measure nor Condition," editorial, *LC* 106 (October 29, 1944): 16–17; Walter Horton, "Christian Ideals and War Guilt," *SA* 9 (November 15, 1943): 8–24; Walter Horton, "Punishment and Forgiveness," *LS* 102 (May 13, 1944): 3–4.

66. Reinhold Niebuhr, "The Religious Level of the World Crisis," *CAC* 5 (January 21, 1946): 4–7.

67. Lawrence S. Price, "The Church, Unequal to Her Task," *LS* 103 (January 20, 1945): 6–7. See also George A. Buttrick, "Prayer and the Return of Faith," *CC* 59 (June 3, 1942): 722–24.

68. Raphael Harwood Miller, "Disciples: Attend to Your Colleges!" *CE* 83 (January 17, 1945): 59.

69. "Need for World Re-Education," editorial, *CE* 82 (August 9, 1944): 759.

70. Sturgis Lee Riddle, "Education Faces the Post-War World," *CH* 158 (May 15, 1944): 6–7. See also Philip Davidson, "Education in the Postwar World," *CA* 119 (June 8, 1944): 699.

71. Clarence P. Sheed, "Religion in Postwar Higher Education," *PS* 35 (February, 1945): 46–47.

72. Henry Schultze, "Post War Education," *BA* 78 (July 2, 1943): 574.

73. Bert H. Davis, "Campus Calling," *CA* 120 (April 5, 1945): 394–95; W. J. Sumpstine, "If G.I. Joe Enters a Christian College," *CE* 83 (January 3, 1945): 8.

74. "A Call to the Churches," *FCB* 28 (October 1945): 7. See also "Our Churches in This Hour," *FCB* 27 (November 1944): 3–4.

75. "Reconstruction of Christian Institutions in Europe," *FCB* 25 (December 1942): 7; "Missions after the War," editorial, *CC* 59 (July 27, 1942): 902–3.

76. For more information about the crusade, see F. Bringle McIntosh, "Danger Signals for Methodism," *CA* 120 (January 25, 1945): 102–3; Bishop Arthur J. Moore, "Methodism, Arise!" *CA* 119 (May 11, 1944): 567; "The Crusade for Christ," *CA* 119 (June 8, 1944): 692–93; "Organizing for Action," *CA* 119 (August 10, 1944): 980–81; "Crusade Approaches a Crisis," *CA* 120 (March 1, 1945): 244–45; Harold H. Cramer, "The Crusade for Christ," *ZH* 122 (November 8, 1944): 707–8; Alford Peckham, "Atomic Christianity," *ZH* 123 (August 22, 1945): 531.

77. Eleanor Lehman, "All Out for Evangelism," *LS* 102 (March 4, 1944): 4–5.

78. "American Lutheran Commissioners Make Plans with World Council," *LS* 103 (May 12, 1945): 15.

79. Abdel Ross Wentz, "The Forward Movement in Missions," *LU* 27 (January 3, 1945): 2. See also Fred J. Fiedler, "Forward in China and Japan," *LU* 27 (January 10, 1945): 8–9.

80. Theodore Graebner, "Lutherans Move toward Union," *LS* 102 (March 25, 1944): 4–5.

81. "We Need a Passion for Souls," editorial, *WE* 32 (August 17, 1944): 801. See also "The Need for Militant Christianity," editorial, *WE* 33 (September 13, 1945): 888–89; J. G. Hughes, "Baptists in This Strategic Hour," *BR* 109 (December 2, 1943): 4–5; W. R. White, "Baptist Principles in This Hour," *BR* 110 (August 31, 1944): 6–7; E. D. Head, "Wanted—Narrow-minded Baptists," *WR* 119 (January 18, 1945): 3–4.

82. J. H. Rushbrooke, "The World Responsibility of Baptists," *BL* 6 (August 1944): 8, and *BL* 6 (September 1944): 10; Stanley I. Stuber, "Postwar Advance among Northern Baptists," *WE* 32 (August 17, 1944): 810; W. Fred Kendall, "Spiritual Objectives for the Centennial Crusade," *WR* 119 (February 22, 1945): 4–5; *Annual of the Southern Baptist Convention* (1945), 53; H. H. Hargrove, "Concerning the Committee for the Preparation for the Post-War Missions," *BR* 108 (August 6, 1942): 4–5.

83. See "Missions after the War," editorial, *CC* 59 (July 27, 1942): 902–3; Marvin O. Sansbury, "Can We Restore Our Evangelistic Passion?" *CE* 82 (September 13, 1944): 885–86; "The Challenge of Wakening Asia," *CS* 80 (March 17, 1945): 1; "The Challenge of Desolated Europe," *CS* 80 (January 20, 1945): 1; Henry St. George Tucker, "Forward in World Service," *LC* 105 (October 10, 1943): 17; John W. Bradbury, "The Mission of the National Association of Evangelicals," *UEA* 3 (April 4, 1944): 6; "Preparation Now for Post-War Missionary Advance," *SST* 85 (July 10, 1943): 555; "70,000 Attend Chicago Youth for Christ Rally," *UEA* 6 (June 15, 1945): 1.

84. See, for example, W. W. Landrum, "If You Are a Christian, Why Not a Baptist?" *BR* 109 (May 6, 1943): 4–5; "Loyal to the Methodist Church," editorial, *ZH* 122 (August 30, 1944): 552; Harold J. Ockenga, "The Reality of Church Unity," *UEA* 3 (August 10, 1943): 3; "An American Council of Churches," *SST* 83 (October 11, 1941): 813; "The St. Louis Convention," *SST* 84 (June 20, 1942): 493; Ernest Gordon, "The Federal Council Arraigned," *SST* 86 (December 2, 1944): 881; Harold J. Ockenga, "The Roman Catholic Hierarchy Challenges Protestant America," parts 1, 2, and 3, *SST* 87 (August 11, 1945): 607, *SST* 87 (August 18, 1945): 627, and *SST* 87 (August 25, 1945): 648; "Protestant Reorientation," editorial, *CC* 60 (October 27, 1943): 1222–24; "Fighting on Two Fronts," editorial, *BA* 80 (July 6, 1945): 628–29; Samuel McCrea Cavert, "Our Protestant Heritage," *FCB* 27 (October 1944): 7–9; Harold Snider, "Why We Should Remain in the Federal Council," *GM* 94 (April 14, 1945): 11; "Is the Council Protestant?" editorial, *ZH* 123 (January 10, 1945): 22; "The Church and the American Council," *PG* 14 (May 10, 1945): 137.

CHAPTER FOURTEEN

1. Fosdick, *Living under Tension*, 2.
2. Ibid., 7.

BIBLIOGRAPHY

RELIGIOUS PERIODICALS

Baptist:

    Baptist and Reflector (Jackson, Tenn.), 1939–45

    Baptist Leader (Valley Forge, Pa.), 1940–45

    Watchman-Examiner (New York), 1939–45

    Western Recorder (Louisville, Ky.) 1939–45

Christian Reformed:

    Banner (Grand Rapids, Mich.), 1939–45

Congregational:

    Advance (Boston), 1939–45

    Social Action (New York), 1939–45

Disciples:

    Christian-Evangelist (St. Louis), 1939–45

    Christian Standard (Cincinnati, Ohio), 1939–45

    Scroll (Chicago), 1939–45

Lutheran:

    Lutheran (Philadelphia), 1939–45

    Lutheran Standard (Columbus, Ohio), 1939–45

    Lutheran Witness (St. Louis), 1939–45

Methodist:

    Christian Advocate (New York), 1939–45

    Christian Index (Jackson, Tenn.), 1939–45

    Zion's Herald (Boston), 1939–45

Nondenominational:

    Christian Century (Chicago), 1939–45

    Christian Herald (Chappaque, N.Y.), 1939–45

    Christianity and Crisis (New York), 1941–45

    Federal Council Bulletin (New York), 1939–45

    Fellowship (New York), 1939–45

    Moody Monthly (Chicago), 1939–45

    Protestant Digest (*Protestant*) (New York), 1939–45

    Radical Religion (New York), 1939–41

Sunday School Times (Philadelphia), 1939–45
United Evangelical Action (Boston), 1942–45
Peace Churches:
Gospel Messenger (Elgin, Ill.), 1939–45
Mennonite (North Newton, Kans.), 1939–45
Presbyterian:
Presbyterian (Philadelphia), 1939–45
Presbyterian Guardian (Philadelphia), 1939–45
Presbyterian Survey (Richmond, Va.), 1939–45
Presbyterian Tribune (New York), 1939–45
Protestant Episcopal:
Churchman (New York), 1939–45
Living Church (Milwaukee, Wis.), 1939–45
Roman Catholic:
America (New York), 1939–45
Catholic Action (Washington, D.C.), 1939–45
Commonweal (New York), 1939–45
Seventh-Day Adventist:
Signs of the Times (Mountain View, Calif.), 1939–45
Unitarian:
Christian Register (Boston), 1939–45

PUBLICATIONS OF DENOMINATIONAL MEETINGS

Annual of the Illinois Conference of the Evangelical Lutheran Augustana Synod, 1940–45
Annual of the Northern Baptist Convention, 1940–45
Annual of the Southern Baptist Convention, 1940–45
Journal of the General Convention of the Protestant Episcopal Church in the United States of America, 1940, 1943
Mennonite Yearbook, 1945
Minutes, General Council of the Congregational and Christian Churches, 1940
Minutes of the Annual Sessions of New York Yearly Meeting of the Religious Society of Friends, 1940–44
Minutes of the Biennial Convention of the United Lutheran Church in America, 1942, 1944
Minutes of the General Assembly of the Presbyterian Church in the United States, 1940–45
Minutes of the General Assembly of the Presbyterian Church in the United States of America, 1940–45
Yearbook of the Evangelical Mission Covenant Church in America, 1940, 1942–45

ARTICLES

Abrams, Ray H., ed. "The American Family in World War II." *Annals of the American Academy of Political and Social Science*, vol. 229 (September 1943).
———. "The Churches and the Clergy in World War II." *Annals of the American Academy of Political and Social Science* 256 (March 1948): 110–19.

Bainton, Roland H. "The Churches and War: Historical Attitudes toward Christian Participation." *Social Action* 11 (January 1945): 32–69.

Brcak, Nancy, and John R. Pavia. "Racism in Japanese and U.S. Wartime Propaganda." *Historian* 56 (Summer 1994): 671–83.

"The Churches and the War." *Time* (December 22, 1941): 67–69.

Conway, John S. "Myron C. Taylor's Mission to the Vatican, 1940–1950." *Church History* 44 (Winter 1975): 85–99.

Ford, John C., S.J. "The Morality of Obliteration Bombing." *Theological Studies* 5 (September 1944): 261–309.

Fox-Genovese, Elizabeth. "Mixed Messages: Women and the Impact of World War II." *Southern Humanities Review* 27 (Summer 1993): 235–45.

Gilbert, Mark. "Pacifist Attitudes to Nazi Germany, 1936–1945." *Journal of Contemporary History* 27 (July 1992): 493–511.

Goldin, C. D. "The Role of World War II in the Rise of Women's Employment." *American Economic Review* 81 (September 1991): 741–57.

Graves, John Temple. "The Southern Negro and the War Crisis." *Virginia Quarterly Review* 18 (Autumn 1942): 500–17.

Hall, Mitchell K. "A Withdrawal from Peace: The Historical Response to War of the Church of God (Anderson, Indiana)." *Journal of Church and State* 27 (Spring 1985): 301–14.

Hepburn, Mary A. "Educating for Democracy: The Years Following World War II." *Social Studies* 81 (July–August 1990): 153–60.

Hopkins, George E. "Bombing and the American Conscience during World War II." *Historian* 28 (May 1966): 451–73.

Hyman, Michael R., and Richard Tansey. "Ethical Codes and the Advocacy Advertisements of World War II." *International Journal of Advertising* 12 (1993): 351–66.

Johnson, F. Ernest. "The Impact of the War on Religion in America." *American Journal of Sociology* 48 (November 1942): 353–61.

Keim, Albert N. "John Foster Dulles and the Protestant World Order Movement on the Eve of World War II." *Journal of Church and State* 21 (Winter 1979): 73–89.

——. "Service or Resistance? The Mennonite Response to Conscription in World War II." *Mennonite Quarterly Review* 52 (Spring 1978): 141–55.

Leff, M. H. "The Politics of Sacrifice on the American Home Front in World War II." *Journal of American History* 77 (March 1991): 1296–1318.

Litoff, Judy Barrett, and David C. Smith. "U.S. Women and the Home Front in World War II." *Historian* 57 (Winter 1995): 349–60.

Lovin, Robin. "Reason, Relativism, and Christian Realism." *Annual of the Society of Christian Ethics* (1985): 57–78.

Ludlow, Peter W. "The International Protestant Community in the Second World War." *Journal of Ecclesiastical History* 29 (July 1978): 311–62.

McEnaney, Laura. "He-men and Christian Mothers: The America First Movement and the Gendered Meanings of Patriotism." *Diplomatic History* 18 (Winter 1994): 47–57.

McNeal, Patricia F. "Catholic Conscientious Objectors during World War II." *Catholic Historical Review* 61 (April 1975): 222–42.

Mathis, Susan. "Propaganda to Mobilize Women for World War II." *Social Education* 58 (February 1994): 94–98.

Meyer, Leisa D. "Creating G.I. Jane." *Feminist Studies* 18 (Fall 1992): 581–602.

Murphy, Dwight D. "The World War II Relocation of Japanese-Americans." *Journal of Social, Political, and Economic Studies* 18 (Spring 1993): 93–117.

Okihiro, Gary Y. "Religion and Resistance in America's Concentration Camps." *Phylon* 45 (Summer 1984): 220–33.

Orser, William Edward. "Racial Attitudes in War: The Protestant Churches during the Second World War." *Church History* 41 (Summer 1972): 337–53.

———. "World War II and the Pacifist Controversy in the Major Protestant Churches." *American Studies* 14 (Spring 1973): 5–24.

Sims-Wood, Janet. "Africans and World War II: An Annotated Bibliography." *Negro History Bulletin* 51 (December 1993): 62–67.

Thompson, Dean K. "World War II, Interventionism, and Henry Pitney Van Dusen." *Journal of Presbyterian History* 55 (Fall 1977): 327–45.

Wensyel, James W. "Home Front." *American History* 30 (June 1995): 44–66.

Westbrook, R. B. "'I Want a Girl, Just Like the Girl That Married Harry James': American Women and the Problem of Political Obligation in World War II." *American Quarterly* 42 (December 1990): 587–614.

Zahn, Gordon C. "Peace Witness in World War II." *Worldview* 18 (Fall 1975): 49–55.

BOOKS

Abell, Aaron I., ed. *American Catholic Thought on Social Questions*. Indianapolis: Bobbs-Merrill Company, Inc., 1968.

Abrams, Ray H. *Preachers Present Arms*. Scottdale, Pa.: Herald Press, 1933.

Albright, Raymond W. *A History of the Protestant Episcopal Church*. New York: Macmillan, 1964.

America's Pacifist Minority. Chicago: Fellowship of Reconciliation, 1942.

Anderson, Karen. *Wartime Women: Sex Roles, Family Relations, and the Status of Women during World War II*. Westport, Conn.: Greenwood Press, 1981.

Arrington, Leonard J. "The Price of Prejudice: The Japanese-American Relocation Center in Utah during World War II." In *Three Short Works on Japanese Americans*, edited by Roger Daniels, 3–43. New York: Arno Press, 1978.

Arrington, Leonard J., and Davis Bitton. *The Mormon Experience: A History of the Latter-Day Saints*. New York: Alfred A. Knopf, 1979.

Atomic Warfare and the Christian Faith: Report of the Commission on the Relation of the Church to the War in the Light of the Christian Faith. New York: Federal Council of Churches, 1946.

Bailey, Kenneth. *Southern White Protestantism in the Twentieth Century*. New York: Harper and Row, 1964.

Bainton, Roland H. *Christian Attitudes toward War and Peace: A Historical Survey and Critical Re-evaluation*. New York: Abingdon Press, 1960.

Baker, Robert Andrew. *A Baptist Source Book: With Particular Reference to Southern Baptists*. Nashville: Boardman Press, 1966.

Balfour, Michael. *Propaganda in War, 1939–1945*. London: Routledge and Kegan Paul, 1979.

Barnes, Roswell P. *A Christian Imperative*. New York: Friendship Press, 1941.

Barnes, William Wright. *The Southern Baptist Convention, 1845–1953*. Nashville: Boardman Press, 1954.

Barnhart, Edward N., Floyd W. Matson, and Jacobus Ten Broek. *Prejudice, War, and the Constitution: Japanese American Evacuation and Resettlement*. Berkeley: University of California Press, 1958.

Bell, G. K. A. *The Church and Humanity*. London: Longmans, Green and Co., 1946.

Bennett, David H. *The Party of Fear: From Nativist Movements to the New Right in American History*. Chapel Hill: University of North Carolina Press, 1988.

Bennett, John C. *Christian Ethics and Social Policy*. New York: Charles Scribner's Sons, 1946.

———. *Christian Realism*. New York: Charles Scribner's Sons, 1941.

Be'rube', Allan. *Coming Out under Fire: The History of Gay Men and Women in World War II*. New York: Free Press, 1990.

Black, John D., Sir Willmott Lewis, and Clarence E. Pickett. *America's Food and Europe's Needs*. Ser. 10. Philadelphia: American Academy of Political and Social Science, 1941.

Blum, John Morton. *V Was for Victory: Politics and American Culture during World War II*. New York: Harcourt Brace Jovanovich, 1976.

Boland, Francis J., and John A. Ryan. *Catholic Principles of Politics*. New York: Macmillan, 1940.

Bosworth, Allan R. *America's Concentration Camps*. New York: W. W. Norton, 1967.

Bowman, B. L., and Dan T. Caldwell. *They Answered the Call*. Richmond, Va.: John Knox Press, 1952.

Bowman, Rufus D. *The Church of the Brethren and War, 1708–1941*. Elgin, Ill.: Brethren Publishing House, 1944.

Brimner, Larry Dane. *Voices from the Camps: Internment of Japanese Americans during World War II*. New York: Franklin Watts, 1994.

Brock, Peter. *Twentieth-Century Pacifism*. New York: Van Nostrand Reinhold Company, 1970.

Brown, William Adams. *A Creed for Free Men*. New York: Charles Scribner's Sons, 1941.

———. *The New Order in the Church*. New York: Abingdon-Cokesbury, 1943.

———. *Toward a United Church: Three Decades of Ecumenical Christianity*. New York: Charles Scribner's Sons, 1946.

Brown, William Adams, Louis Finkelstein, and J. Elliot Ross. *The Religions of Democracy: Judaism, Catholicism, Protestantism in Creed and Life*. New York: Devin-Adair Company, 1943.

Buchanan, A. Russell. *Black Americans in World War II*. Santa Barbara, Calif.: Clio Books, 1977.

Bucke, Emory Stevens, ed. *The History of American Methodism*. 3 vols. New York: Abingdon Press, 1964.

Campbell, D'Ann. *Women at War with America: Private Lives in a Patriotic Era*. Cambridge: Harvard University Press, 1984.

Carmer, Carl, ed. *The War against God*. New York: Henry Holt and Company, 1943.

Casdorph, Paul D. *Let the Good Times Roll: Life at Home in America during World War II.* New York: Paragon House, 1989.

Catlin, George, Vera Brittain, Sheila Hodges, Gert Spindler, and Devere Allen, comps. *Above All Nations.* New York: Harper and Brothers, 1945.

Cavert, Samuel McCrea. *On the Road to Christian Unity: An Appraisal of the Ecumenical Movement.* Westport, Conn.: Greenwood Press, 1961.

Chafe, William H. *Women and Equality: Changing Patterns in American Culture.* New York: Oxford University Press, 1977.

Chapman, Robert. *Tell It to the Chaplain.* New York: Exposition Press, 1952.

Chatfield, Charles. *For Peace and Justice: Pacifism in America, 1914–1941.* Boston: Beacon Press, 1971.

Cianfarra, Camille M. *The Vatican and the War.* New York: Literary Classics, Inc., 1944.

Clifford, J. Garry, and Samuel R. Spencer Jr. *The First Peacetime Draft.* Lawrence: University Press of Kansas, 1986.

Clinard, Marshall B. *The Black Market: A Study of White Collar Crime.* New York: Rinehart and Company, Inc., 1952.

Coe, George A. *What Is Religion Doing to Our Consciences?* New York: Charles Scribner's Sons, 1943.

Cole, Wayne S. *America First: The Battle against Intervention, 1940–1941.* Madison: University of Wisconsin Press, 1953.

——. *Roosevelt and the Isolationists, 1932–1945.* Lincoln: University of Nebraska Press, 1983.

Conrat, Maisie, and Richard Conrat. *Executive Order 9066: The Internment of 110,000 Japanese Americans.* Cambridge: MIT Press, 1972.

Conscientious Objection. Special Monograph 11, Vol. 1. Washington, D.C.: Government Printing Office, 1950.

Costello, John. *Virtue under Fire: How World War II Changed Our Social and Sexual Attitudes.* Boston: Little, Brown and Company, 1985.

Cripps, Thomas. *Making Movies Black: The Hollywood Message Movie from World War II to the Civil Rights Era.* New York: Oxford University Press, 1993.

Crosby, Donald F. *Battlefield Chaplains: Catholic Priests in World War II.* Lawrence: University Press of Kansas, 1994.

Cross, Christopher. *Soldiers of God.* New York: E. P. Dutton and Company, Inc., 1945.

Dalfiume, Richard M. *Desegregation of the U.S. Armed Forces: Fighting on Two Fronts, 1939–1953.* Columbia: University of Missouri Press, 1969.

——. "The 'Forgotten Years' of the Negro Revolution." In *The Negro in Depression and War: Prelude to Revolution, 1930–1945,* edited by Bernard Sternsher, 298–316. Chicago: Quadrangle Books, 1969.

Daniels, Roger. *The Decision to Relocate the Japanese Americans.* Malabar, Fla.: Robert E. Krieger Publishing Company, 1986.

——. *The Politics of Prejudice: The Anti-Japanese Movement in California and the Struggle for Japanese Exclusion.* Berkeley: University of California Press, 1962.

——. *Prisoners without Trial: Japanese Americans in World War II.* New York: Hill and Wang, 1993.

Daniels, Roger, Harry H. L. Kitano, and Sandra C. Taylor. *Japanese Americans: From Relocation to Redress.* Salt Lake City: University of Utah Press, 1986.

Davie, Maurice R. *Refugees in America: Report of the Committee for the Study of Recent Immigration from Europe*. New York: Harper and Brothers, 1947.

Davis, Derek, and James E. Wood, eds. *The Role of Religion in the Making of Public Policy*. Waco, Tex: J. M. Dawson Institute, 1991.

Davis, Kenneth S. *Experience of War: The United States in World War II*. Garden City, N.Y.: Doubleday and Company, 1965.

Divine, Robert A. *The Illusion of Neutrality*. Chicago: University of Chicago Press, 1962.

——. *The Reluctant Belligerent: American Entry into World War II*. New York: John Wiley and Sons, 1965.

——. *Second Chance: The Triumph of Internationalism in America during World War II*. New York: Atheneum, 1967.

Dohen, Dorothy. *Nationalism and American Catholicism*. New York: Sheed and Ward, 1967.

Doherty, Thomas. *Projections of War: Hollywood, American Culture, and World War II*. New York: Columbia University Press, 1993.

Dolan, Edward F., Jr. *Hollywood Goes to War*. New York: Gallery Books, 1985.

Dolan, Jay. *The American Catholic Experience*. New York: Doubleday, 1985.

Douglas, Paul. *The City Church in the War Emergency*. New York: Friendship Press, 1945.

Drury, Clifford Merrill. *The History of the Chaplain Corps, United States Navy*. Vol. 2, *1939–1949*. Washington, D.C.: U.S. Government Printing Office, n.d.

Dulles, John Foster. *War, Peace, and Change*. New York: Harper and Brothers, 1939.

Dulles, John Foster, et al. *A Righteous Faith for a Just and Durable Peace*. New York: Commission to Study the Bases of a Just and Durable Peace, 1942.

Dunham, Arthur. *Friends and Community Service in War and Peace*. Philadelphia: American Friends Service Committee, 1942.

Dunn, David, et al. *A History of the Evangelical and Reformed Church*. Philadelphia: Christian Education Press, 1961.

Eller, Cynthia. *Conscientious Objectors and the Second World War: Moral and Religious Arguments in Support of Pacifism*. New York: Praeger, 1991.

Ellis, John Tracy. *American Catholicism*. Rev. ed. Chicago: University of Chicago Press, 1969.

Ellwood, Charles A. *The World's Need of Christ*. New York: Abingdon-Cokesbury Press, 1940.

Enforcement of the Selective Service Law. Washington, D.C.: U.S. Government Printing Office, 1951.

Enser, A. G. S. *A Subject Bibliography of the Second World War, 1939–1974*. Boulder, Colo.: Westview Press, 1977.

——. *A Subject Bibliography of the Second World War, 1975–1983*. Brookfield, Vt.: Gower Publishing Company, 1985.

Fehrenbach, T. R. *F.D.R.'s Undeclared War, 1939–1941*. New York: David McKay Company, Inc., 1967.

Fein, Helen. *Accounting for Genocide: National Responses and Jewish Victimization during the Holocaust*. Chicago: University of Chicago Press, 1979.

Feingold, Henry L. *The Politics of Rescue: The Roosevelt Administration and the Holocaust, 1938–1945*. New Brunswick, N.J.: Rutgers University Press, 1970.

Feldblum, Esther Yolles. *The American Catholic Press and the Jewish State, 1917–1959.* New York: KTAV Publishing House, Inc., 1977.

Filene, Peter Gabriel. *Him/Her/Self: Sex Roles in Modern America.* New York: Harcourt Brace Jovanovich, 1974.

Finkle, Lee. *Forum for Protest: The Black Press during World War II.* Cranbury, N.J.: Associated University Presses, Inc., 1975.

Fitch, Robert E. *A Certain Blind Man.* New York: Charles Scribner's Sons, 1944.

Fitzpatrick, Edward A., ed. *Selective Service in Wartime: Second Report of the Director of Selective Service, 1941–1942.* Washington, D.C.: U.S. Government Printing Office, 1943.

Fosdick, Harry Emerson. *A Great Time to Be Alive: Sermons on Christianity in Wartime.* New York: Harper and Brothers, 1944.

——. *The Living of These Days: An Autobiography.* New York: Harper and Brothers, 1956.

——. *Living under Tension.* New York: Harper and Brothers, 1941.

——. *On Being Fit to Live With.* New York: Harper and Brothers, 1946.

Fox, Frank W. *Madison Avenue Goes to War: The Strange Military Career of American Advertising, 1941–1945.* Provo, Utah: Brigham Young University Press, 1975.

Fox, Richard Wightman. *Reinhold Niebuhr: A Biography.* San Francisco: Harper and Row, 1985.

Franklin, John Hope. *From Slavery to Freedom: A History of American Negroes.* New York: Alfred A. Knopf, 1947.

Frazier, E. Franklin. *The Negro in the United States.* Rev. ed. New York: Macmillan, 1957.

Freeman, Harrop A. *The Constitutionality of Peacetime Conscription.* Ser. 7, no. 2. Philadelphia: Pacifist Research Bureau, 1945.

——, ed. *Peace Is the Victory.* New York: Harper and Brothers, 1944.

French, Paul Comly. *Civilian Public Service.* Washington, D.C.: National Service Board for Religious Objectors, 1944.

——, ed. *Common Sense Neutrality: Mobilizing for Peace.* New York: Hastings House, 1939.

Friedman, Saul S. *No Haven for the Oppressed: United States Policy toward Jewish Refugees, 1938–1945.* Detroit: Wayne State University Press, 1973.

Funk, Arthur L. *The Second World War: A Bibliography of Books in English since 1975.* Claremont, Calif.: Regina Books, 1985.

Gardiner, C. Harvey. *Pawns in a Triangle of Hate: The Peruvian Japanese and the United States.* Seattle: University of Washington Press, 1981.

Garfinkel, Herbert. *When Negroes March: The March on Washington Movement in the Organizational Politics for FEPC.* Glencoe, Ill.: Free Press, 1959.

Garrenton, John S. *The Flying Chaplain.* New York: Vantage Press, 1957.

Genizi, Haim. *American Apathy: The Plight of Christian Refugees from Nazism.* Jerusalem: Bar-Ilan University Press, 1983.

Gilbert, Martin. *Auschwitz and the Allies.* New York: Holt, Rinehart and Winston, 1981.

——. *The Holocaust: A History of the Jews of Europe during the Second World War.* New York: Holt, Rinehart and Winston, 1985.

Gilkey, James Gordon. *God Will Help You.* New York: Macmillan, 1943.

Gingerich, Melvin. *Service for Peace: A History of the Mennonite Civilian Public Service.* Akron, Pa.: Mennonite Central Committee, 1949.

Girdner, Audrie, and Anne Loftis. *The Great Betrayal: The Evacuation of the Japanese-Americans during World War II*. New York: Macmillan, 1969.

Glaberman, Martin. *Wartime Strikes: The Struggle against the No-Strike Pledge in the UAW during World War II*. Detroit: Bewick Editions, 1980.

Gluck, Sherna. *Rosie the Riveter Revisited: Women, War, and Social Change*. Boston: Twayne, 1987.

Goodman, Jack, ed. *While You Were Gone: A Report on Wartime Life in the U.S.* New York: Simon and Schuster, 1946.

Goodwin, Doris Kearns. *No Ordinary Time: Franklin and Eleanor Roosevelt: The Home Front in World War II*. New York: Simon and Schuster, 1994.

Gordon, Linda. *Woman's Body, Woman's Right: A Social History of Birth Control in America*. New York: Grossman Publishers, 1976.

Gray, Joseph M. *The Postwar Strategy of Religion*. New York: Abingdon-Cokesbury Press, 1944.

Gregg, Richard B. *The Power of Non-Violence*. Philadelphia: J. B. Lippincott Company, 1934.

Gregory, Chester W. *Women in Defense Work during World War II*. New York: Exposition Press, 1974.

Gruhzit-Hoyt, Olga. *They Also Served: American Women in World War II*. New York: Card Publishing, 1995.

Gunnemann, Louis H. *The Shaping of the United Church of Christ*. New York: United Church Press, 1977.

Gushwa, Robert L. *The Best and Worst of Times: The U.S. Army Chaplaincy, 1920–1945*. Washington, D.C.: U.S. Government Printing Office, 1977.

Handy, Robert T. *The American Religious Depression, 1925–1935*. Philadelphia: Fortress Press, 1968.

———. *A Christian America: Protestant Hopes and Historical Realities*. New York: Oxford University Press, 1984.

———. *A History of the Churches in the United States and Canada*. New York: Oxford University Press, 1977.

Hartmann, George W. *A Plea for an Immediate Peace by Negotiation*. New York: War Resisters League, 1942.

Hartmann, Susan M. *The Home Front and Beyond: American Women in the 1940s*. Boston: Twayne Publishers, 1982.

Haselden, Kyle. *The Racial Problem in Christian Perspective*. New York: Harper and Brothers, 1959.

Haskell, Molly. *From Reverence to Rape: The Treatment of Women in the Movies*. Chicago: University of Chicago Press, 1973.

Hennesey, James, S.J. *American Catholics: A History of the Roman Catholic Community in the United States*. New York: Oxford University Press, 1981.

Herber, Will. *Protestant-Catholic-Jew: An Essay in American Religious Sociology*. Garden City, N.Y.: Doubleday and Company, Inc., 1956.

Herman, Steward W., Jr. *It's Your Souls We Want*. New York: Harper and Brothers, 1943.

Hershberger, Guy Franklin. *The Mennonite Church in the Second World War*. Scottdale, Pa.: Mennonite Publishing House, 1951.

———. *War, Peace, and Nonresistance*. Scottdale, PA: The Herald Press, 1944.

Holmes, John Haynes. *I Speak for Myself: The Autobiography of John Haynes Holmes*. New York: Harper and Brothers, 1959.

Holt, Arthur E. *Christian Roots of Democracy in America*. New York: Friendship Press, 1941.

Homrighausen, Elmer George. *Let the Church Be the Church*. New York: Abingdon Press, 1940.

Honey, Maureen. *Creating Rosie the Riveter: Class, Gender, and Propaganda during World War II*. Amherst: University of Massachusetts Press, 1984.

Honeywell, Roy J. *Chaplains of the U.S. Army*. Washington, D.C.: U.S. Government Printing Office, 1958.

Hopkins, C. Howard. *History of the Y.M.C.A. in North America*. New York: Association Press, 1951.

Hopper, Stanley Romaine. *The Crisis of Faith*. New York: Abingdon-Cokesbury Press, 1944.

Horton, Walter Marshall. *Can Christianity Save Civilization?* New York: Harper and Brothers, 1940.

Hough, Lynn Harold. *Living Democracy*. New York: Fleming H. Revell Company, 1943.

Hudnut-Beumler, James. "The American Churches and U.S. Interventionism." In *The Church's Public Role*, edited by Dieter T. Hessel, 125–42. Grand Rapids, Mich.: William B. Eerdmans Publishing Company, 1993.

Hughes, Philip. *The Pope's New Order*. New York: Macmillan, 1944.

Hunter, James Davison. *Culture Wars*. New York: Basic Books, 1991.

Hutchison, John A. *We Are Not Divided: A Critical Historical Study of the Federal Council of the Churches of Christ in America*. New York: Round Table Press, 1941.

Hutchinson, Paul. *The New Leviathan*. New York: Willett, Clark and Company, 1946.

Hutchison, William R., ed. *Between the Times: The Travail of the Protestant Establishment in America, 1900–1960*. New York: Cambridge University Press, 1989.

An Introduction to Friends Civilian Public Service. Philadelphia: American Friends Service Committee, 1945.

Ironside, H. A. *The Lamp of Prophecy, or Signs of the Times*. Grand Rapids, Mich.: Zondervan Publishing House, 1940.

Janeway, Eliot. *The Struggle for Survival: A Chronicle of Economic Mobilization in World War II*. New Haven: Yale University Press, 1951.

Johnson, Charles S. *To Stem This Tide: A Survey of Racial Tension Areas in the United States*. Boston: Pilgrim Press, 1943.

Johnson, F. Ernest, ed. *Religion and the World Order*. New York: Institute for Religious Studies, 1944.

Johnson, Walter. *The Battle against Isolation*. Chicago: University of Chicago Press, 1944.

Jonas, Manfred. *Isolationism in America, 1935–1941*. Ithaca, N.Y.: Cornell University Press, 1966.

Jones, Peter G. *War and the Novelist: Appraising the American War Novel*. Columbia: University of Missouri Press, 1976.

Jorgensen, Daniel B. *The Service of Chaplains to Army Air Units, 1917–1946*. Washington, D.C.: U.S. Government Printing Office, n.d.

Kanawada, Leo V., Jr. *Franklin D. Roosevelt's Diplomacy and American Catholics, Italians, and Jews.* Ann Arbor, Mich.: UMI Research Press, 1982.

Kandel, I. L. *The Impact of the War upon American Education.* Chapel Hill: University of North Carolina Press, 1948.

Kean, Charles Duell. *Christianity and the Cultural Crisis.* New York: Association Press, 1945.

Keim, Albert N., and Grant M. Stoltzfus. *The Politics of Conscience: The Historic Peace Churches and America at War, 1917–1955.* Scottdale, Pa.: Herald Press, 1988.

Kennett, Lee. *For the Duration: The United States Goes to War, Pearl Harbor—1942.* New York: Charles Scribner's Sons, 1985.

——. *G.I.: The American Soldier in World War II.* New York: Charles Scribner's Sons, 1987.

Kernan, W. F. *We Can Win This War.* Boston: Little, Brown and Company, 1943.

Kesselman, Louis Coleridge. *The Social Politics of FEPC: A Study in Reform Pressure Movements.* Chapel Hill: University of North Carolina Press, 1948.

Kinsella, William E., Jr. *Leadership in Isolation: FDR and the Origins of the Second World War.* Cambridge: Schenkman Publishing Company, 1978.

Landis, Benson Y., ed. *Religion and the Good Society: an Introduction to Social Teachings of Judaism, Catholicism, and Protestantism.* New York: The National Conference of Christians and Jews, 1942.

Langer, William L., and S. Everett Gleason. *The Challenge to Isolation, 1937–1940.* New York: Harper and Brothers, 1952.

Latourette, Kenneth Scott. *The Unconquerable Light.* New York: Harper and Brothers, 1941.

Leber, Charles Tudor. *The Church Must Win!* New York: Fleming H. Revell Company, 1944.

——. *The Unconquerable: Concerning the Christian Mission in a World at War.* New York: Fleming H. Revell Company, 1943.

Lee, Robert. *The Social Sources of Church Unity: An Interpretation of Unitive Movements in American Protestantism.* New York: Abingdon Press, 1960.

Lee, Umphrey. *The Historic Church and Modern Pacifism.* New York: Abingdon-Cokesbury Press, 1943.

Levin, Nora. *The Holocaust: The Destruction of European Jewry, 1933–1945.* New York: Thomas Y. Crowell Company, 1968.

Lichtenstein, Nelson. *Labor's War at Home: The CIO in World War II.* New York: Cambridge University Press, 1982.

Lingeman, Richard R. *Don't You Know There's a War On? The American Home Front, 1941–1945.* New York: G. P. Putnam's Sons, 1970.

Litoff, Judy Barrett, and David C. Smith, eds. *We're in This War, Too: World War II Letters from American Women in Uniform.* New York: Oxford University Press, 1994.

Lloyd-Jones, D. Martyn. *The Plight of Man and the Power of God.* Grand Rapids, Mich.: William B. Eerdmans Publishing Company, 1945.

Logan, Rayford W., ed. *What the Negro Wants.* Chapel Hill: University of North Carolina Press, 1944.

Logan, Spencer. *A Negro's Faith in America.* New York: Macmillan, 1946.

Lotz, David W., editor. *Altered Landscapes: Christianity in America, 1935–1985.* Grand Rapids, Mich.: William B. Eerdmans Publishing Company, 1989.

Lynn, Rita LeBille. *The National Catholic Community Service in World War II*. Washington, D.C.: Catholic University of America Press, 1952.

McConnell, Francis J., ed. *A Basis for the Peace to Come*. New York: Abingdon-Cokesbury Press, 1942.

Mackay, John. *Heritage and Destiny*. New York: Macmillan, 1943.

McNeal, Patricia F. *The American Catholic Peace Movement, 1928–1972*. New York: Arno Press, 1978.

Malkin, Richard. *Marriage, Morals, and War*. New York: Arden Book Company, 1943.

Maritain, Jacques. *Christianity and Democracy* (1943) and *The Rights of Man and Natural Law* (1942). San Francisco: Ignatius Press, 1986.

——. *The Twilight of Civilization*. New York: Sheed and Ward, 1943.

Marrin, Albert, ed. *War and the Christian Conscience: From Augustine to Martin Luther King, Jr.* Chicago: Henry Regnery Company, 1972.

Marsden, George M. *Fundamentalism and American Culture: The Shaping of Twentieth-Century Evangelicalism, 1870–1925*. New York: Oxford University Press, 1980.

——. *Reforming Fundamentalism: The History of Fuller Seminary*. Grand Rapids, Mich.: William B. Eerdmans Publishing Company, 1987.

Marsh, Mabel. *Service Suspended*. New York: Carlton Press, 1968.

Martin, Hugh, Douglas Newton, H. M. Waddams, and R. R. Williams. *Christian Counter-Attack: Europe's Churches against Nazism*. New York: Charles Scribner's Sons, 1944.

Marty, Martin E. *Modern American Religion*. Vol. 1, *The Irony of It All, 1893–1919*. Chicago: University of Chicago Press, 1986.

——. *A Nation of Behavers*. Chicago: University of Chicago Press, 1976.

——. *Righteous Empire: The Protestant Experience in America*. New York: Harper and Row, 1970.

Matsumoto, Toru. *Beyond Prejudice: A Story of the Church and Japanese Americans*. New York: Friendship Press, 1946.

May, Henry F. *Protestant Churches and Industrial America*. New York: Harper and Brothers, 1949.

Mead, Frank S. *Handbook of Denominations in the United States*. 6th ed. Nashville: Abingdon Press, 1975.

Mead, Sidney E. *The Lively Experiment: The Shaping of Christianity in America*. New York: Harper and Row, 1963.

Merrill, Francis E. *Social Problems on the Home Front: A Study of War-time Influences*. New York: Harper and Brothers, 1948.

Meyer, Donald B. *The Protestant Search for Political Realism, 1919–1941*. Berkeley: University of California Press, 1960.

Miller, Robert Moats. *American Protestantism and Social Issues, 1919–1939*. Chapel Hill: University of North Carolina Press, 1958.

Miller, William D. *A Harsh and Dreadful Love: Dorothy Day and the Catholic Worker Movement*. New York: Liveright, 1973.

Mitchell, Hobart. *We Would Not Kill*. Richmond, Ind.: Friends United Press, 1983.

Moellering, Ralph Luther. *Modern War and the American Churches: A Factual Study of the*

Christian Conscience on Trial from 1939 to the Cold War Crisis of Today. New York: American Press, 1956.

Moomaw, I. W. *Crusade against Hunger.* New York: Harper and Row, 1977.

Moore, R. Laurence. *Religious Outsiders and the Making of Americans.* New York: Oxford University Press, 1986.

Morella, Joe, Edward Z. Epstein, and John Griggs. *The Films of World War II.* Secaucus, N.J.: Citadel Press, 1973.

Morrison, Charles Clayton. *Can Protestantism Win America?* New York: Harper and Brothers, 1948.

———. *The Christian and the War.* New York: Willett, Clark and Company, 1942.

Morse, Arthur D. *While Six Million Died: A Chronicle of American Apathy.* New York: Random House, 1967.

Morton, Malvin. *The Development and Structure of the War Relief Agencies.* Pittsburgh: Bureau of Social Research, 1945.

Motley, Mary Penick. *The Invisible Soldier: The Experience of the Black Soldier, World War II.* Detroit: Wayne State University Press, 1975.

Muelder, Walter G. *Methodism and Society in the Twentieth Century.* New York: Abingdon Press, 1961.

Murray, Andrew E. *Presbyterians and the Negro—A History.* Philadelphia: Presbyterian Historical Society, 1966.

Muste, A. J. *Non-Violence in an Aggressive World.* New York: Harper and Brothers, 1940.

———. *War Is the Enemy.* Pendle Hill Pamphlets, 10–16. New York: Fellowship of Reconciliation, n.d.

———. *The World Task of Pacifism.* Pendle Hill Pamphlets, 10–16. New York: Fellowship of Reconciliation, n.d.

Myrdal, Gunnar. *An American Dilemma: The Negro Problem and Modern Democracy.* 2 vols. New York: Harper and Brothers, 1944.

Nance, Ellwood C., ed. *Faith of Our Fighters.* St. Louis: Bethany Press, 1944.

Nash, Gerald D. *The Great Depression and World War II: Organizing America, 1933–1945.* New York: St. Martin's Press, 1979.

Nelson, Clifford E. *Lutheranism in North America, 1914–1970.* Minneapolis: Augsburg Publishing House, 1972.

Nelson, John K. *The Peace Prophets: American Pacifist Thought, 1919–1941.* Chapel Hill: University of North Carolina Press, 1967.

Niebuhr, Reinhold. *Christianity and Power Politics.* New York: Charles Scribner's Sons, 1940.

Nixon, Justin Wroe. *Protestantism's Hour of Decision.* Philadelphia: Judson Press, 1940.

O'Brien, David J. *Public Catholicism.* New York: Macmillan, 1989.

———. *The Renewal of American Catholicism.* New York: Oxford University Press, 1972.

Offner, Arnold A. *The Origins of the Second World War: American Foreign Policy and World Politics, 1917–1941.* New York: Praeger Publishers, 1975.

Outka, Gene, and John P. Reeder, Jr., eds. *Prospects for a Common Morality.* Princeton, N.J.: Princeton University Press, 1992.

Oxnam, G. Bromley. *Facing the Future Unafraid*. New York: Fleming H. Revell Company, 1944.

——. *Labor and Tomorrow's World*. New York: Abingdon-Cokesbury Press, 1945.

Paton, William. *The Church and the New Order*. New York: Macmillan, 1941.

——. *The Church Calling*. New York: Macmillan, 1942.

Paullin, Theodore. *Introduction to Non-Violence*. Philadelphia: Pacifist Research Bureau, 1944.

Peachey, Urbane, ed. *Mennonite Statements on Peace and Social Concerns, 1900–1978*. Akron, Pa.: Mennonite Central Committee, 1980.

Peck, Jim. *We Who Would Not Kill*. New York: Lyle Stuart, 1958.

Perrett, Geoffrey. *Days of Sadness, Years of Triumph: The American People, 1939–1945*. Madison: University of Wisconsin Press, 1973.

Pickard, Bertram. *Pacifist Diplomacy in Conflict Situations*. Philadelphia: Pacifist Research Bureau, 1943.

Piper, John F., Jr. *The American Churches in World War I*. Athens: Ohio University Press, 1985.

Polenberg, Richard. *War and Society: The United States, 1941–1945*. New York: J. B. Lippincott Company, 1972.

Poling, Daniel A. *A Preacher Looks at War*. New York: Macmillan, 1943.

Pope, Liston. *Religious Proposals for World Order: An Analysis of Thirty-Four Statements*. New York: Church Peace Union, 1941.

Poteat, Edwin McNeill. *Four Freedoms and God*. New York: Harper and Brothers, 1943.

Pratt, Henry J. *The Liberalization of American Protestantism: A Case Study in Complex Organizations*. Detroit: Wayne State University Press, 1972.

Pruessen, Ronald W. *John Foster Dulles: The Road to Power*. New York: Free Press, 1982.

Rauschning, Hermann. *The Redemption of Democracy: The Coming Atlantic Empire*. New York: Alliance Book Corporation, 1941.

Reichley, A. James. *Religion in American Public Life*. Washington, D.C.: Brookings Institute, 1985.

Reimers, David M. *White Protestantism and the Negro*. New York: Oxford University Press, 1965.

Rhodes, Anthony. *The Vatican in the Age of the Dictators, 1922–1945*. New York: Holt, Rinehart and Winston, 1973.

Ribuffo, Leo P. *The Old Christian Right: The Protestant Far Right from the Great Depression to the Cold War*. Philadelphia: Temple University Press, 1983.

Rice, John R. *World-Wide War and the Bible*. Wheaton, Ill.: Sword of the Lord Publishers, 1940.

Rickenbacker, Captain Edward V. *Seven Came Through*. Garden City, N.Y.: Doubleday, Doran and Company, Inc., 1943.

Rogers, Carl R., and John L. Wallen. *Counseling with Returned Servicemen*. New York: McGraw-Hill Book Company, Inc., 1946.

Rose, Lisle A. *Dubious Victory: The United States and the End of World War II*. Kent, Pa.: Kent State University Press, 1973.

——. *The Long Shadow: Reflections on the Second World War Era*. Westport, Conn.: Greenwood Press, 1969.

Rosen, Margorie. *Popcorn Venus: Women, Movies, and the American Dream*. New York: Coward, McCann and Geoghegan, 1973.

Ross, Robert W. *So It Was True: The American Protestant Press and the Nazi Persecution of the Jews*. Minneapolis: University of Minnesota Press, 1980.

Rouse, Ruth, and Stephen Charles Neill, eds. *A History of the Ecumenical Movement, 1517–1948*. Philadelphia: Westminster Press, 1967.

Roy, Ralph Lord. *Communism and the Churches*. New York: Harcourt, Brace and Company, 1960.

Ruchames, Louis. *Race, Jobs, and Politics: The Story of FEPC*. New York: Columbia University Press, 1953.

Rupp, Leila J. *Mobilizing Women for War: German and American Propaganda, 1939–1945*. Princeton: Princeton University Press, 1978.

Ryan, John K. *Modern War and Basic Ethics*. Washington: Catholic University of America, 1933.

Salomon, George, ed. *Jews in the Mind of America*. New York: Basic Books, Inc., 1966.

Sappington, Roger E. *Brethren Social Policy, 1908–1958*. Elgin, Ill.: Brethren Press, 1961.

Schlissel, Lillian, ed. *Conscience in America: A Documentary History of Conscientious Objection in America, 1757–1967*. New York: E. P. Dutton and Company, Inc., 1968.

Schoenfeld, Seymour J. *The Negro in the Armed Forces*. Washington, D.C.: Associated Publishers, 1945.

Scott, Colonel Robert L., Jr. *God Is My Co-Pilot*. New York: Charles Scribner's Sons, 1943.

Seaton, Douglas P. *Catholics and Radicals: The Association of Catholic Trade Unionists and the American Labor Movement, from Depression to Cold War*. Lewisburg, Pa.: Bucknell University Press, 1981.

Selective Service and Victory: The 4th Report of the Director of Selective Service, 1944–1945. Washington, D.C.: U.S. Government Printing Office, 1948.

Seymour, Harold J. *Design for Giving: The Story of the National War Fund, Inc., 1943–1947*. New York: Harper and Brothers, 1947.

Sheen, Fulton J. *Philosophies at War*. New York: Charles Scribner's Sons, 1943.

——. *Seven Pillars of Peace*. New York: Charles Scribner's Sons, 1944.

Sherrill, Rowland A., ed. *Religion and the Life of the Nation*. Urbana: University of Illinois Press, 1990.

Shindler, Colin. *Hollywood Goes to War: Films and American Society, 1939–1952*. Boston: Routledge and Kegan Paul, 1979.

Short, K. R. M., ed. *Film and Radio Propaganda in World War II*. Knoxville: University of Tennessee Press, 1983.

Shotwell, James T. *The Great Decision*. New York: Macmillan, 1945.

Sibley, Mulford. *The Political Theories of Modern Pacifism*. Ser. 5, no. 1. Philadelphia: Pacifist Research Bureau, 1944.

Sibley, Mulford Q., and Philip E. Jacob. *Conscription of Conscience: The American State and the Conscientious Objector, 1940–1947*. Ithaca, N.Y.: Cornell University Press, 1952.

Sibley, Mulford, and Ada Wardlaw. *Conscientious Objectors in Prison, 1940–1945*. Ser. 5, no. 2. Philadelphia: Pacifist Research Bureau, 1945.

Silk, Mark. *Spiritual Politics: Religion and America since World War II*. New York: Simon and Schuster, 1988.

Silvera, John D. *The Negro in World War II*. New York: Arno Press, 1969.

Simmons, Clifford, ed. *The Objectors*. London: Times Press, n.d.

Sklar, Robert. *Movie-Made America: A Cultural History of American Movies*. New York: Random House, 1994.

Smyth, The Right Honorable Sir John. *In This Sign Conquer: The Story of the Army Chaplains*. London: A. R. Mowbray and Company Ltd., 1968.

Snoek, Johan M. *The Grey Book: A Collection of Protests against Anti-Semitism and the Persecution of Jews Issued by Non-Roman Catholic Churches and Church Leaders during Hitler's Rule*. Assen: Koninklijke Van Gorcum and Comp. N.V., 1968.

Snyder, Louis L., ed. *Masterpieces of War Reporting: The Great Moments of World War II*. New York: Julian Messner, Inc., 1962.

Sockman, Ralph W. *Date with Destiny: A Preamble to Christian Culture*. New York: Abingdon-Cokesbury Press, 1944.

Spellman, Francis J. *No Greater Love: The Story of Our Soldiers*. New York: Charles Scribner's Sons, 1945.

——. *The Road to Victory*. New York: Charles Scribner's Sons, 1942.

Spencer, Lyle M., and Robert K. Burns. *Youth Goes to War*. Chicago: Science Research Associates, 1943.

Sperry, Willard L. *Rebuilding Our World*. New York: Harper and Brothers, 1943.

——, ed. *Religion in America*. Boston: Beacon Press, 1946.

——. *Religion in the Postwar World*. 4 vols. Cambridge: Harvard University Press, 1945.

Stenehjem, Michele Flynn. *An American First: John T. Flynn and the America First Committee*. New Rochelle, N.Y.: Arlington House Publishers, 1976.

Sternsher, Bernard, ed. *The Negro in Depression and War: Prelude to Revolution, 1930–1945*. Chicago: Quadrangle Books, 1969.

Stillman, Richard J. *Integration of the Negro in the U.S. Armed Forces*. New York: Frederick A. Praeger, 1968.

The Story of Christian Science Wartime Activities, 1939–1946. Boston: Christian Science Publishing Society, 1947.

Stover, Gerald L., ed. *The Plight of the Jews*. New York: Loizeaux Brothers, n.d.

Street, T. Watson. *The Story of Southern Presbyterians*. Richmond, Va.: John Knox Press, 1960.

Susman, Warren, ed. *Culture and Commitment, 1929–1945*. New York: George Braziller, 1973.

Suzuki, Lester E. *Ministry in the Assembly and Relocation Centers of World War II*. Berkeley: Yardbird Publishing Company, 1979.

Taft, Philip. *The A.F. of L. from the Death of Gompers to the Merger*. New York: Harper and Brothers, 1959.

Taylor, A. Margorie, comp. *The Language of World War II: Abbreviations, Captions, Quotations, Slogans, Titles, and Other Terms and Phrases*. New York: The H. W. Wilson Company, 1944.

Thomas, Evan W. *The Way to Freedom*. New York: War Resisters League, 1943.

Thompson, Donald A. *American Army Chaplaincy: A Brief History*. Washington, D.C.: Chaplains Association, 1946.

Toulouse, Mark G. "The Open Membership Controversy." In *A Case Study of Main-*

stream Protestantism, edited by D. Newell Williams, 194–235. Grand Rapids, Mich.: William B. Eerdmans Publishing Company, 1991.

——. *The Transformation of John Foster Dulles: From Prophet of Realism to Priest of Nationalism*. Atlanta: Mercer University Press, 1985.

Tuttle, William M., Jr. *"Daddy's Gone to War": The Second World War in the Lives of America's Children*. New York: Oxford University Press, 1993.

Uchida, Yoshiko. *Desert Exile: The Uprooting of a Japanese American Family*. Seattle: University of Washington Press, 1982.

Unruh, John D. *In the Name of Christ: A History of the Mennonite Central Committee and Its Services, 1920–1951*. Scottdale, Pa.: Herald Press, 1952.

Van Dusen, Henry P. *What Is the Church Doing?* New York: Charles Scribner's Sons, 1943.

——, ed. *The Christian Answer*. New York: Charles Scribner's Sons, 1945.

Van Kirk, Walter W. *A Christian Global Strategy*. Chicago: Willett, Clark and Company, 1945.

——. *Religion Renounces War*. Chicago: Willett, Clark and Company, 1934.

Van Paassen, Pierre. *The Forgotten Ally*. New York: Dial Press, 1943.

Walker, F. A. *The Blunder of Pacifism*. London: Hodder and Stoughton, 1940.

Wallenberg, Harry A., Jr. *Whither Freedom?: A Study of the Treatment of Conscientious Objectors in the United States during World Wars I and II and Its Relation to the Concept of Freedom*. New York: Fellowship of Reconciliation, 1954.

Ware, Susan. *Beyond Suffrage: Women in the New Deal*. Cambridge: Harvard University Press, 1981.

Washburn, Patrick S. *A Question of Sedition: The Federal Government's Investigation of the Black Press during World War II*. New York: Oxford University Press, 1986.

Waskow, Arthur I. *From Race Riot to Sit-In, 1919 and the 1960s: A Study in the Connections between Conflict and Violence*. Garden City, N.Y.: Doubleday and Company, Inc., 1966.

Weatherhead, Doris. *American Women and World War II*. New York: Facts on File, 1990.

Wells, Ronald A. *The Wars of America: Christian Views*. Grand Rapids, Mich.: William B. Eerdmans Publishing Company, 1981.

Wentz, Abdel Ross. *A Basic History of Lutheranism in America*. Philadelphia: Fortress Press, 1964.

What about the Conscientious Objector? Philadelphia: American Friends Service Committee, 1940.

White, Walter. *A Rising Wind*. Garden City, N.Y.: Doubleday, Doran and Company, Inc., 1945.

Whittacker, Lieutenant James C. *We Thought We Heard the Angels Sing*. New York: E. P. Dutton and Company, Inc., 1943.

Whyte, John H. *Catholics in Western Democracies: A Study in Political Behavior*. New York: St. Martin's Press, 1981.

Wieman, Henry Nelson. *Now We Must Choose*. New York: Macmillan, 1941.

Wilson, E. Raymond. *Uphill for Peace: Quaker Impact on Congress*. Richmond, Ind.: Friends United Press, 1975.

Winkler, Allan M. *The Politics of Propaganda: The Office of War Information, 1942–1945*. New Haven: Yale University Press, 1978.

Wise, Nancy Baker, and Christy Wise. *A Mouthful of Rivets: Women at Work in World War II.* San Francisco: Jossey-Bass, 1994.

Wittner, Lawrence S. *Rebels against War: The American Peace Movement, 1933–1983.* Philadelphia: Temple University Press, 1984.

Woll, Allen L. *The Hollywood Musical Goes to War.* Chicago: Nelson-Hall, 1983.

Woodbridge, George, ed. *UNRRA: The History of the United Nations Relief and Rehabilitation Administration.* 3 vols. New York: Columbia University Press, 1950.

Wuthnow, Robert. *The Restructuring of American Religion: Society and Faith since World War II.* Princeton, N.J.: Princeton University Press, 1988.

——. *The Struggle for America's Soul: Evangelicals, Liberals, and Secularism.* Grand Rapids, Mich.: William B. Eerdmans Publishing Company, 1989.

Wyman, David S. *The Abandonment of the Jews: America and the Holocaust, 1941–1945.* New York: Pantheon Books, 1984.

——. *Paper Walls: America and the Refugee Crisis, 1938–1941.* Amherst: University of Massachusetts Press, 1968.

Wynn, Neil A. *The Afro-American and the Second World War.* New York: Holmes and Meier Publishers, 1975.

Zahn, Gordon C. *Another Part of the War: The Camp Simon Story.* Amherst: University of Massachusetts Press, 1979.

——. *War, Conscience, and Dissent.* New York: Hawthorne Books, Inc., 1967.

DISSERTATIONS

Burroway, Jessie J. "Christian Witness Concerning World Order: The Federal Council of Churches and Postwar Planning, 1941–1947." Ph.D. diss., University of Wisconsin, 1954.

Camp, William D. "Religion and Horror: The American Religious Press Views Nazi Death Camps and Holocaust Survivors." Ph.D. diss., Carnegie-Mellon University, 1981.

Carpenter, Joel A. "The Renewal of American Fundamentalism, 1930–1945." Ph.D. diss., John Hopkins University, 1984.

Collins, Johnnie Andrew. "Pacifism in the Churches of Christ: 1866–1945." Ph.D. diss., Middle Tennessee State University, 1984.

Grimsrud, Theodore G. "An Ethical Analysis of Conscientious Objectors to World War II." Ph.D. diss., Graduate Theological Union, 1988.

Hafer, Harold Franklin. "The Evangelical and Reformed Churches and World War II." Ph.D. diss., University of Pennsylvania, 1947.

Kegel, James D. "A Church Come of Age: American Lutheranism and National Socialism, the German Church Conflict, and the Reconstitution of the Church: 1933–1948." Ph.D. diss., Lutheran School of Theology, 1988.

Kohlhoff, Dean W. "Missouri Synod Lutherans and the Image of Germany, 1914–1945." Ph.D. diss., University of Chicago, 1973.

Lund, Doniver A. "The Peace Movement among the Major American Protestant Churches, 1919–1939." Ph.D. diss., University of Nebraska, 1955.

MacCarthy, Esther J. "The Catholic Periodical Press and Issues of War and Peace: 1914–1946." Ph.D. diss., Stanford University, 1977.

Magden, Ronald E. "Attitudes of the American Religious Press toward Soviet Russia, 1933–1941." Ph.D. diss., University of Washington, 1964.

Murphy, Frederick. "The American Christian Press and Pre-War Hitler's Germany, 1933–1939." Ph.D. diss., 1970.

Nawyn, William E. "American Protestant Churches Respond to the Plight of Germany's Jews and Refugees, 1933–41." Ph.D. diss., University of Iowa, 1980.

Orser, William Edward. "The Social Attitudes of the Protestant Churches during the Second World War." Ph.D. diss., University of New Mexico, 1969.

Pangborn, Cyrus Ransom. "Free Churches and Social Change: A Critical Study of the Council for Social Action of the Congregational Christian Churches of the United States." Ph.D. diss., Columbia University, 1951.

Robinson, Mitchell L. "Civilian Public Service during World War II: The Dilemmas of Conscience and Conscription in a Free Society." Ph.D. diss., Cornell University, 1990.

Sparks, Donald Tennyson. "The Influence of Official Protestant Church Groups on the Formulation and Conduct of American Foreign Policy." Ph.D. diss., University of Chicago, 1954.

Wachs, Theodore R. "Conscription, Conscientious Objection, and the Context of American Pacifism, 1940–1945." Ph.D. diss., University of Illinois at Urbana, 1976.

Wentz, Frederick K. "The Reaction of the Religious Press in America to the Emergence of Nazism." Ph.D. diss., Yale University, 1954.

Weston, W. Moran. "Social Policy of the Episcopal Church in the Twentieth Century." Ph.D. diss., Columbia University, 1954.

Whyatt, Nelson Thomas. "Planning for the Postwar World: Liberal Journalism during World War II." Ph.D. diss., University of Minnesota, 1971.

Zahn, Gordon. "A Descriptive Study of the Sociological Background of Conscientious Objectors in Civilian Service Camps during World War II." Ph.D. diss., Catholic University of America, 1953.

Zeitzer, Glen. "The American Peace Movement during World War II." Ph.D. diss., Bryn Mawr College, 1978.

INDEX

Executive Order 8802, 182–84
Executive Order 9066, 170–72

Fagley, Frederick L., 119, 162, 221
Fair Employment Practices Commission, 180–82
Family: in wartime, 195–98
Fascists, 189–91
Federal Council of Churches, 18, 20–21, 120, 121
—civil liberties, 169; and Japanese Americans, 177; and opposition to racism and anti-Semitism, 182, 212–13; and Catholics, 265 (n. 33)
—mission to the nation: and National Christian Mission, 126–27; unity of, 128–29; and citizenship, 129–30
—peacetime work: and atomic bomb, 220–21; and Christian Mission on World Order, 237; and Commission to Study the Basis of a Just and Durable Peace, 238–40, 243
—wartime ministry: and conscientious objectors, 132, 143; in defense communities, 143, 151; and chaplains, 143, 161; relief work of, 207–8
Fellowship, 122–24
Fellowship of Reconciliation, 60; and opposition to war, 122–24; Refugee Committee of, 214
Ferre, Nels, 60, 123
Fey, Harold, 52, 57
Fisher, Galen, 174
Fosdick, Harry Emerson: and pacifism in 1930s, 17, 23, 26; pacifist arguments of, 55; and opposition to bombing, 220; and postwar peace, 238; and living in wartime, 251–52
Frantz, Edward, 118
Fraternal Council of Negro Churches of America, 185, 201
Friends of Israel Refugee Relief Committee, 78, 214
Fundamentalists: and view of war, 85, 88–92; revivals of, 125–26; wartime

work of, 148, 153; and civil liberties, 189, 191–92; and support of bombing, 220; and world government, 232–33

General Commission on Army and Navy Chaplains, 143, 156, 166
Germany, 242–43
GI Bill of Rights, 228–29
Gilroy, William E., 113, 188

Harkness, Georgia, 23, 26, 35
Hartman, L. O.: and view of war, 4–5; and view of democracy, 100, 104–5; and civil liberties, 187
Hershberger, John, 124
Hitler, Adolph, 42, 64, 87, 90
Holmes, John Haynes: pacifism of, 54–55, 65, 123; and opposition to bombing, 220
Holocaust, 212–16
Holt, Ivan Lee, 23, 26, 121
Holy Name Society, 154
Horton, Walter Marshall, 13
Houghton, Will, 85
Humanitarianism, 113
Hume, Theodore, 13, 23

Inflation, 229–30
Interfaith Declaration on World Peace, 235
Internationalism, 20, 223
Interventionism, 63–76
Ironside, H. A., 94

Japanese Americans: internment of, 169–71; Christian support for, 172–76; resettlement of, 177–78
Jehovah's Witnesses, 186–88
Johnson, F. E., 105
Jones, E. Stanley, 26, 205, 220
Juvenile delinquency, 198–200

Kershner, Frederick, 117
Kershner, Howard E., 206
Knubel, F. H., 110

228–29; and view of reconversion, 229; peace proposals of, 235–36

Rood, Paul W., 125

Roosevelt, Franklin Delano: third term of, 57–58; and Taylor appointment, 110–13, 122; and conscientious objectors, 131–32; and rationing, 138; and Japanese Americans, 170–72, 177; executive orders of, 171, 183; and African Americans, 182–84; and liquor, 199; relief policies of, 209–10; and Jews, 215; and bombing, 216–17

Russia, 189–91, 241

Ryan, John A., 111

Schewe, Edward F., 88

Schmoe, Floyd, 176

Schramm, Edward, 114

Segregation, 179–82

Selective service. *See* Conscription

Separation Centers, 226

Separation of church and state, 110–13

Service Men's Christian League, 153–54

Service Prayer Books, 148

Sheppard Bill, 200

Shipler, Guy Emery, Jr., 183

Skillin, Edward, Jr.: and debate over entry into war, 40; and Taylor appointment, 111; and conscientious objectors, 131; and labor, 140; and civil liberties, 183, 187; and family life, 195; and opposition to bombing, 219; and Russia, 241

Smith, Frank Herron, 176

Smith, Gerald L. K., 189, 215

Smith, Roy L., 37, 188, 191

Smith, Wilbur M., 89

Southern Baptist Convention: and debate over entry into war, 48; and Taylor appointment, 110; opportunities for ministry of, 119; and view of war, 122; Home Mission Board of, 152–53; and chaplaincy controversies, 165–66; and opposition to peacetime conscription, 201; and postwar peace, 235; Centennial Crusade of, 248

Sovereignty of God, 78–81

Spellman, Cardinal Francis J., 149

Stewart, Brooke Hilary, 41

Stewart, Luther, 118

Stonehouse, Ned B., 114, 202–3

Supreme Court cases, 175, 187

Takagi, Yoshitaka, 175

Talbot, Francis X., 65; and debate over entry into war, 41–43, 52–59; and opposition to Roosevelt, 57–58; and Catholic unity, 128; and labor, 140–41; anticommunism of, 189, 241; and civil liberties, 190; and GI Bill of Rights, 228–29

Tanis, E. J., 114, 195, 218

Taylor, Myron, 109–13

Theodicy, 77–98

Thompson, Everett W., 176

Tittle, Ernest Fremont, 26, 35, 220

Totalitarianism, 4, 21–22, 57, 83–84, 99–101

Trapp, Jacob, 101

Unitarians, 20, 101, 138

United Nations Organization, 238–40

United Nations Relief and Rehabilitation Administration, 206, 208

United Service Organization, 154–56

Van Dusen, Henry Pitney, 64, 121, 230

Van Kirk, Walter, 23, 131–32, 238

Vatican, 109–13

Versailles, Treaty of, 17, 226, 230, 243

Veterans, 225–30

Villard, Oswald Garrison, 50, 218

Ward, Harry F., 241

War Relocation Authority, 172, 177

War-Time Service Commission, 143–44

Weigle, Luther A., 177

Western civilization, 2–6, 21–22, 51

Whitaker, Robert, 109, 241

White, William Allen, 50–51

Williams, John Paul, 101